Lecture Notes in Computer Science 1656
Edited by G. Goos, J. Hartmanis and J. van Leeuwen

Springer

Berlin
Heidelberg
New York
Barcelona
Hong Kong
London
Milan
Paris
Singapore
Tokyo

Siddhartha Chatterjee   Jan F. Prins
Larry Carter   Jeanne Ferrante   Zhiyuan Li
David Sehr   Pen-Chung Yew (Eds.)

Languages
and Compilers
for Parallel Computing

11th International Workshop, LCPC'98
Chapel Hill, NC, USA, August 7-9, 1998
Proceedings

Springer

Volume Editors

Siddhartha Chatterjee, Jan F. Prins
Department of Computer Science, The University of North Carolina
Chapel Hill, NC 27599-3175, USA
E-mail: {sc/prins}@cs.unc.edu

Larry Carter, Jeanne Ferrante
Department of Computer Science and Engineering
University of California at San Diego
9500 Gilman Drive, La Jolla, CA 92093-0114, USA
E-mail: {carter/ferrante}@cs.ucsd.edu

Zhiyuan Li
DEpartment of Computer Science, Purdue University
1398 Computer Science Building, West Lafayette, IN 47907, USA
E-mail: li@cs.purdue.edu

David Sehr
Intel Corporation
2200 Mission College Boulevard, RN6-18, Santa Clara, CA 95052, USA
E-mail: dsehr@gomez.sc.intel.com

Pen-Chung Yew
Department of Computer Science and Engineering, University of Minnesota
Minneapolis, MN 55455, USA
E-mail: yew@cs.umn.edu

Cataloging-in-Publication data applied for

Die Deutsche Bibliothek - CIP-Einheitsaufnahme

Languages and compilers for parallel computing : 11th
international workshop ; proceedings / LCPC '98, Chapel Hill, NC,
USA, August 7 - 9, 1998. S. Chatterjee ... (ed.). - Berlin ; Heidelberg
; New York ; Barcelona ; Hong Kong ; London ; Milan ; Paris ;
Singapore ; Tokyo : Springer, 1999
  (Lecture notes in computer science ; Vol. 1656)
  ISBN 3-540-66426-2

CR Subject Classification (1998): D.1.3, D.1.3, D.3.4, F.1.2, B.2.1, C.2

ISSN 0302-9743
ISBN 3-540-66426-2 Springer-Verlag Berlin Heidelberg New York

© Springer-Verlag Berlin Heidelberg 1999
Printed in Germany

Typesetting: Camera-ready by author
SPIN: 10704088   06/3142 – 5 4 3 2 1 0   Printed on acid-free paper

Preface

The year 1998 marked the eleventh anniversary of the annual Workshop on Languages and Compilers for Parallel Computing (LCPC), an international forum for leading research groups to present their current research activities and latest results. The LCPC community is interested in a broad range of technologies, with a common goal of developing software systems that enable real applications. Among the topics of interest to the workshop are language features, communication code generation and optimization, communication libraries, distributed shared memory libraries, distributed object systems, resource management systems, integration of compiler and runtime systems, irregular and dynamic applications, performance evaluation. and debuggers. LCPC'98 was hosted by the University of North Carolina at Chapel Hill (UNC-CH) on 7 - 9 August 1998, at the William and Ida Friday Center on the UNC-CH campus. Fifty people from the United States, Europe, and Asia attended the workshop.

The program committee of LCPC'98, with the help of external reviewers, evaluated the submitted papers. Twenty-four papers were selected for formal presentation at the workshop. Each session was followed by an open panel discussion centered on the main topic of the particular session. Many attendees have come to regard the open panels as a very effective format for exchanging views and clarifying research issues. Using feedback provided both during and after the presentations, all of the authors were given an opportunity to improve their papers before submitting the final manuscript contained in this volume. This collection documents important research activities from the past year in the design and implementation of programming languages and environments for parallel computing.

The major themes of the workshop included both classical issues (Fortran, instruction scheduling, dependence analysis) as well as emerging areas (Java, memory hierarchy issues, network computing, irregular applications). These themes reflect several recent trends in computer architecture: aggressive hardware speculation, deeper memory hierarchies, multilevel parallelism, and "the network is the computer." In this final editing of the workshop papers, we have grouped the papers into these categories.

In addition to the regular paper sessions, LCPC'98 featured an invited talk by Charles Leiserson, Professor of Computer Science at the MIT Laboratory for Computer Science, entitled "Algorithmic Multithreaded Programming in Cilk". This talk was the first exposure to the Cilk system for many of the participants and resulted in many interesting discussions. We thank Prof. Leiserson for his special contribution to LCPC'98.

We are grateful to the Department of Computer Science at UNC-CH for its generous support of this workshop. We benefited especially from the efforts of Linda Houseman, who ably coordinated the logistical matters before, during, and after the workshop. Thanks also go out to our local team of volunteers: Brian Blount, Vibhor Jain, and Martin Simons. Special thanks are due to the

LCPC'98 Steering and Program Committes for their time and energy in reviewing the submitted papers. Finally, and most importantly, we thank all the authors and participants of the workshop. It is their significant research work and their enthusiastic discussions throughout the workshop that made LCPC'98 a success.

May 1999   Siddhartha Chatterjee
                                                                   Program Chair

Steering Committee

Utpal Banerjee	*Intel Corporation*
David Gelernter	*Yale University*
Alex Nicolau	*University of California at Irvine*
David Padua	*University of Ilinois at Urbana-Champaign*

Program Committee

Larry Carter	*University of California at San Diego*
Siddhartha Chatterjee	*University of North Carolina at Chapel Hill*
Jeanne Ferrante	*University of California at San Diego*
Zhiyuan Li	*Purdue University*
Jan Prins	*University of North Carolina at Chapel Hill*
David Sehr	*Intel Corporation*
Pen-Chung Yew	*University of Minnesota*

Organizing Committee

Linda Houseman	*University of North Carolina at Chapel Hill*

External Reviewers

George Almasi	Asheesh Khare
Ana Azevedo	Jaejin Lee
Brian Blount	Yuan Lin
Calin Cascaval	Yunheung Paek
Walfredo Cirne	Nick Savoiu
Paolo D'Alberto	Martin Simons
Vijay Ganesh	Weiyu Tang
Xiaomei Ji	

Table of Contents

Dependence Analysis

From Flop to MegaFlops:
Java for Technical Computing

J. E. Moreira, S. P. Midkiff, and M. Gupta

IBM T.J. Watson Research Center
P.O. Box 218, Yorktown Heights, New York 10598, USA
{jmoreira,smidkiff,mgupta}@us.ibm.com

Abstract. Although there has been some experimentation with Java as a language for numerically intensive computing, there is a perception by many that the language is not suited for such work. In this paper we show how optimizing array bounds checks and **null** pointer checks creates loop nests on which aggressive optimizations can be used. Applying these optimizations by hand to a simple matrix-multiply test case leads to Java compliant programs whose performance is in excess of 500 Mflops on an RS/6000 SP 332MHz SMP node. We also report in this paper the effect that each optimization has on performance. Since all of these optimizations can be automated, we conclude that Java will soon be a serious contender for numerically intensive computing.

1 Introduction

The scientific programming community has recently demonstrated a great deal of interest in the use of Java for technical computing. There are many compelling reasons for such use of Java: a large supply of programmers, it is object-oriented without excessive complications (in contrast to C++), and it has support for networking and graphics. Technical computing is moving more and more towards a network-centric model of computation. In this context, it can be expected that Java will first be used where it is most natural: for visualization and networking components. Eventually, Java will spread into the core computational components of technical applications.

Nevertheless, a major obstacle remains to the pervasive use of Java in technical computing: performance. Let us start by looking into the performance of a simple matrix-multiply routine in Java, as shown in Fig. 1. This routine computes $C = C + A \times B$, where C is an $m \times p$ matrix, A is an $m \times n$ matrix, and B is an $n \times p$ matrix. We use that routine to multiply two 500×500 matrices ($m = n = p = 500$) on an RS/6000 SP 332MHz SMP node. This machine contains 4×332 MHz PowerPC 604e processors, each with a peak performance of 664 Mflops. We refer to this simple benchmark as MATMUL.

The Java code is compiled into a native executable by the IBM High Performance Compiler for Java (HPCJ) [10], and achieves a performance of 5 Mflops on a 332 MHz PowerPC 604e processor. The equivalent Fortran code, compiled by the IBM XLF compiler, achieves 265 Mflops! A 50-fold performance

S. Chatterjee (Ed.): LCPC'98, LNCS 1656, pp. 1–17, 1999.
© Springer-Verlag Berlin Heidelberg 1999

```
static void matmul(double[][] A, double[][] B, double[][] C,
                   int m, int n, int p) {

    int i, j, k;
    for (i=0; i<m; i++)
      for (j=0; j<p; j++)
        for (k=0; k<n; k++)
          C[i][j] += A[i][k]*B[k][j];
}
```

Fig. 1. Simple matrix-multiply code in Java.

degradation makes it hard to justify using Java for a technical application. The single-threaded version of ESSL (Engineering and Scientific Subroutine Library[22]), carefully hand-tuned to achieve optimum performance, executes the matrix multiplication at 289 Mflops. The multi-threaded version of ESSL achieves 1183 Mflops!

Why is the performance of Java so bad, relative to Fortran? In the case of matrix-multiply, the IBM XLF Fortran compiler uses several high-order transformations to achieve high-performance, including: blocking (for better cache reuse), loop unrolling, and scalar replacement. Because of Java's strict sequential semantics, combined with the generation of precise exceptions when an array index is out-of-bounds, these same transformations are not legal in Java.

The goal of this paper is to show that we can close the performance gap between Java and Fortran or C++. The key to achieving high-performance in Java is a new transformation that creates regions of an iteration space in which all array indices are guaranteed to be in-bounds. This has both direct and indirect benefits. First, the actual checks for array bounds can be removed in those regions. More importantly, though, because all iterations in these *safe* regions will execute without exceptions, many of the high-order transformations applicable to Fortran and C++ (including parallelization) can be used. In the particular case of MATMUL on a RS/6000 SP 332MHz SMP node, we have achieved fully-compliant Java performance in excess of 500 Mflops.

The rest of this paper is organized as follows. Section 2 discusses one of our methods to create safe regions, without out-of-bounds array indices. Section 3 then discusses how to apply high-order transformations to these regions and lists performance improvements obtained with Java. Section 4 shows how we can parallelize MATMUL and presents more performance results. In Section 5 we discuss some related work. In particular, we show that speculative execution is an alternative strategy to enable many of the high-order transformations. Finally, in Section 6 we conclude this paper and discuss some future work.

2   Optimization of Array Bounds Checking

A major impediment to optimizing Java is the requirement that exceptions be thrown precisely. An exception must be thrown for any attempt to dereference a **null** pointer or perform an out-of-bounds array access [18]. Because most references in computationally intense Java loops are to arrays or via pointers, most references have the potential to generate an exception. Because of the precise exception requirement, it is impossible to do code motion across potential exceptions, and in general it is impossible to perform many optimizations.

Our solution to this problem is to transform the program so that most computation, in programs that perform few or no invalid accesses, is in loops that are provably free of invalid accesses. Intuitively, these loops are formed by tiling the iteration space of the loop nest with *regions*. A region is a set of adjacent iterations in the loop nest such that either (i) all accesses in the region are provably safe, *i.e.* will not cause an exception to be thrown, or (ii) one or more accesses may be invalid. An iteration i is placed into a type (i) region (also called a *safe region*) if no reference in iteration i causes an invalid access exception. Otherwise the iteration is placed into a type (ii) region (also called an *unsafe* region).

To execute the two types of regions, two versions of the loop nest are formed. One version, which executes the iterations in safe regions, has no code to check for access violations. The second version, which executes the iterations in the unsafe regions, performs all access violation checks explicitly mandated by the Java VM specification. By executing the regions and the iterations within the regions in proper order, the iteration space of the loop is executed in the original execution order. However, checks are only performed in unsafe regions.

2.1 Determining iterations with safe accesses

Let $A[f(i)]$ be the reference for which the safe bounds are being found. Let i be the loop index variable of a normalized loop with stride one. We refer to this loop as loop i. We discuss the case where $f(i)$ is a linear function of the form $c \cdot i + b$, where c and b are invariant within the loop, and $c > 0$. In [27,26], we discuss other methods for forming safe regions, and describe a variety of techniques to handle subscripted subscripts, constant subscript, general affine subscripts, and subscripts involving modulo operators. In the case of arrays of arrays, used in Java to simulate multi-dimensional arrays, we treat the access to each dimension of the array as a separate access.

Let lo(A) and up(A) be the lower and upper bounds of array A, respectively. Note that in Java programs, lo(A) will always be zero, but we specify it symbolically for generality. Let l_i and u_i be the lower and upper bounds of the iteration space of i, respectively. The safe iterations of i are defined as all iterations i such that $f(i) \geq$ lo(A) and $f(i) \leq$ up(A). Solving these two inequalities for i, and intersecting with the loop iteration space, gives the range of i that will not cause access violations in reference $A[c \cdot i + b]$:

$$\left(\left\lceil \frac{\text{lo}(A) - b}{c} \right\rceil \leq i \leq \left\lfloor \frac{\text{up}(A) - b}{c} \right\rfloor \right) \bigcap (l_i \leq i \leq u_i) \qquad (1)$$

The intersection of all ranges defined by Eq. 1, for all references in loop i indexed by i, defines the lower and upper bounds of the *safe region* for i. We denote these

(a) A d-dimensional loop nest:

$$
\begin{array}{l}
\textbf{for } (i_1 = l_{i_1}; i_1 \le u_{i_1}; i_1\text{++}) \\
\quad \textbf{for } (i_2 = l_{i_2}; i_2 \le u_{i_2}; i_2\text{++}) \\
\quad\quad \dots \\
\quad\quad\quad \textbf{for } (i_d = l_{i_d}; i_d \le u_{i_d}; i_d\text{++}) \\
\quad\quad\quad\quad B(i_1, i_2, \dots, i_d)
\end{array}
$$

(b) The loop-nest transformed:

$$
\begin{array}{l}
\textit{regions}(1,\ (\,),\ (\,),\ d,\ \mathcal{B},\ \mathcal{R},\ u_\delta = 0) \\
\textbf{for } (\delta = 1; \delta \le u_\delta; \delta\text{++})\ \{ \\
\quad \textbf{if } (\mathcal{R}[\delta].\tau == \textbf{test})\ \{ \\
\quad\quad \textbf{for } (i_1 = l_{i_1}(\delta); i_1 \le u_{i_1}(\delta); i_1\text{++}) \\
\quad\quad\quad \textbf{for } (i_2 = l_{i_2}(\delta); i_2 \le u_{i_2}(\delta); i_2\text{++}) \\
\quad\quad\quad\quad \dots \\
\quad\quad\quad\quad\quad \textbf{for } (i_d = l_{i_d}(\delta); i_d \le u_{i_d}(\delta); i_d\text{++}) \\
\quad\quad\quad\quad\quad\quad B_{\textbf{test}}(i_1, i_2, \dots, i_d) \\
\quad \}\ \textbf{else}\ \{ \\
\quad\quad \textbf{for } (i_1 = l_{i_1}(\delta); i_1 \le u_{i_1}(\delta); i_1\text{++}) \\
\quad\quad\quad \textbf{for } (i_2 = l_{i_2}(\delta); i_2 \le u_{i_2}(\delta); i_2\text{++}) \\
\quad\quad\quad\quad \dots \\
\quad\quad\quad\quad\quad \textbf{for } (i_d = l_{i_d}(\delta); i_d \le u_{i_d}(\delta); i_d\text{++}) \\
\quad\quad\quad\quad\quad\quad B_{\textbf{notest}}(i_1, i_2, \dots, i_d) \\
\quad \} \\
\}
\end{array}
$$

Fig. 2. Bounds optimization code generation

bounds l_i^s and u_i^s, respectively. The safe region for the loop i implicitly defines two other regions for loop i. One is the lower unsafe region, $l_i \le i < l_i^s$, the other is the upper unsafe region $u_i^s < i \le u_i$.

We note that if the array is known to be rectangular, then l_i^s and u_i^s need be computed only once per dimension. If the array is ragged then computing l_i^s and u_i^s for some reference requires computing it for each possible value of the other indices. That is, in a nested (i, j) loop, the values of l_j^s and u_j^s can, in general, be functions of i.

Null pointer checks can be performed on array base pointers and other pointers while computing the safe region. If a **null** is found, the safe region is made empty, and all of the iterations placed in either the lower or upper unsafe region. Details on **null** pointer issues, handling the situation where the intersection of safe regions is empty, and other boundary cases, are found in [27].

2.2 Tiling the iteration space with regions

Consider a general d-dimensional rectangular loop nest, as shown in Fig. 2(a). The body of the loop is denoted by $B(i_1, i_2, \dots, i_d)$. Fig. 2(b) shows the form in which the transformed code is generated. We use the full $(l_{i_k},\ u_{i_k})$ and safe $(l_{i_k}^s,\ u_{i_k}^s)$ bounds of the loops to tile the iteration space. As shown in Fig. 2(b), a call is first made to a procedure *regions*, which computes the safe and unsafe regions that tile the iteration space of the given loop nest. The interested reader is referred to [27] for details on how these regions are computed. The δ driver loop iterates over the regions. If a region is not safe and requires tests, the first loop, whose body, $B_{\textbf{test}}(i_1, i_2, \dots, i_d)$, contains all necessary tests, is executed.

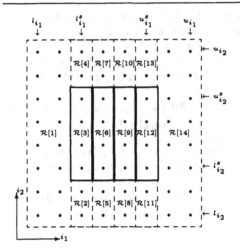

$l_{i_1}^s$ $l_{i_1}^s$ $u_{i_1}^s$ u_{i_1}

u_{i_2}

$\mathcal{R}[4]$ $\mathcal{R}[7]$ $\mathcal{R}[10]$ $\mathcal{R}[13]$

$u_{i_2}^s$

$\mathcal{R}[1]$ $\mathcal{R}[3]$ $\mathcal{R}[6]$ $\mathcal{R}[9]$ $\mathcal{R}[12]$ $\mathcal{R}[14]$

$l_{i_2}^s$

$\mathcal{R}[2]$ $\mathcal{R}[5]$ $\mathcal{R}[8]$ $\mathcal{R}[11]$

l_{i_2}

i_1

- $\mathcal{R}[1]$: tests in i_1 and i_2

- $\mathcal{R}[2], \mathcal{R}[5], \mathcal{R}[8], \mathcal{R}[11]$: tests in i_2

- $\mathcal{R}[3], \mathcal{R}[6], \mathcal{R}[9], \mathcal{R}[12]$: no tests

- $\mathcal{R}[4], \mathcal{R}[7], \mathcal{R}[10], \mathcal{R}[13]$: tests in i_2

- $\mathcal{R}[14]$: tests in i_1 and i_2

(a) Partitioning the iteration space into regions   (b) Mandatory tests in each region

Fig. 3. Example of iteration space for a perfectly nested two-dimensional loop.

Otherwise, the second, check-free loop nest, with body $B_{\mathbf{notest}}(i_1, i_2, \ldots, i_d)$, is executed.

An example of such tiling is shown in Fig. 3 for a 2-dimensional iteration space. The outer i_1 loop is divided into at most two unsafe regions, plus its safe regions. The inner i_2 loop is, in the worst case, divided into at most three regions for each iteration of the safe region of the outer loop. In the example, there are four iterations in the outer loop safe region (i.e., those iterations between $l_{i_1}^s$ and $u_{i_1}^s$).

Because each instance of the loop invoked by the driver corresponds to exactly one region as illustrated in Fig. 3, the code generation strategy facilitates code transformations. Within a region, and the corresponding loop nest, the iteration space is a contiguous subset of the original loop nest's iteration space. Thus if some iteration I' is adjacent to some iteration I in the loop nest instantiating a region, then I' is also adjacent to iteration I in the original loop nest. Stated differently, and referring to Fig. 3, the regions $\mathcal{R}[1]$ through $\mathcal{R}[14]$ are lexicographically ordered:

$$\mathcal{R}[1] < \mathcal{R}[2] < \mathcal{R}[3] < \mathcal{R}[4] < \ldots < \mathcal{R}[14]. \tag{2}$$

Because of this ordering, transformations within the loop nest corresponding to the safe regions are not constrained by exceptions thrown in the loop nest corresponding to an unsafe region. Furthermore, any orderings required to honor Java semantics in the presence of exceptions (thrown in iterations corresponding to unsafe regions) are enforced by the order in which regions are instantiated by the driver loop.

2.3   Thread safety

Threads are an integral part of the Java language specification. In general, it is not possible to determine at compile-time if a method will be sharing data with other concurrent threads as it executes. Therefore, it is necessary that our optimization be thread safe. Thread safety of the bounds checking optimization can be ensured if the bounds of an array used during the execution of procedure *regions* is the same as the bounds of the array when it is accessed in the **notest** loop.

Fig. 4(a) shows the layout of a 2-dimensional Java array (as mentioned earlier, non-zero lower bounds are used for generality). Each vector (either data vector or pointer vector) contains information about its extent. The bounds of an array change when an element of a pointer vector is assigned to point to another (data or pointer) vector, whose bounds are different than what originally existed. Issues of thread safety arise when another thread is changing the bounds of an array that is accessed by a concurrently executing thread running code optimized by the transformation of this section. We denote the thread changing the array bound as T_c, and the thread executing optimized code that accesses array elements as T_o, and give a worst case scenario. We stress that while asynchronously changing array extents may be poor programming practice, it is legal Java.

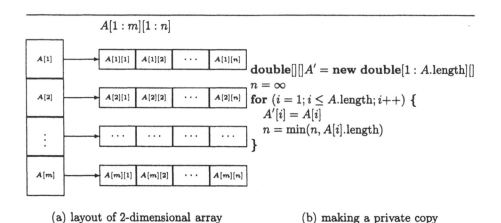

(a) layout of 2-dimensional array   (b) making a private copy

Fig. 4. Thread-safety issues are handled by privatizing data.

First, T_o executes *regions*, and computes l_i^s and u_i^s for the loop index i. Thread T_c then changes the extent of one vector of floating point numbers (v) to be shorter (so much shorter that u_i^s is no longer valid) by replacing it with v'. The storage after v' happens to be filled with values that are illegal floating point numbers. Next, during the execution of the **notest** loop, the value of the subscript function $f(i)$ exceeds the length of v', and a value that is an illegal floating point number is fetched. An operation is executed on the value, and the program generates an incorrect result (*e.g.*, NaN). Two non-compliant events have occurred: (i) an out-of-bounds access was performed and no exception was thrown, and (ii) the result of the optimized program does not correspond to a valid execution of the original program.

Fortunately, the Java memory model provides a solution to this problem. Java allows keeping copies of shared (or *main memory*) values in thread-private memory (or *working memory*) between synchronization points. To guarantee thread safety, we keep the vectors of pointers in private memory. Thus, referring to Fig. 4(a), (the values of) the $A[1 : m]$ vector will be kept in private memory during computation. These private values are then used by procedure *regions*, and the **test** and **notest** loops. Thus, any races and asynchronous changes in the size of the array will occur before the computation of l_i^s and u_i^s, and these values will be consistent throughout the execution of the modified code.

We show how to implement the privatization by copying array $A[1 : m]$ into a private array $A'[1 : m]$ in Fig. 4(b). While copying we can find the minimum extent of a row of A. In computing the safe bounds, A can be treated as rectangular, with this minimum extent as its second-axis extent. (In other words, this is the number of columns of A.) Matrix multiplication of $n \times n$ matrices is an $O(n^3)$ operation. The cost of privatizing and verifying the extents of one of the matrices is only $O(n)$. This is certainly insignificant for $n = 500$. We discuss some approaches to deal with very small n or less intensive computations in Section 5.

2.4   An alternate approach

Finally, we discuss here an alternative to this regions approach. A normal execution of a method such as matmul in Fig. 1 is expected to generate no exceptions. With current programming styles, an execution that causes an exception is most likely a misuse and it is not really important to optimize. Optimization of the normal case (no exceptions) can be achieved by a simple set of range tests before the execution of a loop nest. Let a loop nest have a reference of the form $A[\sigma]$ in its body. Let $\min(\sigma)$ and $\max(\sigma)$ be the smallest and largest values, respectively, that σ evaluates to during execution of the loop nest. A simple evaluation of $(\min(\sigma) \geq \mathrm{lo}(A)) \wedge (\max(\sigma) \leq \mathrm{up}(A))$ can tell if $A[\sigma]$ is guaranteed to always be safe or not. In the particular case of MATMUL, the triple-nested loop of Fig. 1 can be transformed to the following two-version code:

```
if (  (m ≤ rows(C)) ∧ (p ≤ cols(C))∧
      (m ≤ rows(A)) ∧ (n ≤ cols(A))∧
      (n ≤ rows(B)) ∧ (p ≤ cols(B))   ) {
   notest version of loop-nest
else {
   test version of loop-nest
}
```

where **rows**(A) and **cols**(A) denote the number of rows and columns of matrix A, respectively.

In loop nests where there are no exceptions (*i.e.*, all iterations of a loop are in a single safe region) the two-version code is, for all practical purposes, equivalent to the regions method. In this situation we have verified that the performance of the two methods (measured using MATMUL) is within our experimental error. Because a hand-implementation of the two-version method is simpler, we have used that approach in our experiments.

If there are bounds exceptions in the loop nest, the difference in performance between the two can be dramatic. For example, if the two version method was used, a single exception in some iteration of the outer loop would force the entire loop to run with checks and without optimizations. This is the case even if the exception is expected and cleanly handled by a **try-catch** clause. Using the regions based methods, the majority of the iteration space can still execute fully optimized. In [29], a programming style that uses array bounds exceptions as loop termination conditions is advanced. Regardless of how offensive this style may appear to a Fortran or C++ programmer, the loop termination condition is apparently simpler. Therefore, it is likely that this and related styles will enjoy some degree of popularity. With this style of programming, the versioning method will see no benefit from optimizations that require safe regions. In contrast, the regions based method will allow code with the best possible level of optimization to be selected dynamically (by the regions driver loop).

3   Optimizations

In this section, we describe the impact of various program transformations on the performance of the MATMUL program executing on a single processor. For completeness, we also analyze another program, MICROSTRIP, which does not have $O(n^3)$ behavior. This study was performed using the IBM HPCJ compiler for the POWER family of architectures [33], which converts the Java bytecode into native code of the target machine. The kernel of the MATMUL program is shown in Fig. 1. The transformations that we applied to this program are described below.

3.1   Program Transformations

The first program transformation reduces the overhead of checking for out-of-bounds array access violations, as described in Section 2. We generate two versions of the loop nest, one in which bounds checking computations are performed for each array reference, and the other in which no such computations are needed. A correctly written program is expected to execute the loop nest without bounds checking. This transformation not only reduces the overhead of array bounds checking, but also creates program regions that are provably free from exceptions. Those regions can now be transformed using standard loop transformation techniques [37,3,35,30] without violating Java semantics.

The next transformation on the program is to tile (block) the loop nest in the exception-free region, to improve the cache-performance by promoting greater reuse of data [36,30]. Tiling requires both strip-mining, which does not change the order of computation, and loop-interchange, which does change the order of computation. Loop-interchange (and tiling) can be legally performed only on that part of a Java program in which no exception may be thrown. Based on the existing algorithm in the IBM XLF compiler [30] to select the loop blocking parameters (which uses estimates of the number of distinct cache lines touched by the computation [15]), we choose strip size of 40 for each of the i, j, and k loops in the PowerPC 604e and strip size of 120 for the same loops in the POWER2.

Following loop tiling, we perform loop-unrolling [30] to increase the size of the loop body. This enables the backend to generate a better schedule that exploits the instruction-level parallelism. It also enhances data reuse within registers. We perform outer loop-unrolling, where both the i and the j loops are unrolled by a factor of 4 each.

The next program version uses scalar replacement [8,30], where references to the array being written, C, are replaced by references to scalar temporary variables in the innermost loop. Additional statements are used to load the temporaries from the array at the beginning of the loop iteration and to store them back at the end. It is well-known that scalar replacement enables the compiler backend to improve register-allocation for the code, as most backends are able to disambiguate scalar references more effectively.

Finally, to determine the performance benefits from the **looseNumerics** extension to Java [17] (described in Section 5), which allows the use of extended-precision (greater than 32- and 64-bit) arithmetic, we modified the compiler options that are passed on by the Java compiler to the backend. We turned on the option that allows the backend to use the fma (fused multiply-add) instruction. The fma instruction in the POWER family of architectures, fma a, b, c, x, computes $x = a + b * c$.

The programs were compiled using the -O option of the IBM HPCJ compiler, and with the -qarch and -qtune options set to turn on code tuning for the respective PowerPC and POWER2 architectures.

3.2   Experimental Results

Fig. 5 shows the performance of different versions of the MATMUL program on a PowerPC 604e and a POWER2 workstation, expressed as a fraction of the performance obtained for the best version written in C++. On the PowerPC, the base-line Java version achieves a performance of only 4.9 MFlops. After the transformation to create a safe region with no array bounds checking, the performance improves to 11.1 MFlops. The indirect impact of that transformation is even more significant. The application of tiling, which is enabled by that transformation, followed by other loop transformations described above, steadily improves the performance of the program. The final Java-compliant optimized program achieves a performance of 144.4 MFlops on the PowerPC, while the version which exploits the proposed **looseNumerics** Java extension (by using fma instructions) achieves 199.9 MFlops. This is is 63.6% of the performance of

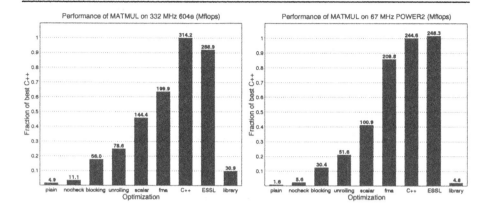

Fig. 5. Summary of results for MATMUL. (Mflop numbers at the top of each bar.)

the equivalent C++ version with identical loop transformations, and 69.2% of the hand-tuned ESSL version.

On the POWER2, the impact of these transformations is even more dramatic. The base-line Java program achieves 1.6 MFlops, whereas the optimized version with fma instructions achieves a performance of 209.8 MFlops, for an improvement by a factor of 131. The fully optimized Java program achieves 85.8% of the performance of the corresponding C++ version, and 84.5% of the ESSL performance.

For both machines, we also show the performance of the best Java version (with fma instructions) where only the transformation to create safe, exception-free, regions is not performed (these are the "library" bars). It would not be legal for a compiler to derive such a version from the given base-line program, as it has different semantics under Java when exceptions are possible. However, this measurement helps quantify the overhead of array bounds checking in an otherwise tuned (BLAS-3 style [14]) matrix-multiply routine. It can be seen that the performance of this version is quite poor on both the machines: 30.9 MFlops on a PowerPC and 4.8 MFlops on a POWER2.

In summary, the transformation to create exception-free regions in the MATMUL program has a large positive impact on the performance of the program, in two ways. First, it eliminates the actual overhead of bounds checking (which is more significant on the higher-performance version of the program). Second, it enables other loop transformations, which can be performed automatically by a compiler.

3.3 The MICROSTRIP benchmark

We use the MICROSTRIP benchmark to demonstrate that bounds checking optimization and the enabled transformations can also improve the performance of non-$O(n^3)$ computation. This benchmark solves the Poisson equation for the potential field in a dielectric. It uses an iterative solver. Each iteration involves two relaxation steps and the computation of an error value. Source code for these operations is shown in Fig. 6. These are both $O(n^2)$ computations.

```
for (int i=1; i<w; i++) {
  for (int j=1; j<h; j++) {
    b[i][j] = 0.25*(a[i+1][j]+
            a[i-1][j]+a[i][j+1]+
            a[i][j-1]);
  }
}

(a) relaxation step
```

```
error = 0.0;
for (int i=0; i<w+1; i++) {
  for (int j=0; j<h+1; j++) {
    error += Math.abs(b[i][j]-
            a[i][j]);
  }
}
error /= (w+1)*(h+1);
                        (b) error computation
```

Fig. 6. Main computations in MICROSTRIP.

The results for MICROSTRIP on both the PowerPC 604e and the POWER2 are shown in Fig. 7 (there is no ESSL version for this benchmark). Also, it does not benefit from the fma instruction (none are generated by the compiler) and that bar is absent as well. The reference performance is that obtained by the Fortran compiler with the highest level of optimization. The benefit of optimizing the checks for Java is more evident on the POWER2, where the performance jumps from 4.0 to 34.0 Mflops. Further optimizing the code with loop unrolling (of both the i and j loops of Fig. 6(a)) and scalar replacement brings Java performance to 87% of peak Fortran performance on the POWER2.

The performance of $O(n^2)$ matrix computations is often constrained by memory bandwidth, rather than processor speed. Therefore, we do not see great improvements in the PowerPC 604e, which has lower memory bandwidth than the POWER2. Nevertheless, optimizing the checks nearly doubles the performance of the Java version of MICROSTRIP. Additional optimizations bring it to 90% of Fortran performance. Again, in both plots we indicate by "library" the performance of the best Java version without checks optimization.

4   Parallelization

The final step in optimizing the performance of MATMUL is parallelization. It is not legal to directly parallelize the (i, j, k) loop nest of the Java version of MATMUL. Because exceptions can be thrown in any iteration of the loop nest, we have to guarantee that the values of $C[i][j]$ are modified in the sequential order of the iterations. Fortunately, the transformation of Section 2 creates regions that are exception-free. The same transformation that enabled blocking, unrolling, and the other optimizations of Section 3 also enables parallelization.

Fig. 8 presents our results from parallelization of MATMUL(see [28] for details). We show the performance of three versions of MATMUL for different number of threads: (i) a version that conforms to current Java semantics (identified by

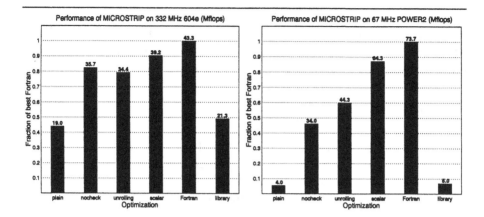

Fig. 7. Summary of results for MICROSTRIP. (Mflop numbers at the top of each bar.)

JAVA), (ii) a version with Java using the `fma` instructions (identified by JFMA), and (iii) a C++ version (identified by C++). The numbers at the top of the bars are the absolute Mflops achieved by each version. The speedup in each case is computed with respect to the best sequential case, 314 Mflops. The peak ESSL performance was 1183 Mflops.

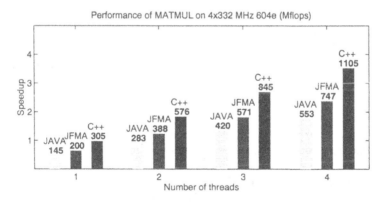

Fig. 8. Performance results comparing Java, Java with `fmas`, and C++.

Overall, we observe good scaling with the number of threads in all three versions: JAVA, JFMA, and C++. The C++ version achieves more than 90% of the peak ESSL performance. The version of Java with `fma` instructions, JFMA, achieves almost 2/3 of the peak ESSL performance. While this is still 30% less than the C++ version, it is a very respectable result. Even the strict Java version, JAVA, achieved more than 500 Mflops. This represents a more than 100-fold improvement in performance over our starting point!

5 Related Work

Examples of projects using Java for substantial numerical computing are described in [2,6,9,31]. In some cases, results have been positive despite the performance disadvantages of Java. As shown in [6], for some computations and certain machine configurations, current Java implementations can achieve within 50% of C performance. We note however, that the best performance reported in [6] for matrix multiplication in Java is only 50 Mflops.

There are four main approaches in the literature to optimizing array bounds checks: (i) the use of static data-flow analysis information to determine that a test is unnecessary [11,21,12,13,32], (ii) the use of data-flow information and symbolic analysis at compile time to reduce the dynamic number of tests remaining in the program [23,20,1,19,24], (iii) the regions based approach discussed in this paper and more generally in [26,27], and (iv) speculative methods discussed in [26].

Work in the first group uses data-flow information to prove at compile time that an array bounds violation cannot occur at run-time, and therefore that the test for the violation is unnecessary. Using the terms of our discussion, the goal of this work is to identify loops that are safe regions. In contrast, the goal of our work is to transform loops in order to *create* safe regions.

Work in the second group attempts to reduce the dynamic and static number of bounds tests. It also attempts to reduce the overhead induced by a test even if it cannot be eliminated. This is done (i) by hoisting tests out of loops when possible [24] and (ii) by also determining that a test is covered by another test [23,20,1,19] and can be eliminated.

Neither of these optimizations are usable with Java in general because the Java semantics requiring precise exceptions make the hoisting and reordering of tests illegal in many situations. Also, when an access violation exception is caught by a **try** block in the loop body, the loop should not be terminated (as would occur when hoisting tests).

The work in the third and fourth groups differs from what is discussed here in the generality of discussion, and in the experiments performed. Specifically, in [26] no benchmarking was performed. In [27] measurements compared the performance of programs with all checks, no checks, and our transformations. The more important effects of the transformation in enabling other optimizations was neither discussed in any detail, nor measured.

We emphasize that creating safe regions has the important effect of enabling an entire set of powerful optimization techniques. These techniques are constrained in Java by the requirement of precise exceptions. An alternative approach that enables this optimizations even in presence of (potential) exceptions is *speculative execution* [26]. A fully transformed and optimized version of a loop nest (or code fragment in general) can be generated and executed speculatively. If an access violation is detected, then the computation is rolled-back and restarted in strict order. This approach is analogous to speculative execution to explore parallelism in the presence of (potential) data dependences. Note that some mechanism to detect violations is necessary, so this approach does not get the benefit of eliminating the actual tests.

Several other projects have looked at aggressively optimizing Java. In [5] and [4], the **javar** and **javab** projects are described. These projects are closely related, with **javar** compiling Java source code and **javab** compiling byte code. The **javar** restructurer supports user specified parallelism, and the **javab** performs automatic parallelization. In [7], a project begun at the JavaSoft division of Sun Microsystems and its follow-on at Rice University are outlined. The work was aimed at a *dynamic* (or *just-in-time*) compilation system, and focused on local scalar optimizations. Hand compilations using a technique called *object inlining* achieved up to a 7-fold speedup on an *Oopack* routine (an object-oriented version of Linpack). The work of both of these projects are complementary to our work, and show the gains that can be made in Java performance.

Several groups have put forth proposals for altering the Java floating point semantics to allow greater freedom in scheduling floating point operations and exploiting floating point hardware. In [17], James Gosling describes a **looseNumerics** and **idealizedNumerics** class and method modifiers. The **looseNumerics** modifier allows a class or method to return floating point results with more precision than allowed by the Java standard. This enables the use of the fma operation on the IBM POWER and PowerPC architectures. For Intel *x86* processors, it allows intermediate and local variables to be kept in full 80-bit precision. As seen in Section 3.2, enabling the fma operation can have a dramatic effect on performance. Similar benefits should accrue to programs compiled for the *x86* processors. The **idealizedNumerics** modifier would allow floating point operations to be reordered as if they were associative, and would, for example, allow parallelization of the inner loop recurrence in the matrix multiply.

Sun has submitted for public review a change to the Java programming language [25,34] that allows extended precision in intermediate results. This proposal is similar to the **looseNumerics** proposal described above, and would allow the use of the fma operation. The Java Grande Forum, which is looking into the use of Java for high performance computing, is also working on proposals (see [16]) to relax Java floating point semantics.

Finally, various researchers have studied the benefit of adding rectangular, multidimensional arrays to Java. True multidimensional arrays have several advantages over Java arrays-of-arrays, such as: better data locality due to contiguous data allocation, simpler address computation of array elements, and better aliasing disambiguation. Specifically, in the context of our work, true multidimensional arrays offer the added advantages of simpler bounds checking optimization due to their fixed shapes, and reduced overhead of privatizing the array for thread-safety while performing the bounds checking optimization.

6   Conclusions

Eliminating and/or reducing the cost of verifying array references for validity is a key factor for achieving high-performance in Java for technical computing. The method we presented in this paper partitions the iteration space of a loop-nest into regions with different access violation characteristics. For technical computing, we expect most or all of the work to be performed in safe and exception-free regions. The benefit of creating safe regions is two-fold: (i) code to explicitly check for valid references is unnecessary in those regions and (ii) operation-reordering optimizations are allowed.

By applying high-order loop transformations (available today in the IBM XLF compiler) we have achieved single-processor Java performance in MATMUL that is within 65–85% of the best library and Fortran/C++ versions. We want to stress the fact that there are no fundamental reasons for the Java code not to achieve the same performance as C++ in the serial and parallel versions of MATMUL. The current differences are due to differences in the compilers, which result in different instructions schedules. As part of our future work, we want to investigate the causes of these differences and to provide the necessary fixes. Furthermore, in the MICROSTRIP application, we achieved 87–90% of the performance of a Fortran version of the code. This shows that the performance gains achieved with MATMUL are also attainable on $O(n^2)$ computations.

The safe regions also open up the possibility of automatic parallelization of Java codes. Automatic parallelization is being developed at IBM within the context of the *Toronto Portable Optimizer* (TPO) framework. This framework operates at an intermediate language level, and it is equally applicable to Fortran, C, C++, and Java. Parallelization of MATMUL yielded almost linear speedup for Java, achieving 750 Mflops on 4×332 MHz PowerPC 604e machine. We are looking forward to soon smashing the 1 Gflop barrier!

Acknowledgments

The authors wish to thank Rick Lawrence and Marc Snir for fruitful technical discussions, and for strongly supporting our research.

References

1. J.M. Asuru. Optimization of array subscript range checks. *ACM Letters on Programming Languages and Systems*, 1(2):109–118, June 1992.
2. C. A. Atwood, R. P. Garg, and D. DeRyke. A prototype computational fluid dynamics case study in Java. *Concurrency, Pract. Exp. (UK)*, 9(11):1311–18, November 1997. Java for Computational Science and Engineering - Simulation and Modeling II Las Vegas, NV, USA 21 June 1997.
3. U. Banerjee. Unimodular transformations of double loops. In *Proc. Third Workshop on Programming Languages and Compilers for Parallel Computing*, Irvine, California, August 1990.

4. A. Bik and D. Gannon. **javab** manual (version 1.0 BETA. In *ACM 1998 Workshop on Java for High-Performance Network Computing.* ACM SIGPLAN, 1998. Available at URL http://www.cs.ucsb.edu/conferences/java98.

5. A. Bik, J. Villacis, and D. Gannon. **javar**: A prototype Java restructuring compiler. *Concurrency, Pract. Exp. (UK)*, 9(11):1181–91, November 1997. Java for Computational Science and Engineering - Simulation and Modeling II Las Vegas, NV, USA 21 June 1997.

6. R. F. Boisvert, J. J. Dongarra, R. Pozo, K. A. Remington, and G. W. Stewart. Developing numerical libraries in Java. In *ACM 1998 Workshop on Java for High-Performance Network Computing.* ACM SIGPLAN, 1998. Available at http://www.cs.ucsb.edu/conferences/java98.

7. Z. Budimlic and K. Kennedy. Optimizing Java: Theory and practice. *Concurrency, Pract. Exp. (UK)*, 9(11):445–63, November 1997. Java for Computational Science and Engineering - Simulation and Modeling II Las Vegas, NV, USA 21 June 1997.

8. D. Callahan, S. Carr, and K. Kennedy. Improving register allocation for subscripted variables. In *Proc. ACM SIGPLAN '90 Conference on Programming Language Design and Implementation*, White Plains, NY, June 1990.

9. H. Casanova, J. Dongarra, and D. M. Doolin. Java access to numerical libaries. *Concurrency, Pract. Exp. (UK)*, 9(11):1279–91, November 1997. Java for Computational Science and Engineering - Simulation and Modeling II Las Vegas, NV, USA 21 June 1997.

10. IBM Corporation. IBM High Performance Compiler for Java, 1997. Available for download at http://www.alphaWorks.ibm.com/formula.

11. P. Cousot and R. Cousot. Abstract interpretation: A unified lattice model for static analysis of programs by construction or approximation of fixpoints. In *Conference Record of the 4'th ACM Symposium on Principles of Programming Languages*, pages 238–252, January 1977.

12. P. Cousot and N. Halbwachs. Automatic discovery of linear restraints among variables of a program. In *Conference Record of the 5'th ACM Symposium on Principles of Programming Languages*, pages 84–96, January 1978.

13. P. Cousot and N. Halbwachs. Automatic proofs of the absence of common runtime errors. In *Conference Record of the 5'th ACM Symposium on Principles of Programming Languages*, pages 105–118, January 1978.

14. J.J. Dongarra, I.S. Duff, D.C. Sorensen, and H.A. van der Vorst. *Solving Linear Systems on Vector and Shared Memory Computers*. Society for Industrial and Applied Mathematics, 1991.

15. J. Ferrante, V. Sarkar, and W. Thrash. On estimating and enhancing cache effectiveness. In *Proc. Fourth Workshop on Programming Languages and Compilers for Parallel Computing*, August 1991.

16. Java Grande Forum. Issues in numerical computing with Java. Document available at URL http://math.nist.gov/javanumerics/issues.html, March 1998.

17. James Gosling. The evolution of numerical computing in Java. Document available at Web-page http://java.sun.com/people/jag/FP.html. Sun Microsystems.

18. James Gosling, Bill Joy, and Guy Steele. *The Java$^{(TM)}$ Language Specification*. Addison-Wesley, 1996.

19. R. Gupta. A fresh look at optimizing array bounds checking. In *Proceedings of the ACM SIGPLAN '90 Conference on Programming Language Design and Implementation*, pages 272–282, June 1990.

20. R. Gupta. Optimizing array bound checks using flow analysis. *ACM Letters on Programming Languages and Systems*, 2(1-4):135–150, March–December 1993.

21. W.H. Harrison. Compiler analysis for the value ranges for variables. *IEEE Transactions on Software Engineering*, SE3(3):243–250, May 1977.
22. International Business Machines Corporation. *IBM Engineering and Scientific Subroutine Library for AIX - Guide and Reference*, December 1997.
23. P. Kolte and M. Wolfe. Elimination of redundant array subscript range checks. In *Proceedings of the ACM SIGPLAN '95 Conference on Programming Language Design and Implementation*, pages 270–278, Jun 1995.
24. V. Markstein, J. Cocke, and P. Markstein. Elimination of redundant array subscript range checks. In *Proceedings of the ACM SIGPLAN '82 Conference on Programming Language Design and Implementation*, pages 114–119, June 1982.
25. Sun Microsystems. Sun proposes modification to Java programming languages's floating point specification. http://www.sun.com/smi/Press/sunflash/9803/sunflash.980324.17.html, 1998.
26. S. P. Midkiff, J. E. Moreira, and M. Gupta. Method for optimizing array bounds checks in programs. Patent pending, IBM Docket #YO-998-052, filed with U. S. Patent Office, April 24th, 1998.
27. S.P. Midkiff, J.E. Moreira, and M. Snir. Optimizing bounds checking in java programs. *IBM Systems Journal*, 37(3):409–453, August 1998.
28. J. E. Moreira, S. P. Midkiff, and M. Gupta. From flop to megaflops: Java for technical computing, 1998. Submitted to ACM TOPLAS, IBM Research Report 21166.
29. D. Orchard. Better peformance with exceptions in Java. *Byte*, pages 53–54, March 1998. In the *Core Programming* feature.
30. V. Sarkar. Automatic selection of high-order transformations in the IBM XL Fortran compilers. *IBM Journal of Research and Development*, 41(3), May 1997.
31. M. Schwab and J. Schroeder. Algebraic java classes for numerical optimization. In *ACM 1998 Workshop on Java for High-Performance Network Computing*. ACM SIGPLAN, 1998. Available at http://www.cs.ucsb.edu/conferences/java98.
32. B. Schwarz, W. Kirchgassner, and R. Landwehr. An optimizer for Ada - design, experience and results. In *Proceedings of the ACM SIGPLAN '88 Conference on Programming Language Design and Implementation*, pages 175–185, June 1988.
33. V. Seshadri. IBM high performance compiler for Java. *AIXpert Magazine*, September 1997. Electronic publication available at URL http://www.developer.ibm.com/library/aixpert.
34. Proposal for extension of java floating point in jdk 1.2. http://java.sun.com/feedback/fp.html, 1998.
35. M. E. Wolf and M. S. Lam. A loop transformation theory and an algorithm to maximize parallelism. *IEEE Transactions on Parallel and Distributed Systems*, 2(4):452–471, October 1991.
36. M. J. Wolfe. Iteration space tiling for memory hierarchies. In *Proc. 3rd SIAM Conference on Parallel Processing for Scientific Computing*, pages 357–361, Philadelphia, PA, 1987.
37. M. J. Wolfe. *Optimizing Supercompilers for Supercomputers*. The MIT Press, 1989.

Considerations in HPJava Language Design and Implementation

Guansong Zhang, Bryan Carpenter, Geoffrey Fox, Xinying Li, and Yuhong Wen

NPAC at Syracuse University
Syracuse, NY 13244, USA
{dbc,zgs,gcf,lxm,xli,wen}@npac.syr.edu

Abstract. This paper discusses some design and implementation issues in the *HPJava* language. The language is briefly reviewed, then the class library that forms the foundation of the translation scheme is described. Through example codes, we illustrate how HPJava source codes can be translated straightforwardly to ordinary SPMD Java programs calling this library. This is followed by a discussion of the rationale for introducing the language in the first place, and of how various language features have been designed to facilitate efficient implementation.

1   Introduction

HPJava is a programming language extended from Java to support parallel programming, especially (but not exclusively) data parallel programming on message passing and distributed memory systems, from multi-processor systems to workstation clusters.

Although it has a close relationship with HPF [5], the design of HPJava does not inherit the HPF programming model. Instead the language introduces a high-level structured SPMD programming style—the *HPspmd* model. A program written in this kind of language explicitly coordinates well-defined process groups. These cooperate in a loosely synchronous manner, sharing logical threads of control. As in a conventional distributed-memory SPMD program, only a process owning a data item such as an array element is allowed to access the item directly. The language provides special constructs that allow programmers to meet this constraint conveniently.

Besides the normal variables of the sequential base language, the language model introduces classes of global variables that are stored collectively across process groups. Primarily, these are *distributed arrays*. They provide a global name space in the form of globally subscripted arrays, with assorted distribution patterns. This helps to relieve programmers of error-prone activities such as the local-to-global, global-to-local subscript translations which occur in data parallel applications.

S. Chatterjee (Ed.): LCPC'98, LNCS 1656, pp. 18–33, 1999.

In addition to special data types the language provides special constructs to facilitate both data parallel and task parallel programming. Through these constructs, different processors can either work simultaneously on globally addressed data, or independently execute complex procedures on locally held data. The conversion between these phases is seamless.

In the traditional SPMD mold, the language itself does not provide implicit data movement semantics. This greatly simplifies the task of the compiler, and should encourage programmers to use algorithms that exploit locality. Data on remote processors is accessed exclusively through explicit library calls. In particular, the initial HPJava implementation relies on a library of collective communication routines originally developed as part of an HPF runtime library. Other distributed-array-oriented communication libraries may be bound to the language later. Due to the explicit SPMD programming model, low level MPI communication is always available as a fall-back. The language itself only provides basic concepts to organize data arrays and process groups. Different communication patterns are implemented as library functions. This allows the possibility that if a new communication pattern is needed, it is relatively easily integrated through new libraries.

The preceding paragraphs attempt to characterize a language independent programming style. This report only briefly sketches the HPJava language. For further details, please refer to [2,15]. Here we will discuss in more depth some issues in the language design and implementation. With the pros and cons explained, the language can be better understood and appreciated.

Since it is easier to comment on the language design with some knowledge of its implementation, this document is organized as follows: section 2 briefly reviews the HPJava language extensions; section 3 outlines a simple but complete implementation scheme for the language; section 4 explains the language design issues based on its implementation; finally, the expected performance and test results are given.

2   Overview of HPJava

Java already provides parallelism through threads. But that model of parallelism can only be easily exploited on shared memory computers. HPJava is targetted at distributed memory parallel computers (most likely, networks of PCs and workstations).

HPJava extends Java with class libraries and some additional syntax for dealing with *distributed arrays*. Some or all of the dimensions of a these arrays can be declared as *distributed ranges*. A distributed range defines a range of integer subscripts, and specifies how they are mapped into a process grid dimension. It is represented by an object of base class Range. Process grids—equivalent to processor arrangements in HPF—are described by suitable classes. A base class Group describes a general group of processes and has subclasses Procs1, Procs2, ..., representing one-dimensional process grids, two-dimensional process grids, and so on. The inquiry function dim returns an object describing a particular dimension of a grid. In the example

```
Procs2 p = new Procs2(3, 2) ;

Range x = new BlockRange(100, p.dim(0)) ;
Range y = new BlockRange(200, p.dim(1)) ;

float [[,]] a = new float [[x, y]] on p ;
```

a is created as a 100×200 array, block-distributed over the 6 processes in p. The Range subclass BlockRange describes a simple block-distributed range of subscripts, analogous to BLOCK distribution format in HPF. The arguments of the BlockRange constructor are the extent of the range and an object defining the process grid dimension over which the range is distributed.

In HPJava the type-signatures and constructors of distributed arrays use double brackets to distinguish them from ordinary Java arrays. Selected dimensions of a distributed array may have a collapsed (sequential) ranges rather than a distributed ranges: the corresponding slots in the type signature of the array should include a * symbol. In general the constructor of the distributed array is followed by an on clause, specifying the process group over which the array is distributed. (If this is omitted the group defaults to the APG, see below.) Distributed ranges of the array must be distributed over distinct dimensions of this group.

A standard library, *Adlib*, provides functions for manipulating distributed arrays, including functions closely analogous to the array transformational intrinsic functions of Fortran 90. For example:

```
float [[,]] b = new float [[x, y]] on p ;
Adlib.shift(b, a, -1, 0, CYCL) ;

float g = Adlib.sum(b) ;
```

The shift operation with shift-mode CYCL executes a cyclic shift on the data in its second argument, copying the result to its first argument. The sum operation simply adds all elements of its argument array. In general these functions imply inter-processor communication.

Often in SPMD programming it is necessary to restrict execution of a block of code to processors in a particular group p. Our language provides a short way of writing this construct

```
on(p) {
  ...
}
```

The language incorporates a formal idea of an active process group (APG). At any point of execution some group is singled out as the APG. An on(p) construct specifically changes its value to p. On exit from the construct, the APG is restored to its value on entry.

Subscripting operations on distributed arrays are subject to some restrictions that ensure data accesses are local. An array access such as

```
a [17, 23] = 13 ;
```

is forbidden because typical processes do not hold the specified element. The idea of a *location* is introduced. A location can be viewed as an abstract element, or "slot", of a distributed range. The syntax x [n] stands for location n in range x. In simple array subscripting operations, distributed dimensions of arrays can only be subscripted using locations (not integer subscripts). These must be locations in the appropriate range of the array. Moreover, locations appearing in simple subscripting operations must be *named locations*, and named locations can only be scoped by *at* and *overall* constructs.

The *at* construct is analogous to *on*, except that its body is executed only on processes that hold the specified location. The array access above can be safely written as:

```
at(i = x [17])
  at(j = y [23])
    a [i, j] = 13 ;
```

Any location is mapped to a particular slice of a process grid. The body of the *at* construct only executes on processes that hold the location specified in its header.

The last *distributed control* construct in the language is called *overall*. It implements a distributed parallel loop, and is parametrized by a range. Like *at*, the header of this construct scopes a named location. In this case the location can be regarded as a parallel loop index.

```
float [[,]] a = new float [[x, y]], b = new float [[x, y]] ;
```

```
overall(i = x)
  overall(j = y)
    a [i, j] = 2 * b [i, j] ;
```

The body of an *overall* construct executes, conceptually in parallel, for every location in the range of its index. An individual "iteration" executes on just those processors holding the location associated with the iteration. Because of the rules about use of subscripts, the body of an *overall* can usually only combine elements of arrays that have some simple alignment relation relative to one another. The idx member of Range can be used in parallel updates to yield expressions that depend on global index values.

Other important features of the language include Fortran-90-style regular array sections (*section construction* operations look similar to simple subscripting operations, but are distinguished by use of double brackets), an associated idea of *subranges*, and *subgroups*, which can be used to represent the restricted APG inside *at* and *overall* constructs.

The language extensions are most directly targetted at data parallelism. But an HPJava program is implicitly an SPMD Java program, and task parallelism is available by default. A structured way to write a task parallel program is to write an overall construct parametrized by a process dimension (which is a particular kind of range). The body of the loop executes once in each process. The body can execute one or more "tasks" of arbitrary complexity. Task parallel programming with distributed arrays can be facilitated by extending the standard library with one-sided communication operations to access remote patches of the arrays, and we are investigating integration of software from the PNNL Global Array Toolset [8] in this connection.

3   Translation scheme

The initial HPJava compiler is implemented as a source-to-source translator converting an HPJava program to a Java node program, with calls to runtime functions. The runtime system is built on the NPAC PCRC runtime library [3], which has a kernel implemented in C++ and a Java interface implemented in Java and C++.

3.1   Java packages for HPspmd programming

The current runtime interface for HPJava is called *adJava*. It consists of two Java packages. The first is the HPspmd runtime proper. It includes the classes needed to translate language constructs. The second package provides communication and some simple I/O functions. These two packages will be outlined in this section.

The classes in the first package include an environment class, distributed array "container classes", and related classes describing process groups and index ranges. The environment class SpmdEnv provides functions to initialize and finalize the underlying communication library (currently MPI). Constructors call native functions to prepare the lower level communication package. An important field, apg, defines the group of processes that is cooperating in "loose synchrony" at the current point of execution.

The other classes in this package correspond directly to HPJava built-in classes. The first hierarchy is based on Group. A *group*, or *process group*, defines some subset of the processes executing the SPMD program. Groups have two important roles in HPJava. First they are used to describe how program variables such as arrays are distributed or replicated across the process pool. Secondly they are used to specify which subset of processes execute a particular code fragment. Important members of adJava Group class include the pair on(), no() used to translate the *on* construct. The most common way to create a group object is through the constructor for one of the subclasses representing a *process grid*. The subclass Procs represents a grid of processes and carries information on process dimensions: in particular an inquiry function dim(r) returns a range object describing the r-th process dimension. Procs is further subclassed by Procs0, Procs1, Procs2, ... which provide simpler constructors for fixed dimensionality process grids. The class hierarchy of groups and process grids is shown in figure 1.

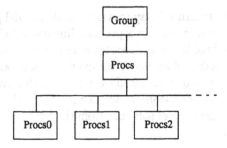

Fig. 1. The HPJava Group hierarchy

The second hierarchy in the package is based on **Range**. A *range* is a map from the integer interval $0, \ldots, n-1$ into some process dimension (ie, some dimension of a process grid). Ranges are used to parametrize distributed arrays and the *overall* distributed loop. The most common way to create a range object

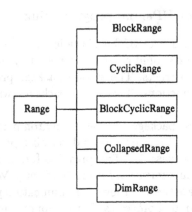

Fig. 2. The HPJava Range hierarchy

is to use the constructor for one of the subclasses representing ranges with specific *distribution formats*. The current class hierarchy is given in figure 2. Simple block distribution format is implemented by **BlockRange**, while **CyclicRange** and **BlockCyclicRange** represent other standard distribution formats of HPF. The subclass **CollapsedRange** represents a sequential (undistributed range). Finally, **DimRange** represents the range of coordinates of a process dimension itself—just one element is mapped to each process.

The related adJava class **Location** represents an individual location in a particular distributed range. Important members of the adJava **Range** class include the function **location(i)** which returns the ith location in a range and its inverse, **idx(1)**, which returns the global subscript associated with a given location. Important members of the Location class include at() and ta(), used in the implementation of the HPJava that *at* construct.

Finally in this package we have the rather complex hierarchy of classes representing distributed arrays. HPJava global arrays declared using [[ ]] are represented by Java objects belonging to classes such as:

```
Array1dI, Array1cI,
Array2ddI, Array2dcI, Array2cdI, Array2ccI,
...
Array1dF, Array1cF,
Array2ddF, Array2dcF, Array2cdF, Array2ccF,
...
```

Generally speaking the class Array*ndc...T* represents n-dimensional distributed array with elements of type T, currently one of I, F, ..., meaning int, float, ...[1]. The penultimate part of the class name is a string of n "c"s and "d"s specifying whether each dimension is collapsed or distributed. These correlate with presence or absence of an asterisk in slots of the HPJava type signature. The concrete Array... classes implement a series of abstract interfaces. These follow a similar naming convention, but the root of their names is Section rather than Array (so Array2dcI, for example, implements Section2dcI). The hierarchy of Section interfaces is illustrated in figure 3. The need to introduce the Section

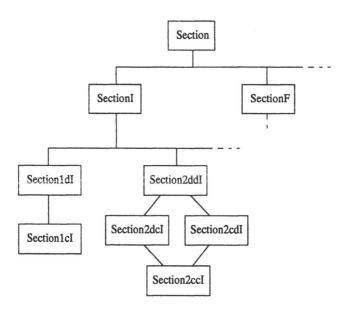

Fig. 3. The adJava Section hierarchy

---

[1] In the inital implementation, the element type is restricted to the Java primitive types.

interfaces should be evident from the hierarchy diagram. The type hierarchy of HPJava involves a kind of multiple inheritance. The array type int [[*, *]], for example, is a specialization of *both* the types int [[*,]] and int [[, *]]. Java allows "multiple inheritance" only from interfaces, not classes.

We will illustrate constructors of the Array classes in later examples. Here we mention some important members of the Section interfaces. The inquiry dat() returns an ordinary one dimensional Java array used to store the locally held elements of the distributed array. The member pos(i, ...), which takes n arguments, returns the local offset of the element specified by its list of arguments. Each argument is either a location (if the corresponding dimension is distributed) or an integer (if it is collapsed). The inquiry grp() returns the group over which elements of the array are distributed. The inquiry rng(d) returns the dth range of the array.

The second package in adJava is the communication library. The adJava communication package includes classes corresponding to the various collective communication schedules provided in the NPAC PCRC kernel. Most of them provide of a constructor to establish a schedule, and an **execute** method, which carries out the data movement specified by the schedule. The communication schedules provided in this package are based on the NPAC runtime library. Different communication models may eventually be added through further packages.

The collective communication schedules can be used directly by the programmer or invoked through invoked through certain wrapper functions. A class named Adlib is defined with static members that create and execute communication schedules and perform simple I/O functions. This class includes, for example, the following methods, each implemented by constructing the appropriate schedule and then executing it.

```
static public void remap(Section dst, Section src)
static public void shift(Section dst, Section src,
                         int shift, int dim, int mode)
static public void copy(Section dst, Section src)
static public void writeHalo(Section src,
                             int[] wlo, int[] whi, int[] mode)
```

Use of these functions will be illustrated in later examples. Polymorphism is achieved by using arguments of class Section.

3.2   Programming in the adJava interface

In this section we illustrate through an example (Fox's algorithm [11] for matrix multiplication) how to program in the adJava interface. We assume A and B are square matrices of order n, so $C = AB$ is also a square matrix of order n. Fox's algorithm organizes A, B and C into sub-matrices on a P by P process array. It takes P steps. In each step, a sub-matrix of A is broadcast across each row of the processes, a local block matrix product is computed, and array B is shifted for computation in the next step.

We can program this algorithm in HPJava, using Adlib.remap to broadcast submatrices, Adlib.shift to shift array B, and Adlib.copy to copy data back after shifting. The HPJava program is given in figure 4. The subroutine `matmul` for local matrix multiplication will be given in the next section.

This HPJava program is slightly atypical: it uses arrays distributed explicitly over process dimensions, rather than using higher-level ranges such as `BlockRange` to describe the distribution of the arrays. Hence, two-dimensional matrices are represented as four dimensional arrays with two distributed ranges (actually process dimensions) and two collapsed ranges (spanning the local block). This simplifies the initial discussion.

```
Procs2 p = new Procs2(P,P);
Range x = p.dim(0), y = p.dim(1);
on(p) {
  float [[,,*,*]] a = new float [[x,y,B,B]];
  float [[,,*,*]] b = new float [[x,y,B,B]];

  ... initialize a, b elements ...

  float [[,,*,*]] c = new float [[x,y,B,B]];
  float [[,,*,*]] tmp = new float [[x,y,B,B]];

  for (int k = 0; k<P; k++) {
    overall(i = x) {
      float [[*,*]] sub = new float [[B,B]];
      Adlib.remap(sub, a[[i, (x.idx(i) + k) % P, :, :]]);
                      // Broadcast sub-matrix of 'a'
      overall(j = y)
        matmul(c[[i, j, :, :]], sub, b[[i, j, :, :]]);
                      // Local matrix multiplication
    }
    Adlib.shift(tmp, b, 1, 0, CYCLIC);
          // Cyclic shift 'b' in first dim, amount 1
    Adlib.copy(b, tmp);
  }
}
```

Fig. 4. Algorithm for matrix multiplication in HPJava

We can rewrite the program in pure Java language using our adJava interface. A translation is given in figure 5. This is an executable Java program. One can use (for example) `mpirun` to start Java virtual machines on P^2 processors and let them simultaneously load the Fox class. This naive translation uses *for* loops plus *at* constructs to simulate the *overall* constructs. The function pairs on,no and at,ta adjust the field `spmd.apg`, which records the current active process group. The dynamic alteration of this group plays an non-trivial role in this program. The call to `remap` implements a broadcast because the temporary `sub` is replicated over the process group active at it's point of declaration. Within the overall(i = x) construct, the locally effective APG is a row of the process grid. The rather complex code for section construction exposes various low-level inquiries (and one auxilliary class, Map) from the adJava runtime. The details are not particulary important here.

3.3   Improving the performance

The program for the Fox algorithm is completed by the definition of matmul. First in HPJava:

```
void matmul (float[[*,*]] c, float[[*,*]] b, float[[*,*]] c) {
  for (int i=0; i<B; i++)
    for (int j=0; j<B; j++)
      for (int k=0; k<B; k++)
        c[i,j]+=a[i,k]*b[k,j];
}
```

Translated naively to the adJava interface, this becomes:

```
public static void matmul(Section2ccF c, Section2ccF a,
                          Section2ccF b) {

  for (int i=0; i<B; i++)
    for (int j=0; j<B; j++)
      for (int k=0; k<B; k++)
        c.dat()[c.pos(i, j)] +=
            a.dat()[a.pos(i, k)] * b.dat()[b.pos(k, j)];
}
```

The methods dat and pos were introduced earlier.

It is clear that the segment of code above will have very poor run-time performance, because it involves many method invocations for each array element access. Because the array data is actually stored in a certain regularly strided section of a Java array, these calls are not really necessary. All that is needed is to find the address of the first array element, then write the other addresses as a linear expression in the loop variable and this initial value. The code above can be rewritten in the form given in figure 6. This optimization again exposes various low-level functions in the runtime—we omit details (see [3]). The effect is to compute the parameters of the linear expressions for the local address offsets. This allows inlining of the element calls. In this case the resulting expressions are linear in the induction variables of the *for* loops. If necessary the multiplications can be eliminated by standard compiler optimizations.

This segment of Java code will certainly run much faster. The drawback is that, compared with the first Java procedure, the optimized code is less readable. This is a simple example of the need for compiler intervention if the HPJava style of programming is to be made acceptable. Similar and more compelling examples arise in optimization of the overall construct. As described in [15] and illustrated in the example of the last section, a trivial implementation of the general overall construct is by a *for* loop surrounding an *at* construct. More sensibly, all the

```
class Fox {
  final static int P=2;
  final static int B=4;

  public static void matmul(Array2Float c,Array2Float a,Array2Float b) {
    ... implemented in next section ...
  };

  public static void main(String argv[]) {
    SpmdEnv spmd = new SpmdEnv(argv);
    Procs2 p=new Procs2(P,P);
    Range x=p.dim(0); Range y=p.dim(1);
    if(p.on()) {
      Section4ddccF a = new Array4ddccF(spmd.apg,x,y,B,B);
      Section4ddccF b = new Array4ddccF(spmd.apg,x,y,B,B);

      ... initialize a, b elements ...

      Section4ddccF c = new Array4ddccF(spmd.apg,x,y,B,B);
      Section4ddccF tmp = new Array4ddccF(spmd.apg,x,y,B,B);

      for (int k=0; k<P; k++) {
        for (int i=0; i<P; i++) {
          Location ii = x.location(i);
          if (ii.at()) {
            Section2ccF sub = new Array2ccF(spmd.apg,B,B);
            Location kk = a.rng(1).location((i + k) % P) ;
            Adlib.remap(sub,
                new Array2ccF(a.grp().restrict(ii).restrict(kk),
                              a.map(2), a.map(3), a.dat(),
                              a.map(0).offset(ii) + a.map(1).offset(kk)) ;
                              // Broadcast sub-matrix of 'a'
            for (int j=0; j<P; j++) {
              Location jj = y.location(j);
              if (jj.at()) {
                matmul(new Array2ccF(c.grp().restrict(ii).restrict(jj),
                                     c.map(2), c.map(3), c.dat(),
                                     c.map(0).offset(ii) + c.map(1).offset(jj)),
                       new Array2ccF(b.grp().restrict(ii).restrict(jj),
                                     b.map(2), b.map(3), b.dat(),
                                     b.map(0).offset(ii) + b.map(1).offset(jj))) ;
                              // Local matrix multiplication
              } jj.ta();
            }
          } ii.ta();
        }
        Adlib.shift(tmp, b, 1, 0, 0);
                              // Cyclic shift 'b' in first dim, amount 1
        Adlib.copy(b, tmp);
      }
    }
  }
}
```

Fig. 5. Algorithm for matrix multiplication in adJava

```
public static void matmul(Section2ccF c, Section2ccF a, Section2ccF b) {

    Map c_u0=c.map(0);
    Map c_u1=c.map(1);

    final int i_c_bas=c_u0.disp();
    final int i_c_stp=c_u0.step();
    final int j_c_bas=c_u1.disp();
    final int j_c_stp=c_u1.step();

    ... similar inquiries for a and b ...

    for (int i=0; i<B; i++) {
      for (int j=0; j<B; j++) {
        for (int k=0; k<B; k++) {
          c.data[i_c_bas+i_c_stp*i+j_c_bas+j_c_stp*j] +=
            a.data[i_a_bas+i_a_stp*i+k_a_bas+k_a_stp*k] *
            b.data[k_b_bas+k_b_stp*k+j_b_bas+j_b_stp*j];
        }
      }
    }
}
```

Fig. 6. Optimized translation of `matmul`

machines across a process dimension should simultaneously execute the body for all locally held locations in the relevant distributed range. Computation of the local offset of the array element can again be reduced to a linear expression in a loop variable instead of a function call.

4   Issues in the language design

With some of the implementation mechanisms exposed, we can better discuss the language design itself.

4.1   Extending the Java language

The first question to answer is why use Java as a base language? Actually, the programming model embodied in HPJava is largely language independent. It can bound to other languages like C, C++ and Fortran. But Java is a convenient base language, especially for initial experiments, because it provides full object-orientation—convenient for describing complex distributed data—implemented in a relatively simple setting, conducive to implementation of source-to-source translators. It has been noted elsewhere that Java has various features suggesting it could be an attractive language for science and engineering [7].

With Java as base language, an obvious question is whether we can extend the language by simply adding packages, instead of changing the syntax. There are two problems with doing this for data-parallel programming.

Our baseline is HPF, and any package supporting parallel arrays as general as HPF is likely cumbersome to code with. The examples given earlier using the adJava interface illustrate this point. Our runtime system needs an (in principle) infinite series of class names

```
Array1dI, Array1cI, Array2ddI, Array2dcI, ...
```

to express the HPJava types

```
int [[]], int [[*]], int [[,]], int [[,*]] ...
```

as well as the corresponding series for char, float, and so on. To access an element of a distributed array in HPJava, one writes

```
a[i] = 3 ;
```

In the adJava interface, it must be written as,

```
a.dat()[a.pos(i)] = 3 ;
```

This is for *simple* subscripting. In passing in section 3.2 we noted how even more complex Fortran-90 style regular section construction appeared using the raw class library interface.

The second problems is that a Java program using a package like adJava in a direct, naive way will have very poor performance, because all the local address of the global array are expressed by functions such as pos. An optimization pass is needed to transform offset computation to a more intelligent style, as suggested in section 3.3. So if a preprocessor must do these optimizations anyway, it makes most sense to design a set of syntax to express the concepts of the programming model more naturally.

4.2   Why not HPF?

The design of the HPJava language is strongly influenced by HPF. It emerged partly out of practices adopted in our efforts to implement an HPF compilation system [14]. For example:

```
!HPF$ POCESSOR     P(4)
!HPF$ TEMPLET      T(100)
!HPF$ DISTRIBUTE   T(BLOCK) ONTO P
      REAL         A(100,100), B(100)
!HPF$ ALIGN        A(:,*) WITH T(:)
!HPF$ ALIGN        B WITH T
```

have their conterparts in HPJava:

```
Procs1 p = new Procs1(4);
Range x = new BlockRange (100, p.dim(0));
float [[,*]] a = new float [[x,100]] on p;
float [[ ]] b = new float [[x]] on p;
```

Both languages provide a globally addressed name space for data parallel applications. Both of them can specify how data are mapped on to a processor grid. The difference between the two lies in their communication aspects. In HPF, a simple assignment statement may cause data movement. For example, given the above distribution, the assignment

```
A(10,10) = B(30)
```

will cause communication between processor 1 and 2. In HPJava, similar communication must be done through explicit function calls[2]:

```
Adlib.remap(a[[9,9]], b[[29]]);
```

Experience from compiling the HPF language suggests that, while there are various kinds of algorithms to detect communication automatically, it is often difficult to give the generated node program acceptable performance. In HPF, the need to decide on which processor the computation should be executed further complicates the situation. One may apply "owner computes" or "majority computes" rules to partition computation, but these heuristics are difficult to apply in many situations.

In HPJava, the SPMD programming model is emphasized. The distributed arrays just help the programmer organize data, and simplify global-to-local address translation. The tasks of computation partition and communication are still under control of the programmer. This is certainly an extra onus, and the language is more difficult to program than HPF[3]; but it helps programmer to understand the performance of the program much better than in HPF, so algorithms exploiting locality and parallelism are encouraged. It also dramatically simplifies the work of the compiler.

Because the communication sector is considered an "add-on" to the basic language, HPJava should interoperate more smoothly than HPF with other successful SPMD libraries, including MPI [6], CHAOS [4], Global Arrays [8], and so on.

4.3   Datatypes in HPJava

In a parallel language, it is desirable to have both local variables (like the ones in MPI programming) and *global* variables (like the ones in HPF programming). The former provide flexibility and are ideal for task parallel programming; the latter are convenient especially for data parallel programming.

In HPJava, variable names are divided into two sets. In general those declared using ordinary Java syntax represent local variables and those declared with [[ ]] represent global variables. The two sectors are independent. In the

---

[2] By default Fortran array subscripts starts from 1, while HPJava global subscripts always start from 0.

[3] The program must meet SPMD constraints, eg, only the owner of an element can access that data. Runtime checking can be added automatically to ensure such conditions are met.

implementation of HPJava the global variables have special data descriptors associated with them, defining how their components are divided or replicated across processes. The significance of the data descriptor is most obvious when dealing with procedure calls.

Passing array sections to procedure calls is an important component in the array processing facilities of Fortran90 [1]. The data descriptor of Fortran90 will include stride information for each array dimension. One can assume that HPF needs a much more complex kind of data descriptor to allow passing distributed arrays across procedure boundaries. In either case the descriptor is not visible to the programmer. Java has a more explicit data descriptor concept; its arrays are considered as objects, with, for example, a publicly accessible length field. In HPJava, the data descriptors for global data are similar to those used in HPF, but more explicitly exposed to programmers. Inquiry functions such as grp(), rng() have a similar role in global data to the field length in an ordinary Java array.

Keeping two data sectors seems to complicate the language and its syntax. But it provides convenience for both task and data parallel processing. There is no need for things like the LOCAL mechanism in HPF to call a local procedure on the node processor. The descriptors for ordinary Java variables are unchanged in HPJava. On each node processor ordinary Java data will be used as local varables, like in an MPI program.

4.4 Programming convenience

The language provides some special syntax for the programmer's convenience. Unlike the syntax for data declaration, which has fundamental significance in the programming model, these extensions are purely provide syntactic conveniences.

There are a limited number of Java operators overloaded. A group object can be *restricted* by a location using the / operation, and a sub-range or location can be obtained from a range using the [ ] operator enclosing a triplet expression or an integer, These pieces of syntax can be considered as shorthand for suitable constructors in the corresponding classes. This is comparable to the way Java provides special syntax support for String class constructor.

Another kind of overloading occurs in *location shift*, which is used to support *ghost regions*. A shift operator + is defined between a location and an integer. It will be illustrated in the examples in the next section. This is a restricted operation—it has meaning (and is legal) only in an array subscript expression.

5   Concluding remarks

In this report, we discussed design and implementation issues in HPJava, a new programming language we have proposed. We claim that the language has the flexibility of SPMD programming, and much of the convenience of HPF. Related languages include F– [9], Spar [12], ZPL [10] and Titanium [13]. They all take different approaches from ours. The implementation of HPJava is straightforwardly supported by a runtime library. In the next step, we will complete the HPJava translator and implement further optimizations. At the same time, we plan to integrate further SPMD libraries into the framework.

References

1. Jeanne C. Adams, Walter S. Brainerd, Jeanne T. Martin, Brian T. Smith, and Jerrold L. Wagener. *Fortran 90 Handbook.* McGraw-Hill, 1992.
2. Bryan Carpenter, Guansong Zhang, Geoffrey Fox, Xinying Li, and Yuhong Wen. Introduction to Java-Ad. http://www.npac.syr.edu/projects/pcrc/HPJava.
3. Bryan Carpenter, Guansong Zhang, and Yuhong Wen. NPAC PCRC runtime kernel definition. Technical Report CRPC-TR97726, Center for Research on Parallel Computation, 1997. Up-to-date version maintained at http://www.npac.syr.edu/projects/pcrc/docs.html.
4. R. Das, M. Uysal, J.H. Salz, and Y.-S. Hwang. Communication optimizations for irregular scientific computations on distributed memory architectures. *Journal of Parallel and Distributed Computing*, 22(3):462–479, September 1994.
5. High Performance Fortran Forum. High Performance Fortran language specification. *Scientific Programming*, special issue, 2, 1993.
6. Message Passing Interface Forum. *MPI: A Message-Passing Interface Standard.* University of Tenessee, Knoxville, TN, June 1995. http://www.mcs.anl.gov/mpi.
7. Geoffrey C. Fox, editor. *ACM 1998 Workshop on Java for High-Performance Network Computing*, February 1998. To appear in Concurrency: Practice and Experience.
8. J. Nieplocha, R.J. Harrison, and R.J. Littlefield. The Global Array: Non-uniform-memory-access programming model for high-performance computers. *The Journal of Supercomputing*, 10:197–220, 1996.
9. R.W. Numrich and J.L. Steidel. F–: A simple parallel extension to Fortran 90. *SIAM News*, page 30, 1997.
10. Lawrence Snyder. A ZPL programming guide. Technical report, University of Washington, May 1997. http://www.cs.washington.edu/research/projects/zpl/.
11. E Pluribus Unum. *Programming with MPI.* Morgan Kaufmann, 1997.
12. Kees van Reeuwijk, Arjan J. C. van Gemund, and Henk J. Sips. Spar: A programming language for semi-automatic compilation of parallel programs. *Concurrency: Practice and Experience*, 9(11):1193–1205, 1997.
13. Kathy Yelick, Luigi Semenzato, Geoff Pike, Carleton Miyamoto, Ben Liblit, Arvind Krishnamurthy, Paul Hilfinger, Susan Graham, David Gay, Phil Colella, and Alex Aiken. Titanium: A high-performance java dialect. In *ACM 1998 Workshop on Java for High-Performance Network Computing. Palo Alto, February 1998*, Concurrency: Practice and Experience, 1998. To appear.
14. Guansong Zhang, Bryan Carpenter, Geoffrey Fox, Xiaoming Li, Xinying Li, and Yuhong Wen. PCRC-based HPF compilation. In *10th International Workshop on Languages and Compilers for Parallel Computing*, volume 1366 of *Lecture Notes in Computer Science*. Springer, 1997.
15. Guansong Zhang, Bryan Carpenter, Geoffrey Fox, Xinying Li, and Yuhong Wen. A high level SPMD programming model: HPspmd and its Java language binding. In *International Conference on Parallel and Distributed Processing Techniques and Applications (PDPTA '98)*, July 1998.

A Loop Transformation Algorithm Based on Explicit Data Layout Representation for Optimizing Locality*

M. Kandemir[1], J. Ramanujam[2], A. Choudhary[1], and P. Banerjee[1]

[1] ECE Dept., Northwestern University,
Evanston, IL 60208, USA
{mtk,choudhar,banerjee}@ece.nwu.edu
[2] ECE Dept., Louisiana State University,
Baton Rouge, LA 70803, USA
jxr@ee.lsu.edu

Abstract. We present a cache locality optimization technique that can optimize a loop nest even if the arrays referenced have different layouts in memory. Such a capability is required for a global locality optimization framework that applies both loop and data transformations to a sequence of loop nests for optimizing locality. Our method finds a non-singular iteration-space transformation matrix such that in a given loop nest spatial locality is exploited in the innermost loops where it is most useful. The method builds inverse of a non-singular transformation matrix column-by-column starting from the rightmost column. In addition, our approach can work in those cases where the data layouts of a subset of the referenced arrays is unknown. Experimental results on an 8-processor SGI Origin 2000 show that our technique reduces execution times by up to 72%.

1 Introduction

As the disparity between processor and memory speeds increases, it is increasingly important to restructure programs so that the time spent in accessing or waiting for memory will be minimized. Previous research has shown that impressive speedups can be obtained if the programs are restructured to take advantage of the memory hierarchy by satisfying as many data references as possible from the cache instead of the main memory. Along these lines, several restructuring techniques have been offered including loop (iteration space) as well as array layout (data space) transformations [9,8,13]. The basic idea is to modify the access pattern of the program such that the data brought into cache is reused as much as possible before being discarded from the cache.

---

* M. Kandemir and A. Choudhary were supported by NSF Young Investigator Award CCR-9357840, NSF grant CCR-9509143 and Air Force contract F30602-97-C-0026. J. Ramanujam was supported by NSF Young Investigator Award CCR-9457768. P. Banerjee was supported by NSF grant CCR-9526325 and by DARPA contract DABT-63-97-C-0035.

S. Chatterjee (Ed.): LCPC'98, LNCS 1656, pp. 34–50, 1999.
© Springer-Verlag Berlin Heidelberg 1999

```
do i = 1, N                      do u = 1, N
  do j = 1, N                      do v = 1, N
    U[i+j,j] = U[j,j] + U[j,i+j]     U[u+v,v] = U[v,v] + U[v,u+v]
      + V[i,i+j]                       + V[u,u+v]
  end do                           end do
end do                           end do


do i = 1, N                      do u = 1-N, N+1
  do j = 1, N                      do v = max(1,1-u), min(N,N-u)
    U[i,i-j] = V[i,i-j] + 1         U[u+v,v] = V[u,u+v] + 1
  end do                           end do
end do                           end do

        (a)                              (b)
```

Fig. 1. (a) Original program. (b) Transformed program.
The transformed program exhibits good spatial locality provided that array U has diagonal memory layout and array V is row-major.

Loop transformations Consider an array reference $U[i, j]$ in a two-deep loop nest where the outermost loop is i and the inner loop is j. Assuming that the array U is stored in memory in column-major order and that the trip counts N of the enclosing loops are very large, successive iterations of the j-loop will touch different columns of array U which will very likely get mapped onto different cache lines. Let us focus on a specific cache line that holds the initial part of a given column. Before that column is accessed again, the j-loop sweeps through N different values; so, it is very likely that this cache line will be discarded from the cache. Consequently, in the worst case, every memory access to array U may involve a data transfer between the cache and memory resulting in high latencies. A solution to this problem is to *interchange* the loops i and j, making the i-loop innermost. As a result, a cache line brought into memory will be reused in a number of successive iterations of the i-loop, provided that the cache line is large enough to hold a number of array elements. Previous research on optimizing compilers [13,8,9,14] has proposed algorithms to detect and perform this loop interchange transformation automatically.

Data transformations Alternately, the same problem can be tackled by a technique called *data transformation* or *array restructuring*. It is easy to see that if the memory layout of array U mentioned above is changed from column-major to row-major, the successive iterations of the j-loop can reuse the data in the cache. Recently, several authors [10,2,7,5] have proposed data transformation techniques. Although these are promising because they are not affected by data dependences, the effect of a layout transformation is global, meaning that it effects the cache behavior of all loop nests that access the array assuming a fixed layout for each array. In this paper, we consider the possibility of different arrays with different layouts. Therefore, in a general case, given a loop nest, the compiler is faced with finding an appropriate loop transformation assuming that the arrays in the nest may have different—perhaps unspecified—layouts; current techniques are unable to handle this.

Combined data and loop transformations Consider the code fragment in Fig. 1(a), assuming that the arrays U and V are column-major by default. In this fragment, there are two disjoint loop nests with different access patterns. The first loop nest accesses array U diagonally and array V as row-major. The second loop nest accesses both arrays as row-major. Due to data dependence and conflicting access patterns of the arrays, the first loop nest cannot be optimized for locality of both arrays using the iteration space transformations alone. Using data layout transformations [4], we can determine that array U should be diagonally stored in memory and array V should be row-major. Now having optimized the first loop nest, we focus on the second loop nest. A simple analysis shows that for the best locality either the loops should be interchanged and the arrays should be stored diagonally in memory, or both the arrays should have row-major layout without any loop transformation. We note that neither of these solutions is satisfactory. The reason is that the layout of U is fixed as diagonal and that of array V as row-major in the first loop nest. Since we do not consider layout changes, accesses to one of the arrays in the second loop nest remain unoptimized in either case. One suggestion may be to use loop skewing [14] in the second loop nest, but this results in poor locality for array V. What we need for this second loop nest is a loop transformation which optimizes both the references under the assumption that the memory layout of the associated arrays are distinct: one of them is diagonal and the other one is row-major, as found in the first nest. This paper shows that such a transformation is possible. The resulting code is shown in Fig. 1(b). Notice that this program exhibits very good locality assuming that array U has diagonal layout and array V is row-major. Notice also that this optimized code requires the derived layouts for arrays U and V. The transformation that implements the desired layouts for arrays is rather mechanical; the associated details are beyond the scope of this paper and can be found elsewhere [7,4,10].

We present a framework which, given a loop nest, derives a transformation matrix for the case where the distinct arrays accessed in the nest may have different memory layouts. In addition, our solution works in the presence of undetermined layouts for a subset of the arrays referenced; this is of particular interest in enhancing locality beyond a single nest. The framework subsumes previous iteration space based linear locality enhancing transformation techniques which assume a fixed canonical memory layout for all arrays.

Outline After a brief review of the necessary terminology in Section 2, we summarize a framework to represent memory layout information mathematically in Section 3. In Section 4, we present a loop transformation framework assuming that the memory layout for all arrays is column-major. In Section 5, we generalize our approach to attack the problem of optimizing a loop nest assuming that the arrays referenced may have distinct memory layouts. Then in Section 6 we show how to utilize the partial layout information. We give our experimental results obtained on an 8-processor SGI Origin 2000 distributed-shared-memory multiprocessor in Section 7. We review the related work on data locality in Section 8 and conclude the paper in Section 9.

2   Terminology

In this paper we consider nested loops. An iteration in an n-nested loop is denoted by the *iteration vector* $\bar{I} = [\imath_1, \imath_2, ..., \imath_n]^T$. We assume that the array subscript expressions and loop bounds are affine functions of enclosing loop indices and symbolic constants. In such a loop nest, each reference to an array U can be modeled by an access (or reference) matrix $\mathcal{L}$ of size $m \times n$ and an m-dimensional offset vector $\bar{o}$ [8,13,14]. For example, a reference $U[i_1 + i_2, i_2 + 1]$ in a loop nest of depth two can be represented by $\mathcal{L}\bar{I} + \bar{o}$ where $\mathcal{L} = \begin{bmatrix} 1 & 1 \\ 0 & 1 \end{bmatrix}$ and $\bar{o} = [0,1]^T$. We focus on iteration space transformations that can be represented by integer non-singular square matrices. Such a transformation matrix is invertible and is of size $n \times n$ for an n-dimensional loop nest. The effect of such a transformation $\mathcal{T}$ is that each iteration vector $\bar{I}$ in the original loop nest is transformed to $\mathcal{T}\bar{I}$. Therefore, loop bounds and subscript expressions should be modified accordingly. Let $\bar{I}' = \mathcal{T}\bar{I}$. Since $\mathcal{T}$ is invertible, the transformed reference can be written as $\mathcal{L}\bar{I} + \bar{o} = \mathcal{L}\mathcal{T}^{-1}\bar{I}' + \bar{o}$. The computation of new loop bounds is done using Fourier-Motzkin elimination [12]. An iteration space transformation is legal if it preserves all data dependences in the original loop nest [14]. A linear transformation represented by $\mathcal{T}$ is legal if, after the transformation, $\mathcal{T}\bar{d}$ is lexicographically non-negative for each dependence $\bar{d}$ in the original nest.

3   Memory layout representation using hyperplanes

In this section, we briefly review the concepts [4] relating to the representation of memory layouts using hyperplanes. A *hyperplane* defines a set of elements $(\jmath_1, \cdots, \jmath_m)$ that satisfies

$$g_1 \jmath_1 + g_2 \jmath_2 + \cdots + g_m \jmath_m = c \tag{1}$$

for a constant c. Here, $g_1, \cdots, g_m$ are rational numbers called hyperplane coefficients and c is a rational number called hyperplane constant [11]. The hyperplane coefficients can be written collectively as a hyperplane vector $\bar{g} = [g_1, \cdots, g_m]^T$. Where there is no confusion, we omit the transpose. A *hyperplane family* is a set of hyperplanes defined by $\bar{g}$ for different values of c. It can be used to *partially* represent the memory layout of an array. We assume that the array elements on a specific hyperplane are stored in consecutive memory locations. Thus, for an array whose memory layout is column-major, each column represents a hyperplane whose elements are stored in memory consecutively. Given a large array, the relative order of hyperplanes with respect to each other may not be important. The relative storage order of columns (although well defined by column-major layout) is not important for the purposes of this paper. The hyperplane vector $(1,0)$ denotes a row-major layout, $(0,1)$ denotes column-major layout, and $(1,-1)$ defines a diagonal layout. Two array elements $\bar{J}$ and $\bar{J}'$ belong to the same hyperplane $\bar{g}$ if

$$\bar{g}^T \bar{J} = \bar{g}^T \bar{J}'. \tag{2}$$

As an example, in a two-dimensional array stored as column-major (hyperplane vector $[0, 1]$), array elements $[4, 5]$ and $[9, 5]$ belong to the same hyperplane (i.e., the same column) but elements $[4, 5]$ and $[4, 6]$ do not. We say that two array elements which belong to the same hyperplane have *spatial locality*. Although this definition of spatial locality is somewhat coarse and does not hold at the array boundaries, it is suitable for our locality optimization strategy.

In a two-dimensional array space, a single hyperplane family is sufficient to partially define a memory layout. In higher dimensions, however, we may need to use more hyperplane families. Let us concentrate on a three-dimensional array U whose layout is column-major. Such a layout can be represented using two hyperplanes: $\bar{g} = [0, 0, 1]^T$ and $\bar{h} = [0, 1, 0]^T$. We can write these two hyperplanes collectively as a *layout constraint matrix* or simply a *layout matrix* $L_U = \begin{bmatrix} \bar{g}^T \\ \bar{h}^T \end{bmatrix} = \begin{bmatrix} 0 & 0 & 1 \\ 0 & 1 & 0 \end{bmatrix}$. In that case, two data elements $\bar{J}$ and $\bar{J}'$ have spatial locality if

$$\bar{g}^T \bar{J} = \bar{g}^T \bar{J}' \quad \text{and} \quad \bar{h}^T \bar{J} = \bar{h}^T \bar{J}'. \tag{3}$$

The elements that have spatial locality should be stored in consecutive memory locations. The idea can easily be generalized to higher dimensions [4]. In this paper, unless stated otherwise, we assume column-major memory layout for all arrays. In Section 5, we show how to generalize our technique to optimize a given loop nest where a number of arrays with distinct memory layouts are accessed. Our optimization technique can work with any memory layout which can be represented by hyperplanes. The layout matrices that we use for column-major storage (starting from two-dimensional case) are as follows: $\underbrace{[0, 1]}_{2D}, \underbrace{\begin{bmatrix} 0 & 0 & 1 \\ 0 & 1 & 0 \end{bmatrix}}_{3D}, \underbrace{\begin{bmatrix} 0 & 0 & 0 & 1 \\ 0 & 0 & 1 & 0 \\ 0 & 1 & 0 & 0 \end{bmatrix}}_{4D}, \cdots$. In general, the column-major layout for an m-dimensional array can be represented by an $(m-1) \times m$ matrix $L = [l_{ij}]$ such that $l_{i(m-i+1)} = 1$ for $1 \leq i \leq (m-1)$ and $l_{ij} = 0$ for the remaining elements. Notice that each row of the layout constraint matrix represents a constraint on the elements that have spatial locality with respect to the associated layout. In some cases, the order of the rows in a layout constraint matrix may be important. But, for the purposes of this paper, we assume they are not. Thus, any row permutation of the layout matrices mentioned before is also considered a legal layout constraint matrix.

4 Transformation for optimizing spatial locality

Our objective is to transform a loop nest such that spatial locality will be exploited in the inner loops in the transformed nest. That is, when we transform a loop nest, we want two consecutive iterations of the innermost loop to access array elements that have spatial locality (i.e., reside on the same column by our definition of spatial locality). In particular, if possible, we want the accessed array elements to be next to each other so that they can be on the same cache

```
   do i = 1, N              do u = 1, N              do u = 1, N
     do j = 1, N              do v = 1, N              do v = 1, N
       do k = 1, N              do w = 1, N              do w = 1, N
         C[i,j] +=                C[w,v] +=                C[w,u] +=
           A[i,k] * B[k,j]          A[w,u] * B[u,v]          A[w,v] * B[v,u]
         end do                   end do                   end do
       end do                   end do                   end do
     end do                   end do                   end do

      (a)                       (b)                       (c)
```

Fig. 2. Matrix multiplication code. (a) Original loop nest. (b)-(c) Transformed loop nests.

line (or neighboring cache lines). This can be achieved if, in the transformed loop nest, the elements accessed by consecutive iterations of the innermost loop satisfy Equation (2) for two-dimensional arrays and the relation in Equation (3) for three-dimensional arrays and so on.

Assume $Q = T^{-1}$ for convenience. Ignoring the offset vector, after transformation T, new iteration vector $\bar{I}$ accesses (through $\mathcal{L}$) the array element $\mathcal{L}Q\bar{I}$. We first focus on two-dimensional arrays. For such an array U, the layout constraint matrix for the column-major layout is $L_U = [0, 1]$. Two consecutive iteration vectors can be written as $\bar{I} = [i_1, \cdots, i_{n-1}, i_n]^T$ and $\bar{I}_{next} = [i_1, \cdots, i_{n-1}, 1 + i_n]^T$. The data elements accessed by $\bar{I}$ and $\bar{I}_{next}$ through a reference represented by access matrix $\mathcal{L}$ will have spatial locality (see equation (2)) if $[0, 1]\mathcal{L}Q\bar{I} = [0, 1]\mathcal{L}Q\bar{I}_{next}$ or $[0, 1]\mathcal{L}Q[0, 0, \cdots, 0, 1]^T = 0$; i.e., $\bar{l}_m\bar{q}_n = 0 \Rightarrow \bar{q}_n \in Ker\{\bar{l}_m\}$, where $\bar{l}_m$ and $\bar{q}_n$ are the last row of matrix $\mathcal{L}$ and last column of matrix Q, respectively. Since $\bar{l}_m$ is known, we can always choose $\bar{q}_n$ from its null set (Ker set). Note that here m is 2.

Consider the matrix-multiplication loop nest shown in Fig. 2(a). The access matrices are $\mathcal{L}_C = \begin{bmatrix} 1 & 0 & 0 \\ 0 & 1 & 0 \end{bmatrix}, \mathcal{L}_A = \begin{bmatrix} 1 & 0 & 0 \\ 0 & 0 & 1 \end{bmatrix}$, and $\mathcal{L}_B = \begin{bmatrix} 0 & 0 & 1 \\ 0 & 1 & 0 \end{bmatrix}$.

For array C: $\bar{q}_3 \in Ker\{[0, 1, 0]\}$ $\Rightarrow$ $\bar{q}_3 = [\times, 0, \times]^T$

For array A: $\bar{q}_3 \in Ker\{[0, 0, 1]\}$ $\Rightarrow$ $\bar{q}_3 = [\times, \times, 0]^T$

For array B: $\bar{q}_3 \in Ker\{[0, 1, 0]\}$ $\Rightarrow$ $\bar{q}_3 = [\times, 0, \times]^T$.

Thus $Q = \begin{bmatrix} \times & \times & \times \\ \times & \times & 0 \\ \times & \times & 0 \end{bmatrix}$. Therefore, $Q_1 = \begin{bmatrix} 0 & 0 & 1 \\ 0 & 1 & 0 \\ 1 & 0 & 0 \end{bmatrix}$ and $Q_2 = \begin{bmatrix} 0 & 0 & 1 \\ 1 & 0 & 0 \\ 0 & 1 & 0 \end{bmatrix}$ are the only suitable permutation matrices. Fig. 2(b) and (c) give the transformed nests obtained using $T_1 = Q_1^{-1}$ and $T_2 = Q_2^{-1}$ respectively. Notice that although the spatial locality is good for both transformed versions, the one in Fig. 2(c) is expected to perform better (see [8]). Next, we will explain why and how the loop nest in Fig. 2(c) is preferred over the one in Fig. 2(b).

Notice that our approach as explained so far determines only (possibly part of) the last column of the matrix Q. The remaining elements can be filled in any way as long as the resulting Q is non-singular and its inverse (T) observes all data dependences. We will focus on how to complete a partially filled Q matrix later. For now, to see why the last column of Q is so important for locality, consider a reference to an m-dimensional array in an n-dimensional loop nest. Assume that $\mathcal{L} = [\bar{l}_1, \bar{l}_2, \cdots, \bar{l}_m]^T$ and $Q = [\bar{q}_1 \, \bar{q}_2 \cdots \bar{q}_n]$, where $\bar{l}_i$ is the ith row of $\mathcal{L}$ and $\bar{q}_j$ is the jth column of Q. Assuming $i_1, i_2, ..., i_n$ are the loops in the nest *after* the transformation, omitting the offset vector, the new reference matrix is of the form $\mathcal{L}Q[i_1, \cdots, i_n]^T = [\bar{l}_1\bar{q}_1i_1 + \cdots + \bar{l}_1\bar{q}_ni_n, \cdots, \bar{l}_m\bar{q}_1i_1 + \cdots + \bar{l}_m\bar{q}_ni_n]$. Since the spatial behavior of a reference is mainly determined by the innermost loop (in our case i_n) and all $\bar{l}_j$ are known, $\bar{q}_n$ is the sole factor determining the spatial locality. Our objective is to select $\bar{q}_n$ such that $\bar{l}_j\bar{q}_ni_n$ will be 0 for each $2 \leq j \leq n$, and $\bar{l}_1\bar{q}_ni_n$ will be (preferably) 1 or a small integer constant.[1] In two-dimensional case, since $m = 2$, selecting $\bar{q}_n$ from $Ker\{\bar{l}_m\}$ achieves precisely this goal.

Using a similar reasoning, we can see that in higher-dimensional cases, for good spatial locality in the innermost loop, the following relations should be satisfied

$$\bar{q}_n \in Ker\{\bar{l}_2\}, \bar{q}_n \in Ker\{\bar{l}_3\}, \cdots, \bar{q}_n \in Ker\{\bar{l}_m\}.$$

So far, we have only concentrated on determining the elements of the last column of Q. While, for most cases, this is sufficient to improve locality, in situations where the trip count of the innermost loop is small and some references exhibit temporal locality in the innermost loop, we may need to pay attention to the spatial locality carried by the outer loops as well. Let us consider the matrix-multiplication code of Fig. 2(a) again. In this example, one of the references exhibits temporal locality in the innermost loop. Consequently, it might be wise to take the second innermost loop into account as well. Recall that for this example previously we ended up with two possible permutation matrices. In fact, the partly filled Q matrix was $Q = \begin{bmatrix} \times & \times & \times \\ \times & \times & 0 \\ \times & \times & 0 \end{bmatrix}$. Now, we focus on the spatial locality in the second innermost loop. This corresponds to determining the elements of the second rightmost column of Q. Let us define $\bar{I}_k = [\imath_1, \cdots, \imath_{k-1}, \imath_k, \imath_{k+1}, \cdots, \imath_n]^T$ and $\bar{I}'_k = [\imath_1, \cdots, \imath_{k-1}, 1 + \imath_k, \imath_{k+1}, \cdots, \imath_n]^T$. This means that iteration vectors $\bar{I}_k$ and $\bar{I}'_k$ have exactly the same values for all loop index positions except the kth index where they differ by one. In this case, we say that $\bar{I}_k$ and $\bar{I}'_k$ are *consecutive in k^{th} loop*. Notice that previously we have considered only the consecutive iterations in the innermost loop. From our experience, we can say that for majority of the loop nests which appear in scientific codes, this is sufficient. For most of the remaining loop nests, it should be enough to consider the spatial locality in the *second* innermost loop. For two-dimensional column-major arrays, we can formalize the idea as follows: $[0, 1]\mathcal{L}Q\bar{I}_{n-1} = [0, 1]\mathcal{L}Q\bar{I}'_{n-1}$, or $[0, 1]\mathcal{L}Q[0, 0, \cdots, 0, 1, 0]^T = 0$; this implies

---

[1] In the case where $\bar{l}_1\bar{q}_ni_n$ is also 0, we have temporal locality in the innermost loop. We do not consider exploiting temporal locality explicitly in this paper. Our approach can be modified to take temporal locality into account as well.

that $\bar{l}_m q_{n-1} = 0$, i.e., $q_{n-1} \in Ker\{\bar{l}_m\}$. For the matrix-multiplication example, we proceed as follows:

$$\text{For array } C: \quad \bar{q}_2 \in Ker\{[0,1,0]\} \quad \Rightarrow \quad \bar{q}_2 = [\times, 0, \times]^T$$
$$\text{For array } A: \quad \bar{q}_2 \in Ker\{[0,0,1]\} \quad \Rightarrow \quad \bar{q}_2 = [\times, \times, 0]^T$$
$$\text{For array } B: \quad \bar{q}_2 \in Ker\{[0,1,0]\} \quad \Rightarrow \quad \bar{q}_2 = [\times, 0, \times]^T.$$

Combining these equations with those obtained on $\bar{q}_3$, we have to ignore one equation. Since the equations on C and B are the same, we favor that equation. Thus, we choose Q as $\begin{bmatrix} \times & \times & \times \\ \times & 0 & 0 \\ \times & \times & 0 \end{bmatrix}$. The only suitable permutation matrix is $Q = \begin{bmatrix} 0 & 0 & 1 \\ 1 & 0 & 0 \\ 0 & 1 & 0 \end{bmatrix}$. The resulting code obtained using $\mathcal{T} = Q^{-1}$ is shown in Fig. 2(c). This code exploits spatial locality for arrays C and A in the innermost loop. Array B, on the other hand, has temporal locality in the innermost loop and spatial locality in the second innermost loop.

5 Algorithm to find the loop transformation for the general case

In this section, we present the formulation of the problem for the most general case where a number of arrays with possibly different memory layouts are referenced in a given loop nest. Our objective is to find a transformation matrix $\mathcal{T}$ such that the spatial locality will be good for as many references as possible. To resolve the conflicts between different references, we assume that prior to our analysis the references are ordered according to their importance. We use the following notation:

ν is the number of distinct references
R_σ is the reference σ where $1 \leq \sigma \leq \nu$.
$L_\sigma = [l_{ij}^\sigma]$ is the layout constraint matrix for the array associated with R_σ (It is an $(m-1) \times m$ matrix for an m-dimensional array)
$\mathcal{L}_\sigma = [a_{ij}^\sigma]$ is the access matrix for R_σ (It is an $m \times n$ matrix for a reference to an m-dimensional array in an n-dimensional loop nest)

Without loss of generality, we also assume that the references are ordered as $R_1,...R_\nu$, where R_1 is the most important reference and R_ν is the least important. Ideally, the references should be ordered according to their access frequencies. Currently, we use profile information for this purpose.

Let us now focus on a single reference R_σ. Assuming $\bar{I}$ and $\bar{I}_{next}$ are two consecutive iteration vectors, *after* the transformation $\mathcal{T} = Q^{-1}$, the two data elements accessed by these iteration vectors through R_σ will have spatial locality if $L\mathcal{L}Q\bar{I} = L\mathcal{L}Q\bar{I}_{next}$ or $L\mathcal{L}\bar{q}_n = \bar{0}$, where $\bar{q}_n$ is the last column of Q.

On expanding, we derive the relation

$$
\begin{bmatrix}
l_{11}^{\sigma} & l_{12}^{\sigma} & \cdots & l_{1m}^{\sigma} \\
l_{21}^{\sigma} & l_{22}^{\sigma} & \cdots & l_{2m}^{\sigma} \\
\vdots & \vdots & \ddots & \vdots \\
l_{(m-1)1}^{\sigma} & l_{(m-1)2}^{\sigma} & \cdots & l_{(m-1)m}^{\sigma}
\end{bmatrix}
\begin{bmatrix}
a_{11}^{\sigma} & a_{12}^{\sigma} & \cdots & a_{1n}^{\sigma} \\
a_{21}^{\sigma} & a_{22}^{\sigma} & \cdots & a_{2n}^{\sigma} \\
\vdots & \vdots & \ddots & \vdots \\
a_{m1}^{\sigma} & a_{m2}^{\sigma} & \cdots & a_{mn}^{\sigma}
\end{bmatrix}
\begin{bmatrix}
q_{1n} \\
q_{2n} \\
\vdots \\
q_{nn}
\end{bmatrix}
=
\begin{bmatrix}
0 \\
0 \\
\vdots \\
0
\end{bmatrix}.
$$

Setting $b_{ij}^{\sigma} = \sum_{k=1}^{m} l_{ik}^{\sigma} a_{kj}^{\sigma}$ $(1 \leq i \leq m-1, 1 \leq j \leq n)$, we rewrite this relation as $B^{\sigma} \bar{q}_n = \bar{0}$ where $B^{\sigma} = [b_{ij}^{\sigma}]$. Then, the determination of the last column of Q can be expressed as the problem of finding a vector from the solution space of this homogeneous system. Notice that this solution takes care of the reference R_{σ} only. In order to obtain a transformation which satisfies all ν references we have to set up and solve the following system $B^1 \bar{q}_n = \bar{0}, B^2 \bar{q}_n = \bar{0}, \cdots, B^{\nu} \bar{q}_n = \bar{0}$. Additionally, as in matrix multiplication code, we might want to add the constraints on q_{n-1} to exploit the spatial reuse in the second innermost loop. Given a large number of references, this homogeneous system may not have a solution. In that case, we drop some equations from consideration starting from those of B^{ν} and repeat the process. The complete algorithm is given in Fig. 3 on page 43. A solution to this homogeneous system is of the form $\bar{q}_n = \delta_1 \bar{x}_1 + \delta_2 \bar{x}_2 + \cdots + \delta_p \bar{x}_p$. We fill out Q of the form

$$
Q =
\begin{bmatrix}
1 & 0 & \cdots & 0 & q_{1n} \\
0 & 1 & \cdots & 0 & q_{2n} \\
\vdots & \vdots & \ddots & \vdots & \vdots \\
0 & 0 & \cdots & 1 & q_{(n-1)n} \\
0 & 0 & \cdots & 0 & q_{nn}
\end{bmatrix}. \text{ Then } \mathcal{T} = Q^{-1} =
\begin{bmatrix}
1 & 0 & \cdots & 0 & -\frac{q_{1n}}{q_{nn}} \\
0 & 1 & \cdots & 0 & -\frac{q_{2n}}{q_{nn}} \\
\vdots & \vdots & \ddots & \vdots & \vdots \\
0 & 0 & \cdots & 1 & -\frac{q_{(n-1)n}}{q_{nn}} \\
0 & 0 & \cdots & 0 & \frac{1}{q_{nn}}
\end{bmatrix}. \tag{4}
$$

Notice that assuming $q_{nn} \neq 0$ such a transformation matrix is non-singular. Moreover, we can set $\delta_1, \cdots, \delta_p$ such that for each $\bar{d} \in \mathcal{D}$, $\mathcal{T}\bar{d} \geq 0$ where $\bar{q}_n = [q_{1n}, \cdots, q_{nn}]^T = \delta_1 \bar{x}_1 + \delta_2 \bar{x}_2 + \cdots + \delta_p \bar{x}_p$ and $\mathcal{D}$ is the original dependence matrix. Let $\bar{d} \in \mathcal{D}$ be a dependence vector as follows $\bar{d} = [d_1, \cdots, d_{n-1}, d_n]^T$. After the transformation $\mathcal{T}$, we have $\mathcal{T}\bar{d} = [d_1 - d_n q_{1n}/q_{nn}, d_2 - d_n q_{2n}/q_{nn}, \cdots, d_{n-1} - d_n q_{(n-1)n}/q_{nn}, d_n/q_{nn}]^T$. We note that if d_n is equal to zero, then this resulting dependence vector is always legal provided that $\bar{d}$ is legal to begin with. Otherwise, the parameters $\delta_1, \cdots, \delta_p$ can be chosen so that $\mathcal{T}\bar{d}$ is lexicographically non-negative.

As an application of this algorithm, we consider the matrix-multiplication code given in Fig. 2(a) once more. This time we assume that arrays A and C are row-major whereas array B is column-major. The equations in our homogeneous system are $[1, 0, 0][q_{13}, q_{23}, q_{33}]^T = 0$; $[1, 0, 0][q_{13}, q_{23}, q_{33}]^T = 0$; and $[0, 1, 0][q_{13}, q_{23}, q_{33}]^T = 0$ corresponding to references to arrays C, A and B re-

Input A loop nest with a number of references, layout matrices for each reference and the data dependence matrix.

Output A non-singular loop transformation matrix which observes all data dependences.

Step 1. Form the following homogeneous system $\{B^1 \bar{q}_n = \bar{0}, \cdots, B^\nu \bar{q}_n = \bar{0}\}$ $\equiv$ $B\bar{q}_n = \bar{0}$ where $B^\sigma = L_\sigma L_\sigma$. Eliminate the redundant equations and let τ be the number of the remaining rows in B

Step 2. Solve the system by row-echelon reduction. This is achieved by transforming the augmented matrix $[B|0]$ of the system to a matrix $[C|0]$ in reduced row echelon form [14].

After the reduction, let r be the number of non-zero rows in C, where $1 \leq r \leq \tau$.

Step 3. If $r \geq n$ the solution space has no basis. In that case, delete the last row of B and repeat **Step 2** until a $r < n$ is found.

Step 4. Write the solution $\bar{x}$ as a linear combination of vectors $\bar{x}_1, \bar{x}_2, ..., \bar{x}_p$ with the corresponding coefficients $\delta_1, \delta_2, ..., \delta_p$:

$$\bar{x} = \delta_1 \bar{x}_1 + \delta_2 \bar{x}_2 + ... + \delta_p \bar{x}_p$$

Step 5. Choose $\delta_1, \delta_2, \cdots, \delta_p$ such that Q is of the form in Equation 4, and for each $\bar{d} \in \mathcal{D}$, $T\bar{d} \geq 0$ where $\bar{q}_n = [q_{1n}, q_{2n}, \cdots, q_{nn}]^T = \delta_1 \bar{x}_1 + \delta_2 \bar{x}_2 + ... + \delta_p \bar{x}_p$ and $\mathcal{D}$ is the original dependence matrix.

Step 6. Return $\mathcal{T} = Q^{-1}$.

Fig. 3. Algorithm for determining the transformation matrix (it is assumed that $q_{nn} \neq 0$).

spectively. The partially filled matrix is $Q = \begin{bmatrix} \times & \times & 0 \\ \times & \times & 0 \\ \times & \times & 1 \end{bmatrix}$, which can be completed

as $\begin{bmatrix} 1 & 0 & 0 \\ 0 & 1 & 0 \\ 0 & 0 & 1 \end{bmatrix}$ and $T = \begin{bmatrix} 1 & 0 & 0 \\ 0 & 1 & 0 \\ 0 & 0 & 1 \end{bmatrix}$.

What this implies is that under the mentioned memory layouts, the original loop order i-j-k is the best loop order from the locality point of view. Table 1 shows the best loop orders for the matrix multiplication nest under all possible (permutation-based) layout combinations. The middle column gives the best order for the sequential execution whereas the rightmost column gives that for the parallel execution. Determining the suitability of a locality-optimized sequential program for a parallel architecture is definitely an important issue that needs to be visited in the future. It should be emphasized that in deriving these best orders we have considered the second column of Q as well.

Table 1. Best loop orders for different layout combinations in the matrix-multiplication code.

A triple x-y-z in the first column refers to memory layouts for arrays C, A, and B respectively, where c means column-major and r means row-major.

C-A-B	best (seq.)	best (par.)
c-c-c	j-k-i	j-k-i
c-c-r	k-j-i	j-k-i
c-r-c	j-i-k	j-i-k
c-r-r	j-k-i	j-k-i
r-c-c	i-k-j	i-k-j
r-c-r	k-i-j	i-k-j
r-r-c	i-j-k	i-j-k
r-r-r	i-k-j	i-k-j

6   Utilizing partial layout information

A direct generalization of the approach presented in the previous section is optimizing a loop nest assuming some of the arrays have fixed but possibly different layouts whereas the remaining arrays have not been assigned memory layouts yet. In the following we summarize our strategy; the details can be found elsewhere [3]. We handle this problem in two steps:

(1) find a loop transformation which satisfies the references to the arrays whose layouts have already been determined, and
(2) taking into account this loop transformation, determine optimal layouts for the remaining arrays referenced in the nest.

The first step is handled as shown in the previous section. The second step is an array restructuring problem and is fully explained in [4]. To illustrate the process, consider the example shown in Fig. 4(a) on page 45. Assuming a two-dimensional array layout represented by hyperplane vector $[g_1, g_2]$ and a reference represented by access matrix $\mathcal{L}$, the spatial locality will be exploited if $[g_1, g_2]\mathcal{L}[q_{1n}, \cdots, q_{nn}]^T = 0$, where $[q_{1n}, q_{2n}, \cdots, q_{nn}]^T$ is the last column of the inverse of the loop transformation matrix. Since both $[g_1, g_2]$ and $[q_{1n}, q_{2n}, \cdots, q_{nn}]^T$ are unknown, this formulation is non-linear. However, if either of them is known, the other can easily be found using the relations:

$$[g_1, g_2] \in Ker\left\{\mathcal{L}[q_{1k}, \cdots, q_{kk}]^T\right\} \tag{5}$$

$$[q_{1k}, q_{2k}, \cdots, q_{kk}]^T \in Ker\left\{[g_1, g_2]\mathcal{L}\right\}. \tag{6}$$

Usually Ker sets may contain multiple vectors in which case we choose the one such that the gcd of its elements is minimum. Let us consider the example in Fig. 4(a), the access matrices for the first nest are as follows: $\mathcal{L}_U = \begin{bmatrix} 1 & 0 \\ 0 & 1 \end{bmatrix}$,

```
      do i = 1, N                      do u = 1, N
        do j = 1, N                      do v = 1, N
          U[i,j] = V[i+j,j]                U[u,v] = V[u+v,v]
        end do                           end do
      end do                           end do

      do i = 1, N                      do u = 1-N, N-1
        do j = 1, N                      do v = max(1,1-u), min(N-u,N)
          W[j,i] = V[i,j] * V[j,i]        W[u,u+v] = V[u+v,v] * V[v,u+v]
        end do                           end do
      end do                           end do
        (a)                              (b)
```

Fig. 4. (a) Original loop nest. (b) Transformed loop nest.

and $\mathcal{L}_V = \begin{bmatrix} 1 & 1 \\ 0 & 1 \end{bmatrix}$. For the second nest: $\mathcal{L}_{V_1} = \begin{bmatrix} 1 & 0 \\ 0 & 1 \end{bmatrix}, \mathcal{L}_{V_2} = \begin{bmatrix} 0 & 1 \\ 1 & 0 \end{bmatrix}$, and $\mathcal{L}_W = \begin{bmatrix} 0 & 1 \\ 1 & 0 \end{bmatrix}$. Let us assume for the first nest we apply only data transformations using the technique in [4]; that is, $[q_{12}, q_{22}]^T = [0, 1]$ (Q is identity matrix). Using (5), for array U,

$$[g_1, g_2] \in Ker\left\{\mathcal{L}_U[0, 1]^T\right\} \qquad \Longrightarrow \qquad [g_1, g_2] \in Ker\left\{[0, 1]^T\right\}.$$

A solution is $[g_1, g_2] = [1, 0]$ meaning that array U should be row-major. For array V,

$$[g_1, g_2] \in Ker\left\{\mathcal{L}_V[0, 1]^T\right\} \qquad \Longrightarrow \qquad [g_1, g_2] \in Ker\left\{[1, 1]^T\right\}.$$

Selecting $[g_1, g_2] = [1, -1]$ results in diagonal layout for array V.

Having fixed the layouts for two arrays, we proceed with the second nest whose optimization is the topic of this section. Assuming again that Q is the inverse of the loop transformation matrix for this nest, using (6), we find the loop transformation which satisfies the both references to array V:

$$[q_{12}, q_{22}]^T \in Ker\left\{[1, -1]\mathcal{L}_{V_1}\right\} \qquad \Longrightarrow \qquad [q_{12}, q_{22}]^T \in Ker\left\{[1, -1]\right\}$$
$$\text{and } [q_{12}, q_{22}]^T \in Ker\left\{[1, -1]\mathcal{L}_{V_2}\right\} \qquad \Longrightarrow \qquad [q_{12}, q_{22}]^T \in Ker\left\{[-1, 1]\right\}$$

$[q_{12}, q_{22}]^T = [1, 1]^T$ satisfies both the equations, and for this, $Q = \begin{bmatrix} 1 & 1 \\ 0 & 1 \end{bmatrix}$. The process so far is exactly what we have done in the previous section. The next task is to determine the optimal memory layout for array W which is referenced only in the second nest. By taking into account the last column of Q and using (5) once more (now for array W), $[g_1, g_2] \in Ker\left\{\mathcal{L}_W[1, 1]^T\right\} \Longrightarrow [g_1, g_2] \in Ker\left\{[1, 1]^T\right\}$ which means that array W should have a diagonal layout. The transformed program is shown in Fig. 4(b).

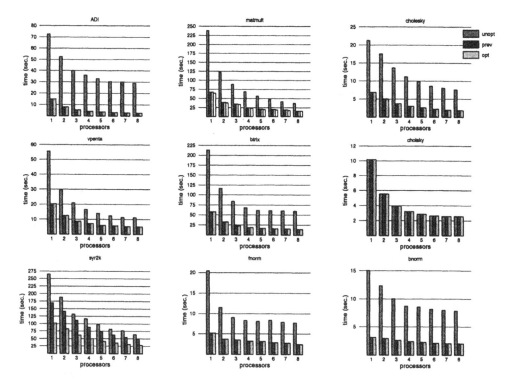

Fig. 5. Execution times on an SGI Origin. [The problem sizes are (in doubles) as follows. ADI: $1000 \times 1000 \times 3$ arrays; matmult: 1200×1200 arrays; cholesky: 1024×1024 arrays; vpenta: $4 \times 720 \times 720$ 3D arrays and 720×720 2D arrays; btrix: size parameter is 150; cholsky: size parameter is 2500; syr2k: 1024×1024 arrays with $b = 400$; fnorm and bnorm: 6144×6144 arrays. The programs from Spec92, the ADI code, and matmult have outer timing loops. The unopt version refers to the original program, the prev version refers to the approach offered by previous work, and the opt version is the code generated by our technique].

7   Experimental Results

In this section, we illustrate how our iteration space transformation technique improves performance on an 8-processor SGI Origin 2000 distributed-shared-memory machine. This machine uses 195MHz R10000 processors, 32KB L1 data cache and 4MB L2 unified cache. The cache line size is 128 bytes and page size is 16KB. Our presentation is in two parts. First, we evaluate the effectiveness of our approach using a set of nine programs assuming a fixed memory layout for all arrays. Then, we focus on two programs, and measure the improvements in execution time with different layout combinations.

For the first part, we experiment with the following programs: ADI from Livermore kernels; matmult, a matrix-multiplication routine; cholesky from [8];

vpenta, btrix, and cholsky[2] from Spec92/NASA benchmark suite; syr2k from BLAS; and finally fnorm and bnorm from ODEPACK, a collection of solvers for the initial value problem for ordinary differential equation systems. We use the C versions of these programs and the hand–optimized programs are compiled by the native compiler using the -O2 option (expect for syr2k).

Fig. 5 shows the performance results for our benchmark programs. For each program, the unopt version refers to the original program, the prev version refers to the approach offered by [8], and finally the opt version is the code generated by our technique. We note that except for cholsky, we have improvements in all programs against the unoptimized versions over all processor sizes. The cholsky code consists of a number of imperfectly nested loops; thus, is difficult to optimize by linear loop transformations. However, loop distribution [14] can substantially improve the performance by enabling linear loop transformations as explained in the second part of our experimental results. In syr2k, fnorm and bnorm the optimized programs do not scale well mostly due to employment of static scheduling for non-rectangular loop bounds. Apart from those, the results reveal that our approach is quite successful in optimizing locality in the Origin 2000. It should be noted that the sizes that we use for the programs from Spec92/NASA are larger than the usual sizes; so the results should not be compared with the previous works. It should also be noted that except for syr2k our approach and the approach offered in [8] result in the same programs. In the syr2k code the access pattern is quite complicated and we perform better than Li's approach with the -O1 compiler option. If the -O2 option is used, however, the two approaches perform very similar. In general, for a fixed permutation-based memory layout for all arrays, we expect that unless the access pattern is complicated both optimization approach will result in either the same or very similar codes. For the case where all the arrays have a uniform diagonal layout, it is not clear to us how Li's approach can be modified. Finally, the fourth bar in performance results of matmult shows the execution time of the best possible layout combination and the associated loop order. In this case, the best time has been obtained with the i-j-k loop order assuming that the arrays C and A have row-major memory layout whereas array B is column-major. We note that given this layout combination our approach can derive the i-j-k loop order automatically.

In the second part, we evaluate the effectiveness of our approach in optimizing loop nests assuming that the memory layouts of the arrays might be different. We focus on two programs: matmult and cholsky. Table 2(a) shows the single processor execution times for all permutation-based layout combinations of matmult. The legend x-y-z means that the memory layouts for C, A and B are x, y and z respectively, where c means column-major and r means row-major. For each combination, we experiment with all possible loop permutations. The boldfaced figures in each row denotes the minimum times (in seconds) under the corresponding memory layout combinations. The preferred loop order detected for each layout combination by our algorithm is marked with a ′. The best loop

---

[2] Different from cholsky; uses two three-dimensional arrays.

order using only loop transformations that work with fixed layouts namely all row-major or all column-major for all arrays (referred to as prev) is denoted by a †. When we compare these results with the best sequential loop orders given in Table 1, it is easy to see that, except for two cases, our technique is able to find the optimal loop orders in every layout combination. In those two cases mentioned our technique results in an execution time which is close to the minimum time. Notice also that a loop transformation approach based on fixed memory layouts can only optimize two cases: c-c-c and r-r-r.

Table 2(b), on the other hand, shows the execution times in eight processors. Except for the two cases, the results are again consistent with those given in the last column of Table 1. Since prev does not offer an optimal layout for the multiprocessor case, it is not shown.

Next, we focus on the cholsky program from Spec92 benchmarks. This program accesses two three-dimensional arrays. First, we applied loop distribution to obtain as many perfectly nested loops as possible. Then we conducted experiments with all four permutation-based layout combinations. The performance results given in Table 3 show that our technique is able to optimize the program for all layout combinations we experiment with. The improvements are between 51% and 72%.

8   Related work

Early work on automating locality enhancing optimizations was done by Abu-Sufah et al. [1]. More recently the interest was on loop restructuring for optimizing cache locality. McKinley et al. [9] present a loop reordering technique to optimize locality and parallelism. Their approach also employs loop distribution and loop fusion. Li [8] and Wolf and Lam [13] developed frameworks where the data reuse information is represented explicitly using reuse vectors. Our technique is different from those mentioned here in the sense that we can optimize a loop nest for locality assuming different arrays referenced in the nest may have distinct memory layouts which include row-major, column-major, higher dimension equivalents of row- and column-major as well as any type of skewed layout that can be expressed by hyperplanes. Extending the approaches presented in [13] and [8] to work with general layouts is non-trivial.

More recently, there is an interest in optimizing locality using data layout transformations. In this context, Leung and Zahorjan [7] and O'Boyle and Knijnenburg [10] present array restructuring algorithms for optimizing locality. Although these techniques may be effective for some cases where locality enhancing loop transformations fail, the question of how to mitigate the global effect of a layout transformation remains to be solved. Leung and Zahorjan [7] and Kandemir et al. [4] propose solutions to handle multiple loop nests. A major problem with the approaches based on pure data transformations is that they cannot optimize temporal locality.

There have been a few attempts at a unified framework for locality optimizations. Cierniak and Li [2] and Kandemir et al. [5] propose algorithms for

Table 2. Execution times (in sec.) of `matmult` under all permutation-based memory layouts and loop orders on SGI origin. [Minimum times for each layout combination are in boldface].

(a) Number of processors = 1

C-A-B	i-j-k	i-k-j	j-i-k	j-k-i	k-i-j	k-j-i
c-c-c	238.749	478.383	237.730	**66.921** † ′	491.833	102.540
c-c-r	417.405	292.398	415.886	68.121	315.801	**68.062** ′
c-r-c	64.798	490.661	**64.435** ′	257.849	513.729	271.467
c-r-r	246.884	286.199	**237.370**	258.202 ′	331.914	270.457
r-c-c	**238.227**	245.415 ′	238.672	291.760	264.998	315.432
r-c-r	416.795	68.123	415.484	292.377	**67.992** ′	315.216
r-r-c	64.006 ′	246.316	64.088	474.004	267.269	498.209
r-r-r	236.539	**66.932** † ′	231.907	478.359	102.558	492.604

(b) Number of processors = 8

C-A-B	i-j-k	i-k-j	j-i-k	j-k-i	k-i-j	k-j-i
c-c-c	37.353	65.910	33.571	**16.803** ′	116.271	58.403
c-c-r	56.988	43.322	55.972	**17.511** ′	157.846	72.857
c-r-c	17.433	68.369	**15.390** ′	38.722	261.163	76.908
c-r-r	39.549	42.305	**34.700**	39.406 ′	342.488	73.710
r-c-c	35.547	34.831 ′	**34.703**	42.235	73.034	130.526
r-c-r	56.227	**17.591** ′	56.042	44.031	74.433	150.590
r-r-c	**15.347** ′	34.907	18.502	64.313	74.986	106.485
r-r-r	32.968	**16.369** ′	35.738	65.271	59.420	99.661

optimizing cache locality using a blend of loop and data transformations, albeit drawn from a restricted set. In contrast, the technique presented in this paper can work with any type of memory layout that can be expressed by hyperplanes, and can derive general non-singular [14] iteration space transformation matrices. Recently Kodukula et al. [6] have proposed *data shackling*, in which data is first blocked and based on the data blocks that are accessed together, iteration space tiling is derived. But, the data is stored in memory using the default layouts.

9 Conclusions

We have presented a technique to improve data locality in loop nests. Our technique uses explicit layout information available to our analysis as layout constraint matrices. This information allows our technique to optimize loop nests in which each array may have a distinct memory layout. We believe that such a capability is needed by a global locality optimization algorithm which optimizes the loop nests in a program by applying an appropriate combination of loop and data transformations.

Table 3. Execution times in seconds of the optimized and unoptimized versions of cholsky and % improvements [p is the number of processors].

version	c-c		c-r		r-c		r-r	
	p=1	p=8	p=1	p=8	p=1	p=8	p=1	p=8
unopt	6.146	3.834	7.010	2.915	8.312	1.391	18.311	2.471
opt	2.904	1.907	2.139	1.359	2.292	0.680	6.352	1.103
imprv.	53%	51%	69%	53%	72%	51%	65%	55%

References

1. A. Abu-Sufah, D. J. Kuck, and D. H. Lawrie. On the performance enhancement of paging systems through program analysis and transformations. *IEEE Trans. Comp.*, C-30(5):341–356, 1981.
2. M. Cierniak and W. Li. Unifying data and control transformations for distributed shared memory machines. *Proc. SIGPLAN Conf. Prog. Lang. Des. & Imp.*, June 1995.
3. M. Kandemir, A. Choudhary, J. Ramanujam, and P. Banerjee. A Matrix-Based Approach to the Global Locality Optimization Problem In *Proc. 1998 Int. Conf. Parallel Architectures & Compilation Techniques (PACT 98)*, October 1998.
4. M. Kandemir, A. Choudhary, N. Shenoy, P. Banerjee, and J. Ramanujam. A hyperplane based approach for optimizing spatial locality in loop nests. In *Proc. 12th ACM Int. Conf. Supercomputing*, July 1998.
5. M. Kandemir, J. Ramanujam, and A. Choudhary. A compiler algorithm for optimizing locality in loop nests. In *Proc. 11th ACM Int. Conf. Supercomputing*, pp. 269–276, July 1997.
6. I. Kodukula, N. Ahmed, and K. Pingali. Data-centric multi-level blocking. In *Proc. SIGPLAN Conf. Prog. Lang. Des. & Imp.*, June 1997.
7. S.-T. Leung and J. Zahorjan. Optimizing data locality by array restructuring. Technical Report TR 95-09-01, CSE Dept., University of Washington, Sep. 1995.
8. W. Li. Compiling for NUMA parallel machines. Ph.D. Thesis, Cornell University, 1993.
9. K. McKinley, S. Carr, and C.W. Tseng. Improving data locality with loop transformations. *ACM Transactions on Programming Languages and Systems*, 1996.
10. M. O'Boyle and P. Knijnenburg. Non-singular data transformations: Definition, validity, applications. In *Proc. 6th Workshop on Compilers for Par. Comp.*, pp. 287–297, Germany, 1996.
11. J. Ramanujam and P. Sadayappan. Compile-time techniques for data distribution in distributed memory machines. In *IEEE Trans. Par. & Dist. Sys.*, 2(4):472–482, Oct. 1991.
12. A. Schrijver. *Theory of linear and integer programming*, John Wiley, 1986.
13. M. Wolf and M. Lam. A data locality optimizing algorithm. In *Proc. ACM SIGPLAN 91 Conf. Programming Language Design and Implementation*, pp. 30–44, June 1991.
14. M. Wolfe. *High performance compilers for parallel computing*, Addison Wesley, 1996.

An Integrated Framework for Compiler-Directed Cache Coherence and Data Prefetching*

Hock-Beng Lim[1] and Pen-Chung Yew[2]

[1] Center for Supercomputing R & D, Univ. of Illinois,
Urbana, IL 61801, USA
[2] Dept. of Computer Science, Univ. of Minnesota,
Minneapolis, MN 55455, USA

Abstract. Cache coherence enforcement and memory latency reduction and hiding are very important and challenging problems in the design of large-scale distributed shared-memory (DSM) multiprocessors. We propose an integrated approach to solve these problems through a compiler-directed cache coherence scheme called the *Cache Coherence with Data Prefetching (CCDP)* scheme. The CCDP scheme enforces cache coherence by prefetching the potentially-stale references in a parallel program. It also prefetches the non-stale references to hide their memory latencies. To optimize the performance of the CCDP scheme, some prefetch hardware support is provided to efficiently handle these two forms of data prefetching operations. We also developed the compiler techniques utilized by the CCDP scheme for stale reference detection, prefetch target analysis and prefetch scheduling. We evaluated the performance of the CCDP scheme via execution-driven simulations of several applications from the SPEC CFP95 and CFP92 benchmark suites. The simulation results show that the CCDP scheme provides significant performance improvements for the benchmark programs studied.

Keywords: Compiler-directed Cache Coherence, Data Prefetching, Memory Latency Hiding, Shared-memory Multiprocessors

1 Introduction

In the recent years, large-scale distributed shared-memory (DSM) multiprocessors have emerged as a promising architecture to deliver high performance computing power. However, to fully realize the potential performance of these systems, designers have to solve two important and challenging problems. First, it is imperative that the cache coherence schemes for such systems be efficient, inexpensive and scalable. Second, it is necessary to develop efficient techniques to hide the large remote memory access latencies in such systems.

* This work is supported in part by the National Science Foundation under Grant No. MIP 93-07910, MIP 94-96320, CDA 95-02979 and MIP 96-10379. Additional support is provided by a gift from Cray Research, Inc and by a gift from Intel Corporation.

S. Chatterjee (Ed.): LCPC'98, LNCS 1656, pp. 51–67, 1999.

The cache coherence techniques used in existing commercially-available multiprocessors are mainly hardware-based, such as a *snoopy cache protocol* or a hardware *directory-based* scheme. These schemes rely on interprocessor communications to determine cache coherence actions. In large-scale DSM systems, the scalability of such schemes might be affected by excessive coherence-related network traffic. Furthermore, their hardware complexity and cost can become quite substantial as the number of processors increases. On the other hand, in *compiler-directed cache coherence* schemes [4], the cache coherence actions are performed locally by each processor as specified by the compiler, without the need for interprocessor communications. They also do not require complicated and expensive hardware directories.

Several techniques have been proposed in the literature to address the memory latency problem in multiprocessors. In particular, previous research has shown that *data prefetching* is an effective technique to hide memory latency and to improve memory system performance. Data prefetching schemes, which can be hardware-controlled or software-initiated, predict the data required during program execution and overlap the fetching of these data with computation.

In fact, compiler-directed cache coherence and data prefetching schemes can be combined in a complementary manner to provide better overall performance. Therefore, we integrate compiler-directed cache coherence with data prefetching under a unified framework. We have developed a compiler-directed cache coherence scheme called the *Cache Coherence with Data Prefetching (CCDP)* scheme as a key part of this framework. The CCDP scheme uses compiler analyses to identify potentially-stale data references in a parallel program, and then enforces cache coherence by prefetching up-to-date data corresponding to these references from the main memory. At the same time, data prefetching implicitly hides the memory latencies of fetching remote up-to-date shared data. The CCDP scheme further improves performance by also prefetching the non-stale data references and hiding their memory latencies.

The performance of the CCDP scheme is greatly influenced by the hardware and compiler support provided. To optimize the performance of the CCDP scheme, we designed some inexpensive prefetch hardware support to handle the two forms of data prefetching operations used by the scheme. We developed compiler techniques to perform stale reference detection, prefetch target analysis and prefetch scheduling for the CCDP scheme. Finally, we evaluated the performance of the CCDP scheme through execution-driven simulations of several benchmark programs from the SPEC CFP95 and CFP92 suites. The results of our experimental study indicate that the CCDP scheme can provide significant performance improvements for the programs studied.

The rest of the paper is organized as follows. Section 2 discusses our framework for integrating compiler-directed cache coherence and data prefetching. The prefetch hardware support to optimize the CCDP scheme is discussed in Section 3. In Section 4, we focus on the compiler support for the CCDP scheme. Section 5 presents the experimental study to evaluate the performance of the

CCDP scheme. Finally, we conclude in Section 6 and outline the future directions of our research.

2   The CCDP Framework

2.1   Background and Motivation

When shared data are cached during execution of a parallel program, multiple copies of a shared memory location might exist in the caches of the processors. Cache coherence schemes must ensure that the processors always access the most up-to-date copies of shared data. The remaining invalid copies are known as *stale data*, and the references to these data are called *stale references*.

Most hardware-based cache coherence schemes prevent stale references at run time by invalidating or updating stale cache entries right before the stale references occur. To do so, they require interprocessor communications to keep track of the cache states and to perform these cache coherence actions. Such coherence-related network traffic can use up excessive amount of interconnection network bandwidth of the system. In directory-based cache coherence schemes, the complexity and hardware costs of the directory can be substantial for large-scale multiprocessors.

In contrast, compiler-directed cache coherence schemes [4] can detect the potentially-stale references using compiler analyses at compile time. The compiler then directs the processors to perform cache coherence actions such as cache invalidations locally, without the need for interprocessor communications. This reduces the traffic load on the interconnection network, and eliminates the need to use hardware directories. The drawback of these schemes is that there might be situations when the compiler has to adopt conservative decisions. Thus, certain data references might be classified as potentially-stale if the compiler cannot confirm that they are non-stale.

Although cache coherence schemes can improve multiprocessor cache performance, they cannot completely eliminate remote memory accesses. In fact, data prefetching can be used to hide the latency of cache coherence operations and memory accesses. However, cache coherence and data prefetching are often treated as separate problems to be addressed. In hardware cache-coherent systems, data prefetching is usually applied as a separate optimization which is not integrated with the underlying cache coherence scheme. The data prefetching operations are determined based on data locality considerations alone. Also, the stale and non-stale data references are treated uniformly by the prefetching schemes.

The main motivation of this work is to develop a framework for integrating compiler-directed cache coherence and data prefetching to improve the memory system performance of large-scale DSM systems which do not have hardware cache coherence support. By using compiler analyses to identify potentially-stale references, the CCDP scheme can predict the need to access up-to-date shared data in advance. Therefore, the compiler can direct the processors to prefetch these data into the caches before they are actually needed. Prefetching the potentially-stale references implicitly hides the memory latencies of fetching remote up-to-date shared data. Further performance improvements can be obtained by prefetching the non-stale references and hiding their memory latencies.

2.2   Overview of the CCDP Scheme

The CCDP scheme consists of three major steps. First, during the *stale reference analysis* step, the compiler identifies the potentially-stale and non-stale data references in a parallel program. However, it might not be necessary or worthwhile to prefetch all of the references in these two categories. Thus, the *prefetch target analysis* step determines which of those references in the two categories should be prefetched. Finally, the *prefetch scheduling* step schedules the prefetch operations and inserts them at appropriate locations in the program. In addition to these steps, the compiler also inserts cache and memory management operations such as cache invalidations and *bypass-cache fetch* operations, which bypass the cache and access the main memory directly, when necessary.

Our scheme makes use of two types of prefetch operations : *vector prefetches* and *cache-line prefetches*. In a vector prefetch, a block of data with a fixed stride is fetched from the main memory. On the other hand, the amount of data being fetched by a cache-line prefetch is equal to the size of a cache line. In theory, vector prefetches should reduce the prefetch overhead by amortizing the fixed initiation costs of several cache-line prefetches.

2.3   Data Prefetching Optimizations

Traditionally, data prefetching has been used solely for hiding memory latency. In this context, the data prefetching operations are just performance hints for the system. However, when data prefetching is used for cache coherence enforcement, it is necessary to address the correctness issue. Such prefetch operations may violate program correctness if they are ignored. Thus, the CCDP scheme uses two types of data prefetching optimizations which we call *coherence-enforcing prefetch (ce-prefetch)* and *latency-hiding prefetch (lh-prefetch)*.

For the *ce-prefetch* operations, a key task is to ensure that the correctness of the memory references of a program is not violated by prefetching the potentially-stale references. First, the *ce-prefetch* operations should respect all control and data dependence constraints. Second, the CCDP scheme has to guarantee that the processors will access the prefetched up-to-date data instead of the potentially-stale data in the caches. This can be achieved with the help of special prefetch hardware support which enables the *ce-prefetch* operations to invalidate the cache entries corresponding to the potentially-stale references. Without such prefetch hardware, the compiler has to insert explicit cache invalidation instructions to invalidate the cache entries before the prefetches are issued. On the other hand, the *lh-prefetch* operations are straight-forward. Since they are used for prefetching the non-stale references, they will not violate cache coherence.

The performance issue of the prefetch operations is also important. As the amount of hardware resources provided by the system to handle prefetch requests is often fixed and limited, it is necessary to prioritize the two types of prefetches used by the CCDP scheme. Since it is more important to prefetch the potentially-stale references and maintain cache coherence as efficiently as possible, the scheme assigns higher priority to the *ce-prefetch* operations.

3 Hardware Support

A major factor which affects the performance of the CCDP scheme is the effectiveness of the hardware support for prefetching on the system. The CCDP scheme can make use of the prefetch hardware on existing systems. In fact, we have already implemented the scheme on the Cray T3D. However, the conventional prefetch hardware of the Cray T3D is not optimized to handle the two types of data prefetching operations used by the CCDP scheme. We also have to adapt the compiler algorithms in order to implement the scheme on the Cray T3D. Although our Cray T3D implementation provided substantial performance improvements for the system [6], the performance of the scheme can be further improved by optimizing the prefetch hardware support.

Several sophisticated hardware prefetching schemes have been developed to dynamically predict the data references to prefetch at run-time. However, these prefetch hardware designs are not suitable for the CCDP scheme because they cannot distinguish between potentially-stale and non-stale references and take proper actions to enforce cache coherence. Thus, we propose some inexpensive and efficient prefetch hardware support to suit the CCDP scheme.

3.1 Architectural Model

In this paper, we assume a large-scale non-cache-coherent DSM multiprocessor. The processing nodes in the system are interconnected by a high-bandwidth network. The modeled architecture is similar to that of the Cray T3D. Figure 1 shows the organization of a processing node in the system.

Each node consists of a processor, a data cache and its associated *Data Coherence Prefetch Unit (DCPFU)*, a local memory module, and various support circuitry. The collection of the local memory modules in all of the nodes form a logically shared global memory. The support circuitry on each node contains address translation logic to transform a virtual address into its physical address, which consists of the node number and the memory address within the node. The support circuitry also contains communication and synchronization logic to support messaging and synchronization activities on the system, such as remote memory access, barrier synchronization, etc. With the support circuitry, a processor can directly access the memory of another processor without involving the remote processor. The data cache and the DCPFU are tightly coupled. We assume that there is one level of cache hierarchy in the node for simplicity. The cache is lock-up free, i.e. it can handle multiple outstanding cache misses.

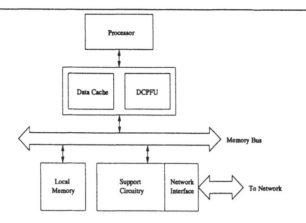

Fig. 1. Organization of a Processing Node

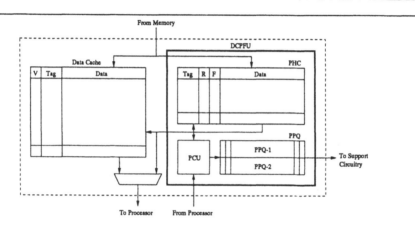

Fig. 2. Organization of the DCPFU

3.2   Organization of the DCPFU

The DCPFU consists of a *Prefetch Control Unit (PCU)*, a *Priority Prefetch Queue (PPQ)* and a *Prefetch Holding Cache (PHC)*. We assume that the DCPFU can handle up to 32 outstanding prefetch requests. The organization of the DCPFU is shown in Figure 2.

The Prefetch Holding Cache (PHC) The PHC is a small, fully-associative cache. A suitable number of PHC cache lines would be the maximum number of outstanding prefetch requests to be handled by the DCPFU, which is assumed to be 32. The PHC holds the up-to-date data corresponding to potentially-stale references which are fetched from the memory by *ce-prefetch* operations. On the other hand, non-stale data fetched by *lh-prefetch* operations are stored directly into the data cache.

The processor checks both the PHC and the data cache simultaneously. If the prefetched data has arrived in the PHC, then the processor loads the data from it. At the same time, the PHC cache lines containing these prefetched data will be moved into the data cache. By requiring the processor to read the data from the PHC, it is guaranteed that the processor will not access potentially-stale data in the data cache. Furthermore, since the prefetched up-to-date data are temporarily buffered in the PHC, the data cache will not be polluted by these prefetched data.

Each PHC cache line contains the following fields : a tag, a *reserved bit*, a *full bit*, and the data. The tag is used to determine if there is a PHC hit. The reserved bit indicates whether the PHC cache line has already been reserved by an earlier prefetch request. The full bit indicates whether the prefetched data for the PHC cache line has arrived from the memory. Before a prefetch request is issued, the PCU has to reserve an available PHC cache line by filling its tag field and setting the reserved bit. Thus, a PHC cache line with the reserved and full bits set holds prefetch data which have arrived but have not been accessed by the processor yet. After the processor accesses such a PHC cache line, its reserved bit will be reset and its content will be moved to the data cache.

The Priority Prefetch Queue (PPQ) The PPQ queues the prefetch operations which are to be issued. It is divided into two sections, PPQ-1 and PPQ-2, each having 16 entries. Each PPQ entry holds a tag to identify the prefetch operation, which is simply the memory address to be prefetched. PPQ-1 is used for *ce-prefetch* operations, while PPQ-2 is used for *lh-prefetch* operations. The PCU inserts the prefetch requests into the PPQ in the order specified by their priority levels. The prefetch requests in the PPQ-1 will be issued first in FIFO order, followed by the prefetch requests in PPQ-2 in FIFO order.

The Prefetch Control Unit (PCU) The PCU is responsible for processing prefetch operations issued by the processor and keeping track of the outstanding prefetch requests handled by the DCPFU. When the PCU accepts a cache-line prefetch operation, it generates a request in the relevant section of the PPQ, depending on whether it is a *ce-prefetch* or *lh-prefetch* operation. As for a vector prefetch operation, the PCU generates individual cache-line prefetch requests based on the starting address, stride, and length of the vector to be prefetched. This relieves the processor from explicitly issuing multiple cache-line prefetches and paying for their initiation overheads.

The PCU helps to reduce the amount of unnecessary prefetches dynamically. For each prefetch operation, the PCU checks if there is already an outstanding prefetch request in the PPQ, or if the cache line has already been prefetched and is still stored in the PHC.

4   Compiler Techniques

The performance of the CCDP scheme is also strongly influenced by the effectiveness of its compiler support. The CCDP scheme relies on the compiler to identify potentially-stale and non-stale data references, and to generate and schedule the appropriate prefetch operations. Several compiler techniques have been developed for software-initiated data prefetching [1,5,8]. However, as these data prefetching schemes are used solely for memory latency hiding, the data prefetching operations are determined based on data locality considerations alone. These techniques do not distinguish between potentially-stale and non-stale references, and so they cannot be applied directly in the CCDP scheme. Therefore, we developed compiler techniques to address this limitation.

4.1   Stale Reference Analysis

Three main program analysis techniques are used in stale reference analysis : *stale reference detection*, *array data-flow analysis*, and *interprocedural analysis*. Extensive algorithms for these techniques were previously developed [3,4], and implemented using the Polaris parallelizing compiler. We make use of these algorithms in the CCDP scheme. Since the detailed algorithms are described in [3], we will only state the functions of the stale reference analysis techniques.

To find the potentially-stale data references, it is necessary to detect the memory reference sequences which might violate cache coherence. The *stale reference detection* algorithm [3] accomplishes this by performing data-flow analysis on the *epoch flow graph* of the program, which is a modified form of the control flow graph. However, not all of the potentially-stale reference patterns actually lead to a stale reference at run time. The stale reference detection can be refined by exploiting some temporal and spatial reuses of memory locations in the program. To do so, two *locality preserving analysis* techniques are used. We use array data-flow analysis [3], which treats different regions of arrays referenced in the program as distinct symbolic variables, to refine the stale reference detection. Procedure calls in a program introduce side effects which complicate stale reference detection. We use interprocedural analysis [3] to further improve the accuracy of stale reference detection. In this way, the CCDP scheme can exploit locality across procedure call boundaries.

4.2   Prefetch Target Analysis

As the prefetch operations introduce instruction execution and network traffic overhead, it is important to minimize the number of unnecessary prefetches. The role of our prefetch target analysis algorithm is to identify the potentially-stale and the non-stale references which should be prefetched. It initially includes all of the potentially-stale and non-stale references in two separate sets of possible prefetch candidates. As the algorithm proceeds, those references which should not be prefetched are removed from the sets.

Our prefetch target analysis algorithm [7] focuses on the potentially-stale and the non-stale references in the inner loops, where prefetching is most likely to be beneficial. Those potentially-stale references which are not in the inner loops will not be prefetched. Instead, they are issued as bypass-cache fetch operations, which fetch the up-to-date data directly from the memory to preserve program correctness. On the other hand, the non-stale references which are not in the inner loops are treated as normal read references.

The algorithm also exploits spatial reuses to eliminate some unnecessary prefetch operations. If cache-line prefetch operations are used for a reference that has self-spatial reuse [10], then we can unroll the inner loop such that all copies of the reference access the same cache line during an iteration. In this manner, only one cache-line prefetch operation is needed to bring in data for all copies of the reference, and thereby eliminating unnecessary prefetch operations. The prefetch target analysis algorithm marks the prefetch target references which exhibit self-spatial locality using a similar approach as in [1,8], so that the prefetch scheduling step can carry out the appropriate loop unrolling.

In addition, a group of references which are likely to refer to the same cache line during the same iteration of the inner loop are said to exhibit *group-spatial reuse* [10]. We only need to prefetch the *leading reference* [10] of such a group of references. The other references in the group are issued as normal reads. If a set of references are *uniformly generated* (i.e. they have similar array index functions which differ only in the constant term), then they have group-spatial reuse.

Finally, note that the potentially-stale references which need not be prefetched due to locality exploitation will be treated as normal read references. This is because the up-to-date data will be brought into the caches by other *ce-prefetch* operations, and thus program correctness will be preserved. Similarly, the non-stale references which are eliminated from the set of prefetch targets are simply issued as normal read operations.

4.3   Prefetch Scheduling

After the prefetch target analysis step, we have the set of potentially-stale and the set of non-stale target references which should be prefetched. The next important task is to schedule these prefetches.

Scheduling Techniques Our prefetch scheduling algorithm makes use of three scheduling techniques : *vector prefetch generation*, *software pipelining*, and *moving back prefetches*. These techniques are similar to some scheduling strategies used in conventional prefetching algorithms for memory latency hiding. However, we have enhanced and adapted the previous techniques to suit the requirements of the CCDP scheme.

Vector prefetch generation Gornish [5] developed an algorithm for conservatively determining the earliest point in a program at which a block of data can be prefetched. It examines the array references in each loop to see if they could be *pulled out* of the loop and still satisfy the control and data dependences. A vector prefetch operation can then be generated for these references if the loop is serial or if the loop is parallel and the loop scheduling strategy is known at compile time.

However, the drawback of Gornish's algorithm is that it tries to pull out array references from as many levels of loop nests as possible, and does not consider important hardware constraints such as the cache size and the size of the prefetch queue or issue buffer. Even if array references can be pulled out of multiple loop levels, the prefetched data might not remain in the cache by the time the data are referenced.

We adapt Gornish's approach to generate vector prefetches. In order to maximize the effectiveness of the vector prefetches, we impose a restriction on the number of loop levels that array references should be pulled out from. Our algorithm pulls out an array reference one loop level at a time. It then constructs a vector prefetch operation and checks if the number of words to be prefetched will exceed the available prefetch queue size or the cache size. The vector prefetch operation will be generated only if these hardware constraints are satisfied and if the array reference should not be pulled further out. The compiler then inserts the prefetch operation into the code just before the appropriate loop.

Software pipelining In Mowry's approach [8], *software pipelining* is used to schedule cache-line prefetch operations. Software pipelining hides memory latency by overlapping the prefetches for a future iteration with the computation of the current iteration of a loop. However, we should ensure that the benefits of software pipelining would exceed the instruction execution overhead introduced. We adapt the software pipelining algorithm to suit the CCDP scheme. First, software pipelining will only be used for inner loops that do not contain recursive procedure calls. The compiler can estimate the loop execution time from the number of clock cycles taken by each instruction. After computing the number of iterations to prefetch ahead, the compiler has to decide whether it is profitable to use software pipelining. This is a design issue which is machine dependent. Our algorithm uses a compiler parameter to specify the range of the number of loop iterations which should be prefetched ahead of time. The value of this parameter can be empirically determined and tuned to suit a particular system. The algorithm also takes the hardware constraints into consideration by not issuing the prefetches when the amount of data to be prefetched exceeds the available prefetch queue size or the cache size.

Moving back prefetches If neither vector prefetch generation nor software pipelining can be applied for a particular loop, then our algorithm attempts to move back the prefetch operations as far away as possible from the point where the data will be used. There are several situations in which this technique is applicable. First, it might not be possible to pull out array references from some loops due to unknown loop scheduling information or control and data dependence constraints. Second, the prefetch hardware resources might not be sufficient if we prefetch the references in certain loops using vector prefetch generation or software pipelining. Third, we can use this technique for prefetch targets in serial code sections, where vector prefetch generation and software pipelining are not applicable.

Gornish's algorithm for pulling back references [5] tries to move references as far back as control and data dependence constraints allow. However, the algorithm might move a prefetch operation so far back that the prefetched data gets replaced from the cache by the time it is needed. Another possible situation is that the distance which a prefetch operation may be moved back is so small that the prefetched data does not arrive in time to be used. Thus, to maximize the effectiveness of the prefetches, our algorithm uses a parameter to decide whether to move back a prefetch operation. The range of values for this parameter indicates the suitable distance to move back the prefetches. This parameter can also be tuned by using an experimental study on the desired system.

Prefetch Scheduling Algorithm Our prefetch scheduling algorithm [7] considers each inner loop or serial code segment of the program. It determines if the prefetch hardware resources can handle all of the potentially-stale and non-stale prefetch target references in the loop. If there is insufficient hardware resources, then it selects the actual prefetch targets to be issued as prefetch operations based on their priority levels. Those potentially-stale prefetch targets which will not be issued are replaced by bypass-cache fetches to preserve program correctness. On the other hand, the non-stale prefetch targets which are not issued are replaced by normal read operations.

Depending on the type of loop or code segment, the algorithm uses a suitable scheduling technique for the prefetch targets. Loop unrolling is performed before software pipelining is applied to a loop if the loop contains prefetch targets which exhibit self-spatial locality. It is unnecessary to perform loop unrolling in conjunction with vector prefetch generation because the latter already exploits spatial locality of prefetch target references.

5   Performance Evaluation

5.1   System Model

In our experiments, we model a 32-processor, non-cache-coherent DSM multiprocessor which is similar to the Cray T3D using the EPGsim [9] execution-driven simulator. The nodes of the system are interconnected via a multistage network. For simplicity, we did not model the actual 3D-torus mesh network of the Cray T3D. The cache hit latency is 1 cycle, while the cache miss latency is 100 cycles if there is no network contention. The network delays are simulated using an analytical model. Each processor is single-issue and all the arithmetic and logical instructions are assumed to take 1 cycle.

Each processor has a 64KB lock-up free direct-mapped data cache. The cache line size is 32 bytes. For all the compiler-directed cache coherence schemes, we use a write-through with write-allocate policy, which is the most suitable one according to previous analysis [2]. On the other hand, a write-back policy should deliver the best performance for a hardware directory scheme [2]. For a system which uses the CCDP scheme, we model a DCPFU in each of its processor. The PPQ of each DCPFU has two sections, each with 16 entries. The PHC has 32 entries, each with line size of 32 bytes. It is fully-associative, with a hit latency of 1 cycle if the prefetched up-to-date data has already arrived.

5.2   Simulated Schemes

We simulated the following cache coherence schemes :

- **BASE** : This scheme does not cache shared data in order to avoid the cache coherence problem.
- **CBP** : This is the Cache Bypass scheme which applies stale reference analysis to detect potentially-stale references, and uses *bypass-cache fetch* operations to bypass the cache and obtain up-to-date data from the main memory.
- **CCDP** : This is the CCDP scheme discussed in this paper.
- **HWD** : This scheme uses a full-map hardware directory with a three-state invalidation-based coherence protocol. The directories are distributed across the nodes and are organized as pointer caches to reduce storage.

The BASE architecture is similar to that of the Cray T3D. Due to the lack of hardware cache coherence mechanisms on the Cray T3D, the shared data in the Cray MPP Fortran (CRAFT) programs are not cached. The CBP scheme is a pure software-controlled cache coherence scheme which can be implemented on existing large-scale DSM systems without requiring additional cache coherence hardware. The performance of the CBP scheme will give an indication of the impact of applying stale reference analysis alone. Finally, the HWD scheme is a standard hardware directory-based cache coherence scheme. We augment the HWD scheme with data prefetching, but it does not use the prefetch hardware of the CCDP scheme. Instead, it prefetches data directly into the data cache.

5.3   Experimental Methodology

First, we automatically parallelize the application codes using the Polaris compiler. With the parallelism and data sharing information of the parallelized codes, we can simulate their execution under the BASE scheme. Next, we use a Polaris implementation of the stale reference analysis algorithm to automatically detect the potentially-stale and the non-stale references in these parallelized programs. For the CBP scheme, the potentially-stale references marked by the compiler are treated as bypass-cache fetch operations by the simulator.

For the CCDP scheme, we manually add prefetch operations into the programs, according to the prefetch target analysis and prefetch scheduling algorithms of the scheme. Our aim in this paper is to use hand compilation to quickly evaluate the performance of the CCDP scheme without sacrificing accuracy. After obtaining the parallel programs with the required cache coherence operations, we instrument these programs [9] to generate events that model the program execution on our target architecture. Finally, we run these instrumented codes through the EPGsim simulator and generate the performance results.

5.4   Application Codes

We selected two programs from the SPEC CFP95 and three programs from the SPEC CFP92 benchmark suites. The two applications from the CFP95 suite are TOMCATV and SWIM. The three programs from the CFP92 suite, namely, MXM, VPENTA, and CHOLSKY, are part of the NASA7 code. These applications are all floating-point intensive and they are written in Fortran.

TOMCATV is a highly vectorizable mesh generation program. The main data structures which it uses are 7 matrices of size 513×513. SWIM solves a system of shallow water equations using finite difference approximations. The main data structures used in the program are 14 matrices of size 513×513. The MXM application multiplies a 256×128 matrix by another 128×64 matrix. The VPENTA application inverts three matrix pentadiagonals. The main data structures used are 7 matrices of size 128×128. CHOLSKY performs the Cholesky decomposition on a set of input matrices. The main matrices used in the program are of size $250 \times 5 \times 41$ and $4 \times 250 \times 41$.

5.5   Performance Results

Cache miss ratio The cache misses consist of *sharing* and *nonsharing* misses. A sharing miss occurs when the cached data item has been invalidated. The other types of usual cache misses such as cold, conflict and capacity misses are considered as nonsharing misses. The sharing misses can be divided into *true sharing* and *false sharing* misses. True sharing misses arise due to the need to enforce cache coherence. On the other hand, the false sharing misses are unnecessary cache misses due to over invalidations.

Figure 3 shows the cache miss ratios of the applications. By using the CBP scheme, a significant amount of false sharing misses in the BASE scheme are eliminated. In absolute terms, the reduction in cache miss ratio ranges from 4.8% in VPENTA to 19.8% in CHOLSKY. The CCDP scheme further reduces the cache miss ratios of the applications, ranging from 3.6% in SWIM to 10.2% in TOMCATV. This is due to the fact that the CCDP scheme prefetches the potentially-stale references, which reduces the amount of cache misses. The CCDP scheme also reduces the amount of false-sharing misses by eliminating some unnecessary *ce-prefetch* operations through prefetch target analysis.

Compared to the HWD scheme, the CCDP scheme has lower cache miss ratios in the SWIM application. This is because of the higher false-sharing effect in the hardware directory protocol. On the other hand, the CCDP scheme has higher cache miss ratios compared to the HWD scheme in the other applications.

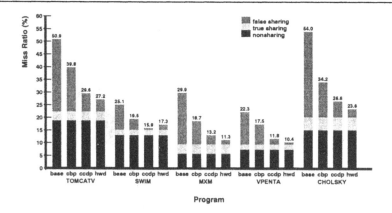

Fig. 3. Cache miss ratios of the applications under various coherence schemes.

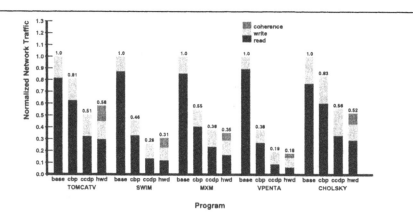

Fig. 4. Normalized network traffic of the applications under various coherence schemes.

This is due to the conservative compiler analyses which lead to higher amount of false sharing misses.

Network traffic The network traffic is made up of read traffic, write traffic and coherence traffic. For each application, we normalize the network traffic under the four cache coherence schemes to that of the BASE scheme. Figure 4 shows the normalized network traffic of the applications. The read traffic is affected by the cache miss ratios. Thus, by reducing the cache miss ratios, the CBP, CCDP and HWD schemes also reduce the read traffic.

The write traffic depends on the cache write policy used. As the BASE, CBP, and CCDP schemes use the write-through policy, they incur similar amounts of write traffic. On the other hand, the HWD scheme uses a write-back policy, which

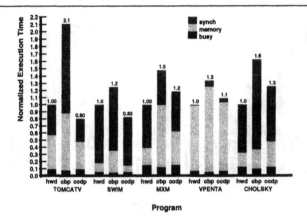

Fig. 5. Normalized execution times of the applications.

incur a lower amount of write traffic than a write-through policy. In absolute terms, the CBP scheme reduces the overall network traffic incurred by the BASE scheme by an amount ranging from 17% in CHOLSKY to 62% in VPENTA. The CCDP scheme further reduces the network traffic from that of the CBP scheme, by an amount ranging from 17% in MXM to 30% in TOMCATV.

The coherence traffic in the compiler-directed cache coherence schemes studied are negligible since they do not require interprocessor communications. On the other hand, the HWD scheme incurs coherence traffic due to the cache coherence transactions specified by the directory protocol. As a result, the overall network traffic of the HWD scheme is higher than that of the CCDP scheme in some applications such as TOMCATV and SWIM. The CCDP scheme incurs higher network traffic than the HWD scheme in the other applications due to the higher amount of false-sharing misses.

Execution time The simulated execution time is composed of the processor busy time, the memory access time, and the synchronization time. For each application, we normalize the execution times under the HWD, CBP and CCDP schemes to that of the HWD scheme. Figure 5 shows the normalized execution times of the applications.

Our results show that the CCDP and HWD schemes outperform the CBP scheme in all of the applications. However, the CCDP and HWD schemes actually incur a higher processor busy time than the CBP scheme since they perform data prefetching operations. The CCDP scheme improves upon the performance of the CBP scheme by reducing the amount of false-sharing misses and network traffic through prefetching both the potentially-stale and non-stale data references.

The HWD scheme requires cache coherence transactions imposed by the coherence protocol. This increases the network traffic, which in turn increases the latency of memory references, especially in applications with a lot of migratory sharing patterns. The CCDP scheme can outperform the HWD scheme in such applications since coherence-related transactions are carried out locally in each processor. Furthermore, it prefetches the potentially-stale references in advance, which hides the latency of accessing these data. In our study, the CCDP scheme outperforms the HWD scheme in the TOMCATV and SWIM applications.

However, the conservative nature of the stale reference detection algorithm used by the CCDP scheme might lead to excessive amount of references being classified as potentially-stale, which in turn increases the amount of *ce-prefetch* operations that incur higher expected memory latency. The experiment results show that the CCDP scheme underperform the HWD scheme in MXM, VPENTA and CHOLSKY. Overall, the CCDP scheme provides comparable performance as the HWD scheme for the applications studied.

6   Conclusions

In this paper, we proposed a framework for integrating compiler-directed cache coherence and data prefetching. The CCDP scheme prefetches the potentially-stale data references in a parallel program to enforce cache coherence, and prefetches the non-stale references to hide memory latency. To optimize the scheme, we designed some inexpensive prefetch hardware to handle the two forms of data prefetching operations. We also developed the compiler techniques used for stale reference detection, prefetch target analysis and prefetch scheduling.

Our results from execution-driven simulations show that the CCDP scheme provides significant performance improvements for the programs studied. The scheme also provides comparable performance to that of a full-map hardware directory-based cache coherence scheme. We are in the process of implementing the prefetch target analysis and prefetch scheduling algorithms using the Polaris compiler. This will enable us to evaluate the extent of performance improvements achievable by automatically transforming programs for cache coherence enforcement and memory latency hiding with the CCDP scheme.

References

1. D. Bernstein, D. Cohen, A. Freund, and D. Maydan. Compiler techniques for data prefetching on the PowerPC. In *Proceedings of the 1995 International Conference on Parallel Architectures and Compilation Techniques*, pages 19–26, June 1995.
2. Y.-C. Chen. *Cache design and performance in a large-scale shared-memory multiprocessor system*. PhD thesis, University of Illinois at Urbana-Champaign, Center for Supercomputing R & D, 1993.
3. L. Choi. *Hardware and Compiler Support for Cache Coherence in Large-Scale Multiprocessors*. PhD thesis, University of Illinois at Urbana-Champaign, Center for Supercomputing R & D, March 1996.
4. L. Choi, H.-B. Lim, and P.-C. Yew. Techniques for compiler-directed cache coherence. *IEEE Parallel & Distributed Technology*, 4(4):23–34, Winter 1996.
5. E. Gornish. Compile time analysis for data prefetching. Master's thesis, University of Illinois at Urbana-Champaign, Center for Supercomputing R & D, December 1989.

6. H.-B. Lim and P.-C. Yew. A compiler-directed cache coherence scheme using data prefetching. *Proceedings of the 1997 International Parallel Processing Symposium*, pages 643–649, April 1997.
7. H.-B. Lim and P.-C. Yew. Maintaining cache coherence through compiler-directed data prefetching. *To appear in Journal of Parallel and Distributed Computing*, 1998.
8. T. Mowry. *Tolerating Latency Through Software-Controlled Data Prefetching*. PhD thesis, Stanford University, Dept. of Electrical Engineering, March 1994.
9. D. Poulsen and P.-C. Yew. Execution-driven tools for parallel simulation of parallel architectures and applications. In *Proceedings of Supercomputing '93*, pages 860–869, November 1993.
10. M. Wolf. *Improving Locality and Parallelism in Nested Loops*. PhD thesis, Stanford University, Dept. of Computer Science, August 1992.

I/O Granularity Transformations*

Gagan Agrawal

Department of Computer and Information Sciences, University of Delaware
Newark DE 19716, USA
agrawal@cis.udel.edu

Abstract. In compiling I/O intensive operations, it is important to pay attention to the operating system features available for enhancing I/O performance. One such useful feature implemented by several current operating system is the *write-back* facility, in which the output data is cached in main memory buffers and then slowly written to disks. Since the buffers are of limited size, this feature can be made much more effective if the compiler can transform very large output operations into a sequence of smaller operations. In this paper, we present a static analysis technique through which the compiler can perform such transformations automatically.

1 Introduction

In recent years, a number of compiler optimizations have been developed for transforming codes and utilizing the features provided by the architecture and the operating system. Such optimizations and transformations allow the application programmers to achieve good performance without paying attention to the low level details of underlying system. Examples of such compiler transformations include a number of cache optimizations, transformations for exploiting coarse grain and fine-grain parallelism and register allocation techniques.

A significant fraction of codes perform large and frequent I/O operations, this includes codes that *snapshot* or *checkpoint* the progress of computation and the *out-of-core* codes in which the primary data structures do not fit in the main memory. Unlike the parallelism transformations or the cache optimizations, the transformations performed by the compilers for I/O need to take into account the operating system features available for I/O operations. An important feature available in several current operating systems is the *write-back* facility. The purpose of this feature is to cache the data output in main memory buffers (called the *write-back buffers*) and allows the computation to proceed without waiting for all data to be written in disks. Since copying data to write-back buffers is significantly cheaper than writing to disks, the write operation can be completed in a smaller amount of time. The output data can be copied from write-back buffers to disk while the computation is in progress. So, the write-back facility

---

* This research was supported by NSF CAREER award ACI-9733520 and NSF grant CCR-9808522

S. Chatterjee (Ed.): LCPC'98, LNCS 1656, pp. 68–82, 1999.

effectively allows for overlap of disk operations with the computations in the program, without explicitly using the asynchronous or non-blocking operations.

Clearly, this facility can only be effective for certain maximum output size only. Some operating systems have a fixed maximum limit for the write-back buffers. Such limit on the size of the buffers is inadequate for improving the performance of real applications that snapshot or checkpoint data or for applications that are out-of-core.

In such codes, the effectiveness of the write-back facility can be significantly enhanced if a single write operation is replaced by a number of smaller operations such that 1) the size of each output does not exceed the size of write-back buffers and 2) there is substantial computation between each such operation. In this paper, we present an automatic compiler transformation technique, which can analyze the source code and replace large output operations with a number of smaller output operations, all of which can effectively use write-back buffers.

The rest of the paper is organized as follows. In Section 2, we formulate the problem we are addressing. Relevant compiler terms and techniques are reviewed in Section 3. Analysis and transformation technique is presented in Section 4. We conclude in Section 5.

2 Granularity Transformations

In this section, we introduce the problem of granularity transformations for utilizing the write-back facility. The compiler analysis for performing such transformations is presented in the next section.

2.1 Example Transformation

```
C     Original Code
Double Precision A(2000000)
do i = 1, 2000000
      A(i) = ....
enddo
Output A(1:2000000)
```

```
C   Transformed Code
Double Precision A(2000000)
do i1 = 1, 4
   do i2 = 1,500000
        A((i1-1)*500000 + i2) = ....
   enddo
   Output A((i1-1)*500000 +1:
   i1*500000 )
enddo
```

Fig. 1. Example of Granularity Transformation

To illustrate the kind of transformation we are interested in, consider the code given in Figure 1. This is a very simple template which shows snapshoting of the progress of computation. In a computational loop, the array A is modified, then the entire array is output. The array A requires 16MB of storage space, and let us assume that the maximum write-back buffer available is 4MB. The code as presented on the left side of Figure 1 cannot use the write-back facility effectively since only a small fraction of the data output can fit in the write-back buffers. However, this code can be easily transformed to make effective use of write-back buffers, as is shown the right side of the figure. Instead of a single output operation, four output operations are performed, and each output operation fits in the write-back buffer. If significant computation is performed between each of these write operations, it is likely that data in the write-back buffer can be written on disks before next output operation is performed.

Though system software issues for I/O intensive applications have been addressed by several research groups [8,7,6,4,5,1], we are not aware of any previous work in performing such compiler transformation.

Obviously, the transformation shown in the Figure 1 is very simple and does not require much analysis. However, any realistic code that performs snapshoting, checkpointing or out-of-core operations is likely to have much more complex flow of control. In particular, the following features may make the transformation challenging for the compiler:

- The sections of the array(s) output may be modified at several different loop-nests in the program.
- The flow of control may be fairly complex between the point(s) where the array is modified to the point where it is output.
- The array output may be multi-dimensional, and the loops in which it is modified may not be perfectly nested.
- The induction variables in these loops may not be trivial to identify, and the subscripts for accessing the arrays elements may be complex functions of the induction variables.

Consider the example given in Figure 2. This code shows some of the difficulties in the analysis mentioned above.

2.2   Problem Definition

Consider the original program written by the application programmer, which has a large write operation. For simplicity, we assume that a rectilinear section of a single array is written in this operation. Our analysis can be easily extended to the cases when several different arrays are output at the same point in the program.

Let the array section output be $A(l_1 : h_1, \ldots, l_m : h_m)$, i.e. the array A is a m-dimensional array, and the section of the array output has a lower bound of l_i and an upper bound of h_i along the ith dimension. We do not consider the possibility that the array section has non-unit strides, since such sections involve

```
            Double Precision A(2000,2000)
            if foo then
                do i = 1, 1000
                    j = 2*i
                    l = 1
                    do k = 1, 2000
                        A(j,l) = ...
                        l = l + 1
                    enddo
                enddo
            else
                ...
            endif
            Output A(1:2000,1:2000)
```

Fig. 2. An Example Code

very high seek time. Our goal is to replace this operation with smaller output operations such that the data output in any of them can fit in the write-back cache. For the analysis presented here, we assume that the size of the write-back cache is known to the compiler. This is true for several operating systems, and for others, this information can be extracted from profiling.

For presenting our analysis, we initially make the following assumptions about the system. We do not expect these assumption to all reasonable for real systems, however, they ease in formulating the problem and presenting our technique. After presenting our analysis, we discuss how it can be modified if these assumptions are not true.

- We assume that the order in which array elements are output is not important for correctness, i.e., each element can be written to the appropriate location in the output file.
- We assume that no additional overheads are incurred if the total number of write operations is increased.
- We assume that no additional disk seek time is introduced by changing the order of output of array elements.

3 Background

Before presenting our transformation algorithm, we briefly review relevant compiler terms and techniques.

3.1 Interval and Interval Partitioning

Consider the CFG representation of a single procedure. The nodes in the CFG can be partitioned into disjoint sets, called intervals, where each interval has a

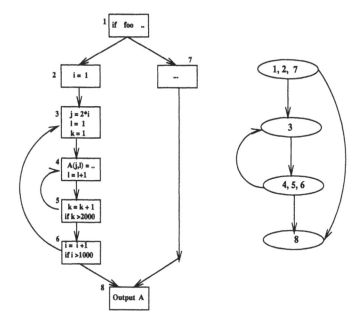

Fig. 3. CFG and Interval Graph for the Example Code

unique header node. The property of the header node is that it dominates all the
nodes in the interval, i.e. there is no path in the CFG from the entry node to a
node in the interval that does not pass through the header node of this interval.
Formally, given a CFG G with an entry node n_0, the interval with header n is
denoted by $I(n)$ and is defined as smallest set of nodes such that:

- n is in $I(n)$
- If all of the predecessors of some node $m \neq n_0$ are in $I(n)$, then m is in $I(n)$.

The interval partition is computed by first determining $I(n_0)$ and then computing $I(n)$ for any node whose predecessor is already in an interval, but n
cannot be added to that interval [2].

Next, using the interval partitioning, we construct the interval graph, $I(G)$,
as follows:

- The nodes of $I(G)$ correspond to the intervals in the interval partition of G.
- The initial node of $I(G)$ is the interval of G that contains the initial node of
  G.
- There is an edge from an interval I to a different interval J if and only if
  there is an edge from some node in I to the header of J.

Consider again the CFG given in Figure 3. The 8 basic blocks in this CFG
can be partitioned into 4 intervals. The intervals are: $(1, 2, 7)$, (3), $(4, 5, 6)$ and
(8). The interval graph is shown on the right hand side in the same Figure.

We can repeat the algorithm for computing intervals on the graph $I(G)$,
and thus obtain a sequence $(G_0, G_1, \ldots, G_m)$ such that $G = G_0$, $G_{i+1} = I(G_i)$,

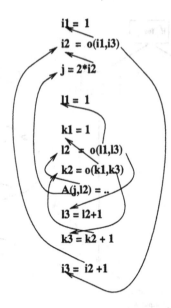

Fig. 4. FUD Graph for the Loop in Example Code

$G_{m-1} \neq G_m$ and $I(G_m) = G_m$. Such a sequence is referred to as the *derived sequence* for G, G_i is called the *derived graph of order i*, and G_m is the limit flow graph of G. If G_m is a single node with no edges, then, G is called a *reducible* graph. Intuitively, a graph is not reducible only if contains jumps inside loops. CFGs for almost all real codes are reducible.

For the interval graph shown in Figure 3, the next derived graph has three nodes: $((1, 2, 7)), ((3), (4, 5, 6))$ and $((8))$.

Consider a node n_1 in the original CFG such that n_1 is an interval header in the interval partition of G_0, $n_2 = I(n_1)$ is an interval header in the interval partition of G_1, and similarly, $n_i = I(n_{i-1})$ is an interval header in the interval partition of G_{i-1}. Moreover, $I(n_i)$ is not an interval header in the interval partition of G_i. If G is a reducible graph, we refer to the node n_i as *heading a loop-nest of depth i*. All nodes of the CFG G that belong to the interval $I(n_i)$ are referred to as *nodes in loop-nest headed by n_i*.

Having determined the interval partitioning, the edges in the CFG can be classified into three categories [2]:

- The edges that branch from nodes in $I(n)$ to n are called the *latches* of $I(n)$.
- The edges that branch from nodes in $I(n)$ to nodes outside the interval are called the *exit edges* of $I(n)$.
- All other edges are called *forward edges*, within the interval their source and sink lies.

3.2   FUD Graph

Next, we define a structure called the Factored-Use-Def (FUD) graph [9]. Consider any use of a variable v in a statement s in a program. There can be multiple statements in the program where the value of v used here could have been defined. The set of such statements is called the set of *reaching definitions* for the use of variable v, in the statement s. A *use-def* graph for a program is a graph in which each use of a variable has links to all its reaching definitions.

FUD graph is a use-def graph with two important properties:

- Each use of a variable has a unique reaching definition
- Special merge operators called ϕ-nodes are added at the control-flow merge points whenever there are multiple reaching definitions

We do not present the algorithms for constructing such chains, they are well documented in the compiler literature [9]. The FUD graph for the loop in Figure 2 is shown in Figure 4.

3.3   Identifying Induction Variables

An important application of FUD graphs is in identifying linear induction variables for a loop nest. By a linear induction variable, we mean a scalar variable assigned in a loop whose value in the next iteration of the loop is the value in the current iteration plus a constant. We briefly explain the standard algorithm for finding linear induction variables here, the formal details are available elsewhere [9]. The main observation in recognizing a linear induction variable for a loop is there is a ϕ node for the definitions of this variable at the beginning of this loop that signifies merge of the value at the start of the loop and the new value assigned inside loop. There must not be any other ϕ nodes, implying that no definition of this variables is enclosed within a conditional inside the loop. The definition inside the loop must be a constant increment to the value in the previous iteration. The main steps are:

- Identify cycles or Strongly Connected Components (SCC) within the FUD graph for the loop-nest.
- Check if the cycle has only one ϕ node at the beginning of the loop.
- Check if the arithmetic operations performed on the variable defined in the cycle are only additions of constant values.

The above steps will identify the linear induction variables, if there exists one.

We can also identify the initial values, the step and the number of iterations of loops associated with each of these induction variables. This is done by starting from the inner most loop and proceeding outwards. The initial value can be determined by looking at the ϕ node, and the edge incident to the ϕ node from the code outside this loop. If it is a countable loop, i.e., the number of iterations of the loop can be determined at compile time, then it must have a single loop exit test that compares two linear induction variables or a linear induction variable and a constant. The number of iterations can then be calculated by determining the lowest value of the linear induction variable that satisfies the test, subtracting the value with the initial value and dividing by the step.

4 Transformation Technique

There are two main steps in our transformation technique. First, we perform data flow analysis on the control flow graph (CFG) to determine the outer-most loop (interval) where the operation is anticipable. Then, we build a representation called Factored Use-Def (FUD) graph within this interval, identify induction variables, analyze the array subscripts and determine how the operation can be split into smaller operations.

4.1 Data Flow Analysis

We use the classical compiler technique of data flow analysis [2] to identify the loop-nest(s) in which the array output is modified.

We use the notion of *anticipability* to determine the outer-most loop on whose exit the output operation can be correctly and safely placed. An operation is anticipable at a point p in the graph if it occurs on all the paths in the CFG leading from p and there is no modification of the operands between p and the point of original occurrence. Thus, if the operation is placed at p instead of the original position, the result of the operation will be the same, and no path that did not have the operation previously will have the operation.

We compute the anticipability of the output operation at the beginning and end of each basic block in G. We denote the anticipability of the operation at the beginning of a basic block b by ANTICIN(b) and the anticipability at the end of a basic block b by ANTICOUT(b).

Computing Anticipability Consider the basic block b_i in which the operation output $A(l_1 : h_1, \ldots, l_m : h_m)$ is initially placed. If the array A is not modified from the start of the basic block to the occurrence of the operation, then we can initialize ANTICIN(b_i) to be array section $(l_1 : h_1, \ldots, l_m : h_m)$. For any basic block b, the anticipability at the end of the basic block is given as:

$$\text{ANTICOUT}(b) = \bigcap_{s \in succ(b)} \text{ANTICIN}(s)$$

Here, $succ(b)$ is the set of successors of the node b in the CFG. The above equation simply states that the rectilinear array section anticipable at the end of a basic block is the intersection of the rectilinear array sections anticipable at the beginning of all the successor basic blocks. Anticipability at the beginning of the basic block where the operation is initially placed has already been determined

and is not modified during the data flow process. For other basic blocks, the
following equation is used.

$$\text{ANTICIN}(b) = MOD_b(\text{ANTICOUT}(b))$$

Here, MOD_b is a function that summarizes the mod information.
$MOD_b(\text{ANTICOUT}(b))$ returns the largest rectilinear section that is unmodified
at the beginning of the basic block b. Determining which array elements are
modified is simple when the array subscript is a constant, e.g., $A(5,6)$. When
the subscripts are not constants, but possibly functions of induction variables,
we use conservative estimates. For example, if the array element modified is
$A(i,6)$, we assume that the entire sixth column of the array has been modified.
We can further improve the accuracy of this when the induction variables and
their bounds have been identified.

Earliest Placement of the Entire Operation If we were just interested in
performing earliest possible output of all the elements in the array section such
that output values do not change, we can determine such a placement using the
above anticipability values. Let PLACE(b) refer to placement inside the basic
block b, and let PLACE(b, c) refer to placement between the basic blocks b and
c, by inserting a new basic block between the two nodes. Using the anticipability
values, we can compute the PLACE terms.

$$\text{PLACE}(b) = \text{ANTICIN}(b) - \text{ANTICOUT}(b)$$

If some elements are anticipable at the end of the basic block b but not at
the beginning of the basic block, this means that these elements are modified
inside this basic block and their earlier possible placement will be within this
basic block.

Next, consider two basic blocks b and c such that $c \in succ(b)$.

$$\text{PLACE}(b, c) = \text{ANTICOUT}(b) - \text{ANTICIN}(c)$$

If a set of elements is anticipable at the beginning of a basic block c but is
not anticipable at the end of the basic block b, where b is a predecessor of c, then
the earlier possible placement can be done by creating a new basic block along
the edge from b to c.

Our final goal is not to do the placement as per the equations presented
earlier, but look for opportunities for placing output of a smaller set of elements.
Consider the PLACE terms as determined by the equations above. We classify
the placement into three categories, as also illustrated in Figure 5.

- PLACE(b), which implies that certain elements of the array output are modified in the basic block b, and therefore, the output of these elements cannot
  be placed any earlier.

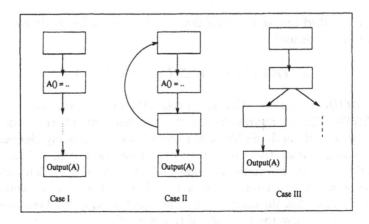

Fig. 5. Three Cases in Placement

- PLACE(b, c), where (b, c) is an exit edge from the interval containing b, and the only other edge from b is a latch (b, d) such that the output is not anticipable at d.
- PLACE(b, c) in all other cases.

The second case above is the most interesting for us, and we discuss the detailed analysis in the next subsection. The edge (b, c) is an exit edge from an interval, which means that b is the exit node within a loop. c is a basic block after the loop and d is the loop header. We know that the operation is anticipable at the beginning of c, but not at the beginning of d. Since the operation is anticipable at the end of an interval, i.e. at the end of a loop, but not at the beginning of the loop, it is likely that the elements of the array output are modified inside this interval in the CFG. Typically, in any code that does snapshoting, checkpointing or out of core computations, we expect that a single loop nest will be modifying all the elements of the array that are output later. By analyzing within this loop-nest, we can insert smaller output operations. We expect that there is sufficient computation within this loop-nest, to ensure that the data written in the write-back buffers can be written to disks before the next operation.

We briefly discuss how the first and third cases can be handled. If output of certain array elements is anticipable at the end of a basic block, but is not anticipable at the beginning of the same basic block, then these array elements cannot be output any earlier than this basic block. So, the easiest solution is to place the output operation within the basic block, just after the instructions where the elements are modified.

Consider the third case. We have an edges in CFG (b, c) and (b, d) such that the operation is anticipable at the beginning of c but not at the beginning of d. Also, b and d do not belong to the same interval. This case represents the situation that the original occurrence of the operation was enclosed by a conditional and there, the operation cannot be moved before the basic block c. So, the operation needs to be placed between the basic blocks b and c.

4.2   Interval Analysis

Consider the second of the three cases mentioned above. Before we can perform further analysis on this interval, we need to make sure that the operation is indeed anticipable at all the exit points of the interval. Recall that an interval has a single entry point, but may have several exit points. We have an exit edge (b, c) such that the operation is anticipable at the beginning of c, the node d is the interval header, and there is a latch (b, d). We examine all the nodes in the interval $I(d)$, and identify all the exit edges, i.e. the edges (e, f), where $e \in I(d)$ and $f \notin I(d)$. For all such nodes f, we check if the operation is anticipable at the beginning.

If the above condition is true, we proceed to analyze the interval $I(d)$. Otherwise, the operation needs to placed between the nodes b and c. Note that multiple exits edges from an interval occur when there is a goto from within the interval to a point outside the interval. In our case, the operation will not be anticipable at all the exits of the interval when this goto leads to a point in the CFG beyond the point of original occurrence of the operation. We believe that such a possibility is not likely for any real code, and therefore, the above restriction does not make our analysis ineffective.

Our further analysis is restricted to analyzing only the loop-nest headed by $I(d)$. We had defined the notion of loop-nest headed by a node in the CFG earlier in this section and the nodes that are included in this loop-nest. Our analysis is based upon the assumption that the CFG is a reducible graph.

4.3   Array Subscript Analysis

Consider a statement s in which the array A is modified. We want to determine the induction variable for each loop, that surrounds the statement s and is within the interval at whose exit the operation was anticipable. For these loops, we will also like to determine the initial value and the step of the induction variable. After we have identified the induction variables in this loop nest, we then relate the array subscripts to the induction variables. Our analysis can be most effective only if the following conditions are met:

– The subscripts for accessing the array A are linear functions of the induction variables, i.e. they are of the form $a + bi$, where a and b are constants or loop invariants, and i is one of the induction variables. Note that a or b can be zero also.
– All the induction variables involved are *linear induction variables*, i.e., they can be defined completely in terms of the initial value (the value during the first iteration of the loop) and its step. The step must be a constant.
– All the loops must be *countable*, i.e., the number of times the loop iterates must not depend upon any value computed in the loop.

For determining the induction variables and their bounds, we construct Factored-Use-Def (FUD) graph within this loop-nest [9]. We gave the definition of the FUD graphs in the previous section. Using the FUD graph, we can determine the induction variables, the initial values of the induction variables and the loop trip counts, as explained in the previous section.

We next relate the array subscripts to the linear induction variables. We classify each subscript in one of the following categories:

- A linear function of a linear induction variable.
- A loop invariant value, i.e. the subscript remains the same during all the iterations within the loop.
- Anything else, which is denoted as a *complex*. This includes possibilities that the subscript depends upon multiple induction variables, or is a higher-order function of the induction variables.

We start analyzing the FUD graph from the nodes for each of the subscripts. We follow the successors in the FUD graph, and perform the following actions on a successor s:

- If s is a ϕ node, then we declare the subscript to be complex.
- If s is a node outside the loop-nest, we declare the subscript to be loop-invariant.
- If s is a node for one of the induction variables, say i, we declare the subscript to be dependent upon the induction variable i.
- For anything else, we continue the same process with all the successors of s.

If we have declared a subscript to be dependent upon a linear induction variable, we need to make sure that the subscript is a linear function of the linear induction variable. Let s be the node where induction variable is defined, and let t be the node for the array subscript. We trace the path in the FUD graph from t to s. Note that this path cannot have any ϕ nodes. Consider any node in this path that denotes an arithmetic operation. We can check that this is only an addition or a multiplication operations. Let the successors of this node be p and q and let p be on the path from t to s. Then, for the subscript to be a linear function of the induction variable, q must be a constant or loop invariant. By analyzing all such nodes along the path from t to s, we can determine the relationship between the array subscripts and the loop variable (say i) and can compute the loop invariants a and b such that the subscript is $a + bi$.

We had earlier determined the initial value and the final value of the induction variables. Let the initial value the final value of the induction variable i be c and d respectively. Along this dimension, the array elements touched range from $(a + bc)$ to $(a + bd)$. If the range of the array section output along this dimension was $l_i : h_i$, then the range of elements that must be output at the end of the current statement is $max(l_i, a + bc) : min(h_i, a + bd)$. We can compute this information for the subscripts along all the array dimensions here.

4.4   Code Generation

For the given statement, we have computed the section of A that is modified here. We know the size of the write-back buffer, so we can determine the number of elements of the array that can fit in this buffer. Let this number be n. We want to place an output of n array elements. Knowing the range of the array elements touched along each dimension, we can compute the iterations in which a section of n elements has been touched since the last output.

Consider the example code in Figure 2. If we know that the size of the write-back buffer is 4MB and each double precision number takes 8 bytes, then we need to place an output as soon as an array section with 500K elements has been touched. We can easily see that this will occur when the value of l is 2000 and the value of j is a multiple of 250. In Figure 6, we have shown the resulting code on the left-hand-side. This code can make much more effective use of the buffers. However, this code also incurs the cost of evaluating conditionals in each iteration.

In most of the codes, the cost of evaluating this conditional can be easily removed. We can choose the iterations of the outer-most loop on whose completion the output must be placed. For example, we can see that the output is placed at the end of the iterations where the value of j is a multiple of 250. We have earlier computed the relationship between the subscript j and the induction variable i. So, we can determine that we need to perform the output at the end of the iterations of the outer-loop, when the value of i is a multiple of 125.

If this outer-most loop is an explicit loop, i.e. it is not formed with goto statements, then we can replace the outer-most loop, with two loops such that we perform the output at the end of the each iteration of the outer loop. The code for the example is shown in the right-hand-side of the Figure 6. This loop does not involve any additional costs of evaluating conditionals.

4.5   Discussion

We now discuss how the assumptions stated earlier while defining the problem can be relaxed. First, we state how our analysis can possibly deteriorate the performance of the code for realistic systems.

- An unnecessarily large number of operations may be placed. While these operations may each utilize the write-back buffers well, the overall cost may be high because of the latency of initiating each operation.
- The smaller operations placed may each be touching non-continuous locations in the disks, and thus the overall seek time may be very high.

Our analysis can be modified or combined with other techniques to avoid the above problems. The first situation arises because of the first placement category, i.e. PLACE(b) may be true for several basic blocks, and a small number of elements may only be output at each of these basic blocks. Consider any such basic block b. Instead of just placing the set of elements in PLACE(b), we

```
Double Precision A(2000,2000)
if foo then
   do i = 1, 1000
      j = 2*i
      l = 1
      do k = 1, 2000
         A(j,l) = ...
         if (j .mod. 250 .eq. 0) .and. (l .eq. 2000)
            Output A(j-249:j,1:2000)
         l = l + 1
      enddo
   enddo
else
   ...
   Output A(1:2000,1:2000)
endif
```

```
Double Precision A(2000,2000)
if foo then
   do i1 = 1, 1000, 125
      do i2 = i1, i1 + 124
         j = 2*i2
         l = 1
         do k = 1, 2000
            A(j,l) = ...
            l = l + 1
         enddo
      enddo
      Output A(j-249:j,1:2000)
   enddo
else
   ...
   Output A(1:2000,1:2000)
endif
```

Fig. 6. The example code with granularity transformations: with conditionals on the left and without conditionals on the right

can output a larger set of elements such that the output is of the size of the write-back buffer. These elements must belong to the set ANTICOUT(b). Also, ANTICIN(b) must be modified to not include any element that is output in this basic block.

The second problem, i.e., larger seek overhead, arises from placement within the interval. Suppose the layout of a two dimensional array is row major, i.e. the elements $A(i, j)$ and $A(i, j + 1)$ are adjacent elements in the memory or the disks. If the loop iterating over j is the outer loop, and the loop iterating over i is the inner loop, then the placement done by our technique will result in higher seek times, as compared to the original operation. The problem can be addressed by doing a loop-interchange on the loop-nest where the array A is modified, so that loop iterating over i becomes the outer loop and the loop iterating over j becomes the inner loop. The techniques for such loop transformations are well documented in the compiler literature [3,9], and we do not discuss them here.

5   Conclusions

In this paper, we have considered the problem of splitting a large output operation into a sequence of smaller operations, to be able to better utilize the write-back buffers. We have presented a general algorithm, which comprises of two major phases. In the first phase, data flow analysis is used to identify the inner-most interval in which the output arrays are modified. In the second phase, we build FUD graph within this interval to identify induction variables within this loop nest, relate the array subscripts to the induction variables, and then transform the code to have smaller granularity outputs.

Acknowledgements

Previous joint work with Anurag Acharya and Joel Saltz lead to the formulation of this problem. Anurag Acharya also helped in extracting the templates used for this work.

References

1. Anurag Acharya, Mustafa Uysal, Robert Bennett, Assaf Mendelson, Michael Beynon, Jeffrey K. Hollingsworth, Joel Saltz, and Alan Sussman. Tuning the performance of I/O intensive parallel applications. In *Proceedings of the Fourth Annual Workshop on I/O in Parallel and Distributed Systems (IOPADS)*. ACM Press, May 1996.
2. Alfred V. Aho, Ravi Sethi, and Jeffrey D. Ullman. *Compilers: Principles, Techniques, and Tools*. Addison-Wesley, 1986.
3. John R. Allen and Ken Kennedy. Automatic loop interchange. In *Proceedings of the ACM Sigplan '84 Symposium on Compiler Construction*, pages 233–246. ACM Press, June 1984.
4. Alok Choudhary, Rajesh Bordawekar, Michael Harry, Rakesh Krishnaiyer, Ravi Ponnusamy, Tarvinder Singh, and Rajeev Thakur. PASSION: Parallel and scalable software for input-output. Technical Report SCCS-636, NPAC, September 1994. Also available as CRPC Report CRPC-TR94483.
5. David Kotz. Disk-directed I/O for MIMD multiprocessors. Technical Report PCS-TR94-226, Department of Computer Science, Dartmouth College, July 1994.
6. Todd C. Mowry, Angela K. Demke, and Orran Krieger. Automatic compiler-inserted i/o prefetching for out-of-core applications. In *Proceedings of the Second Symposium on Operating Systems Design and plementation (OSDI '96)*, Nov 1996.
7. M. Paleczny, K. Kennedy, and C. Koelbel. Compiler support for out-of-core arrays on parallel machines. In *Proceedings of the Fifth Symposium on the Frontiers of Massively Parallel Computation*, pages 110–118. IEEE Computer Society Press, February 1995.
8. Rajeev Thakur, Rajesh Bordawekar, and Alok Choudhary. Compilation of out-of-core data parallel programs for distributed memory machines. In *Proceedings of the IPPS'94 Second Annual Workshop on Input/Output in Parallel Computer Systems*, pages 54–72, April 1994. Also appears in ACM Computer Architecture News, Vol. 22, No. 4, September 1994.
9. Michael Wolfe. *High Performance Compilers for Parallel Computing*. Addison-Wesley, 1995.

Stampede
A Programming System for Emerging Scalable Interactive Multimedia Applications

Rishiyur S. Nikhil[1], Umakishore Ramachandran[2], James M. Rehg[1], Robert H. Halstead, Jr.[3], Christopher F. Joerg[1], and Leonidas Kontothanassis[1]

[1] Compaq Computer Corporation, Cambridge Research Laboratory,
One Kendall Square, Bldg. 700, Cambridge MA 02139, USA
{nikhil,rehg,cfj,kthanasi}@crl.dec.com
[2] College of Computing, Georgia Institute of Technology,
Atlanta GA 30332, USA
rama@cc.gatech.edu
[3] Curl Corporation, 4 Cambridge Center, 7th floor,
Cambridge MA 02142, USA
rhh@curl.com

Abstract. Stampede is a programming system for emerging scalable applications on clusters. The goal is to simplify the programming of applications that are interactive (often using vision and speech), that have highly dynamic computation structures, and that must run on platforms consisting of a mix of front-end machines and high-performance back-end servers with a variety of processors and interconnects. We approach this goal by retaining, as far as possible, the well-known POSIX threads model currently in use on SMPs.
Stampede offers cluster-wide threads with optional loose temporal synchrony, and consistently-cached distributed shared objects. A higher-level sharing/ communication mechanism called *Space-Time Memory*, with automatic garbage collection, is particularly suited to the complex buffer management that arises in real-time analysis hierarchies based on video and audio input. In this paper, we describe an example of our target class of applications, and describe features of Stampede that support cluster-based implementations of such applications.

1 Introduction

There is an emerging class of applications that are computationally very demanding, but which have many features different from the scientific/ engineering applications that have traditionally driven research in parallel processing. An example of this class is a future "Smart Kiosk" for public spaces [3, 11, 14]. It is computationally demanding because it employs sophisticated vision, speech and learning algorithms to track people in front of the kiosk, to recognize them, to gauge facial expressions, gaze and gestures, and to understand their queries. The kiosk's responses may involve sophisticated 3-d graphics, animation and

S. Chatterjee (Ed.): LCPC'98, LNCS 1656, pp. 83–99, 1999.

synthesized speech. Being interactive, it must perform these recognition tasks and generate and render responses at sufficient speed to hold up a convincing "conversation". The structure and demands of the computation are dynamic, depending on the current state of the interaction, if any. Such applications are often based on codes originally written in C. If they have been parallelized, it is often for an explicitly parallel SMP model such as POSIX threads.

The computing platform for a kiosk, or for multiple kiosks scattered throughout an airport or railway station, can be quite heterogeneous. The kiosks may contain front-end computers for low-level vision, speech and rendering tasks, while sharing one or more back-end servers for additional compute power, for database access, for high-speed Internet access, for maintenance, *etc.* These computers may have different processor architectures and operating systems, different numbers of processors, and interconnection networks of uneven capability.

There is a significant programming difficulty for this application and platform scenario. The dynamic structure and complex sharing patterns of the application by themselves make it difficult to use the message-passing programming model (such as MPI). The dynamic application structure, together with the heterogeneity of the platform makes it infeasible to use a flat/ transparent shared memory programming model.

Stampede is our solution to this programming problem. We refer to the heterogeneous platforms described above as "clusters". Stampede offers cluster-wide threads with optional loose temporal synchrony, and consistently-cached distributed shared objects. A higher-level sharing/ communication mechanism called *Space-Time Memory*, with automatic garbage collection, is particularly suited to the complex buffer management that arises in interactive applications with analysis hierarchies based on video and audio input [12]. One of our general design philosophies is to retain, as far as possible, the traditional POSIX threads paradigm for parallel processing on a single SMP.

In this paper, we describe the Smart Kiosk application in more detail, we describe the features of Stampede that make it suitable for such applications on heterogeneous platforms, and conclude with a description of the current status and plans (we have built a prototype and have begun to run the vision component of the Smart Kiosk on it).

2   The Smart Kiosk: An Example Target Application

The goal of Cambridge Research Laboratory's (CRL's) Smart Kiosk project [3] is to develop a kiosk for public spaces– such as a store, museum, or airport– that interacts with people in a natural, intuitive fashion. A Smart Kiosk may contain a variety of input and output devices: video cameras, microphones, loudspeakers, touch screens, infrared and ultrasonic sensors, *etc.* Two or more cameras may be used to produce stereo images of the scene before the kiosk. Microphone arrays accept stereo speech input from customers. Computer vision techniques are used to track, identify and recognize one or more customers in the scene. The kiosk may initiate and conduct conversations with customers. Recognition of customer gestures and speech may be used for customer input. Synthetic emotive speaking faces and sophisticated graphics, in addition to Web-based information displays, may be used for the kiosk's responses.

We believe that the Smart Kiosk has features that are typical of many emerging scalable applications, including robots, smart vehicles, and interactive animation. These applications all have advanced input/ output modes (such as computer vision), very computationally demanding components with dynamic structure, and real-time constraints because they interact with the real world.

Figure 1 shows the software architecture of a Smart Kiosk. The input analysis hierarchy attempts to understand the environment immediately in front of the kiosk. At the lowest level, sensors provide regularly-paced streams of data, such as images at 30 frames per second from a camera. In the quiescent state, a blob tracker does simple repetitive image-differencing to detect activity in the field of view. When such an activity is detected, a color tracker can be initiated that checks the color histogram of the interesting region of the image, to refine the hypothesis that an interesting object (*i.e.*, a human) is in view. If successful, this in turn can invoke higher-level analyzers to detect faces, human (articulated) bodies, *etc.* Still higher-level analyzers look for gaze, gestures, and so on. Similar hierarchies can exist for audio and other input modalities, and these heirarchies can merge as multiple modalities are combined to further refine the understanding of the environment.

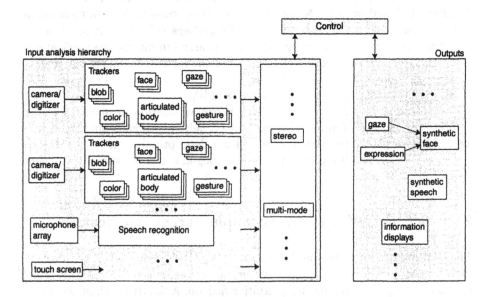

Fig. 1. Software architecture of the Smart Kiosk

The parallel structure of this application is highly dynamic. The environment in front of the kiosk (number of customers, and their relative position) and the state of its conversation with the customers affect which threads are running, their relative computational demands, and their relative priorities (*e.g.*, threads that are currently part of a conversation with a customer are more important than threads searching the background for more customers).

A major problem in implementing this application is "buffer management". Even though the lowest levels of the analysis hierarchy produce regular streams of data items, four things contribute to complexity in buffer management as we move up to higher levels:

- The datasets become temporally sparser and sparser, because they correspond to higher- and higher-level hypotheses of interesting events. For example, the lowest-level event may be: "a new camera frame has been captured", whereas a higher-level event may be: "John has just pointed at the bottom-left of the screen". Nevertheless, we need to keep track of the "time of the hypothesis" because of the interactive nature of the application.
- Threads may not access their input datasets in a strict stream-like manner. In the interests of conducting a convincing real-time conversation with a human a thread may prefer to receive the "latest" input item available, skipping earlier items. The conversation may even result in cancelling activities initiated earlier, so that they no longer need their input data items.
- Datasets from different sources need to be combined, correlating them temporally. For example, stereo vision combines data from two or more cameras, and stereo audio combines data from two or more microphones. Higher-level hypotheses may be generated multi-modally, *i.e.*, by combining vision, audio, gestures and touch-screen inputs.
- Newly created threads may have to re-analyze earlier data. For example, when a thread hypothesizes human presence, this may create a new thread that runs a more sophisticated articulated-body or face-recognition algorithm on the region of interest, beginning again with the original camera images that led to this hypothesis.

These algorithmic features bring up two requirements. First, data items must be meaningfully associated with time and, second, there must be some discipline of time, in order to allow reclamation of storage for data items (garbage collection).

Even a single kiosk is computationally demanding (vision, speech, graphics) and scalable (tracking multiple customers and conducting multiple conversations); in addition, multiple kiosks may be installed in a facility, sharing back-end servers for additional compute power, models (color histograms, face models, articulated body models, ...), databases, high-speed Internet access, *etc.*.

The design of Stampede is aimed at making it easier to program such applications on such platforms. An equally important goal is portability, to allow flexibility in the choice of in-kiosk computers, back-end servers, and their interconnection networks.

3   Overview of Stampede

Figure 2 shows an overview of the Stampede programming model. The control model includes an unlimited number of dynamically created *threads* running in an unlimited number of dynamically created *Address Spaces*. Stampede's threads are an extension of POSIX threads for multiple address spaces.

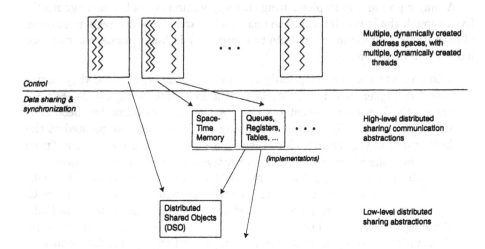

Fig. 2. Overview of the Stampede cluster programming system

All threads within an address space can share data using ordinary shared memory (for example, C global static data, malloc'd data, *etc.*). Threads across all address spaces can share data using consistently-cached *Distributed Shared Objects (DSO)*, described in Section 6. DSO is similar to the Midway shared memory system [2], but with an object-based programming interface (instead of memory-based).

Threads across all address spaces can also share/ communicate data using higher-level distributed data structures, the most novel of which is *Space-Time Memory (STM)*, described in Section 5. STM is particularly useful for managing temporally indexed collections of data, as found in the analysis hierarchies of the Smart Kiosk. The figure also illustrates that STM and the other higher-level data structures can be implemented using DSO, or directly using lower-level "raw" communication mechanisms.

Stampede is currently based entirely on C library calls, *i.e.*, it is implemented as a run-time system, with calls from standard C. Many aspects of the calls could be simplified, prettified, hidden completely, or made more robust (with type-checking), by designing language extensions or a new language. Our initial interest is in proving the concepts and quickly bringing up the Smart Kiosk application, whose existing components are written in C. We have some ideas for high-level descriptions of dynamic thread and communication structures (such as those in Fig. 1) from which we can automatically compile the actual thread creation and Space-Time Memory calls.

4   Address Spaces and Threads

We chose to make multiple Address Spaces (AS's) visible to the application programmer because we believe that, for our target environment, it is infeasible realistically to provide the illusion of a single, shared address space. In the Smart Kiosk, for example, the application may be split between a front-end machine on the kiosk and one or more back-end servers located in a machine room, and these machines may have different processors and operating systems. In addition, the Smart Kiosk application contains a mixture of components, some written in C and some written in Tcl/Tk. The latter components are not thread-safe, and need to be jacketed in their own address space if we are to avoid a major porting job.

The number of Address Spaces has no direct relation to the number of physical machines or processors in the system. An Address Space must be contained completely within a single machine (which may be an SMP), and there can be more than one Address Space on a machine. An Address Space stays on the machine on which it is created– it cannot migrate. Address spaces may be created dynamically, although we expect this to be very infrequent (only for dynamically created thread-unsafe computations).

Stampede threads are based on the POSIX "pthreads" model [6]. A program's execution begins with a single thread at an application-supplied routine named spd_app_main(argc,argv). Through recursive thread creation, an application can create an arbitrary number of threads. A Stampede thread always runs entirely within an address space, and does not migrate, once created. Because we are supporting arbitrary C code and libraries, which can involve pointers into the stack, OS-provided handles, *etc.*, migration would be extremely difficult and expensive (if not impossible).

The spd_thread_create() call in Stampede extends the POSIX call pthread_create() with a few extra parameters. One of them is an integer that specifies which address space the child thread should run in. This number can be in the range 0 to (spd_num_ASs-1), where spd_num_ASs is a Stampede-provided variable equal to the current number of address spaces. Alternatively, a special wild-card argument allows the Stampede run-time system to choose one of the existing address spaces for this thread; this choice may depend, for example, on the current loads on the participating machines. The semantics of thread creation are the same as in POSIX: the parent thread blocks on the creation call until the child thread has been created and is ready to run, no matter which address space it occupies.

Stampede's argument-passing convention during thread creation differs from the POSIX model, because the parent and child threads may be on different address spaces. POSIX thread creation passes only a "one word" argument (coerced to the (void *) type) from the parent thread to the root function of the child thread. Larger arguments are passed by reference, by passing a pointer to the real argument in this one word argument. This is adequate in POSIX since threads occupy a single address space. We have found that a simple extension subsumes the POSIX system, with very little intellectual or performance overhead. Stampede thread creation takes an additional integer arg_size parameter.

When arg_size is zero, the usual (void *) parameter is passed exactly as in POSIX. When arg_size > 0, the (void *) parameter is interpreted as a pointer to arg_size bytes. These bytes are copied to the destination address space, and the child receives a (void *) pointer to this copy. For uniformity, this copy is performed even if the child and parent are on the same address space (so, the child never has to synchronize with the parent to access the copy).

The thread-creation call returns a Stampede thread identifier that is unique across all address spaces in the application. Thread identifiers may be used for thread control and synchronization. For example, if a thread A must wait for another thread B to complete, whether or not they are on the same address space, it can call Stampede's analog to POSIX's pthread_join(), supplying the Stampede thread identifier for B.

In summary, in order to simplify porting of existing applications to Stampede, we have sought to retain the POSIX threads model as far as possible, making only the minimal changes necessary in order to extend it to multiple address spaces.

5 Space-Time Memory

Perhaps the most novel aspect of Stampede is Space-Time Memory (STM), a distributed data structure that addresses the complex "buffer management" problem that arises in managing temporally indexed data items as in the Smart Kiosk application. To recap the description in Section 2, there are four complicating features: streams become temporally sparser as we move up the analysis hierarchy; threads may not access items in strict stream order; threads may combine streams using temporal correlation, and the hierarchy itself is dynamic, involving newly created threads that may re-examine earlier data.

Traditional data structures such as streams, queues and lists are not sufficiently expressive to handle these features. In addition to the issue of associating data items with time, these features also make garbage collection a challenging problem.

Stampede's Space-Time Memory (STM) is our solution to this problem. The key construct in STM is the *channel*, which is a location-transparent collection of objects indexed by time. The API has operations dynamically to create a channel, and for a thread to *attach* and *detach* a channel. Each attachment is known as a *connection*, and a thread may have multiple connections to the same channel. Figure 3 shows an overview of how channels are used. A thread can *put* a data item into a channel *via* a given output connection using the call:

```
spd_channel_put_item (o_conn, timestamp, buf_p, buf_siz, ...)
```

The item is described by the pointer buf_p and its buf_size in bytes. A channel cannot have more than one item with the same timestamp, but there is no constraint that items be put into the channel in increasing or contiguous timestamp order. Indeed, to increase throughput, a module may contain replicated threads that pull items from a common input channel, process them, and put items into

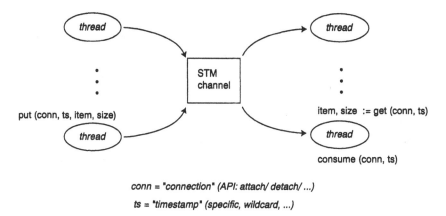

conn = "connection" (API: attach/ detach/ ...)

ts = "timestamp" (specific, wildcard, ...)

Fig. 3. Overview of Stampede channels

a common output channel. Depending on the relative speed of the threads and the particular events they recognize, it may happen that items are placed into the output channel "out of order". Channels can be created to hold a bounded or unbounded number of items. The put call takes an additional flag that allows it to block or to return immediately with an error code, if a bounded output channel is full.

A thread can *get* an item from a channel *via* a given input connection using the call:

```
spd_channel_get_item (i_conn, timestamp,
                      & buf_p, & buf_siz,
                      & timestamp_range, ...);
```

The timestamp can specify a particular value, or it can be a wildcard requesting the newest/oldest value currently in the channel, or the newest value not previously gotten over any connection, *etc.*. As in the put call, a flag parameter specifies whether to block if a suitable item is currently unavailable, or to return immediately with an error code. The parameters buf_p and buf_size can be used to pass in a buffer to receive the item or, by passing NULL in buf_p, the application can ask Stampede to allocate a buffer. The timestamp_range parameter returns the timestamp of the item returned, if available; if unavailable, it returns the timestamps of the "neighboring" available items, if any.

The put and get operations are atomic. Even though a channel is a distributed data structure and multiple threads on multiple address spaces may simultaneously be performing operations on the channel, these operations appear to all threads as if they occur in a particular serial order.

The semantics of put and get are copy-in and copy-out, respectively. Thus, after a put, a thread may immediately safely re-use its buffer. Similarly, after a successful get, a client can safely modify the copy of the object that it received without interfering with the channel or with other threads. Of course, an application can still pass a datum by reference– it merely passes a reference to the object through STM, instead of the datum itself. The reference can be a DSO "global pointer" (described in Section 6) or, if the application exploits knowledge about address spaces, it can even be an ordinary C pointer.

Puts and gets, with copying semantics, are of course reminiscent of message-passing. However, unlike message-passing, these are location-independent operations on a distributed data structure. These operations are one-sided: there is no "destination" thread/ process in a put, nor any "source" thread/ process in a get. The abstraction is one of putting items into and getting items from a temporally ordered collection, concurrently, not of communicating between processes.

5.1   Garbage Collection in STM

The question of garbage collection of items in channel is difficult, in light of the fact that a thread may get and put items sparsely, and even out of order, and the fact that Stampede threads may fork new threads that revisit old data. Stampede imposes rules on thread times and generation of item timestamps that make garbage collection feasible.

An object X in a channel is in one of three states with respect to each input connection ic connecting that channel to some thread. Initially, X is "unseen". If the thread performs a get operation on X over connection ic, then X is in the "open" state with respect to ic. Finally, the thread can perform a consume operation on the object, transitioning it to the "consumed" state. We also say that an item is "unconsumed" if it is unseen or open.

The consume operation can specify a particular object (*i.e.*, with a particular timestamp), or it can specify all objects up to and including a particular timestamp. In the latter case, some objects will move directly into the consumed state, even though the thread never performed a get operation on them.

Every thread has a variable called its "virtual time". At each point in time, each thread has a "virtual time lower bound", which is the lesser of:

- its own virtual time, and
- the smallest timestamp of all unconsumed objects in channels to which the thread has input connections (this number of course may vary as new items are put into those channels by other threads).

A thread can change its virtual time to any specific value $\geq$ this lower bound. Alternatively, a thread can set its own virtual time to the special value INFINITY, in which case its virtual time lower bound is determined purely by what is available on its input channels. This strategy is typically adopted by threads that just compute output item timestamps based on input item timestamps.

When a thread put's an object into a channel *via* an output connection, it can specify any timestamp $\geq$ its virtual time lower bound (subject, of course, to the normal restriction that two objects in a channel cannot have the same timestamp).

Similarly, when a thread creates a new child thread, the parent can specify the child's initial virtual time, using an extra argument in the spd_thread_create() call described in Section 4, to any time $\geq$ the parent's virtual time lower bound.

These rules transitively imply a *global* lower bound timestamp ts_{min}, which is the global minimum of:

- virtual times of all the threads, and
- timestamps of all unconsumed items on all input connections of all channels.

It is impossible for any current thread, or any subsequently created thread, ever to refer to an object with timestamp $< ts_{min}$. Thus, all objects in all channels with lower timestamps can safely be garbage collected. Stampede's runtime system has a distributed algorithm that periodically recomputes this value and garbage collects dead items.

Although this general-purpose global lower-bound computation eventually picks up all garbage in all channels, there is a common case that accelerates garbage collection. Frequently, a producer thread knows exactly how many consumer threads will consume each item (which may be different from the number of input connections to the channel). This information can be passed to Stampede in the form of an additional *reference count* parameter in the put call. As soon as that item has been consumed the requisite number of times, Stampede can garbage collect it immediately.

The copy-in/copy-out semantics allows Stampede to reclaim *all* the space used internally in channels. However, since an item passed through STM may contain references to other application data structures that are unknown to Stampede, Stampede invokes a user-supplied cleanup handler before finally disposing of the item. This "upcall" is always done in the context of the thread that originally put that item into the channel (it is piggy-backed on to other Stampede calls performed by that thread), because that thread is best suited to interpret the contents of the item.

5.2 Communicating Complex Data Structures through STM

The put and get mechanisms described above are adequate for communicating contiguously allocated objects through channels, but what about linked data structures? In the Smart Kiosk vision code, for example, a "color model" data structure is actually a complex of four or more separately allocated components linked with C pointers. We wish to treat them as a single unit that can be communicated through an STM channel. The C pointers are of course meaningless in a different address space.

To solve this, Stampede extends the basic STM system with a notion of "object types". The following call:

```
spd_dcl_type (type, marshall_hook, unmarshall_hook, ...)
```

declares a new object type (represented by an integer), with an associated set of methods, or procedures. Two of these are hooks that assist in marshalling and unmarshalling objects for transmission between address spaces.

A variant of the channel put procedure is based on types instead of object sizes. Its parameters include a pointer to the data structure, as before, and its type, instead of its size (which is not particularly meaningful for a linked data structure). Similarly, a variant of the get call returns a pointer to the linked data structure, and its type instead of size. Figure 4 shows an overview of how these facilities are used. Stampede takes care of the marshalling, communication and unmarshalling of the data structure, using the supplied hooks to decompose and reconstitute the "object". These actions are done lazily, *i.e.*, only when a consumer actually attempts to get an item, and intermediate results are cached to avoid repeating this work in the presence of multiple get's. The normal garbage collection process, described in the previous section, is extended to reclaim any such cached intermediate results.

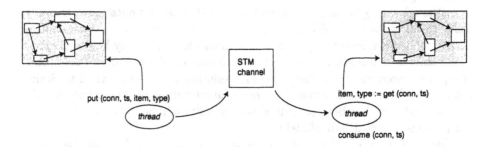

Fig. 4. Communicating complex objects through channels, based on "types"

If we implement Stampede in a language with a richer type system, the application programmer could perhaps be relieved of the burden of specifying these hooks (*cf.* "serializer" mechanisms in Java). However, even in this case, it would be useful to have the ability to override these default methods. For example, image data structures in the Smart Kiosk vision code include a linked list of attributes which can, in fact, be recomputed from the object during unmarshalling, and therefore do not need to be transmitted at all. Further, the image data itself can be compressed during marshalling and decompressed during unmarshalling. Such application- and type-specific generalizations of "marshalling" and "unmarshalling" cannot be provided automatically in the default methods.

5.3 Synchronizing with Real Time

The "virtual time" and "timestamps" described above with respect to STM are merely an indexing system for data items, and do not have any direct connection with real time. For pacing a thread relative to real time, Stampede provides an API for loose temporal synchrony that is borrowed from the Beehive system [13]. Essentially, a thread can declare real time "ticks" at which it will re-synchronize with real time, along with a tolerance and an exception handler. As the thread executes, after each "tick", it performs a Stampede call attempting to synchronize with real time. If it is early, the thread waits until that synchrony is achieved. It if is late by more than the specified tolerance, Stampede calls the thread's registered exception handler which can attempt to recover from this slippage.

Using these mechanisms, for example, a thread in the Smart Kiosk at the bottom of the analysis hierarchy can pace itself to grab images from a camera and put them into an output channel at 30 frames per second, using absolute frame numbers as timestamps.

6   Cluster-Wide Distributed Shared Objects (DSO)

Space-Time Memory is well suited for managing temporally indexed collections of data that are processed in a pipeline manner. But what about ordinary, shared, updatable data? Stampede provides a lower-level, "shared memory-like" mechanism called Distributed Shared Objects (DSO). This mechanism is borrowed from our earlier work on Cid [8], and is also closely related to the Midway shared memory system [2].

Figure 5 shows an overview of DSO usage. First, a thread dynamically declares an object as a global object using the call:

```
spd_dso_gptr  gp;     void *p;     int  size;

gp = spd_dso_make_global (p, size);
```

The returned value gp is an application-wide unique identifier for the object. Once declared global, all threads (including the thread that declared it global) must only access the object between get and release calls:

```
spd_dso_get (gp, mode, & p', & size, ...);

... arbitrary code to manipulate the object using p'-> ...

spd_dso_release (gp, ...);
```

In the get call, the thread specifies the desired object using gp, and the desired access mode in which to obtain the object, such as READ (shared) or WRITE (exclusive). The get call returns an ordinary C pointer to a local copy of the object (p'), and the object's size. The Stampede runtime system implements, in software, a roving-owner consistency protocol to implement the access mode semantics. Each address space contains at most one copy of the object (shared by all threads in that address space).

How does a thread "know" about a global object that may have been created by another thread? The base mechanism is that a gp may be passed as an argument during thread creation. Then, inductively, an object may contain other gptr's as fields.

This is a different programming interface from that in the Midway system, with which it shares the idea that each synchronization action is associated with specific shared data. Midway has the traditional notions of locks and data, and the application program makes explicit calls to associate a lock with the

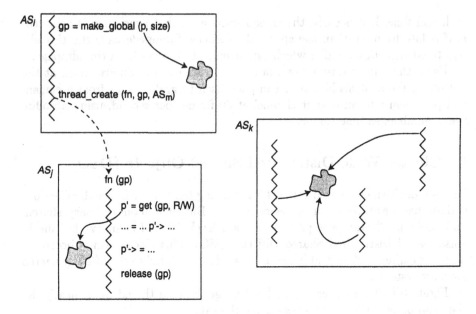

Fig. 5. Overview of Stampede's Distributed Shared Objects (DSO)

data that it guards. This association is exploited in the consistency protocol to decide exactly what data needs to be moved to a processor that acquires a lock to enter a critical section (Midway calls this "entry consistency"). In Stampede's DSO, there is no separate notion of locks. Instead, the programmer directly thinks in terms of shared objects, to which a thread at various times has exclusive, shared, or no access. Unlike flat transparent shared memory systems, DSO does not perform a "check-for-miss" or global-to-local address translation on every memory reference; essentially, this is done once, during the **get** call, which transforms the global name **gp** to a local name **p'**. Subsequent accesses to the object, prior to the **release** call, are just ordinary pointer dereferences, at full speed. The actual addresses **p'** at which an object is replicated by the protocol may in fact vary across different **get**'s. This also makes it easy for the object manager on an address space to evict objects that are not currently in use, and to reuse the freed storage for other objects. When the application no longer needs a DSO object **gp**, it can call **spd_dso_free(gp)** on any address space; the protocol consistently frees all replicas and calls a user-supplied free() routine on the address space where it was originally made global.

In addition to the usual READ and WRITE modes, Stampede's DSO design includes other modes such as RECENT_COPY, PRODUCER and CONSUMER. The former is useful when the application is resilient to accessing a perhaps stale (but consistent) copy of the object, and the latter modes are useful when two threads access an object in the producer-consumer idiom.

Stampede also has an asynchronous variant of the **get** call. This can be used to "prefetch" an object and also to initiate concurrent **get**'s for multiple objects, instead of obtaining them serially. The constructs for these split-phase transactions originated in dataflow languages [1], and were subsequently used in languages like Split-C [4] and Cid [8].

Finally, DSO also supports the distributed sharing of linked data structures, just like the system described for STM in Section 5.2, using type-specific marshalling and unmarshalling hooks. These methods are called automatically, and lazily, by the consistent replication protocol. The cacheing and management of marshalling/unmarshalling intermediate results are a little more complicated in DSO than in STM because of their different semantics: STM has copy-in/copy-out semantics, whereas DSO objects are truly shared and updatable.

The Stampede application programmer has a spectrum of choices in making a linked data structure available cluster-wide. At one extreme, he can have the the entire data structure moved *en masse* using marshall/unmarshall hooks. At the other extreme he can replace every C pointer by a gptr, and access individual elements of the data structure across the cluster at a fine grain by using get and release to traverse gptr links. Or, in between, he can define *regions* of the data structure that are to be treated as single units, use gptr's to link between regions, and provide marshall/unmarshall hooks to have regions moved as units. The choice, on this spectrum, is clearly going to depend on the application.

7   Status and Plans

Essentially all the features of Stampede described above have been implemented for clusters as of this writing. The only pieces still missing are dynamic creation of address spaces, and the non-standard sharing modes in DSO: RECENT_COPY, PRODUCER, CONSUMER, *etc.* We are currently able to run, on a cluster, a prototype of the compute-intensive vision component of the Smart Kiosk, using color models to track multiple targets in front of a single camera.

Earlier, this color-based tracking application and an image-based rendering application exhibited good performance and speedups on a single SMP version of Stampede. Experimental results and pseudo-code can be found in [12].

Stampede is implemented as a C library under Digital Unix. Our main backend compute server is a cluster of four AlphaServer 4100's, each being an SMP with four 400 MHz Alpha processors and 1.5 GB main memory. The SMPs are interconnected with Digital's Memory Channel, Myricom's Myrinet, and an 100 Mb/s FDDI ring. Memory Channel is an extremely low-latency "protected remote write" cluster interconnect [5]. Stampede runs on each of these, and indeed runs on any mix of Alpha Digital Unix workstations and SMPs, resorting to UDP sockets when no better interconnect is available. The Stampede system uses CRL's CLF substrate [9] which provides basic cluster services such as process startup and standard I/O, debugging, and high-speed communication. We cannot yet run on other processor architectures and operating systems, but we have begun porting it to Windows NT on Alpha and x86 machines.

On an experimental basis, Stampede also incorporates the Cashmere Distributed Shared Memory (DSM) system [7] as an alternative to DSO for ordinary shared data. While the rest of Stampede is very portable (it can even work on workstations over UDP sockets), Cashmere is quite closely tied to Digital's Memory Channel. Thus, we view this as an experimental feature only, allowing us to compare the costs of data sharing over DSM and DSO. If DSM is found to be a valuable component of Stampede, we can consider either porting Cashmere to be independent of Memory Channel, or replacing it with some other portable DSM system.

We also have three separate implementations of Space-Time Memory (STM): on top of DSO, a direct implementation using CLF messaging, and on top of Cashmere. Again, this is an experimental setup to allow us to compare the costs of communication and sharing in these three implementations.

We have nearly completed the installation of extensive and detailed instrumentation code in the Stampede system. We will shortly be able to measure Stampede's performance on several micro-benchmarks, and to conduct performance studies to understand the behavior of the application and the system under various choices: the relative performance of Space-Time Memory over its three implementations; the relative performance of ordinary data sharing over DSO and DSM; the effects of thread placement, *etc.* We will of course be tuning and optimizing the implementation continuously.

In a related project, we are studying the integration of dynamic task and data parallelism in Stampede [10]. Many opportunities for data parallelism exist in the Smart Kiosk. For example, images can be partitioned into regions and processed by parallel threads, with each thread looking for all color models in a region. Alternatively, the color models can be partitioned, with each thread looking at entire images for a single color model. Stampede currently has task parallelism only (thread creation), but it is sufficiently flexible to enable manual construction of data parallel structures. However, the book-keeping necessary to split datasets into data parallel chunks and then to recombine the results, can be quite onerous. We have many ideas for higher-level support for data parallelism, but first we intend to conduct some experiments using manually constructed data parallelism to understand where it is most effective.

Further out, we will also be expanding the application on Stampede from the current one-camera vision algorithm towards a full Smart Kiosk system, including stereo vision, more sophisticated vision algorithms, speech recognition and other sensor technologies. As this evolution happens, we expect Stampede's focus to shift towards issues of dynamic thread creation, load balancing, *etc.*

8 Conclusion

There is an emerging class of "smart" applications that monitor a variety of sensors; perform sophisticated, computationally demanding "recognition" algorithms involving individual sensors and combined information from multiple sensors; and, have real-time constraints in that they must react to events in the real-world. The platforms for these applications may combine low power front-end machines together with powerful back-end servers. We have described one such application, CRL's Smart Kiosk, but the description could equally well fit robots, autonomously navigating vehicles, interactive animation for entertainment and training, *etc.*

We have described Stampede, a portable programming system for such applications and platforms, that we are building at CRL. Stampede has dynamic threads that can share data uniformly across multiple distributed address spaces. A key novel feature of Stampede is Space-Time Memory, which permits these applications easily to manage time-sensitive data in the presence of real-time constraints and dynamic thread structure.

Acknowledgements

We would like to thank Kath Knobe for detailed comments that improved this paper substantially. Kath, Jamey Hicks, David Panariti and Mark Tuttle have also been excellent sounding boards for ideas during our design discussions.

References

[1] Arvind, R. S. Nikhil, and K. K. Pingali. I-Structures: Data Structures for Parallel Computing. *ACM Transactions on Programming Languages and Systems*, 11(4):598–632, October 1989.

[2] B. N. Bershad, M. J. Zekauskas, and W. A. Sawdon. The Midway Distributed Shared Memory System. In *Proceedings of the IEEE CompCon Conference*, 1993. Also CMU Technical Report CMU-CS-93-119.

[3] A. D. Christian and B. L. Avery. Digital Smart Kiosk Project. In *ACM SIGCHI '98*, pages 155–162, Los Angeles, CA, April 18–23 1998.

[4] D. E. Culler, A. Dusseau, S. C. Goldstein, A. Krishnamurthy, S. Lumetta, T. von Eicken, and K. Yelick. Parallel Programming in Split-C. In *Proc. Supercomputing 93, Portland, Oregon*, November 1993.

[5] R. Gillett. MEMORY CHANNEL Network for PCI: An Optimized Cluster Interconnect. *IEEE Micro*, pages 12–18, February 1996.

[6] IEEE. Threads standard POSIX 1003.1c-1995 (also ISO/IEC 9945-1:1996), 1996.

[7] L. Kontothanassis, G. Hunt, R. Stets, N. Hardavellas, M. Cierniak, S. Parthasarathy, W. Meira, S. Dwarkadas, and M. Scott. VM-Based Shared Memory on Low-Latency Remote-Memory-Access Networks. In *Proc. Intl. Symp. on Computer Architecture (ISCA) 1997, Denver, Colorado*, June 1997.

[8] R. S. Nikhil. *Cid*: A Parallel "Shared-memory" C for Distributed Memory Machines. In *Proc. 7th. An. Wkshp. on Languages and Compilers for Parallel Computing (LCPC), Ithaca, NY, Springer-Verlag LNCS 892*, pages 376–390, August 8–10 1994.

[9] R. S. Nikhil and D. Panariti. *CLF*: A common Cluster Language Framework for Parallel Cluster-based Programming Languages. Technical Report (forthcoming), Digital Equipment Corporation, Cambridge Research Laboratory, 1998.

[10] J. M. Rehg, K. Knobe, U. Ramachandran, and R. S. Nikhil. Integrated Task and Data Parallelism for Dynamic Applications. In *LCR98: Fourth Workshop on Languages, Compilers, and Run-time Systems for Scalable Computers, Carnegie Mellon University, Pittsburgh, PA, USA*, May 28–30 1998.

[11] J. M. Rehg, M. Loughlin, and K. Waters. Vision for a Smart Kiosk. In *Computer Vision and Pattern Recognition*, pages 690–696, San Juan, Puerto Rico, June 17–19 1997.

[12] J. M. Rehg, U. Ramachandran, R. H. Halstead, Jr., C. Joerg, L. Kontothanassis, and R. S. Nikhil. Space-Time Memory: A Parallel Programming Abstraction for Dynamic Vision Applications. Technical Report CRL 97/2, Digital Equipment Corp. Cambridge Research Lab, 1997.

[13] A. Singla, U. Ramachandran, and J. Hodgins. Temporal Notions of Syncrhonization and Consistency in Beehive. In *Proc. 9th An. ACM Symp. on Parallel Algorithms and Architectures (SPAA)*, June 1997.

[14] K. Waters, J. M. Rehg, M. Loughlin, S. B. Kang, and D. Terzopoulos. Visual Sensing of Humans for Active Public Interfaces. In R. Cipolla and A. Pentland, editors, *Computer Vision for Human-Machine Interaction*. Cambridge University Press, 1998. In press.

Network-Aware Parallel Computing with Remos*

Bruce Lowekamp, Nancy Miller, Dean Sutherland, Thomas Gross**, Peter
Steenkiste, and Jaspal Subhlok***

School of Computer Science, Carnegie Mellon University,
Pittsburgh, PA 15213, USA
{lowekamp,nam,dfsuther,trg,prs,jass}@cs.cmu.edu

Abstract. Networked systems provide a cost-effective platform for parallel computing, but the applications have to deal with the changing
availability of computation and communication resources.
Network-awareness is a recent attempt to bridge the gap between the
realities of networks and the demands of applications. Network-aware
applications obtain information about their execution environment and
dynamically adapt to enhance their performance. Adaptation is especially important for synchronous parallel applications since a single busy
communication link can become the bottleneck and degrade overall performance dramatically. This paper presents Remos, a uniform API that
allows applications to obtain relevant network information, and reports
on the development of parallel applications in this environment. The
challenges in defining a uniform interface include network heterogeneity,
diversity and variability in network traffic, and resource sharing in the
network and even inside an application. The first implementation of the
Remos system is hosted on an IP-based network testbed. The paper reports on our methodology for developing adaptive parallel applications
for high-speed networks with Remos, and presents results that highlight
the importance and effectiveness of adaptive parallel computing.

1   Introduction

Clusters of networked computers are an attractive and ubiquitous platform for
a wide range of parallel and distributed applications. However, effective use
of networked resources is still a major challenge. A networked system consists
of compute nodes (hosts), network nodes (routers and switches), and communication links. Network conditions change continuously due to the sharing of
resources, and when resource demands exceed resource availability, application

---

* Effort sponsored by the Advanced Research Projects Agency and Rome Laboratory, Air Force Materiel Command, USAF, under agreement number F30602-96-
  1-0287. The U.S. Government is authorized to reproduce and distribute reprints
  for Governmental purposes notwithstanding any copyright annotation thereon.
** Thomas Gross is also with ETH, Zurich, Switzerland
*** Jaspal Subhlok is currently with University of Houston, Houston, TX.

S. Chatterjee (Ed.): LCPC'98, LNCS 1656, pp. 100–119, 1999.

performance suffers. Computation load as well as congestion on network nodes and links can reduce the application response time dramatically. An attractive way of dealing with such changes is to make applications *network-aware*, i.e., the application periodically adapts to the network execution environment in an application-specific manner. E.g., an application may select the optimal set of nodes for execution based on compile time information about the kind of communication steps that are included in the program and based on runtime information about the system state. An application may periodically check the resource availability of other nodes and decide to migrate the computation. Or an application may want to select one of several links to transfer data, based on dynamic properties of the links.

The Remos system developed at Carnegie Mellon provides applications with an interface to their execution environment, which includes the network state. Remos is designed for the development of network-aware parallel and distributed applications on diverse network architectures; portability across network architectures and network installations were among the key design considerations. Efficiency is another important consideration, and the cost that an application pays in terms of runtime overhead is low and directly related to the depth and frequency of its requests for network information. The Remos system has its roots in two separate projects: an investigation of resource management in application-aware networks (Darwin) and an effort to support system-aware applications through libraries, frameworks, and tools (Remulac).

Remos allows network-aware applications to obtain information about resource availability, in particular, the network's capabilities and status. Unfortunately, network architectures differ significantly in their ability to provide such information to a host or to an executing application. To avoid dependences on the idiosyncrasies of particular network architectures and communication systems, application development for networks requires a system-independent interface between applications and networks. Remos provides a uniform interface that allows the development of portable applications that can adapt on a range of network architectures. A system-independent interface is also crucial for allowing applications to adapt on heterogeneous networks, where subnets are realized with different network technologies.

Clusters of workstations are an increasingly popular platform for parallel computing but suffer from the problem that sharing of network resources can lead to poor and unpredictable performance. For many synchronous parallel applications, the communication performance is determined by the speed of the *bottleneck* link, and therefore, if even one communication link is busy, the application performance can degrade dramatically. Remos can help in solving this problem by reporting network conditions to applications, and thus allowing applications to adapt dynamically to network conditions. We present the framework for developing network-aware parallel applications with Remos and present preliminary results. In particular, we demonstrate that Remos driven node selection is important and effective for parallel computing on a shared high-speed network.

2 Usage models

Remos targets networked systems that consist of *compute nodes* (or hosts) and *network nodes* (or switches) that are connected by physical communication links. The network nodes and links jointly form the network computing environment. We summarize some scenarios in parallel and distributed computing that can exploit network status information provided by Remos.

- *Node selection:* When mapping an application onto a distributed system, it is necessary to determine the number of nodes (hosts) to be employed, and to select specific nodes for the computation. Many applications are developed so that they work with a variable number of nodes, but increasing the number of nodes may drive up communication costs, while a certain minimum number of nodes are often required to fit the data sets into the physical memory of all participating nodes. Many large-scale scientific simulations fit this pattern, for instance earthquake modelling (the Quake project [2] at Carnegie Mellon) and pollution modeling (Airshed [24]).
- *Application migration:* Changes in the environment may render the initial selection of nodes and connections unattractive. If the application is designed appropriately, the application mapping can be modified during execution to take the changes into account. The Fx programming environment at Carnegie Mellon [26] allows dynamic mapping of programs, and one goal of this research is to provide Fx with network information to drive mapping and migration.
- *Optimization of communication:* Closely related to the application mapping issues is the problem of exploiting low-level system information, such as network topology. As an example, if an application relies heavily on broadcasts, some subnets (with a specific network architecture) may be better platforms than others. This aspect is particularly important for heterogeneous networks.
- *Application quality metrics:* Some applications must meet an application-specific quality model, e.g., jitter-free display of an image sequence, or synchronized delivery of audio and video signals. There may exist a variety of ways to comply with the demands, e.g., by trading off computation for communication. As the network environment changes, the application has to adjust its mix of communication and computation.
- *Function and data shipping:* In some scenarios, a tradeoff is possible between performing a computation locally and performing the computation remotely, and such tradeoffs depend on the availability of network and compute capacity, based on a specific cost model, e.g., when deciding whether to perform a simulation locally or on a remote server.

In the above usage examples, applications will in general have to be aware of all system resources, including both network and computation resources. The Remos interface focuses on providing applications with information about networking resources. System-aware applications typically require information about computation and memory resources available on the network nodes, and there exist a variety of approaches to obtain such information for different time windows (e.g., a real-time operating system may maintain information about immediate resource usage, or a database of historical load information can be used [6]). The focus of this paper is the use of network information, so we do not pursue the issue of dealing with other system resources further. However, Remos does include a simple interface to computation and memory resources.

The Remos interface does not include communication *operations*, only information about communication performance. Many communication frameworks, such as PVM [10] and MPI [8], provide a wealth of communication primitives, so there is no need to duplicate this aspect of parallel computing. Remos can be used in conjunction with such communication libraries, e.g., to optimize primitives in a communication library by customizing the implementation of group communication operations for a particular network.

3   Remos design challenges

In this section we briefly summarize the problems that a uniform, portable network interface like Remos must address:

- *Dynamic behavior*: Network conditions can change quickly, so the interface must characterize this dynamic aspect. Different applications may want this information in different formats, e.g., some applications are more interested in burst bandwidth while others primarily care about long term average bandwidth. Furthermore, applications are most interested in future network behavior not historical information, and hence it is important to provide future information, particularly when a reasonable basis for prediction (e.g., existing reservations) exist.
- *Sharing (internal and external)*: Connections (as seen by the application) share physical links with other connections. This dynamic sharing of resources with entities external to an application is the major reason for the variable network performance experienced by applications. Parallel and distributed computations often simultaneously transfer data across multiple point-to-point connections, so there is also internal sharing as these connections compete with each other for resources. An interface that provides performance data must therefore consider the network's sharing policy when estimating bandwidth availability.
- *Information diversity*: Applications may be interested in a wide variety of information, ranging from static network topology, dynamic bandwidth estimations on a variety of times scales, and latency information. This information may have to be retrieved through diverse mechanisms, ranging from querying information databases using standard protocols, to direct measurement for the network interface.
- *Network heterogeneity*: Network architectures differ significantly in their ability to collect information and make it available. The kind of information that

is available from the network architecture impacts the design and overheads associated with a query interface.

- *Level of abstraction*: One of the thorny issues in designing an interface between applications and networks is to decide what aspects of the network should be exposed to applications. The simplest solution seems to be to expose as much information as possible. However, such a solution conflicts with other goals, particularly the portability of the API across heterogeneous networks. It also raises both ease of use and scalability concerns (the Internet is too huge for exposing all information). An alternative is to provide the information at a much higher level, with focus on performance characteristics of interest to the application. A high level of abstraction can make the interface easier to use and avoid information overload, but it can also result in vagueness and inaccuracies.

- *Accuracy and fidelity:* The information provided by such an interface may not be completely accurate, e.g., the estimates of the future bandwidth may not take all traffic into account. Nor may the information be of high fidelity, e.g., if the average bandwidth over a large interval is computed based on a small number of measurements. The issue then is how much accuracy and fidelity should be demanded (from the network) or promised (to the application).

The challenge for the interface designer is to balance practicality and elegance. These challenges affect both the definition of the interface and its implementation(s). In the next section, we describe the design decisions. Our goal is to support high-level network-independent parallel programming, so we must ensure that the requirements of such programs are satisfied.

4   Remos API

We sketch the main features of the Remos API and explain how they address the challenges presented above. A complete API is published in [5]. We organize our discussion around the major design issues: query based interface, the level of abstraction, dynamic behavior and sharing, and accuracy.

4.1   Query based interface

The most fundamental design decision was to build Remos as a query-based interface instead of alternatives like exporting a comprehensive database of information. The applications specifies the kind of information it needs and Remos supplies the "best effort" information. To limit the scope of the query, the application may select network parameters and parts of a larger network, that are of interest.

The major considerations in favoring a query based interface are overheads and portability. The costs associated with an interface to a network are inherently system and implementation specific, and there is generally a fixed cost associated with routine monitoring. However, a query-based interface connects a major portion of the cost to actual usage of the interface. In particular, a query-based design allows an application to limit the cost of using the interface by determining the frequency of interaction with the network performance monitoring system. This is an important consideration for parallel programs, since the cost of naively gathering and processing the performance data on a large number of nodes can easily exceed the benefits of network-awareness.

Network architectures differ in the support they offer to collect or record of performance information. E.g., some network architecture may maintain detailed, fine-grained information about link utilization at the switches, whereas another network architecture may provide this information only for a coarser time scale. By adopting a model that supports system independent queries that are answered with "best-effort" information, Remos can support portability and avoid the problem of maintaining and exporting excessive information that may be of no value to applications.

4.2   Level of abstraction

To accommodate the diverse application needs, the Remos API provides two levels of abstraction.

Remos supports flow-based queries. A *flow* is an application-level connection between a pair of computation nodes, and queries about bandwidth and latency on sets of flows form the core of the Remos interface. Using flows instead of physical links provides a level of abstraction that makes the interface portable and independent of system details. Flow-based queries provide the challenge of translating network specific information into a general form, but they allow the application developer to write adaptive network applications that are independent of heterogeneity inherent in a network computing environment. Past experience indicates that the flow abstraction should be easy to use by application developers. We describe the basic form of flow queries later in this section.

Remos also supports queries about the network *topology*. The reason we expose a network-level view of connectivity is that certain types of questions are more easily or more efficiently answered based on topology information. For example, finding the pair of nodes with the highest bandwidth connectivity may be expensive if only flow-based queries are allowed. The topology information provided by Remos consists of a graph with compute nodes, network nodes, and links, each annotated with their physical characteristics, e.g., available bandwidth. Topology-based queries are in general harder to use, since the complexity of translating network-level data into application-level information is partially left to the user.

Topology queries return a *logical* interconnection topology in the form of a graph. This graph represents the network behavior as seen by the application; the graph does not necessarily reflect the physical topology. Using a logical topology gives Remos the option of hiding network features that do not affect the application. E.g., if the routing rules imply that a physical link is not used, or can be used only up to a fraction of its capacity, then that information is reflected in the graph. Similarly, if two sets of hosts are connected by a complex network (e.g. the Internet), Remos can represent this network by a single link with appropriate characteristics.

Figure 1 shows a simple example of a logical topology graph. Circles represent network nodes (e.g., routers) and squares indicate compute nodes (endpoints). Nodes and links carry a capacity (and we do not care if a switch's capacity is determined by its backplane or by its processing power). Figure 1 presents a simple topology consisting of two routers, eight endpoints, and nine physical links. However, since Figure 1 is a *logical* topology, it represents a much broader set of (physical) networks. E.g., the link between A and B could represent a complex network. However, the internal details of that network are not relevant to the communication performance between the eight endpoints, so Remos turns this network into a single link with the bandwidth set to what the network can offer to this application.

The basic network topology query has the following form:

```
remos_get_graph(nodes, graph, timeframe)
```

The query fills a graph that is relevant in connecting the nodes set. The information annotated to the graph is relevant for the specified timeframe.

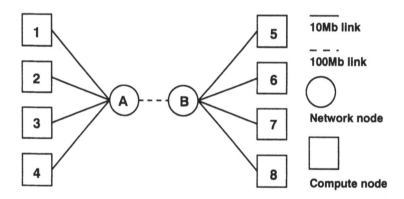

Fig. 1. Remos graph representing the structure of a simple network.

4.3 Dynamic resource sharing

Applications can generate flows that cover a broad spectrum, ranging from constrained low-bandwidth audio to bursty high-bandwidth data flows. Remos collapses this broad spectrum into three types of flows. *Fixed flows* have a specific bandwidth requirement and cannot make use of additional bandwidth. *Variable flows* have related requirements and demand maximum available bandwidth that can be provided to all such flows in a given ratio, e.g., all flows in an all-all communication operation have the same requirements. Finally, *independent flows* simply want maximum available bandwidth.

Applications specify all flow requirements in their request simultaneously, and Remos takes internal resource sharing into account when responding to the queries. E.g., if five application flows share the $A - B$ link in Figure 1, then Remos will take into account that the bandwidth of the link must be shared.

A general flow query has the following form:

```
remos_flow_info(fixed_flows, variable_flows,
            independent_flow, timeframe)
```

Remos tries to satisfy the `fixed_flows`, then the `variable_flows` simultaneously, and finally the `independent_flow`. The corresponding data structures will be filled with the extent to which the flow requests can be satisfied, based on the `timeframe` parameter.

Determining how the throughput of a flow is affected by other messages in transit is very complicated and network specific, and it is unrealistic to expect Remos to characterize these interactions accurately. In general, Remos assumes that, all else being equal, the bottleneck link bandwidth is shared equally by all flows (that are not bottlenecked elsewhere). If other information is available, Remos can use different sharing policies when estimating flow bandwidths. The basic sharing policy assumed by Remos corresponds to the max-min fair share policy [15], which is the basis of ATM flow control for ABR traffic [17,1], and is also used in other environments [13].

Note that users of the topology interface are responsible for accounting for sharing effects, both across application flows and between application flows and other competing flows.

4.4   Accuracy

Applications ideally want information about the level of service they receive in the future, but most users today must use past performance as a predictor of the future. Different applications are also interested in activities on different timescales. A synchronous parallel application expects to transfer bursts of data in short periods of time, while a long running data intensive application may be interested in throughput over an extended period of time. For this reason, relevant queries in the Remos interface accept a timeframe parameter that allows the user to request data to be collected and averaged for a specific time window.

Network information like available bandwidth varies dynamically due to sharing, and often cannot be measured accurately. As a result, characterizing these metrics by a single number can be misleading. E.g., knowing that bandwidth availability has been quite stable represents a different scenario from it being an average of rapidly changing instantaneous bandwidths. To address these aspects, the Remos interface adds statistical information (variability and estimation accuracy measures) to all dynamic quantitative information. Since the distribution is not known, we present the variability of network parameters using quartiles [16].

The level of abstraction, the handling of resource sharing, and an approach to deal with the varying degrees of accuracy are key issues that must be handled by any network performance interface. Further details on other aspects, as well as a complete API, are discussed in other publications [5]. The current Remos API does not provide support for multicast or reservations. These features can be added when they are more widely available to applications. The current Remos API focuses on performance aspects. At a later time, other dimensions like cost (of transmitting data via a specific link) and security (of physical links in the network) can be included.

5   Implementation

The Remos implementation has two components, a Collector and Modeler; they are responsible for network-oriented and application-oriented functionality, respectively. The Collector consists of a process that retrieves information from routers using SNMP [4]. The information obtained covers both static topology and dynamic bandwidth. For latency, the Collector currently assumes a fixed per-hop delay. (A reasonable approximation as long as we use a LAN testbed.) The Collector is implemented in Java, since we envision that in the future it may be down-loaded across the network. A large environment may require multiple cooperating Collectors. The Modeler is a library that can be linked with applications. It satisfies application requests based on the information provided by the Collector. The primary tasks of the modeler are as follows: generating a logical topology, associating appropriate static and dynamic information with each of the network components, and satisfying flow requests based on the logical topology. The modeler exports Remos information through a Java and a C interface.

This prototype Remos implementation has been tested on a dedicated IP-based testbed at Carnegie Mellon, a portion of which is illustrated in Figure 2. The testbed uses a variety of routers (PCs running NetBSD and FreeBSD and Cisco routers), 100Mbps and 10Mbps point-to-point Ethernet segments as links, and DEC Alpha systems as endpoints. An important advantage of using SNMP is that it is widely supported implying that the implementation is portable to many network environments. The portability is illustrated by the diversity of routers in our testbed.

We would like to point out that the Remos API is independent of its implementation, and suitable implementation techniques will be different for networks of different types and sizes. For example, we are developing collectors that use benchmarks to probe the network for environments where the use of SNMP is not possible or practical. We are also looking into the problem of dealing with very large networks, where multiple collectors will have to collaborate to collect the network information.

6   Parallel Application Development with Remos

In this section we examine how Remos can help in meeting specific challenges in parallel computing in a networked environment. We first discuss the adaptation

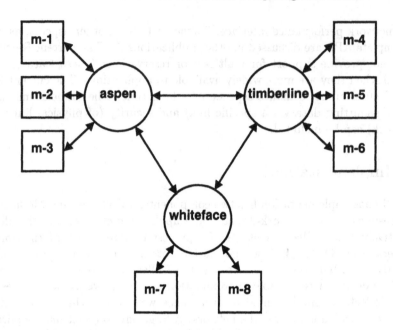

Links: 100Mbps point-to-point ethernet

Endpoints: DEC Alpha Systems *(manchester-* labeled m-*)*

Routers: Pentium Pro PCs running NetBSD *(aspen,timberline, whiteface)*

Fig. 2. IP-based testbed for Remos implementation and experiments

process and sketch some of the design choices for network-aware parallel programs. In the following sections, we discuss how a specific parallelizing compiler and runtime system (the Fx tool chain [12,26]) were enhanced to support the development of Remos driven adaptive parallel programs and present experimental results demonstrating how programs adapt to changing network conditions.

A network-aware parallel application typically consists of a computation module and an adaptation module. The computation module implements the core functionality of the application, that is, its structure is similar to that of the complete application in a dedicated environment. The adaptation module collects information about the status of the network and decides how to best organize execution. In general, only the adaptation module interacts with tools like Remos that collect and deliver network information. Execution is controlled by setting specific parameters such as the number of nodes or the granularity of the computation between communication phases. An important goal of the adaptation module is to determine values for these "adaptation parameters" that optimize application performance (e.g. minimize execution time) given the current network conditions. Making this decision often requires some information from the computation module, e.g. input data sizes. The adaptation step can be very complex and application-specific, although support can often be provided through frameworks[3].

One of the main design decisions for network-aware applications is what parameters to adjust based on network conditions. Most previous work in this area has focused on video streaming applications. Video streaming has the property that the parameters to adjust to changes in the network are fairly obvious (typically the frame rate or frame size), can be adjusted easily, and appropriate values can be selected fairly easily. e.g. if the available bandwidth drops, the frame rate should be reduced. In contrast, parallel computing applications tend to be much more complex. They have a wide variety of parameters and the relationship between these parameters and application performance can be difficult to characterize. For example, the optimal number of nodes for a parallel computation often depends on network performance, but characterizing this relationship precisely is challenging [27]. Alternatively, the adaptation module may select which nodes should be used from a larger pool of available nodes, which is the problem we address in our experiments. Finally, the adaptation parameter may be internal to the application. For example, in [22] an adaption modules selects the optimal pipeline depth for a pipelined SOR application based on network and CPU performance.

Some existing programming tools are well suited to support network-aware adaptation [22]. Many tools such as parallelizing compilers and distributed object libraries already have information on the application properties which may be useful in selecting the parameters that are most sensitive to application performance, at what points during execution is adaptation legal and potentially profitable, or what network properties is the application most sensitive to (e.g., bandwidth or latency). Many tools in fact already optimize application performance based on system properties. parallelizing compilers often map the application considering system characteristics [25] and load balancing systems manage computations based on CPU loads on the different hosts in an environment. The contribution of this research is to allow consideration of communication load under dynamic network conditions, which is a fairly natural extension. Finally, one of the critical steps in using an interface like Remos is the specification of the communication pattern. Programming tools often have this information either because they generate the communication statements (e.g. parallelizing compilers) or because they use specific inbuilt traffic patterns (e.g. object libraries).

Adaptation to network conditions using Remos is a three step process. First, the parallel application has to formulate its computation and communication requirements and specify the network parameters and nodes that are of interest. Second, Remos is invoked to collect the network information. Finally, the application adapts by selecting appropriate runtime parameters. The easiest time to take network conditions into account is when the application starts up, although applications can adapt periodically at runtime in response to changes in the environment. Adaptation at runtime can be more complex since it often requires the use of more complex data structures that can be dynamically redistributed [21]. Moreover, runtime adaptation with distributed data structures is possible only if the state of the computation can be redistributed across the nodes. This can be expensive, and this overhead has to be considered when evaluating adaptation options, thereby complicating the adaptation process.

7 Remos Usage Framework

In this section we describe a framework in use at Carnegie Mellon for developing adaptive parallel programs, along with a set of applications developed in this framework. The tool-chain consists of Remos, Fx compiler system [12,26], and a clustering module. The goal is that the applications should have the ability to migrate to different parts of the network in response to changes in the network traffic. In the next section we discuss the results and experience with developing applications in this framework.

7.1 Fx compiler

The Fx compiler system developed at Carnegie Mellon supports integrated task and data parallel programming. The user writes a sequential program with annotations to assist parallelization, and the compiler generates the programs for the nodes of the parallel system. Fx is based on a variant of the HPF language [18].

The Fx runtime system was enhanced so that the assignment of nodes to tasks in a program could be modified during execution. In this model, a program is invoked on all nodes that may be potentially used for execution. The *task parallelism* support in Fx is used to map the core computation onto an *active task*. The set of processors assigned to the active task can be changed at runtime, thereby effectively migrating the program. The nodes can be reassigned without changing the semantics of the program at any program point where there is no live distributed data. Note that live distributed data can be copied as replicated data to create legal migration points. This step can be expensive in terms of memory usage and copying time, but it makes it possible to create legal migration points in programs with no migration points or, insufficient frequency of migration points to support effective network-aware execution.

7.2 Clustering

An important problem in developing a network aware application is selecting a set of nodes that are well connected in terms of available communication resources. The goal is to select nodes with low latency and high available bandwidth between them. The bandwidth and latency measurements can be obtained from Remos, but the problem of determining the optimal set of nodes is computationally hard [1], which is especially a cause for concern for runtime migration.

For the purpose of our experiments, we have chosen a simple greedy heuristic for clustering. The application provides an initial *start node*, which is the first

---

[1] It is equivalent to a k-clique problem which is known to be NP-hard.

node that is added to the selected *cluster* of nodes. Next , the node with the *shortest distance* to the existing nodes in the cluster is determined and added to the cluster. The basis for *distance* between a pair of nodes is the current latency and bandwidth between the nodes, which is obtained from Remos. The above step is repeated until the cluster contains the number of nodes needed for execution.

We will show in the next section that this clustering procedure leads to good results even though it is based on a simple heuristic. However, it is clear that improved procedures will be needed to achieve good and fast clustering in more complex situations. In particular, we have focused on communication resources, but in general, tradeoffs between computation and communication resources would have to be considered for clustering.

7.3   Application structure

We describe the procedure for developing a network-aware parallel program that can migrate in response to changing network conditions. We restrict ourselves to iterative applications that adapt (if necessary) at the beginning of every iteration of an outer loop. At these migration points, the application calls an adaptation module with parameters for migration, and this adaptation module determines the potential profitability of migration and performs migration if necessary.

When the adaptation module is invoked, it checks if Remos is active on the set of nodes the application is interested in, and starts it up if needed. Next, it calls a Remos routine to obtain the logical topology of the relevant graph. For our experiments, this routine `remos_get_graph` is called for the set of nodes in the testbed shown in Figure 2, and returns the logical network topology connecting these nodes, along with available network bandwidth on the links based on current traffic conditions. We state this call to `remos_get_graph`, along with a summary of the relevant parameters.

`remos_get_graph(nodes, graph, timeframe)`

nodes = **m1,m2,m3,m4,m5,m6,m7,m8**
graph = *logical topology of the testbed shown in Figure 2 with current traffic*
timeframe = **current:** *most recent measurements are used*

The logical topology graph is used to compute a matrix representing *distance* between all pairs of nodes. For our testbed, the distance is based only on bandwidth since latency between any pair of nodes is virtually the same. Note that the information to compute available bandwidth between pairs of nodes could have been obtained with flow queries also, but $O(nodes^2)$ queries would have been needed, implying a much higher overhead which deteriorates rapidly for larger networks.

The communication distance matrix, the number of nodes required for the application, and an application specified initial node are the inputs to the clustering routine discussed earlier. The clustering routine returns the estimated optimal set of nodes for execution along with a measure of the expected communication performance. This communication performance is compared to the estimated performance on the current set of executing nodes, and if the potential improvement is above a specified threshold, the application is migrated to the new set of nodes by providing a new list of nodes to the Fx runtime system.

8   Usage Examples and Experimental Results

We present a preliminary report on the usage of the Remos framework in the context of parallel programs generated by the Fx compiler [12,26]. We present results from network-aware versions of the following two programs: *fast Fourier transforms (FFT)* and *Airshed pollution modelling*. The FFT program performs a two dimensional FFT, which is parallelized such that it consists of a set of independent 1 dimensional row FFTs, followed by a transpose, and a set of independent 1 dimensional column FFTs. Airshed contains a rich set of computation and communication operations, as it simulates diverse chemical and physical phenomena [24]. Both are data parallel programs developed using the Fx compiler system. All experiments were performed on the IP-based testbed illustrated in Figure 2.

The remainder of this section is organized as follows. We first present results that highlight the importance of node selection in an unloaded network, followed by similar results for networks with communication loads. Finally we discuss the dynamically migrating implementations of these applications.

Application		Nodes with Remos		Other Representative Node Sets					
Name of Program	No. of Nodes	Node set	Exec. Time (secs)	Node set	Exec. Time (secs)	Percent increase	Node set	Exec. Time (secs)	Percent increase
FFT (512)	2	m-4,5	.462	m-1,4	.468	1.3	m-4,8	.481	4.1
FFT (512)	4	m-4,5, 6,7	.266	m-1,2, 4,5	.287	3.7	m-1,4, 6,7	.268	.03
FFT (1K)	2	m-4,5	2.63	m-1,4	2.66	1.1	m-4,8	2.68	1.9
FFT (1K)	4	m-4,5, 6,7	1.51	m-1,2, 4,5	1.62	7.3	m-1,4, 6,7	1.61	6.6
Airshed	3	m-4,5,6	908	m-4,6,8	907	-.1	m-1,4,7	917	1.1
Airshed	5	m-4,5,6, 7,8	650	m-1,2,3, 4,5	647	-.4	m-1,2,4, 5,7	657	1.1

Table 1. Performance of programs on nodes selected using Remos on the IP based testbed

8.1   Node selection in a static environment

We first examine the value of node selection when there are no competing applications on the testbed. We should point out that our testbed presents a difficult test for the clustering routine using Remos. Since the testbed is connected with high performance links and switches throughout, and any node can be reached from any other node with at most 3 hops, it is difficult to judge what sets of nodes are better connected than others.

The FFT program and the Airshed program were developed in the framework described in the previous section and executed on sets of nodes selected by Remos based clustering at the time of invocation. For comparison, they were also executed on other representative sets of nodes. In all examples, the programs gave node *m-4* as a start node and used clustering to select remaining nodes. The results are presented in Table 1. We observe that the execution time on the Remos selected nodes was generally (but not always) lower than for other node sets, but only by relatively small amounts. As noted earlier, this is a hard case for Remos based clustering, but our toolchain is doing a good job of node selection. However, we note that node selection has limited importance on a small network with fast routers and links and no external traffic.

8.2   Node selection in a dynamic environment

To study the importance of node selection in the presence of competing applications, we performed another set of experiments. We added a synthetic program that generates communication traffic between nodes *m-6* and *m-8* on our testbed, and performed node selection in the presence of this traffic. The process is illustrated in Figure 3. The figure shows our testbed with communication traffic between nodes *m-6* and *m-8*. The links that carry this traffic are highlighted. The node selection procedure is given *m-4* as the start node, and it selects nodes *m-1,m-2,m-4,m-5* as the cluster most appropriate for execution. Note that this is one of the sets for which the application traffic does not interfere with the external traffic on the network. Selection of either of nodes *m-6, m-7* or *m-8* would imply that at least one link is shared between the application traffic and the external traffic.

Fend me a note when you are back and ready to play.or our measurements, we first executed the program on Remos selected nodes as discussed above. For comparison, the programs were re-executed on a set of nodes that the clustering routine could have potentially selected if it only used the static physical capabilities of the testbed communication nodes and links and ignored the traffic The results are presented in Table 2.

We observe that the execution times are larger by 80-200 percent when dynamic traffic information is not used for node selection. The reason is that the selection of nodes using Remos measured dynamic traffic makes it possible to avoid links with heavy traffic. The table also shows the performance of the programs in the absence of the external traffic (last column). We observe that with our dynamic node selection, the performance degrades only marginally in the

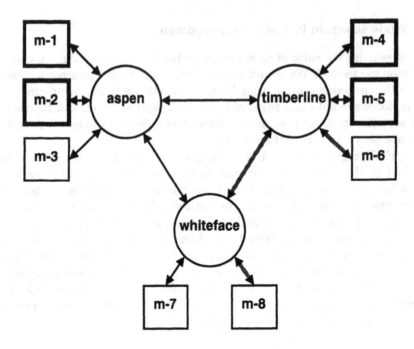

Traffic Route: m-6 -> timberline -> whiteface -> m-8

Start Node: m-4

Selected Nodes: m-1, m-2, m-4, m-5

Fig. 3. Selection of nodes on the testbed with busy communication links

presence of traffic, but can degrade dramatically for a naively selected set of nodes. The conclusion is that node selection is very important for good performance of data parallel programs in dynamic environments with competing traffic, and that our clustering routine using Remos is effective in selecting good sets of nodes in such realistic situations.

8.3 Runtime adaptation

Our final set of experiments consisted of developing applications that periodically select a new set of nodes for execution and migrate to those nodes during execution. This process is significantly more complex than selection of nodes at the start of execution, as the program state has to be migrated. For easing the process of migration, we assume that the active data set at migration points is replicated and all previous communication has completed. Hence, no data copying or explicit synchronization is necessary for migration.

For the experiments, we started the applications, and repeatedly changed the pattern of the external communication during execution. We observed that the set of nodes actively executing the application changed to minimize the impact

Application		Execution Time with External Traffic					Exec. time without External Traffic (secs)
		Remos selected Nodes (Dynamic Measurements)		Nodes selected with only Static Measurements			
Name of Program	No of Nodes	Node Set	Time (secs)	Node Set	Time (secs)	Percent increase	
FFT (512)	2	m-4,5	.475	m-4,6	1.40	194	.462
FFT (512)	4	m-1,2,4,5	.322	m-4,5,6,7	.893	177	.266
FFT (1K)	2	m-4,5	2.68	m-4,6	7.38	175	2.63
FFT (1K)	4	m-1,2,4,5	2.07	m-4,5,6,7	3.71	79	1.51
Airshed	3	m-1,4,5	905	m-4,5,6	2113	133	908
Airshed	5	m-1,2,3,4,5	674	m-4,5,6,7,8	1726	156	6 50

Table 2. Performance implications of node selection using Remos in the presence of external traffic. Measurements use a synthetic program that generates significant traffic between nodes m-6 and m-8 on the IP-based testbed

of external traffic whenever possible. That is, if the new external traffic began to interfere with the program generated traffic, the program migrated to eliminate the interference.

There are a number of issues that are important for runtime adaptation. The application framework has to determine the minimum potential improvement in performance before deciding to migrate. In our experiments, migration was done whenever the potential improvement was positive. One undesirable consequence that was observed was that the program would often migrate between sets of nodes that were equally desirable for execution. A more insidious problem is that the traffic generated by the application would make some links busy, and since Remos does not distinguish between different types or sources of traffic, the result would be that the application would migrate to avoid its own traffic, which is clearly a decision based on an inherent fallacy. This can be avoided if the application knows how much communication traffic it generates and factors that into making migration decisions.

9   Related Work

A number of resource management systems allow applications to make queries about the availability of computation resources, some examples being Condor [19] and LSF (Load Sharing Facility). In contrast, Remos focuses on network resources. More recently, resource management systems have been designed for large scale internet-wide computing, e.g., Globus [9] and Legion [11]. These systems provide support for a wide range of functions such as resource location and reservation, authentication, and remote process creation mechanisms. The Remos interface focuses on providing good abstractions and support for giving applications access to network status information, and allow for a much closer coupling of applications and networks. The Remos interface could be used to extend the functionality of the above systems.

A number of groups have looked at the benefits of explicit feedback to simplify and speed up adaptation [14,7]. However, the interfaces developed by these efforts have been designed specifically for the scenarios being studied.

A number of sites are collecting Internet traffic statistics. This information is not a in form that is usable for applications, and it is typically also at a coarser grain than what applications are interested in using. Another class of related research is the collection and use of application specific performance data, e.g., a Web browser that collects information on what sites had good response times [23].

Parallelizing compilers and runtime systems attempt to balance load across the processors using a variety of adaptive techniques for partitioning computation and communication, an example being [20]. However, such techniques are generally limited to the nodes pre-selected for the application and do not involve other nodes in the system.

10   Concluding Remarks

Remos is an example of a performance monitoring interface that allows parallel applications to inquire about the capabilities of their host network. Remos provides a uniform interface between networks and network-aware applications that covers a range of network architectures. It allows applications to discover, at runtime, the properties of their execution environments. Such interfaces are of great value to compilers and tools that manage placement of computations onto network nodes, or that attempt to maximize performance. The topology and behavior of networks will change from application invocation to invocation and may even change during execution. Hence, it is not practical for the compiler to model the network, so any attempt to optimize performance based on network conditions must be based, at least in part, on runtime information. The Remos interface allows tools and applications to obtain the information they need to make performance optimizations.

An initial implementation of the Remos API demonstrates that the interface can be realized and our initial evaluation using a small set of applications suggests that applications can easily use the interface and benefit from the the the information it provides. In this paper we focused on parallel applications that were developed using parallel programming tools, specifically the Fx compiler and runtime system. In such an environment, the runtime library can use Remos to collect information about network conditions, and simple network aware adaptation decisions can be performed by the tools in a transparent fashion. However, more research is needed to establish the role of such adaptation support tools for different types of application and network behavior.

A uniform interface for network-aware applications significantly reduces the difficulty of coupling an application to a network. As network architectures continue to evolve, we anticipate that interfaces like Remos will play an increasingly important role in raising the acceptability and practicality of network-aware applications.

References

1. ATM User-Network Interface Specification. Version 4.0, 1996. ATM Forum document.
2. BAO, H., BIELAK, J., GHATTAS, O., O'HALLARON, D. R., KALLIVOKAS, L. F., SHEWCHUK, J. R., AND XU, J. Earthquake ground motion modeling on parallel computers. In *Proceedings of Supercomputing '96* (Pittsburgh, PA, Nov. 1996).
3. BOLLIGER, J., AND GROSS, T. A framework-based approach to the development of network-aware applications. *IEEE Trans. Softw. Eng. 24*, 5 (May 1998), 376 – 390.
4. CASE, J., McCLOGHRIE, K., ROSE, M., AND WALDBUSSER, S. Protocol Operations for Version 2 of the Simple Network Management Protocol (SNMPv2), January 1999. RFC 1905.
5. DEWITT, T., GROSS, T., LOWEKAMP, B., MILLER, N., STEENKISTE, P., SUBHLOK, J., AND SUTHERLAND, D. Remos: A resource monitoring system for network-aware applications. Tech. Rep. CMU-CS-97-194, Carnegie Mellon University, Dec 1997.
6. DINDA, P. Statistical properties of host load in a distributed environment. In *Fourth Workshop on Languages, Compilers, and Run-time Systems for Scalable Computers* (Pittsburgh, PA, May 1998).
7. ECKHARDT, D., AND STEENKISTE, P. A Wireless MAC with Service Guarantees. In preparation, 1998.
8. FORUM, T. M. MPI: A Message Passing Interface. In *Proceedings of Supercomputing '93* (Oregon, November 1993), ACM/IEEE, pp. 878–883.
9. FOSTER, I., AND KESSELMAN, K. Globus: A metacomputing infrastructure toolkit. *Journal of Supercomputer Applications 11*, 2 (1997), 115–128.
10. GEIST, G. A., AND SUNDERAM, V. S. The PVM System: Supercomputer Level Concurrent Computation on a Heterogeneous Network of Workstations. In *Proceedings of the Sixth Distributed Memory Computing Conference* (April 1991), IEEE, pp. 258–261.
11. GRIMSHAW, A., WULF, W., AND LEGION TEAM. The Legion vision of a worldwide virtual computer. *Communications of the ACM 40*, 1 (January 1997).
12. GROSS, T., O'HALLARON, D., AND SUBHLOK, J. Task parallelism in a High Performance Fortran framework. *IEEE Parallel & Distributed Technology 2*, 3 (Fall 1994), 16–26.
13. HAHNE, E. L. Round-robin scheduling for max-min fairness in data networks. *IEEE Journal on Selected Areas in Communication 9*, 7 (September 1991).
14. INOUYE, J., CEN, S., PU, C., AND WALPOLE, J. System support for mobile multimedia applications. In *Proceedings of the 7th International Workshop on Network and Operating System Support for Digital Audio and Video* (St. Louis, May 1997), pp. 143–154.
15. JAFFE, J. M. Bottleneck flow control. *IEEE Transactions on Communications 29*, 7 (July 1981), 954–962.
16. JAIN, R. *The Art of Computer Systems Performance Analysis*. John Wiley & Sons, Inc., 1991.
17. JAIN, R. Congestion control and traffic management in ATM networks: Recent advances and a survey. *Computer Networks and ISDN Systems* (February 1995).
18. KOELBEL, C., LOVEMAN, D., STEELE, G., AND ZOSEL, M. *The High Performance Fortran Handbook*. The MIT Press, Cambridge, MA, 1994.

19. LITZKOW, M., LIVNY, M., AND MUTKA, M. Condor — A hunter of idle workstations. In *Proceedings of the Eighth Conference on Distributed Computing Systems* (San Jose, California, June 1988).

20. SHARMA, S., PONNUSAMY, R., MOON, B., HWANG, Y., DAS, R., AND SALTZ, J. Run-time and compile-time support for adaptive irregular problems. In *Proceedings of Supercomputing '94* (Washington, DC, Nov 1994), pp. 97–106.

21. SIEGELL, B. *Automatic Generation of Parallel Programs with Dynamic Load Balancing for a Network of Workstations.* PhD thesis, Department of Computer and Electrical Engineering, Carnegie Mellon University, 1995. Also appeared as technical report CMU-CS-95-168.

22. SIEGELL, B., AND STEENKISTE, P. Automatic selection of load balancing parameters using compile-time and run-time information. *Concurrency - Practice and Experience 9*, 3 (1996), 275–317.

23. STEMM, M., SESHAN, S., AND KATZ, R. Spand: Shared passive network performance discovery. In *USENIX Symposium on Internet Technologies and Systems* (Monterey, CA, June 1997).

24. SUBHLOK, J., STEENKISTE, P., STICHNOTH, J., AND LIEU, P. Airshed pollution modeling: A case study in application development in an HPF environment. In *12th International Parallel Processing Symposium* (Orlando, FL, April 1998).

25. SUBHLOK, J., AND VONDRAN, G. Optimal latency–throughput tradeoffs for data parallel pipelines. In *Eighth Annual ACM Symposium on Parallel Algorithms and Architectures* (Padua, Italy, June 1996), pp. 62–71.

26. SUBHLOK, J., AND YANG, B. A new model for integrated nested task and data parallel programming. In *Proceedings of the Sixth ACM SIGPLAN Symposium on Principles and Practice of Parallel Programming* (June 1997), ACM.

27. TANGMUNARUNKIT, H., AND STEENKISTE, P. Network-aware distributed computing: A case study. In *Second Workshop on Runtime Systems for Parallel Programming (RTSPP)* (Orlando, March 1998), IEEE, p. Proceedings to be published by Springer. Held in conjunction with IPPS '98.

Object-Oriented Implementation of Data-Parallelism on Global Networks

Jan Borowiec

GMD FIRST (www.first.gmd.de)
Research Institute For Computer Architecture and Software Technology
Rudower Chaussee 5, 12489 Berlin, Germany
borowiec@first.gmd.de

Abstract. An alternative approach to the SPMD implementation of data parallelism is described. In this approach, the data–parallel program is executed on a collection of processors that can be located anywhere on a global network. On each of these processors a *server* is installed that hosts one or more *servants* – objects intended for performing parallel operations. One of the servers, the *conductor*, plays a special role: it executes the whole program except for operations on mapped arrays; to execute such operations, the conductor employs the servants mentioned above. The conductor executes on a chosen processor, the *host*.
In addition to the parallel execution model, a framework is described that makes possible experiments with remotely executed data–parallel programs. This framework combines a High Performance Fortran (HPF) subset with the infrastructure of CORBA. It is implemented in Java. Occasionally, we quote the kernel of the algorithm generating communication sets, which was designed for the framework's implementation.

1 The Parallel Execution Model

With the advances in network technology allowing independent workstations to communicate, and thus – among other things – to solve problems in parallel, a new dimension of computational power is attainable. Our approach designed to exploit this power comprises a collection of concepts that are briefly described in the following sections (cf. also Fig. 1).

The program to be executed is parallelized using proven program parallelization mechanisms designed for data mapping, as defined e.g. in High Performance Fortran(HPF) ([1]).

The processors involved can be located anywhere on a global network; they are used to store local portions of the mapped data, i.e. have the same function as processors declared in an HPF program.

Unmapped data, which in HPF implementations is broadcasted over all co-operating processors, is mapped onto a single processor, the *host*. In HPF terms, the host should therefore be considered as representing one or more (as needed) multidimensional arrays of abstract processors with extent 1 at each dimension;

S. Chatterjee (Ed.): LCPC'98, LNCS 1656, pp. 120–130, 1999.

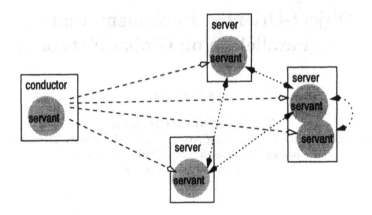

Fig. 1. The parallel execution model. Dashed arrows: conductor prompts servants' execution; dotted arrows: servants send and receive data.

the unmapped data is then processed as if it were mapped onto these arrays of processors.

On each of the cooperating processors, a server is installed that – among other things – creates one or more *servants*.

Computation progress is supervised by a chosen server, the *conductor*, which is also a client. The conductor is installed on the host. It executes the whole program except for operations on mapped arrays; to execute such operations, the conductor employs appropriate collections of servants (dashed arrows in Fig. 1) using remote method calls. Operations executed on servants at a single call are described below (Section 3.4).

The program fragments that a servant is meant to execute are sequences of one or more *array operations*. HPF compilers create and decompose such statements from source language constructs such as array assignments, INDEPENDENT DO loops, WHERE statements/constructs, FORALL statements/constructs as well as from I/O statements[1].

Servants communicate by remotely calling operations on other servants (dotted arrows in Fig. 1). Communication is implemented using the infrastructure provided by CORBA [2], [3]. The creation of communication operations is described below (Sections 3.2, and 3.3).

If assemblies of data mapped onto the same processor may be processed independently of each other, more than one servant may be created; such servants may then be activated and executed in parallel.

After performing its job, a servant may be disposed of by the conductor.

---

[1] For example, the HPF statement WRITE (6, *) A where A is a mapped array, is transformed into two statements: T = A and WRITE (6, *) T, where T is an unmapped array.

2   The Framework

To allow experiments to be performed with the parallel–execution model, a prototypical computational framework was implemented. Given a data–parallel program, this framework creates the whole parallel–execution infrastructure described above, i.e. the programs that implement the constructor, servers and the servants.

To write data–parallel programs, we defined a small subset of HPF called a "mini HPF" (mHPF for short) – and implemented its compiler. EBNF syntax of mHPF is given in Appendix A; the meaning of its individual constructs is the same as in HPF. The compiler is called m2j.

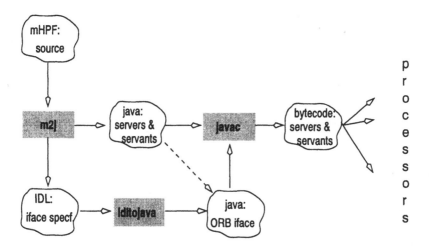

Fig. 2. Transformation of an mHPF Program. (The dashed arrow should be read as "imports and extends".)

Figure 2 shows how the framework brings together mHPF, which defines the data–parallelization mechanisms and operations on mapped arrays, with Java and a Java binding of CORBA which covers network communication. Given an mHPF program, the compiler m2j produces two kinds of output: (i) a collection of Java classes defining both the servers and the servants, and (ii) an IDL file specifying the signatures of public methods the servants can be called to perform. The IDL specification is then transformed, using the idltojava tool, into a Java package containing ORB declarations and the run–time interface. Finally, the javac tool transforms all .java files obtained so far into a collection of server class files implementing both the servers and the servants. These files can then be installed on the processors designated to perform the parallel computations. The command line of each server's installation identifies, among other things, the processor on which a server is being installed, the server's port number, etc.

The whole framework is implemented in Java.

3   Program Transformation

This section briefly describes how the m2j compiler transforms a data–parallel program.

3.1   Mapping Unmapped Data

Unmapped data, which in HPF implementations is broadcasted over all cooperating processors, is in our framework mapped onto the host processor. This mapping is implemented as follows: first, for all n-dimensional unmapped arrays, a PROCESSORS directive is generated that declares an n-dimensional processor collection, $\_H_n$, with extent 1 at each dimension; then, a DISTRIBUTE $(\ldots)$ ONTO $\_H_n$ directive is generated for each of these arrays with CYCLIC(e_j) on position j of the distribution tail list if the respective array's extent at dimension j is e_j.

3.2   Specializing Array Operations: Iterations and Communications

mHPF offers two operations that can be executed in parallel: the array assignment and the FORALL statement. In general, each of these operations can be internally represented as an array assignment with multiple array sections on the right–hand side. Let us call these right–hand–side array sections, which are identical in shape and mapping to the assignment's left–hand–side, *adequate*. Then, the initial internal representation of the above parallel operations is as follows: In the assignment, each inadequate right–hand–side array section $S(\ldots)$ is replaced by an adequate temporary section $T(\ldots)$, and the original assignment is prepended with the auxiliary assignment $T(\ldots) = S(\ldots)$.

A sample mHPF program and its transformed counterpart are shown in Fig. 3.

After the initial transformation, we get two inherently different kinds of array assignments: those with all adequate arguments, and those with a single inadequate argument on the right–hand side. Below, we call the former assignments *iterations* and the latter ones *communications*.

The implementation of iterations depends on the applied global-to-local mapping scheme. An excellent review of such schemes is given in [7]. For our implementation, we have chosen the pattern–cyclic enumeration scheme developed by Chatterjee et al. [8]. In this scheme, an iteration ι is implemented with a nested loop whose depth is equal to the rank of any component of the iteration. If ι is to be executed in parallel on a collection P of processors, then on each processor $p \in P$ this loop is controlled by an *iteration space* determined by transitions of finite–state machines (ΔM tables). The m2j compiler produces an array of iteration spaces, *global-ispace*, containing iteration spaces for each iteration on each processor. If σ_p is a servant installed on a processor p, then one of the first actions performed in the constructor of σ_p is the reduction of the *global-ispace* array to an array *ispace[p]* containing only iteration spaces used in σ_p. Thus, if P is the collection of processors onto which components of an iteration ι are

```
program                                    program
  integer, dimension(46)      :: A, B;       integer, dimension(46)      :: A, B;
  integer, dimension (8)      :: C, D;       integer, dimension (8)      :: C, D;
                                             integer, dimension(46)      :: T;

  processors P(3);                           processors P(3);
                                             processors _H1(1);

  distribute (cyclic(6)) onto P  :: A, B;    distribute (cyclic(6)) onto P  :: A, B;
                                             distribute (cyclic(6)) onto P  :: T;
                                             distribute (cyclic(8)) onto _H1 :: C, D;

  B(1:22:3)  = C;                            B(1:22:3)  = C;
                                             T(12:26:2) = C;
  B(12:26:2) = C + A(12:26:2);               B(12:26:2) = T(12:26:2) + A(12:26:2);
  D          = B(12:26:2);                   D          = B(12:26:2);
end                                        end
```

             (a)   (b)

Fig. 3. A sample mHPF program: (a) Original text, (b) After initial transformation. Shadowed Boxes in (b) expose execution blocks.

mapped, then on each processor $p \in P$ the same loop is executed at runtime, which is controlled by $ispace[p][\iota]$.

Note that an iteration is always initialized (and exclusively executed) on the collection of processors on which the iteration's components are mapped.

In a communication, data is to be sent between two collections of processors. Suppose that

$$\kappa : R = S \qquad (1)$$

is a communication in which the receiver R is mapped on a processor collection Q, and the sender S is mapped on a processor collection P^2. Then, on each $p \in P$ data is to be sent to each $q \in Q$ (which in turn has to receive this data), and all these operations are to be performed in parallel. For each pair (p, q), where $p \in P$ and $q \in Q$, the code sequences implementing κ are controlled by a *communication space* which is a pair of lists of local indices:

$$(send[p][\kappa][q], recv[q][\kappa][p]) \qquad (2)$$

whereby the first component is associated with the code for κ executed on the sender p, and the second component with the code executed on the receiver q (cf. also [9], [10], and [11]). If σ_p is the servant residing on p that is responsible for sending the data to be communicated, and σ_q is the servant on q that has to receive this data, then the communication s is performed as follows:

---

^{2} P and Q may denote the same collection.

1. σ_p creates – using the $send[p][\kappa][q]$ set – a buffer $cbuf$ and packs into it those elements of S that are to be placed in R
2. σ_p issues the remote call $\sigma_q.receive(\kappa, p, cbuf)$
3. σ_q executes its $receive$ method, which uses the $recv[q][\kappa][p]$ set to unpack the buffer $cbuf$ into R.

Note that all the data that σ_p has to send to σ_q is communicated using a single remote method call, all communication problems – such as identifying and finding the (potentially) remote target, marshaling arguments of the call, etc. – being managed by the ORB interface.

Note also that in a communication, the active side, i.e. the side that initializes the communication process, is the sender side.

The m2j compiler produces two arrays, *global-send* and *global-recv*, yielding communication spaces for each communication on each processor. As with iteration spaces above, transitions of finite–state machines using ΔM sequences are used to perform this task.

If σ_p is a servant installed on a processor p, then one of the first actions performed in the constructor of σ_p is the reduction of the *global-send* and *global-recv* spaces to their subspaces, $send[p]$ and $recv[p]$, used exclusively in σ_p.

The next Section (3.3) presents the algorithm that evaluates all communication spaces controlling a single communication (1) when the arrays involved are one–dimensional. Generalization to the multidimensional case is similar to ([8], Algorithm 3).

3.3   Generation of Communication Sets: Algorithm

The algorithm given below evaluates the communication spaces (2) for all pairs of processors involved in a communication (1) when R and S are one–dimensional.

Let n_S (n_R) be the number of processors onto which S (R) is mapped. Two ΔM sequences are used, one for the sender (ΔM_S) and one for the receiver (ΔM_R). To evaluate the successive local indices on the sender side, two vectors are maintained, λ_S and δ_S, each of length n_S. The former stores the current local indices of S on (successive processors from) P; the latter stores the indices of the next ΔM_S entries to be added to λ_S to yield the next vector of local indices[3]. Two vectors are also maintained, λ_R and δ_R, each of length n_R, that play the same role on the receiver side.

The algorithm produces two arrays, $send[n_S][n_R]$ and $recv[n_R][n_S]$, containing communication spaces (2) for each $p = 0, \ldots, n_S - 1$ and $q = 0, \ldots, n_R - 1$. Elements of these arrays are lists of local indices of sections' elements to be sent or received[4].

The resulting arrays are generated in a single loop over the sections' global indices. First, for each pair of global indices, the receiving processor (q) and the

---

[3] As an alternative, a separate ΔM could be used for each processor involved.

[4] In the algorithm, we therefore use a type **intlist** that abstracts lists of integers, and an operation: *append* : **intlist** $\times$ **int** $\rightarrow$ **intlist** that appends an integer to a list of integers.

sending processor (p) are determined. Next, the ΔM_S and ΔM_R sequences are used to determine the sender's and receiver's vectors of successive local indices; both λ vectors and both δ vectors are utilized and modified at this step.

The layout constants m_R and m_S are as declared in the corresponding CYCLIC(m) directives.

Input

R (Receiver): regular section $(l_R : u_R : s_R)$, alignment (a_R, b_R), layout (m_R, n_R), ΔM_R, initial settings of λ_R and δ_R.

S (Sender): regular section $(l_S : u_S : s_S)$, alignment (a_S, b_S), layout (m_S, n_S), ΔM_S, initial settings of λ_S and δ_S.

Output

$recv[n_R][n_S]$ the communication space component to be associated with the Receiver,

$send[n_S][n_R]$ the communication space component to be associated with the Sender.

Algorithm

1. Declare variables and communication space components
   int r, loc_R, s, loc_S, p, q;
   intlist $recv[n_R][n_S]$;
   intlist $send[n_S][n_R]$;

2. Perform the proper loop
   for $(r = l_R,\ s = l_S;\ r <= u_R;\ r += s_R,\ s += s_S)$
   // Determine next receiver–sender processor pair
   $q = ((a_R * r + b_R) / m_R) \% n_R$;
   $p = ((a_S * s + b_S) / m_S) \% n_S$;
   // Evaluate the receiver side
   $loc_R\ \ = \lambda_R[q]$;
   $\lambda_R[q]\ +=\ \Delta M_R[\delta_R[q]]$;
   $\delta_R[q]\ \ = (\delta_R[q] + 1) \% \Delta M_R.length$;
   $append(recv[q][p],\ loc_R)$;
   // Evaluate the sender side
   $loc_S\ \ = \lambda_S[p]$;
   $\lambda_S[p] += \Delta M_S[\delta_S[p]]$;
   $\delta_S[p]\ \ = (\delta_S[p] + 1) \% \Delta M_S.length$;
   $append(send[p][q],\ loc_S)$;

For the communication B(1:22:3) = C in Fig. 3, the algorithm's input is:

	reg. sect.	alignm.	layout	ΔM	λ	δ
receiver:	$(1 : 22 : 3)$	$(1, 0)$	$(6, 3)$	$\{3, 3\}$	$\{1, 1, 1\}$	$\{0, 0, 0\}$
sender:	$(0 : 7 : 1)$	$(1, 0)$	$(8, 1)$	$\{1, 1, 1, 1, 1, 1, 1, 1\}$	$\{0\}$	$\{0\}$

The result produced is:

$recv_{B(1:22:3)}[0][0]\ = \{1, 4, 7, 10\}$ $\qquad$ $send_C[0][0] = \{0, 1, 6, 7\}$
$recv_{B(1:22:3)}[1][0]\ = \{1, 4\}$ $\qquad$ $send_C[0][1] = \{2, 3\}$
$recv_{B(1:22:3)}[2][0]\ = \{1, 4\}$ $\qquad$ $send_C[0][2] = \{4, 5\}$

3.4 Creation of Execution Blocks

In order to minimize the number of calls by which the conductor initializes the execution of operations on cooperating servant collections, the compiler ties together – where possible – sequences of iterations and communications that can be executed *en bloc*. Below, we call these tied–together program pieces *execution blocks*.

The algorithm creating execution blocks relies on the fact that if the creation of an execution block for a processor collection has already begun, then it may be continued until an operation occurs that has to be initialized on a different processor collection. Let us recall that an iteration is always initialized (and executed) on the processor collection on which its components are mapped, whereas a communication is initialized on the processor collection on which the sender is mapped. Thus, for the example in Fig. 3 (b), two execution blocks are created – as indicated by the shadowed boxes: the first is associated with a servant installed on the host _H1, the second with servants installed on processors from the collection P.

After identifying an execution block b, the **m2j** compiler transforms it into a parameterless public method that becomes part of all servants with which b is associated. At program execution, the conductor calls this method remotely at the appropriate time.

Below, we denote execution blocks as $b_1()$, $b_2()$, etc.

3.5 Creation of the IDL Specification

So far, we have identified two kinds of servants' methods that are called remotely: *receive(...)* and execution blocks $b_i()$. One more method is used, *resolve()*, which resolves remote references to servants cooperating in the parallel execution environment; this is not, however, dealt with in more detail here.

As mentioned in Section 2, in addition to Java source files specifying both the servers' and the servants' classes, the **m2j** compiler produces an IDL file specifying the ORB interface, i.e. signatures of the public methods that are implemented by servants and can be remotely called.

The IDL specification generated for the mHPF program in Fig. 3 (b) is shown in Fig. 3.5.

The IDL specification states that any servant has a *resolve()* method as well as a *receive(...)* method. Only the methods corresponding to execution blocks are different.

4 Concluding Remarks

In our framework, three important modern programming paradigms are brought together: *data parallelism* as a means of parallelizing sequential programs, *network technology* allowing geographically remote workstations to communicate, and *object–orientedness* allowing the production of robust, extendable, and reu-

```
module DataParRun {
  interface _AnyServant {
    void resolve();
    void dispose():
    typedef sequence <long> array;
    boolean receive(in long sid, in long pid, in array elems);
  };

  interface _H1Servant : _AnyServant {
    boolean b_1();
  };

  interface _PServant : _AnyServant {
    boolean b_2();
  };
};
```

Fig. 4. Generated IDL specification. Input: mHPF program from Fig. 3 (b).

sable programs. Our first step was to prove that this combination really works. As our next step, we would like to incorporate in the framework profiling tools and conduct performance measurements. We also plan to extend mHPF by adding irregular mapping schemes.

However, some of the framework's advantages and disadvantages are already evident:

Massive Parallelism. If a servant σ remotely calls a method $m(\ldots)$ of each servant σ_p ($p \in P$), then all these calls are issued as independent threads, and σ therefore executes them in parallel. As in a group of remote method calls, each individual call is addressed to a different (remote) servant σ_p, the callee is always executing the called method in parallel with other callees. An additional level of parallelism can be achieved when two or more data-flow–independent array calculations are to be performed: an independent servant may be created for each of these calculations and perform them in parallel with other servants.

Autonomy. An servant residing on a processor p performs only that part of the task concerning data stored on p. After doing its job, a servant may free the processor resources, and the conductor may dispose of it.

Manageability. As a decentralized and presumably small fragment of program code with a fairly simple interface, a servant is easier to manage, profile, and – if required – understand and tune by hand.

Increased Communication Demand. Each initialization of an execution block requires a parameterless remote method call. Additional data communication may be needed to perform operations on unmapped data.

Acknowledgments

The author wishes to thank Thilo Ernst and Gerd Kock for their valuable comments on the first draft of this paper. In addition, he is indebted to the GMD FIRST for providing time and technical means needed to perform this work.

References

1. High Performance Fortran Forum: *High Performance Fortran Language Specification*. Technical Report, Version 2.0.delta, Rice University, October 20, 1996.
2. Object Management Group: *The Common Object Request Broker: Architecture and Specification*. Revision 2.2, February 1998. http://www.omg.org/corba/
3. A. Vogel, K. Duddy: *Java Programming with CORBA*. Wiley Computer Publishing, 1997.
4. *JDK1.2 Documentation*.
   http://www.javasoft.com:80/products/jdk/1.2/docs/index.html
5. K. Arnold, J. Gosling: *The Java Programming Language*. The Java Series. Addison Wesley, Publ. Company. 1996.
6. *Java IDL Documentation*.
   http://www.javasoft.com/products/jdk/idl/docs.html
7. H.J. Sips, C. van Reeuwijk, W. Denissen: *Analysis of local enumeration and storage schemes in HPF*. 1996 International Conference on Supercomputing, May 1996, Philadelphia, ACM Press, 1996.
8. S. Chatterjee, J.R. Gilbert, F.J.E. Long, R. Schreiber, S.-H. Teng: *Generating Local Addresses and Communication Sets for Data-Parallel Programs*. Journal of Parallel and Distributed Computing, vol.26, pp. 72–84, 1995.
9. S. Benkner: *Vienna Fortran 90 and its Compilation*. Ph.D. thesis submitted to the Technical University of Vienna, 1994.
   http://www.vcpc.univie.ac.at/activities/language/Literature.html
10. C. Koelbel: *Compile-time generation of regular communication patterns*. Proceedings of Supercomputing'91, Albuquerque, 1991.
11. S.D. Kaushik, C.-H. Huang, P. Sadayappan: *Efficient Index Set Generation for Compiling HPF Array Statements on Distributed Memory Machines*. Journal of Parallel and Distributed Computing, vol.38, pp. 237–247, 1996.

A   The Input Language mHPF

The EBNF syntax of the input language mHPF is given below. Note that all
"-name" non-terminals represent identifiers. The m2j compiler ignores the case
of keywords.

program	=	**PROGRAM** *stmt* { ";" *stmt* } **END**.
stmt	=	**INTEGER** *at-decls* |
		TEMPLATE *at-decls* |
		PROCESSORS *procs-decls* |
		ALIGN *align-tail* |
		DISTRIBUTE *distr-tail*|
		FORALL *forall-tail* |
		assign-stmt .
at-decls	=	*at-exts* "::" *at-name* {"," *at-name*} .
at-exts	=	"," **DIMENSION** "(" *extent* {"," *extent*} ")" .
procs-decls	=	*procs-name* "(" *extent* {"," *extent*} ")" .
align-tail	=	"(" *dummy-name* {"," *dummy-name*} ")" *align-with-clause*
		"::" *array-name* {"," *array-name*} .
align-with-clause	=	**WITH** *at-name* "(" *align-subscr* { "," *align-subscr* } ")" .
align-subscr	=	[*integer* "*"] *dummy-name* ["+" *integer*] .
distr-tail	=	"(" **CYCLIC** "(*integer* ")" { "," **CYCLIC** "(*integer* ")"
		" } ")" **ONTO** *procs-name* "::" *at-name* { ";" *at-name* } .
at-name	=	*iarr-name* | *tmpl-name* .
forall-tail	=	"(" *forall-triplet-spec* { "," *forall-triplet-spec* } ")"
		assign-stmt .
forall-triplet-spec	=	*index-name* "=" *lower-bound* ":" *upper-bound* [":" *stride*] .
assign-stmt	=	*array-ref* "=" *expr* .
array-ref	=	array-name ["(" *index-expr* { "," *index-expr* } ")"] .
index-expr	=	*integer* ["*" *index-tail* | ":" *section-tail*] |
		index-tail .
index-tail	=	*index-name* ["+" *integer*] .
section-tail	=	*integer* [":" *integer*] .
expr	=	*term* { ("+" | "-") *term* } .
term	=	*factor* { ("*" | "/" *factor* } .
factor	=	"(" *expr* ")" | *array-ref* | *integer* .

Optimized Execution of Fortran 90 Array Language on Symmetric Shared-Memory Multiprocessors

Vivek Sarkar

IBM Thomas J. Watson Research Center
P. O. Box 704, Yorktown Heights, NY 10598, USA
vsarkar@us.ibm.com

Abstract. Past compilers have found it challenging to implement Fortran 90 array language on symmetric shared-memory multiprocessors (SMPs) so as to match, let alone beat, the performance of comparable Fortran 77 scalar loops. This is in spite of the fact that the semantics of array language is *implicitly concurrent* and the semantics of scalar loops is *implicitly sequential.* A well known obstacle to efficient execution of array language lies in the overhead of using array temporaries to obey the fetch-before-store semantics of array language. We observe that another major obstacle to supporting array language efficiently arises from the fact that most past compilers attempted to compile and optimize each array statement in isolation.

In this paper, we describe a solution for optimized compilation of Fortran 90 array language for execution on SMPs. Our solution optimizes scalarized loops and scalar loops in a common framework. Our solution also adapts past work on array temporary minimization so as to avoid degradation of parallelism and locality. This solution has been implemented in the IBM XL Fortran product compiler for SMPs. To the best of our knowledge, no other Fortran 90 compiler performs such combined optimizations of scalarized loops and scalar loops. Our preliminary experimental results indicate that the performance of Fortran 90 array language can match, and even beat, the performance of comparable scalar loops. In addition to Fortran 90 array language, the approach outlined in this paper will be relevant to similar array language extensions that might appear in Java and other programming languages in the future.

Keywords: compilers, code optimization, array language, scalarization, parallelization.

1 Introduction

The array language in Fortran 90 [10] provides greater expressive power and conciseness for writing array computations, compared to Fortran 77. A valid implementation of a Fortran 90 array construct must satisfy the "fetch-before-store" semantics *i.e.,* must be equivalent to an execution in which the entire right

S. Chatterjee (Ed.): LCPC'98, LNCS 1656, pp. 131–147, 1999.

hand side of an array assignment statement is fetched from storage and evaluated before any results are stored for the array variable on the left hand side. The fetch-before-store semantics precludes the possibility of there being a true (flow) loop-carried data dependence [1] in the array computation. Therefore, Fortran 90 array constructs are guaranteed to contain concurrency — the challenge lies in exploiting this concurrency efficiently on a given target machine.

Despite its implicit concurrency, past compilers have found it challenging to implement Fortran 90 array language on symmetric shared-memory multiprocessors (SMPs) so as to match, let alone beat, the performance of comparable Fortran 77 scalar loops. A well known obstacle to efficient execution of array language lies in the overhead of using array temporaries to obey the fetch-before-store semantics of array language. We observe that another major obstacle to supporting array language efficiently arises from the fact that most past compilers attempted to compile and optimize each array statement in isolation. In many cases, it becomes important to optimize the loops for an array statement collectively with other (containing or adjacent) loops in the program so as to increase the scope of loop transformations that enhance parallelism and data locality.

In this paper, we describe a solution for optimized compilation of Fortran 90 array language for execution on SMPs. Our solution optimizes scalarized loops and scalar loops in a common framework for automatic selection of loop transformations [13,14]. This common loop transformation framework is essential for making the uniprocessor performance of Fortran 90 array constructs competitive with that of comparable Fortran 77 loops. For SMPs, the performance advantage of using Fortran 90 array language can then come from its guaranteed concurrency. Our solution also adapts past work on array temporary minimization so as to avoid degradation of parallelism and locality. We show how prior techniques for minimizing the size of array temporaries can actually conflict with the goals of enhanced parallelism and locality and describe how we resolve this conflict.

This solution has been implemented in version 5.1 of the the IBM XL Fortran product compiler for SMPs [7]; to the best of our knowledge, no other Fortran 90 compiler performs such combined optimizations of scalarized loops and scalar loops. Our preliminary experimental results indicate that the performance of Fortran 90 array language can match, and even beat, the performance of comparable scalar loops. In addition to Fortran 90 array language, the approach outlined in this paper will be relevant to similar array language extensions that might appear in Java and other programming languages in the future (e.g., see [3]).

The rest of the paper is organized as follows. Section 2 uses example programs to illustrate the key issues addressed by our approach. Section 3 outlines our solution for optimized compilation of Fortran 90 array language for execution on shared-memory multiprocessors. Section 4 contains some preliminary experimental results and section 5 discusses related work. Finally, section 6 contains the conclusions of this paper.

2   Examples

In this section, we use a few simple example programs to illustrate the key issues addressed by our solution for optimized compilation of Fortran 90 array language for execution on SMPs. As in past work [1], we use the term, *scalarization*, to describe the translation of an array computation into scalar (sequential) code, and view a translation of an array construct to parallel code as consisting of an initial translation to scalar code followed by parallelization of the scalar code. As motivation, we also present performance measurements of different code configurations discussed for the examples. The performance measurements were made using version 5.1 of the product IBM XL Fortran SMP compiler on an IBM RS/6000 SMP workstation containing four PowerPC 604 processors. Performance measurements for larger Fortran 90 benchmark programs are presented later in section 4.

2.1   Conflict between efficient parallelization and array temporary minimization

Consider the two-dimensional array assignment statement in figure 1(a) which performs a matrix addition. A naive rewrite of the array statement into a two-dimensional scalar loop nest is shown in figure 1(b). It is easy to verify see that this scalarization violates the fetch-before-store semantics of array language *e.g.*, the value stored by iteration $i2 = 1, i1 = 1$ into $A(2,2)$ is later fetched by iteration $i2 = 2, i1 = 2$. Loop reversal cannot help in this case — the scalarization in figure 1(b) remains illegal after reversing either the $i1$ loop or the $i2$ loop (or both). However, the compiler can create an array temporary and generate two loop nests to preserve the fetch-before-store semantics as shown in figure 1(c).

Given the array language statement in figure 1(a), array temporary minimization algorithms from past work, such as the algorithm in [1], will apply the loop interchange transformation in conjunction with a reversal of the $i1$ loop to obtain a legal scalarization without using an array temporary, as shown in figure 1(d). While this array temporary minimization is a good choice for the vector computers that the algorithm in [1] was designed for, it leads to inefficient parallelization on SMPs for two reasons. First, only the inner loop is parallelizable thus contributing to increased scheduling and synchronization overhead compared to the outer loop parallelism in figure 1(c). Second, the loop nest in figure 1(d) has poor spatial locality which leads to false sharing overhead in SMP execution.

This example illustrates the conflict between array temporary minimization and efficient parallelization, and the limitations of directly using the array temporary minimization algorithm from [1] when targeting SMPs. As discussed in section 3, we resolve this conflict by restricting array temporary minimization so that it preserves the loops that belong to the "locality group" in the innermost position.

(a) Example array assignment statement:
```
----------------------------------------
A(2 : n+1, 2 : n+1) = A(1 : n, 1 : n) + A(1 : n, 3 : n+2)
```

(b) Illegal scalarization:
```
--------------------------
do i2 = 1, n
   do i1 = 1, n
      A(i1+1,i2+1) = A(i1,i2) + A(i1,i2+2)
   end do
end do
```

(c) Legal scalarization with array temporary
    (outer loop parallelism and good spatial locality):
```
--------------------------------------------------------
do i2 = 1, n     ! parallelizable loop
   do i1 = 1, n  ! parallelizable loop
      temp(i1,i2) = A(i1,i2) + A(i1,i2+2)
   end do
end do
do i2 = 1, n     ! parallelizable loop
   do i1 = 1, n  ! parallelizable loop
      A(i1+1,i2+1) = temp(i1,i2)
   end do
end do
```

(d) Legal scalarization after loop interchange
    (temp is eliminated but only the inner loop is
    parallelizable, and the loop nest has poor spatial locality):
```
------------------------------------------------------------------
do i1 = n, 1, -1  ! serial loop
   do i2 = 1, n    ! parallelizable loop
      A(i1+1,i2+1) = A(i1,i2) + A(i1,i2+2)
   end do
end do
```

Fig. 1. Matrix add example

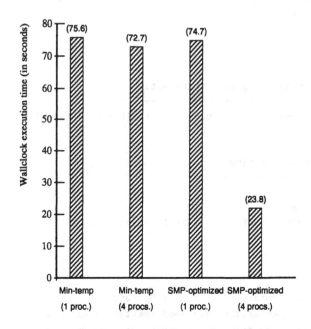

Fig. 2. Performance measurements for matrix add example

Figure 2 summarizes the wallclock (real) execution time measured for 100 repetitions of the following two configurations of the matrix addition computation in figure 1 on 1 processor and 4 processors with $n = 1000$:

Min-temp — scalarized code (figure 1(d)) obtained by array temporary minimization (reversal and interchange), followed by parallelization of the inner (i2) loop.
SMP-optimized — scalarized code (figure 1(c)) obtained by following the approach outlined in this paper and parallelizing only the outer (i2) loop.

The SMP-optimized configuration showed a 3.4× speedup, while the Min-temp configuration showed no speedup (due to false sharing). The uniprocessor execution times for SMP-optimized and Min-temp were comparable for this example, showing that the benefit from array temporary minimization in the Min-temp configuration was cancelled by its loss of data locality. For processors with a larger cache line size than that of the PowerPC 604 (32 bytes), we expect the relative performance improvement of the SMP-optimized code compared to the Min-temp code to be larger, even on one processor.

2.2   Collective optimization of scalarized loops and scalar loops

Consider the scalar k loop shown in figure 3(a) which contains an array assignment statement. For convenience, we chose an example that performs a familiar computation, matrix multiply[1]. In reality, a Fortran 90 programmer is likely to

---

[1] For simplicity, we do not show the initialization of array A to zero in figure 3.

```
(a) Example loop containing an array assignment statement:
---------------------------------------------------------------
do k = 1, n
   A(1:n,1:n) = A(1:n,1:n) + spread(B(1:n,k),2,n) *
                               spread(C(k,1:n),1,n)
end do

(b) After unoptimized scalarization:
-------------------------------------
do k = 1, n
   do i1 = 1, n   ! parallelizable loop
      T1(i1) = B(i1,k)
   end do

   do i2 = 1, n   ! parallelizable loop
      do i1 = 1, n   ! parallelizable loop
         T2(i1,i2) = T1(i1)
      end do
   end do

   do i1 = 1, n   ! parallelizable loop
      T3(i1) = C(k,i1)
   end do

   do i2 = 1, n   ! parallelizable loop
      do i1 = 1, n   ! parallelizable loop
         T4(i1,i2) = T3(i2)
      end do
   end do

   do i2 = 1, n   ! parallelizable loop
      do i1 = 1, n    ! parallelizable loop
         T5(i1,i2) = A(i1,i2) + T2(i1,i2) * T4(i1,i2)
      end do
   end do

   do i2 = 1, n   ! parallelizable loop
      do i1 = 1, n    ! parallelizable loop
         A(i1,i2) = T5(i1,i2)
      end do
   end do
end do
```

Fig. 3. Matrix multiply example

(c) After optimized scalarization:

```
do k = 1, n
   do i2 = 1, n   ! parallelizable loop
      do i1 = 1, n    ! parallelizable loop
         A(i1,i2) = A(i1,i2) + B(i1,k) * C(k,i2)
      end do
   end do
end do
```

(d) After collective transformation of loop nest (c):

```
do bb$_i2=1,n,b$_i2    ! parallelizable loop
   do bb$_i1=1,n,b$_i1     ! parallelizable loop
      do bb$_k =1,n,b$_k
         do i2=max(1,bb$_i2),min(n,bb$_i2+b$_i2-1)
            do i1=max(1,bb$_i1),min(n,bb$_i1+b$_i1-1)
               do k=max(1,bb$_k),min(n,bb$_k+b$_k-1),1
                  A(i1,i2) = A(i1,i2) + B(i1,k) * C(k,i2)
               end do
            end do
         end do
      end do
   end do
end do
```

Fig. 4. Matrix multiply example (contd.)

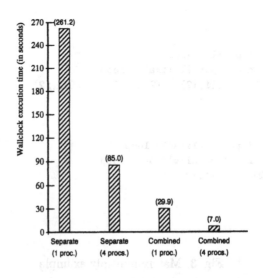

Fig. 5. Performance measurements for matrix multiply example

use the MATMUL intrinsic function for expressing a matrix multiply computation, but the principles illustrated in this example apply to any code structure where there is an opportunity for collective optimization of scalarized loops and scalar loops.

Figure 3(b) shows the result of *unoptimized scalarization* performed on the the code in figure 3(a). The array language statement is expanded into six loop nests, all of which are contained within the outer k loop. Array temporaries $T2$ and $T4$ capture the output of the two calls to the SPREAD intrinsic [10]; many compilers generate calls to a library routine for SPREAD for the computation of $T2$ and $T4$, which would incur even greater overhead than the in-line code for the SPREAD intrinsic shown in figure 3(b).

Figure 4(c) shows the result of *optimized scalarization* performed on the code in figure 3(a). Optimized scalarization performs data dependence analysis and forward substitution to generate a single loop nest for the array language statement, as opposed to the six loop nests in figure 3(b). The two inner loops (i2 and i1) in figure 4(c) can both be parallelized, but these parallel loops will not be moved to the outermost position if the scalarized loops are optimized and parallelized independent of the outer k scalar loop.

Figure 4(d) shows the result of collectively optimizing the scalar k loop and the scalarized i1 and i2 loops. Now, the optimizer can tile all three loops, and also move parallel loops bb_i2 and bb_i1 to the outermost position. Further, loop k is moved to the innermost position so as to make the loop-invariant A(i1,i2) references eligible for scalar replacement. To the best of our knowledge, no other Fortran 90 compiler performs collective optimization on scalar loops and scalarized loops so as to automatically derive the optimized code structure in figure 4(d) from the input program in figure 3(a).

Figure 5 summarizes the wallclock (real) execution time measured for two configurations of the matrix multiply example:

Separate — optimized scalarized code (figure 4(c)) obtained by transforming only the scalarized (i1 and i2) loops, with parallelization of the i2 loop.

Combined — optimized scalarized code (figure 4(d)) obtained by following the approach outlined in this paper and collectively transforming the scalar (k) loop and the scalarized (i1 and i2) loops, with parallelization of the outer bb$_i2 loop.

The wallclock time was measured for $n = 1000$ on one processor and four processors for both configurations. We see a dramatic $8\times$ performance improvement on one processor by using the combined approach outlined in this paper due to the enhanced locality optimization of all three loops. We also get an ideal $4\times$ speedup for the combined approach, which is a multiplicative factor over the $8\times$ uniprocessor performance improvement.

The collective optimization of scalarized loops and scalar loops discussed in this section focused on transformations of a single perfect loop nest containing scalar loops and scalarized loops. Our compiler also uses the loop distribution and loop fusion transformations to perform collective transformations across multiple loop nests as described in [13,9].

3   Optimized Parallelization of Fortran 90 Array Constructs

In this section, we describe our solution for optimized compilation of Fortran 90 array language for execution on shared-memory multiprocessors. A high-level description of the entire algorithm is outlined in figures 6 and 7. Step 1 performs scalarization of array language statements using full-sized array temporaries as needed (*i.e.*, without attempting to minimize the size of array temporaries as in [1]). Steps 2, 3, 4 perform loop distribution, identification of perfect loop nests, and identification of reduction operations respectively, as preparatory steps before optimization of locality and paralleli sm. Step 5 performs locality optimization by following the approach outlined in [14]; the output of this step is a sequence of unimodular and block/tile loop transformations selected in step 5e for each perfect loop nest. Step 6 performs SMP parallelization by following the approach outlined in [14,4]; the output of this step is a further sequence of unimodular, parallelize, and coalesce loop transformations selected in step 6d for each perfect loop nest. Step 7 performs loop fusion [19,9] to exploit opportunities for further optimizing locality and reducing parallel loop overhead across multiple loop nests (this includes undoing unnecessary loop distribution transformations from step 2). Finally, step 8 performs scalar replacement and loop unrolling transformations to improve uniprocessor performance by following the approach described in [13].

For the sake of illustration, we now describe how the algorithm operates on a single k-dimensional array language statement of the form, $LHS = RHS^2$. We first observe that a simple solution (without using the algorithm in figures 6 and 7) might be to parallelize all loops by introducing a full-sized k-dimensional array temporary as shown in figure 8. (It may not always be necessary to introduce a k-dimensional array temporary to parallelize all the loops *e.g.*, no array temporary is needed if the *LHS* array variable does not occur in the *RHS* expression.) However, parallelizing all scalarized loops as in figure 8 creates two serious overhead problems in practice:

1. The fine grain parallelism in the innermost loop(s) interferes with the spatial locality optimization, and causes the same cache line from *LHS* to bounce from processor to processor due to false sharing.
2. There is an overhead incurred due to the barrier synchronization that must be performed at the end of each `parallel do` statement. Parallelization of all loops in figure 8 results in an excessive number of barrier synchronizations (due to nested parallel loops).

Instead, our algorithm in figures 6 and 7 avoids the interference between parallelism and spatial locality by considering the innermost g loops to be

---

[2] *RHS* need not be a single array variable. $RHS(i_1, \ldots, i_k)$ just represents the computation of element $(i_1, \ldots, i_k)$ of the array expression denoted by *RHS*. For simplicity, we assume in this example that *RHS* does not contain any transformational intrinsic functions (TIFs).

Input: Intermediate representation containing a mix of Fortran 77 statements/loops and Fortran 90 array constructs.

Output: Transformed intermediate representation in which all Fortran 90 array constructs have been scalarized and optimized in conjunction with Fortran 77 statements/loops.

Method:

1. Translate each array language statement into scalar code without performing any loop interchange/reversal transformations. Create full-sized array temporaries as needed.
2. Perform maximal loop distribution [19].
3. Identify perfect loop nests [19].
4. Identify loop-carried flow dependences that correspond to associative reduction operations *e.g.*, sum reductions [19]. These reductions are used to relax data dependence constraints on loop transformations.
5. **for each** set of perfectly nested loops $\mathcal{L} = (L_1, \ldots, L_n)$ **do** /* Optimize locality */
   (a) Compute $F(b_1, \ldots, b_n)$, the estimated memory cost per iteration [5,13] assuming symbolic block sizes $b_1, \ldots, b_n$ for loops $L_1, \ldots, L_n$.
   (b) Identify the locality group G consisting of loops L_k such that $\delta F/\delta b_k < 0$ (*i.e.*, such that loop L_k carries spatial or temporal locality) and loop L_k can be interchanged with loop L_n.
   (c) Compute block sizes $b_1, \ldots, b_n$ so as to minimize $F(b_1, \ldots, b_n)$, while obeying the following constraints:
       − If loop L_k is in the locality group, G, then b_k must satisfy $1 \leq b_k \leq N_k$, otherwise b_k is set $= 1$. (N_k is the estimated number of iterations for loop L_k.)
       − The number of distinct cache lines accessed by a single tile of $b_1 \times \ldots \times b_n$ iterations must not exceed the effective cache size. (Similar constraints are imposed for the TLB and the L2-cache.)
   (d) Update the locality group G by removing any loops assigned $b_k = 1$ in step 5c.
   (e) **if** $|G| > 0$ **then** /* Locality group G is non-empty */
       i. Block/tile each loop L_k in G such that $b_k < N_k$. After blocking, the inner blocked loop is retained in G but the outer loop is not. (Loops with $b_k = N_k$ are also retained in G, but are not blocked.)
       ii. Select iteration-reordering loop transformations [16,14] to bring all loops in G together in the innermost position.
       end if
   end for

Fig. 6. Algorithm for optimized parallelization of Fortran 90 array constructs (Part 1 of 2)

6. **for each** set of perfectly nested loops $\mathcal{L} = (L_1, \ldots, L_n)$ **do**
   /* Optimize SMP parallelism */
   (a) Let $\mathcal{L}' = (L'_1, \ldots, L'_{n'})$ be the transformed version of $\mathcal{L}$ obtained after the locality optimization in step 5 was performed on loop nest $\mathcal{L}$. We will only consider loops $L'_1, \ldots, L'_{n'-g}$ to be eligible for parallelization, where $g = |G|$ is the size of the locality group identified for $\mathcal{L}'$.
   (b) Use the algorithm from [18] to find the (unique) largest fully permutable outermost loop nest in loops $L'_1, \ldots, L'_{n'-g}$.
   (c) Find C, the largest set of *coalescable parallel* loops from the fully permutable outermost loop nest identified in step 6b, such that each loop in C is parallel and can be moved to the outermost position and all loops in C can be coalesced.
   (d) Select iteration-reordering loop transformations [16,14] to bring all loops in C to the outermost position, and to parallelize and coalesce them.
   end for
7. Perform loop fusion on the transformed loop nests to improve locality and reduce overhead of parallel loops [19,9]. Unnecessary array temporaries are removed via the *array contraction* transformation [15] after loop fusion.
8. Perform scalar replacement and loop unrolling transformations to improve uniprocessor performance [13].

Fig. 7. Algorithm for optimized parallelization of Fortran 90 array constructs (Part 2 of 2)

```
parallel do ik = . . .
   . . .
      parallel do i2 = . . .
         parallel do i1 = . . .
            temp(i1,i2,...,ik) = RHS(i1,i2,...,ik)
         end do
      . . .
   end do
end do

parallel do ik = . . .
   . . .
      parallel do i2 = . . .
         parallel do i1 = . . .
            LHS(i1,i2,...,ik) = temp(i1,i2,...,ik)
         end do
      . . .
   end do
end do
```

Fig. 8. Simple approach: Use of a k-dimensional temporary to parallelize all loops of an array language statement

ineligible for parallelization (step 6a), where g is the size of the *locality group*. For the *LHS = RHS* statement that is being discussed in this section, the dominant source of locality is spatial locality rather than temporal locality. In fact, the criteria for selection of the locality group (determining if $\delta F/\delta b_k < 0$ in step 5b) can be stated as follows for this special case:

> If a dimension has (*stride < cache block size*) or (*stride < page size*) for any array section in the array statement, then add the dimension to the spatial locality group.

It is easy to see that if the above rule includes dimension i in the locality group, then it must include all dimensions $< i$ in the locality group as well. Therefore, the locality group can be defined by a single dimension number, $S \geq 0$, denoting the innermost set of dimensions that carry spatial locality, $\{1, \dots, S\}$. Often, we find that $g = S = 1$ in practice.

Further, our algorithm in figures 6 and 7 addresses the problem of excessive barrier synchronization overhead by coalescing [11,16] all parallel loops outside the locality group, $i_{S+1}, \dots, i_k$, into a single parallel loop with $N = \prod_{j=S+1}^{k} N_j$ iterations in step 6d (where N_j is the number of iterations in loop i_j). Compared to the configuration in figure 8, the coalesced configuration reduces the number of barrier synchronizations needed per loop nest from $N_{S+2} \times \dots \times N_k$ to just one.

In summary, the algorithm in figures 6 and 7 transforms and optimizes scalarized loops and scalar loops collectively using the high-order transformations implemented in the IBM XL Fortran compiler [13]. These transformations include loop distribution, unimodular transformations, loop tiling/blocking (with compiler-selected tile sizes), loop fusion, unrolling of multiple loops (with compiler-selected unroll factors), and scalar replacement of selected array references. of the IBM XL FORTRAN SMP compiler. An overview of the framework for selection of transformations can be found in [13,14], and brief descriptions of the use of this framework for SMP parallelization can be found in [4,7].

4   Experimental Results

In this section, we summarize some preliminary experimental results for our solution to optimized compilation of Fortran 90 array language for execution on shared-memory multiprocessors. The performance measurements were made using version 5.1 of the product IBM XL Fortran SMP compiler on an IBM RS/6000 SMP workstation containing four PowerPC 604 processors. The two benchmark programs used in our experimental results were taken from the publicly available subset of the Quetzal Fortran 90 Benchmark Suite [12].

Figure 9 summarizes the performance measurements for the Fortran 77 and Fortran 90 versions of the **gas_dynamics** benchmark from the Quetzal suite. The labels on the x-axis in figure 9 refer to different compiler optimization options that were used to obtain the performance measurements, as follows (in order of increasing optimization levels):

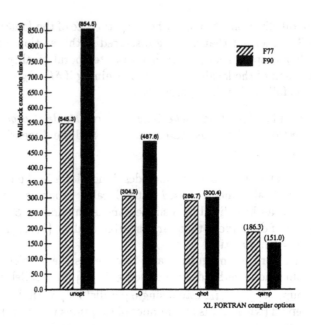

Fig. 9. Performance measurements for Quetzal benchmark, **gas_dynamics**

unopt Compile command: `xlf -qarch=604 ...`
   The compiler generates unoptimized code in the absence of any optimization
   option. The `-qarch=604` option directs the compiler to generate code for the
   PowerPC 604 processor.

-O Compile command: `xlf -O -qarch=604 ...`
   This is the default level of optimization performed by the XL FORTRAN
   compiler. Array language statements are optimized individually and not
   collectively at this optimization level.

-qhot Compile command: `xlf -qhot -O3 -qarch=604 ...`
   The `-qhot -O3` combination can be viewed as the next level of optimization
   beyond `-O` that is supported by the compiler. The `-qhot` option enables
   high order transformations in the XL FORTRAN compiler, using the collective
   transformation approach described in this paper for scalarized loops and
   original loops.

-qsmp Compile command: `xlf -qsmp -qhot -O3 -qarch=604 ...`
   The `-qsmp -qhot -O3` combination includes automatic SMP parallelization
   in conjunction with the optimizations and transformations performed in
   the `-qhot` case. The SMP parallelization is performed using the collective
   transformation approach described in this paper for scalarized loops and
   original loops.

   As can be seen from figure 9, the gap between the F77 and F90 versions is
much larger in the unopt and `-O` cases, compared to the `-qhot` and `-qsmp` cases.
For this benchmark, the combined approach described in this paper enables the
performance of the F90 version to beat the performance of the F77 version when

parallelized for an SMP, even though the performance of the unoptimized F90 version is significantly worse than that of the unoptimized F77 version. These results also underscore the importance of performing a high level of optimization for Fortran 90 programs.

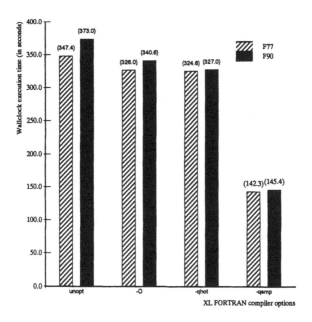

Fig. 10. Performance measurements for Quetzal benchmark, **scattering**

Figure 10 summarizes the performance measurements for the Fortran 77 and Fortran 90 versions of the **scattering** benchmark from the Quetzal suite. As can be seen from figure 10, the gap between the F77 and F90 versions is much larger in the unopt and -O cases, compared to the -qhot and -qsmp cases. For this benchmark, the combined approach described in this paper enables the performance of the F90 version to match the performance of the F77 version.

5   Related Work

The work that is most closely related to this paper is the chapter on "Sectioning" in Allen's Ph.D. dissertation [1]. That chapter addressed the problem of translating Fortran 90 style array assignment statements into sectioned code for vector computers with fixed-size hardware vector lengths. If we consider a vector length of just one, the sectioned code will essentially be the same as scalar code. The main contribution of that chapter was an algorithm for finding a correct scalarization with a reduced number and size of array temporaries.

The work presented in this paper extends Allen's results in two significant ways for effective SMP parallelization. First, our framework allows for collective optimization and transformation of scalar loops and scalarized loops. The transformations performed in this framework include loop distribution, unimodular transformations, loop tiling/blocking (with compiler-selected tile sizes), loop fusion, unrolling of multiple loops (with compiler-selected unroll factors), and scalar replacement of selected array references. Second, we showed how array temporary minimization and optimization of parallelism and locality can be conflicting goals, and described our approach in resolving these conflicts.

There are several papers that have been published in the literature related to transforming scalar loop nests for optimizing parallelism and locality Space limitations prevent us from discussing all these references; instead, we outline a representative subset. Though these references do not address the issue of optimizing Fortran 90 array language, their techniques are related to the combined framework reported in this paper for optimizing scalarized loops and scalar loops.

Irigoin and Triolet [6] described a framework for iteration-reordering transformations based on *supernode partitioning*, an aggregation technique achieved by hyperplane partitioning, followed by iteration space tiling across hyperplane boundaries. Their framework incorporates loop interchange, hyperplane partitioning, and loop tiling (blocking) in a unified way, for loop nests with linear bounds expressions. Our framework takes its inspiration from this kind of unified approach to loop transformations. Their framework is more general than ours in its ability to support non-rectangular tiling through hyperplane partitioning. Our framework is more general than theirs in its ability to support non-linear transformations like loop parallelization and loop coalescing. Our framework is also more practical because it is based on dependence vectors rather than dependence cones.

Recently, *unimodular transformations* (a restricted case of supernode partitioning) has gained popularity as a practical framework for iteration-reordering transformations. Unimodular transformations are attractive because any combination of loop interchange, loop reversal, and loop skewing can be represented by a single unimodular transformation matrix [2,18]. An algorithm that uses unimodular transformations to decompose a perfect loop nest into maximal sets of fully permutable loops as the basis for loop parallelization can be found in [18]. In related work [17], the tiling (blocking) transformation was incorporated into this framework by proposing a two-step approach for locality optimization, in which a unimodular transformation is followed by a tiling transformation. However, there have been no results reported on a compiler implementation that combines the parallelization proposed in [18] with the locality optimization proposed in [17]. More recently, McKinley, Carr, and Tseng [8] studied improvements in data locality by using the loop permutation, fusion, distribution, and reversal transformations. Their experimental results show wide applicability of these locality-improving transformations for existing Fortran 77 programs. However, this study was performed in the uniprocessor context and did not include SMP parallelization.

A key advantage of the approach reported in this paper over past work is that it allows arbitrary composition of a large class of unimodular and non-unimodular (*e.g.,* blocking, parallelization, coalescing) loop transformations for both locality and parallelization optimizations. The algorithm described in section 3 (figures 6 and 7) relies on this generality. To the best of our knowledge, there is no prior work that reports on this form of combined optimization of locality and parallelization for SMP targets.

6   Conclusions and Future Work

In this paper, we described a solution for optimized compilation of Fortran 90 array language for execution on shared-memory multiprocessors. This solution has been implemented in version 5.1 of the XL Fortran product compiler for SMPs. The highlights of our solution include resolving the conflicts between array temporary minimization and parallelization and locality optimizations, as well as a robust framework for collectively transforming and optimizing scalar and scalarized loops. These extensions are essential if the performance of Fortran 90 array constructs is to be competitive with that of Fortran 77 loops. For future work, we plan to apply these techniques to optimization of future array language extensions to Java [3].

Acknowledgments

The author would like to thank Roy Ju, Michael Lai, John Ng, and Jin-Fan Shaw for their contributions to the initial design and implementation of combined scalarization and transformation in the ASTI optimizer built at the IBM Santa Teresa Laboratory during 1991–1993. The author would also like to thank members of the Fortran Language and Parallel Development groups in the IBM Toronto Laboratory for their ongoing work on shipping the ASTI scalarizer and optimizer as components of the IBM XL FORTRAN compiler products [7]. Finally, the author is grateful for the review feedback from the anonymous referees.

References

1. John R. Allen. *Dependence Analysis for Subscripted Variables and its Application to Program Transformation.* PhD thesis, Rice University, Houston, TX, 1983.
2. Utpal Banerjee. Unimodular Transformations of Double Loops. *Proceedings of the Third Workshop on Languages and Compilers for Parallel Computing,* August 1990.
3. B. Carpenter, Y.-J. Chang, G. Fox, and X. Li. Java as a Language for Scientific Parallel Programming. In *Languages and compilers for parallel computing. Proceedings of the 10th international workshop. Held Aug., 1997 in Minneapolis, MN.,* Lecture Notes in Computer Science. Springer-Verlag, New York, 1998.

4. Jyh-Herng Chow, Leonard E. Lyon, and Vivek Sarkar. Automatic Parallelization for Symmetric Shared-Memory Multiprocessors. *CASCON '96 conference*, November 1996.
5. Jeanne Ferrante, Vivek Sarkar, and Wendy Thrash. On Estimating and Enhancing Cache Effectiveness. *Lecture Notes in Computer Science*, (589):328–343, 1991. Proceedings of the Fourth International Workshop on Languages and Compilers for Parallel Computing, Santa Clara, California, USA, August 1991. Edited by U. Banerjee, D. Gelernter, A. Nicolau, D. Padua.
6. Francois Irigoin and Remi Triolet. Supernode Partitioning. *Conference Record of Fifteenth ACM Symposium on Principles of Programming Languages*, 1988.
7. D.H. Kulkarni, S. Tandri, L. Martin, N. Copty, R. Silvera, X. Tian, X. Xue, and J. Wang. XL Fortran Compiler for IBM SMP Systems. *AIXpert*, pages 312–322, December 1997.
8. Kathryn S. McKinley, Steve Carr, and Chau-Wen Tseng. Improving Data Locality with Loop Transformations. *ACM Transactions on Programming Languages and Systems*, 18:423–453, July 1996.
9. Nimrod Megiddo and Vivek Sarkar. Optimal Weighted Loop Fusion for Parallel Programs. *Proceedings of the Ninth Annual ACM Symposium on Parallel Algorithms and Architecture*, pages 282–291, June 1997.
10. M. Metcalfe and J. Reid. *Fortran 90 Explained*. Oxford Science Publishers, 1990.
11. Constantine D. Polychronopoulos and David J. Kuck. Guided Self-Scheduling: A Practical Scheduling Scheme for Parallel Supercomputers. *IEEE Transactions on Computers*, C-36(12), December 1987.
12. John K. Prentice. Performance Benchmarks for Optimizing Fortran 90 Compilers. *Fortran Journal*, pages 6–12, May/June 1995.
13. Vivek Sarkar. Automatic Selection of High Order Transformations in the IBM XL Fortran Compilers. *IBM Journal of Research and Development*, 41(3), May 1997.
14. Vivek Sarkar. Loop Transformations for Hierarchical Parallelism and Locality. *Lecture Notes in Computer Science*, 1151, 1998. Proceedings of LCR98: Fourth Workshop on Languages, Compilers, and Run-time Systems for Scalable Computers. Held in May 1998 at Carnegie Mellon University, Pittsburgh, PA, USA.
15. Vivek Sarkar and Guang R. Gao. Optimization of Array Accesses by Collective Loop Transformations. *Proceedings of the ACM 1991 International Conference on Supercomputing*, pages 194–205, June 1991. Cologne, Germany.
16. Vivek Sarkar and Radhika Thekkath. A General Framework for Iteration-Reordering Loop Transformations. *Proceedings of the ACM SIGPLAN '92 Conference on Programming Language Design and Implementation*, pages 175–187, June 1992.
17. Michael E. Wolf and Monica S. Lam. A Data Locality Optimization Algorithm. *Proceedings of the ACM SIGPLAN Symposium on Programming Language Design and Implementation*, pages 30–44, June 1991.
18. Michael E. Wolf and Monica S. Lam. A Loop Transformation Theory and an Algorithm to Maximize Parallelism. *IEEE Transactions on Parallel and Distributed Systems*, 2(4):452–471, October 1991.
19. Michael J. Wolfe. *Optimizing Supercompilers for Supercomputers*. Pitman, London and The MIT Press, Cambridge, Massachusetts, 1989. In the series, Research Monographs in Parallel and Distributed Computing.

Fortran RED — A Retargetable Environment for Automatic Data Layout*

Ulrich Kremer

Department of Computer Science, Rutgers University
New Bruswick, NJ, USA
uli@cs.rutgers.edu

Abstract. The proliferation of parallel platforms over the last ten years has been dramatic. Parallel platforms come in different flavors, including desk–top multiprocessor PCs and workstations with a few processors, networks of PCs and workstations, and supercomputers with hundreds of processors or more. This diverse collection of parallel platforms provide not only computing cycles, but other important resources for scientific computing as well, such as large amounts of main memory and fast I/O capabilities. As a result of the proliferation of parallel platforms, the "typical profile" of a potential user of such systems has changed considerably. The specialist user who has a good understanding of the complexities of the target parallel system has been replaced by a user who is largely unfamiliar with the underlying system characteristics. While the specialist's main concern is peak performance, the non–specialist user may be willing to trade off performance for ease of programming.

Recent languages such as High Performance Fortran (HPF) and SGI Parallel Fortran are a significant step towards making parallel platforms truly usable for a broadening user community. However, non-trivial user input is required to produce efficient parallel programs. The main challenge for a user is to understand the performance implications of a specified data layout, which requires knowledge about issues such as code generation and analysis strategies of the HPF compiler and its node compiler, and the performance characteristics of the target architecture. This paper discusses our preliminary experiences with the design and implementation of Fortran RED , a tool that supports Fortran as a deterministic, sequential programming model on different parallel target systems. The tool is not part of a compiler. Fortran RED uses HPF as its intermediate program representation since the language is portable across many parallel platforms, and commercial and research HPF compilers are widely available. Fortran RED is able to support different target HPF compilers and target architectures, and allows multi–dimensional distributions in addition to dynamic remapping. This paper focuses on the discussion of the performance prediction component of the tool and reports preliminary results for a single scientific kernel on two target systems, namely PGI's and IBM's HPF compilers with IBM's SP–2 as the target architecture.

* This research was supported by DARPA contract DABT 63-93-C-0064 and experiments were conducted using resources at the Cornell Theory Center.

S. Chatterjee (Ed.): LCPC'98, LNCS 1656, pp. 148–165, 1999.

1   Introduction

Parallel platforms not only provide computing cycles, but also supply large amounts of main memory[1] and fast I/O capabilities. The increase in availability of parallel computing resources to a larger user community is far from being matched with the availability of software tools that allow easy access and use of these resources. The potential user of a parallel system may not be familiar or willing to deal with the complexities of efficient parallel programming. As a consequence, valuable computing resources may be underutilized or even wasted.

Languages such as High Performance Fortran (HPF) [19] or SGI Parallel Fortran [38] provide a shared name space programming model augmented by directives that specify how the data is mapped onto the individual processors. The user of such languages is able to avoid many complexities of explicit parallel programming. Based on the user supplied data layout specifications, the compiler and/or operating system ensure the correct computation and data placements. However, the user is still faced with the difficult problem of choosing an efficient data layout. An efficient data layout minimizes communication while maximizing exploitable parallelism. The best choice of a data layout depends on many factors including the program's computation characteristics, the number of processors used, the performed compiler optimizations, the target machine characteristics, and the problem size. All these factors and their interactions make it extremely hard for a user to choose an efficient data layout.

In this paper, we discuss and evaluate techniques for automatic data layout in the context of a programming environment that can target different compilers and different parallel platforms. Portability across different target compilers and platforms is necessary to achieve the goal of efficient, platform independent programming. A crucial challenge for our automatic data layout approach is the design of a performance predictor that is portable across different target systems and is able to rank correctly a given set of data layout alternatives, while being as simple and efficient as possible. This paper describes the design of a compositional performance predictor for an automatic data layout tool.

A prototype tool based on our framework for automatic data layout has been implemented on top of the D System compiler infrastructure developed at Rice University [1]. The Fortran RED (*Retargetable Environment for Datalayout*) tool takes sequential Fortran programs as input and generates HPF programs as output. The input Fortran programs solve regular problems, i.e., use dense arrays as their main data structures. Regular problems allow computation and communication requirements of the application to be derived at compile time. The overall structure of the Fortran RED tool is shown in Figure 1.

Fortran RED builds and examines search spaces of candidate data layouts. A candidate layout is an efficient layout for some part of the program. These program parts are called *program phases* and are automatically determined by

---

[1] In fact, some researchers argue that machines with a large main memory should always have multiple processors in order to make cost–effective use of the memory's capacity and bandwidth [41].

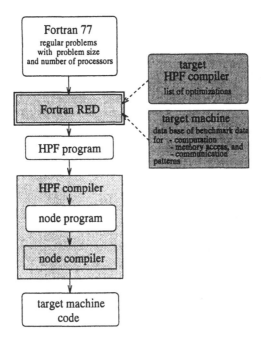

Fig. 1. Overview of Fortran RED

the tool. After the generation of candidate layout search spaces for each phase, a single candidate layout is selected from each search space, resulting in a data layout for the entire program. Note that the optimal selection may consist of candidate data layouts that are each suboptimal for their phases, or may require the remapping of arrays between program phases. A compositional performance estimator based on a compiler, execution, and a machine model is used to predict the execution time of each candidate layout and the costs of possible remappings between candidate data layouts. The compiler model is parameterized with respect to the optimizations performed by the target HPF compiler, including its node compiler. The execution model classifies program parts according to their communication and synchronization patterns in order to identify the critical path for its execution. The machine model uses a set of HPF benchmark kernels to measure the performance of basic computation, memory access, and communication patterns. The benchmark kernels are compiled with the target compiler and executed on the target machine once at tool installation time. The resulting measurements are stored in a performance data base and accessed by the tool during program analysis. A detailed discussion of our general framework for automatic data layout can be found in [22].

The paper is organized as follows. Section 2 presents the scientific program kernel used in our preliminary experiments. The example program that shows the need for a tool such as Fortran RED . Section 3 discusses our compositional performance prediction approach in detail. The paper concludes with a discussion

```
REAL c(N, N), a(N, N), b(N, N)

// loop nest performing READ (c, a, b) operation

DO  iter = 1, max
   // Forward and backward sweeps along rows

   DO j = 2, N
      DO i = 1, N
         c(i, j) = c(i, j) - c(i, j - 1) * a(i, j) / b(i, j - 1)
         b(i, j) = b(i, j) - a(i, j) * a(i, j) / b(i, j - 1)
      ENDDO
   ENDDO

   DO i = 1, N
      c(i, N) = c(i, N) / b(i, N)
   ENDDO

   DO j = N - 1, 1, -1
      DO i = 2, N
         c(i, j) = ( c(i, j) - a(i, j + 1) * c(i, j + 1) ) / b(i, j)
      ENDDO
   ENDDO
   // Downward and upward sweeps along columns

   DO i = 2, N
      DO j = 1, N
         c(i, j) = c(i, j) - c(i - 1, j) * a(i, j) / b(i - 1, j)
         b(i, j) = b(i, j) - a(i, j) * a(i, j) / b(i - 1, j)
      ENDDO
   ENDDO

   DO j = 1, N
      c(N, j) = c(N, j) / b(N, j)
   ENDDO

   DO i = N - 1, 1, -1
      DO j = 1, N
         c(i, j) = ( c(i, j) - a(i + 1, j) * c(i + 1, j) ) / b(i, j)
      ENDDO
   ENDDO

ENDDO

// loop nest performing WRITE (c, b) operation
```

Fig. 2. ADI integration kernel with computation illustration

of experimental results in Section 4, related work in Section 5, and our overall conclusions and directions for future work in Section 6.

2 Example Scientific Program

ADI integration is a technique frequently used to solve partial differential equations (PDEs). Figure 2 shows the code of an ADI kernel computation. The execution of the ADI integration kernel consists of a repeated sequence of forward and backward sweeps along rows, followed by downward and upward sweeps along columns. For the sweeps along the rows, a row layout has the best performance. The same holds for a column layout for the column sweeps. Transposing the arrays between the all row and all column sweeps eliminates communication within the sweeps. In contrast, choosing the same data layout for both, row and column sweeps will avoid communication between the sweeps but will make communication necessary either in the row or column sweeps.

The best data layout choice will depend on the speed of the communication hardware and software of the parallel target architecture, and the ability of the compiler to exploit the available parallelism efficiently. In addition to the compiler dependence, the performance characteristics of the underlying I/O system may be considered in the data layout choice since the program performs read and write disk accesses. Finally, the actual size N of the arrays and the number of available processors may influence the data layout choice. The prototype implementation of Fortran RED generates a data layout for ADI for a given target system, number of available processors, and problem size. The current implementation does not consider the characteristics of the underlying I/O subsystem of the target system.

3   Performance Model

Any optimizing compiler relies on some form of performance prediction to guide its decision process between optimization alternatives. The precision of the performance prediction has to allow the correct ranking of the optimization alternatives, i.e., the relative ranking should match the measured performance improvements of the optimization alternatives. The performance model in Fortran RED has to be able to rank correctly the different candidate data layouts for the entire program or single program segments in most cases. This is a non-trivial challenge since the performance of a candidate layout is compiler, problem size, machine architecture and machine size dependent. Clearly, there is a tradeoff between prediction cost and prediction quality. The performance model has to be portable across different target systems. In fact, the key to the portability of Fortran RED is the portability of its underlying performance prediction model.

The performance model used in Fortran RED is compositional in the sense that it first models the optimizations performed by the compiler, followed by a model for the execution of the generated, message–passing node programs. In turn, the execution model itself relies on a machine model that produces performance numbers for basic computation, communication, and memory access patterns. Based on the machine model predictions, the problem size, and the number of processors, the execution model aggregates the costs along the critical path of the execution.

The compiler model is parameterized with respect to a set of optimization transformations, in particular communication optimizations such as message vectorization and message coalescing. The execution model is target compiler and target architecture independent, but uses the problem size and number of processors to look–up the corresponding performance predictions in the machine model data base. The machine model consists of a collection of kernel programs written in HPF. These programs are compiled with the target compiler, and executed

```
Do i = 1, N
   do j = 1, N
      b(i,j) = a(i-1,1)
```

Fig. 3. Candidate layout dependent communication patterns

on the target system for ranges of different parameter values. These parameters include message length, unit or non-unit stride memory accesses, and number of processors. Retargeting the machine model to a new target system consists of rebuilding the performance data base by compiling and executing all HPF kernel patterns on the new system. This has only to be done once at tool installation time. It is important to note that the same HPF kernel patterns are used for all target systems, allowing true portability. The following sections discuss the compiler, execution, and machine models in more detail.

3.1   Compiler Model

The compiler simulation module analyzes RHS and LHS of assignment statements for each program phase and candidate data layout. In the first step, local iteration sets are computed that represent local loop iterations that have to be executed by each node processor. Based on these iterations, a data structure is built for each phase that maps phase loop levels to a sets of regular section descriptors (RSDs [7,17]) that describe the generated communication patterns. Currently supported communication patterns are shift, send_receive, broadcast, and reduction. Compiler flags are used to enable communication optimizations such as message vectorization, message coalescing, and message aggregation [39,15,4]. These optimizations are simulated using array subscript dependence analysis to determine *when* the communication occurs and RSDs information to describe *what* data elements have to be communicated. A communication pattern that is marked as loop carried at a loop level will lead to a pipelined execution at the entire phase loop nest, where a single execution of the loop at the communication level and the levels below is a single stage of the pipeline.

RSDs are constructed for each distributed dimension of an array separately and stored at the appropriate phase nesting level. The subsequent execution model interprets the overall interactions of the communication patterns. A single array reference, such as $a(i - 1, 1)$ shown in Figure 3, may lead to different communication patterns for different candidate layouts. It is important to note that the goal of the compiler model is not to determine the best communication optimizations or compilation strategy possible, but to be able to simulate the transformation and optimization process performed by a set of target compilers. Clearly, the compiler model has to make tradeoffs between simulation cost and precision.

Assuming that all candidate layouts have the perfect alignment (Align a With b) for the program segment shown in Figure 3, the (*,block) distribution will require the first column of array a to be broadcast to all processors.

In the case of a (block,*) distribution, a single element, nearest neighbor shift communication is sufficient. A (block,block) distribution may result in a multicast and shift communication. The placement of the communication within the loop is compiler dependent.

3.2   Execution Model

Once locations and types of compiler generated communications are known for a candidate layout and its phase, an *execution model* is used to estimate the performance effects of synchronizations induced by the communications. Communication inside a phase may lead to a pipelined execution of the loop. Communication outside of the phase may result in a loosely synchronous execution scheme [12]. In addition, special communication patterns may be recognized that represent global operations such as reductions. Based on the synchronization schemes and the costs for simple communication patterns and basic computations, the execution model determines the overall cost estimate for a candidate layout and its phase.

In a loosely synchronous phase, all processors operate in a loose lockstep, consisting of alternating steps of parallel asynchronous computation and synchronous communication. The performance of the overall program can be estimated by predicting the cost of the "representative" node program that operates on the largest local data segment. This performance model assumes that the largest segment has the highest computation and communication costs and therefore represents the critical path in a loosely synchronous execution of the entire program. The computation and communication costs for the largest local data segment are just added up to determine the overall phase performance.

Performance prediction of a pipelined phase execution is more complicated than in the loosely synchronous case due to the structure of the underlying critical execution path. Execution models that can estimate pipelines of different granularity have been discussed in the literature, for instance in [26,32]. For a pipelined phase, Fortran RED uses the innermost level that carries a true dependence to determine the granularity of the pipeline. This level is referred to as the pipeline level. The performance estimate for a single pipeline stage is the predicted computation and memory access cost for a single iteration at the pipeline level. The number of stages executed by each processor is the number of iterations of the outer loops within the phase that enclose the pipeline level. The execution time for the entire pipeline is determined by the time needed by the last processor to finish all its stages and by its starting delay relative to the first processor of the pipelined execution. The pipeline model implemented in Fortran RED is similar to the model described by Mellor-Crummey, Adve, and Koelbel [26], and allows pipelined execution across different distributed dimensions, i.e., multi-dimensional pipelines. For the special case of a reduction phase, Fortran RED determines the kind of reduction operation and its data type, for instance min, max, or sum of type double_precision. The costs of the global reductions are derived from corresponding HPF reduction benchmark kernels.

PATTERN	NAME	HPF CODE†	PREDICTION

COMMUNICATION

PATTERN	NAME	HPF CODE†	PREDICTION

shift
unit stride
message size=N
#processors=P
	$shift_{unit}(N,P)$	`Dimension x(N,P), y(N,P)`
		`Align x With y`
		`Processors t(P)`
		`Distrib (*,block)x Onto t`
		`do j=2,P`
		`do i=1,N`
		`  x(i,j) = y(i,j-1)`
			$exec\_time$

broadcast
unit stride
message size=N
#processors=P
	$broadcast_{unit}(N,P)$	`Dimension x(N,P), y(N)`
		`Align y(i) With x(i,1)`
		`Processors t(P)`
		`Distrib (*,block)x Onto t`
		`do j=1,P`
		`do i=1,N`
		`  x(i,j) = y(i)`
			$exec\_time$

MEMORY ACCESS

PATTERN	NAME	HPF CODE†	PREDICTION

write array ref.
unit stride
	$cache\_hit_{write}$	`do j=1,N`
		`do i=1,N`
		`  x(i,j)=1.0`
			$exec\_time/N^2$

read array ref.
unit stride
	$cache\_hit_{read}$	`do j=1,N`
		`do i=1,N`
		`  x(i,j)=y(i,j)`
			$(exec\_time/N^2) -$
			$\quad cache\_hit_{write}$

write array ref.
nonunit stride
	$cache\_miss_{write}$	`do i=1,N‡`
		`do j=1,N`
		`  x(i,j)=1.0`
			$exec\_time/N^2$

read array ref.
nonunit stride
	$cache\_miss_{read}$	`do i=1,N‡`
		`do j=1,N`
		`  x(i,j)=y(i,j)`
			$(exec\_time/N^2) -$
			$\quad cache\_miss_{write}$

COMPUTATION

PATTERN	NAME	HPF CODE†	PREDICTION

addition	$cost_+$	`do j=1,N`
		`do i=1,N`
		`  x(i,j)=x(i,j)+y(i,j)`
			$(exec\_time/N^2) -$
			$(cache\_hit_{read} +$
			$cache\_hit_{write})$

multiplication	$cost_*$	`do j=1,N`
		`do i=1,N`
		`  x(i,j)=x(i,j)*y(i,j)`
			$(exec\_time/N^2) -$
			$(cache\_hit_{read} +$
			$cache\_hit_{write})$

† Unless stated otherwise, arrays are declared of size (N,N) and stored in column–major order.

‡ The value of N is big enough to generate cache misses for each innermost j iteration.

Table 1. Example communication, memory access, and computation benchmark kernels

3.3 Machine Model

The machine model consists of a set of HPF programs that measure the execution times of basic computations, memory access, and communication patterns. A single pattern may generate a set of different performance numbers. For example, each global communication pattern is executed for different message sizes and numbers of processors.

Communication Model For each communication pattern, the actual size of the messages and the number of processors involved have to be determined. The current model does not consider contention between groups of processors. If two groups of processors have logically independent communication operations, each operation is predicted separately for the number of processors in each group. Table 1 shows two benchmark kernels, for nearest neighbor *shift* communication and for global *broadcast* communication.

Computation Model Two computation benchmark kernels are listed in Table 1. Based on the timings, the computation costs of basic operations are determined by subtracting out the memory access costs. The measured computation costs may be interpreted differently for different target architectures. For example, if the target architecture has two floating point units, the benchmark kernel may represent the ideal situation where computations are independent. Additional analysis may be needed to model computation that is not independent, i.e., may lead to stalls in the different floating point units. The current prototype of Fortran RED does not contain an instruction scheduling simulator, but adds up the individual costs of of operations.

Memory Hierarchy Model The memory model tries to capture the cost for the address computation and the cost resulting from possible cache misses. This is done by assigning *each* array reference a unit stride array reference cost ($cache\_hit_{read/write}$), and in the case of a cache miss, add an additional cache miss penalty ($cache\_miss_{read/write}$). The cache model to determine the overall cache miss penalty is based on the work by McKinley, Carr and Tseng [27]. Our model is simpler in the sense that it relies on basic pattern matching to identify spatial and temporal reuse. Spatial or temporal reuse across iterations of the innermost loop, or cache conflict misses [18] are not considered in the current model. However, a model to predict the number of capacity misses is used similar to the model introduced by Ferrante, Sarkar, and Thrash [11].

All array references in the loop are partitioned into RefGroups, where each RefGroup contributes a single cache miss penalty to the overall cache miss penalty for an innermost loop iteration. The RefGroup partitioning avoids the overcounting of cache misses since only the first reference in the group will result in a cache miss, followed by cache hits for the remaining references in the group. RefGroups that contain only references that are invariant within the innermost loop, or have only unit stride accesses do not contribute to the cache miss penalty. The remaining groups contain non–unit stride accesses and are classified as either

```
Do i = 2, N      // e.g., parameter (N = 256)
   Do j = 1, N
      c(i,j) = c(i,j) - c(i-1,j) * a(i,j) / b(i-1,j)
      b(i,j) = b(i,j) - a(i,j) * a(i,j) / b(i-1,j)
```

Fig. 4. Example loop with non–unit stride accesses

read or write. A write group contains at least one array reference that occurs on the left–hand–side of an assignment statement.

A simple model for capacity misses determines whether cache misses occur for non-unit stride accesses. Basically, the model determines the number of distinct cache lines touched by an innermost iteration. If this number exceeds the available number of lines in the cache, a cache miss is predicted.

Assuming column-major order allocation of multi-dimensional arrays, the example loop of our ADI kernel in Figure 4 has three RefGroups, namely $\{c(i,j), c(i-1,j)\}$, $\{b(i,j), b(i-1,j)\}$, and $\{a(i,j)\}$. The first two groups are write groups, and the last is a read group. All three groups are non-unit stride. For each group, the number of cache misses is determined based on the cache architecture of the target machine and the sizes of the data segments allocated on each processor. The current Fortran RED implementation uses the following simple model to determine cache capacity misses of a reference group in an innermost loop with n iteration:

$$
\# \text{ cache misses} = \begin{cases} n & \text{if } s \geq l \text{ and } n > S \\ \frac{n*s}{l} & \text{if } s < l \text{ and } \frac{n*s}{l} > S \\ 0 & \text{otherwise} \end{cases}
$$

where s is the access stride, l is the cache line size, and S is the number of cache sets available for the reference group. In the current implementation, the number of available sets is the total number of sets in the cache divided by the number of arrays referenced in the loop. In the example of Figure 4, a perfect alignment and column distribution of all three arrays onto two processors[2] will result in local innermost iterations of size $n = 128$ and a stride $s = 256$. Assuming a cache with 256 sets and a line size $l = 32$, the available number of sets for each array is set to $S = \lfloor 256/3 \rfloor = 85$. As a result, each reference group contributes one cache misses to each innermost iteration. The final memory access cost, including the cache miss penalty for capacity misses is

$$
2 * cache\_hit_{write} + 8 * cache\_hit_{read} +
$$

$$
2 * (cache\_miss_{write} - cache\_hit_{write}) +
$$

$$
cache\_miss_{read} - cache\_hit_{read}
$$

Each of the 10 references in the loop is assigned a cache hit cost, with additional penalties for three cache misses, two due to write accesses and one due to read accesses.

---

[2] Processor procs(2); Align a With b,c ; Distribute (*,block) a Onto procs

	PGI pghpf/xlf-1.1	IBM xlhpf/xlf-1.3
message vectorization	✓	✓
message coalescing	✓	✓
message aggregation		✓
communication routine calls	✓	
explicit send/receive		✓
software pipeling	✓	✓

Table 2. Characteristics of the HPF target compilers

4   Experiments

The alternating direction implicit integration kernel (Adi) as shown in Figure 2 was the basis for our preliminary experiments. There were two target systems for Fortran RED , PGI's HPF compiler with IBM's xlf version 1.1 compiler as its node compiler, and IBM's HPF compilers with IBM's xlf version 1.3 node compiler. In both cases, the IBM SP–2 distributed memory multiprocessor was the target architecture. Experiments were performed for 4, 8, and 16 thin nodes (PowerPC2). Both target compilers were used at the highest compiler optimization level (-O3). The two commercially available HPF compilers (IBM's xlhpf/xlf-1.3 and PGI's pghpf/xlf-1.1) use different communication generation strategies. For a nearest neighbor *shift* communication pattern, PGI's pghpf compiler generates a single call to a global communication routine that implements the pattern. In contrast, IBM's xlhpf compiler generates explicit calls to lower level send and receive communication routines for the pattern. Using a single global communication routine allows runtime communication optimization since the decisions regarding execution order and type of lower level send and receive routines may be postponed until the global routine is actually called. Inserting send and receive communications directly into the program allows compile time optimizations such as message latency hiding by moving sends ahead of receives across program segments. However, runtime optimizations are more restricted since the placement and type of communication routines are determined at compile time. Both HPF compilers use message vectorization and message coalescing, but only IBM's compiler performs message aggregation [39]. Both compilation systems perform software pipeling at the node program level.

A summary of the HPF compiler characteristics is given in Table 2. These characteristics were provided to Fortran RED as the description of the target compiler. For the experiments, our prototype system simulated message vectorization and coalescing. In addition to the results of the benchmark kernels in the performance data base, Fortran RED exploited knowledge about the structure of the PowerPC2 node architecture such as the cache design of the IBM SP–2. The data cache size is 126Kbytes, with 256bytes for each cache line (512 sets).

For the Adi code, Fortran RED generated candidate layouts consisting of perfect alignments of the two dimensional arrays (Align a With b, c) and all possible combinations of one and two dimensional block distributions for 4, 8, and 16 processors. In order to validate the precision of the performance prediction component of the tool, we hand coded the corresponding static global layouts in HPF and measured their execution times on the target systems. In addition, a dynamic layout was considered that performed array transposes between the row and column sweeps of the computation. Figures 5 and 6 show the measured and predicted execution times of the different global data layouts for Adi for the two target system on 4, 8 and 16 processors. Each figure shows four data points: problem sizes (144x144), (272x272), (400x400), and (528x528) of double precision.

For the xlhpf/xlf-1.3 target compiler, the best data layout varied with the number of processors and problem sizes. In contrast, PGI's pghpf/xlf-1.1 compiler always performed best using a dynamic data layout. Fortran RED was able to predict the performance of all measured data layouts with high accuracy. This is a remarkable result, considering the complexity of the target compiler and target architecture. In particular, the tool always selected the best data layout. For the pghpf/xlf-1.1 target compiler, Fortran RED failed to predict the best layout in four cases (see Figure 6, 4 processors), which resulted in an execution time increase of up to 89% due to the suboptimal selection. In all other cases, the best data layout was selected. Although the predictions for most data layouts were much lower than the actual measurements, this underestimations was not significant enough to lead to the wrong data layout selection (with the exception of the four cases mentioned above). In addition, the ranking of some suboptimal data layouts were not preserved in the prediction. As it turned out, the 1.1 version of the xlf compiler generated redundant code within software pipelined and unrolled loops[3]. This problem has been fixed in version 1.3. Unfortunately, we were not able to rerun the experiments with the PGI compiler and the updated version of the xlf compiler due to the closure of the Cornell Theory Center. However, it is interesting to note that we were able to find this bug because of our performance prediction results.

5 Related Work

The problem of automatic data layout has been addressed by many researchers [3,9,16,20,23,24,25,34,6,21]. The presented solutions differ significantly in the assumptions that are made about the input language, the possible set of data layouts, the compilation system, and the target machine architecture.

Our work is similar in nature to the recent work done by Anderson and Lam at Stanford University [3,2], Chatterjee, Gilbert, Schreiber, Sheffler, and Pugh at RIACS, Xerox Parc, and the University of Maryland [37,8], Palermo and Banerjee at the University of Illinois at Urbana Champaign [31,30], Ayguadé, Garcia, Girones, Labarta, Torres and Valero at the University of Catalunya in Barcelona, [14,13], and Ning, Van Dongen, and Gao at CRIM and McGill University [28]. In contrast to previous work, Fortran RED is design to target different compilation systems and parallel architectures, allowing program portability across a

---

[3] Source: Henry Zongaro, XL Fortran/XL HPF Compiler Development, IBM Toronto

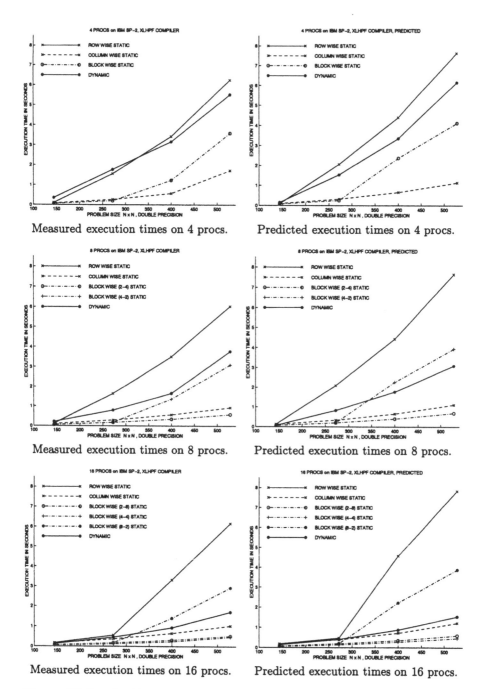

Fig. 5. IBM's xlhpf/xlf-1.3 compiler and 4, 8, and 16 processors of IBM SP-2.

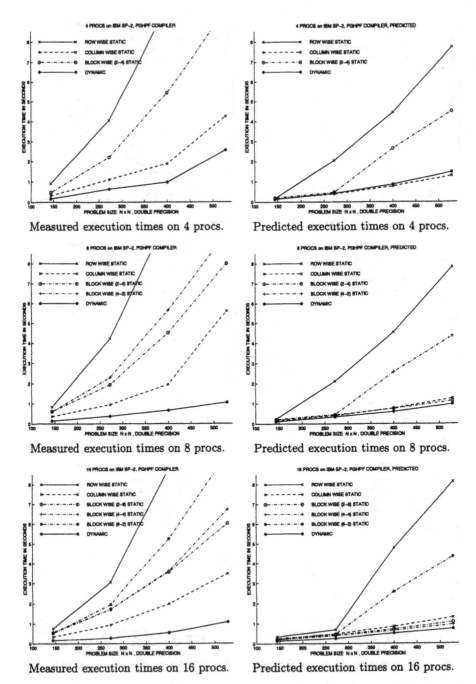

Fig. 6. PGI's pghpf/xlf-1.1 compiler and 4, 8, and 16 processors of IBM SP-2.

range of parallel platforms. A crucial component within Fortran RED is performance prediction. Our work on performance prediction in the context of Fortran RED has been based on our previous work on "training sets" [5]. This work is very similar to the *micro-benchmarking* approach developed by Saavedra and Smith [36,35]. The importance of performance prediction for optimizing compilers has been recognized by many researchers and several proposals have been published in the literature, such as [40,33,10,29]. However, accurate and cost efficient performance prediction, in particular for superscalar architectures, is still an open research problem.

6   Conclusion

This paper discussed preliminary experiences with Fortran RED , a tool designed to support Fortran on a variety of different parallel target platforms. The tool uses HPF as an intermediate program representation. The portability requires that Fortran RED is able to predict the quality of data layouts across different HPF compilers and target architectures. The performance prediction component within the tool uses benchmarks of communication, computation, and memory access patterns to determine the expected performance of a given data layout. These benchmark patterns are written in HPF to allow portability. Experiments were performed for two different target systems consisting of PGI's and IBM's HPF compilers for the IBM SP–2 multiprocessor, and a single scientific application. For 20 out of 24 test cases, Fortran RED determined the best data layout, where a test case is a particular problem size and number of processors used. For most test cases, the data layout choices were non-trivial, and a wrong data layout choice would result in a dramatic reduction in program performance. For the IBM-xlhpf/SP–2 target system, the performance predictions had very high accuracy. However, in particular for the PGI-pghpf/SP–2 target system, the tool failed to rank subsets of suboptimal data layout alternatives correctly. We believe that this problem resulted from a previously unknown compiler performance bug in the IBM xlf-1.1 compiler and should disappear by using the updated version xlf-1.3.

Clearly, more experimental results are needed to validate our overall approach. The preliminary experiments showed that one of the main challenges in designing a tool such as Fortran RED is accurate performance prediction. A compositional performance prediction approach is needed to model the different components of a target system such as the HPF and node compilers, and the cache. We are currently investigating performance prediction at the node compiler level that takes superscalar optimizations and processor characteristics such as multiple functional units into account. In addition, models to predict cache conflict misses will be included.

References

1. V. Adve, A. Carle, E. Granston, S. Hiranandani, K. Kennedy, C. Koelbel, U. Kremer, J. Mellor-Crummey, C-W. Tseng, and S. Warren. Requirements for data-parallel programming environments. *IEEE Parallel and Distributed Technology*, 2(3):48–58, 1994.

2. J. Anderson. *Automatic Computation and Data Decomposition for Multiprocessors.* PhD thesis, Stanford University, March 1997.
3. J. Anderson and M. Lam. Global optimizations for parallelism and locality on scalable parallel machines. In *Proceedings of the SIGPLAN '93 Conference on Programming Language Design and Implementation,* pages 112–125, 1993.
4. V. Balasundaram, G. Fox, K. Kennedy, and U. Kremer. An interactive environment for data partitioning and distribution. In *Proceedings of the 5th Distributed Memory Computing Conference,* pages 1160–1170, 1990.
5. V. Balasundaram, G. Fox, K. Kennedy, and U. Kremer. A static performance estimator to guide data partitioning decisions. In *Proceedings of the Third ACM SIGPLAN Symposium on Principles and Practice of Parallel Programming,* pages 213–223, 1991.
6. D. Bau, I. Kodukula, V. Kotlyar, K. Pingali, and P. Stodghill. Solving alignment using elementary linear algebra. In *Proceedings of the Seventh Workshop on Languages and Compilers for Parallel Computing,* Ithaca, New York, August 1994.
7. D. Callahan and K. Kennedy. Analysis of interprocedural side effects in a parallel programming environment. In *Proceedings of the First International Conference on Supercomputing.* Springer-Verlag, Athens, Greece, June 1987.
8. S. Chatterjee, J. R. Gilbert, R. Schreiber, and T. Sheffler. Array distribution in data-parallel programs. In *Proceedings of the Seventh Workshop on Languages and Compilers for Parallel Computing,* Ithaca, New York, August 1994.
9. S. Chatterjee, J.R. Gilbert, R. Schreiber, and S-H. Teng. Automatic array alignment in data-parallel programs. In *Proceedings of the Twentieth Annual ACM Symposium on the Principles of Programming Languages,* pages 16–28, 1993.
10. T. Fahringer and H.P. Zima. A static parameter based performance prediction tool for parallel programs. In *Proceedings of the 1993 ACM International Conference on Supercomputing,* Tokyo, Japan, July 1993.
11. J. Ferrante, V. Sarkar, and W. Thrash. On estimating and enhancing cache effectiveness. *Proceedings of the Fourth Workshop on Languages and Compilers for Parallel Computing – LNCS, Springer Verlag,* 589:328–343, 1991.
12. G. Fox, M. Johnson, G. Lyzenga, S. Otto, J. Salmon, and D. Walker. *Solving Problems on Concurrent Processors.* Prentice-Hall, Englewood Cliffs, NJ, 1988.
13. J. Garcia. *Automatic Data Distribution for Massively Parallel Processors.* PhD thesis, Universitat Politècnica de Catalunya, Barcelona, April 1997.
14. J. Garcia, E. Ayguadé, and J. Labarta. Dynamic data distribution with control flow analysis. In *Proceedings of Supercomputing '96,* 1996.
15. M. Gerndt. Updating distributed variables in local computations. *Concurrency—Practice & Experience,* 2(3):171–193, September 1990.
16. M. Gupta. *Automatic Data Partitioning on Distributed Memory Multicomputers.* PhD thesis, University of Illinois at Urbana-Champaign, September 1992.
17. P. Havlak and K. Kennedy. An implementation of interprocedural bounded regular section analysis. *IEEE Transactions on Parallel and Distributed Systems,* 2(3):350–360, July 1991.
18. J. Hennessy and D. Patterson. *Computer Architecture A Quantitative Approach (2nd edition).* Morgan Kaufmann Publishers, San Mateo, CA, 1996.
19. High Performance Fortran Forum. High Performance Fortran language specification. *Scientific Programming,* 2(1-2):1–170, 1993.
20. D. Hudak and S. Abraham. Compiler techniques for data partitioning of sequentially iterated parallel loops. In *Proceedings of the 1990 ACM International Conference on Supercomputing,* pages 187–200, 1990.

21. W. Kelly and W. Pugh. Minimizing communication while preserving parallelism. In *Proceedings of the 1996 ACM International Conference on Supercomputing*, pages 52–60, Philadelphia, PA, May 1996.

22. K. Kennedy and U. Kremer. Automatic data layout for distributed memory machines. *ACM Transactions on Programming Languages and Systems*, 20(4):869–916, July 1998.

23. K. Knobe, J.D. Lukas, and W.J. Dally. Dynamic alignment on distributed memory systems. In *Proceedings of the Third Workshop on Compilers for Parallel Computers*, Vienna, Austria, July 1992.

24. P. Lee and T-B. Tsai. Compiling efficient programs for tightly-coupled distributed memory computers. In *Proceedings of the 1993 International Conference on Parallel Processing*, pages II161–II165, St. Charles, IL, August 1993.

25. J. Li and M. Chen. Index domain alignment: Minimizing cost of cross-referencing between distributed arrays. In *Frontiers90: The 3rd Symposium on the Frontiers of Massively Parallel Computation*, College Park, MD, October 1990.

26. J. Mellor-Crummey, V. Adve, and C. Koelbel. The Compiler's Role in Analysis and Tuning of Data-Parallel Programs. In *Proceedings of The Second Workshop on Environments and Tools for Parallel Scientific Computing*, pages 211–220, 1994.

27. K. S. McKinley, S. Carr, and C.-W. Tseng. Improving data locality with loop transformations. *ACM Transactions on Programming Languages and Systems*, 18(4):424–453, July 1996.

28. Q. Ning, V. V. Dongen, and G. R. Gao. Automatic data and computation decomposition for distributed memory machines. In *Proceedings of the 28th Annual Hawaii International Conference on System Sciences*, Maui, Hawaii, January 1995.

29. D.B. Noonburg and J.P. Shen. Theoretical modeling of superscalar processor performance. In *Proceedings of the 27th Annual International Symposium on Microarchitecture*, San Jose, CA, December 1994.

30. D. Palermo. *Compiler Techniques for Optimizing Communication and Data Distribution for Distributed–Memory Multicomputers*. PhD thesis, University of Illinois at Urbana–Champaign, June 1996. Available as CRHC-96-09.

31. D. Palermo and P. Banerjee. Automatic selection of dynamic data partitioning schemes for distributed-memory multicomputers. Technical Report CRHC-95-09, University of Illinois at Urbana-Champaign, April 1995.

32. D. Palermo, E. Su, J. A. Chandy, and P. Banerjee. Communication optimizations used in the PARADIGM compiler for distributed-memory multicomputers. In *Proceedings of the 1994 International Conference on Parallel Processing*, 1994.

33. M. Parashar, S. Hariri, H. Haupt, and G. Fox. Interpreting the performance of HPF/Fortran90D. In *Proceedings of Supercomputing '94*, 1994.

34. J. Ramanujam and P. Sadayappan. A methodology for parallelizing programs for multicomputers and complex memory multiprocessors. In *Proceedings of Supercomputing '89*, pages 637–646, Reno, NV, November 1989.

35. R.H. Saavedra and A.J. Smith. Performance characterization of optimizing compilers. *IEEE Transactions on Software Engineering*, 21(7):615–628, July 1995.

36. R.H. Saavedra-Barrera. *CPU Performance Evaluation·and Execution Time Prediction Using Narrow Spectrum Benchmarking*. PhD thesis, U.C. Berkeley, February 1992. UCB/CSD-92-684.

37. T. Sheffler, R. Schreiber, W. Pugh, J.R. Gilbert, and S. Chatterjee. Efficient distribution analysis via graph contraction. *International Journal of Parallel Programming*, 24(6):599–620, December 1996.

38. Silicon Graphics Inc. *F77 User's Manual: Chapter 6 – Parallel Programming on Origin2000*, 1997.

39. C-W. Tseng. *An Optimizing Fortran D Compiler for MIMD Distributed-Memory Machines*. PhD thesis, Rice University, January 1993. Rice COMP TR93-199.
40. K-Y. Wang. Precise compile-time performance prediction for superscalar-based computers. In *Proceedings of the SIGPLAN '94 Conference on Programming Language Design and Implementation*, Orlando, FL, June 1994.
41. D. Wood and M. Hill. Cost–effective parallel computing. *IEEE Computer*, 1995.

Automatic Parallelization of C by Means of Language Transcription

Richard L. Kennell and Rudolf Eigenmann*

School of Electrical and Computer Engineering, Purdue University
West Lafayette, IN 47907-1285, USA
{kennell,eigenman}@ecn.purdue.edu

Abstract. The automatic parallelization of C has always been frustrated by pointer arithmetic, irregular control flow and complicated data aggregation. Each of these problems is similar to familiar challenges encountered in the parallelization of more rigidly-structured languages, such as FORTRAN77. By creating a mapping from one language to the other, we can expose the capabilities of existing automatically parallelizing compilers to the C language. In this paper, we describe our approach to mapping applications written in C to a form suitable for the Polaris source-to-source FORTRAN compiler. We also describe the improvements in the compiled applications realized by this second level of transformation and show results for a small application in comparison to commercial compilers. We describe our model of a Virtual Speculative Parallel Machine as the target of our compiler.

1 Introduction

Polaris is an automatically parallelizing source-to-source FORTRAN compiler. It accepts FORTRAN77 input and produces a FORTRAN output in a new dialect that supports explicit parallelism by means of embedded directives such as the OpenMP [12] or Sun FORTRAN Directives [14]. The benefit that Polaris provides is in automating the analysis of the loops and array accesses in the application to determine how they can best be expressed to exploit available parallelism. The analysis of typical FORTRAN77 applications is more straightforward than with other languages, because parallelism is commonly expressed using a limited set of loop constructs and array declarations. This allows Polaris to perform complicated interprocedural and global analysis without risk of misinterpretation of programmer intent. Experimental results show that Polaris is able to markedly improve the run-time of applications without additional programmer direction [8,4].

The expressiveness and low-level memory access primitives of C make it ideally suited for translation into efficient machine language. However, these

---

* This work was supported in part by U. S. Army contract #DABT63-95-C-0097, an NSF CAREER award, and Purdue Research Foundation. This work is not necessarily representative of the positions or policies of the U. S. Army or the Government.

S. Chatterjee (Ed.): LCPC'98, LNCS 1656, pp. 166–180, 1999.

low-level operations interfere with further optimizations such as parallelization, software pipelining and various types of loop transformations. Much research has been performed in the areas of pointer analysis [6,7,9] and control-flow analysis to not only ensure the correctness of program transformations, but also to achieve efficient execution on a given target architecture [3]. Despite these significant contributions, state-of-the-art C compilers are not able to optimize C programs to the level possible in Fortran compilers. For obvious reasons, rewriting C programs in Fortran is not an option. To take advantage of higher optimization levels nevertheless, in this paper, we study the transcription of C programs into the representation used by a Fortran optimizer.

The immediate question we attempt to answer is the following: to what degree is available Fortran compiler technology capable of optimizing C programs? A secondary, long-term goal of this work is to develop a C optimizer that generates efficient code for a Virtual Speculative Parallel Machine (VSPM). Such execution engines have recently been proposed [10,13]. However, their compiler interface is an open issue. For our purposes, the VSPM is modeled as an engine that can execute parallel regions correctly, even if they contain data dependences. However, if there are many dependence violations at runtime, the performance may degrade (because the VSPM may perform roll backs and re-execute serially). The VSPM interface permits the compiler to identify provable data dependences and provably independent loops. In these cases, the VSPM may insert synchronizations or execute in parallel without speculation, respectively. In all other cases, speculative parallel execution is used, potentially incurring overhead. To keep this overhead low, the compiler identifies as many provable data dependences and independent references as possible and leaves the resolution of *may dependences* up to the VSPM. In this paper, we do not yet provide such dependence information. However the VSPM execution model is important in that we can view the compiler's task solely as a performance optimization rather than a strict enforcement of correctness. This is crucial for optimizing C programs, where otherwise conservative assumptions may severely limit performance.

The remainder of this paper is organized as follows. In Section 2, we describe the construction of our transcription system. We examine related research in Section 3, describe performance benefits of the system in Section 4 and conclude with Section 5.

2   The Cepheus Transcriber

We have created a tool that transcribes C programs into a FORTRAN-like representation. For the sake of presentation we choose actual FORTRAN text as the target language. In actuality, the ultimate representation is a FORTRAN intermediate form–specifically, the representation of the Polaris compiler. Our transcriber uses three basic ideas:

- A pointer is simply an index into an array that spans the entire memory. In this sense, pointer analysis can then be reduced to array region analysis. By creating overlapping arrays–one for each basic type and one for each field of each structure type–we further subdivide the analysis.

- Many for loops in C can be transformed into Fortran DO loops using standard control flow analysis techniques. More esoteric control-flow can be expressed with GOTO statements.
- Arrays of aggregate data declarations may be translated as separate (overlapping) array declarations, allowing the FORTRAN compiler to use traditional analysis techniques.

We call our transcriber Cepheus[1], and, though it is separate now, we expect to integrate it with the Polaris translator in the near future. The current implementation of Cepheus does not transcribe the full C semantics. Consequently, some programs will not be able to take advantage of the subsequent Polaris optimization step. One goal of this research is to determine how successful such a transcription can be and where C-language-specific optimization methods become necessary.

2.1   Representation of data

FORTRAN77 does not have the flexibility of lexical scoping that C does. The two primary means of sharing "global" data between two functions or subroutines is by either passing values through formal parameters or by sharing *common blocks*. Cepheus allocates a common block to represent each variable declared outside of any function's scope. The semantics of the storage class (e.g. extern, static) and initialization are also represented in the transcribed code.

Function arguments in C are *passed by value* but arguments in FORTRAN are *passed by address*. In the transcribed output, all variables are passed in the natural FORTRAN manner, except that data that must conform to pass-by-value semantics is copied to a temporary value within the function that is used in place of the formal argument. This ensures that the callee cannot modify the caller's value.

Cepheus translates an aggregate data structure, such as a struct or union, into a generic block of data that has an EQUIVALENCE relationship with each of the variables and arrays that represent its fields at the proper offsets. The interaction between global data, formal arguments and structure elements is a complex relationship. Many of the transformations that Cepheus performs are devoted to making sure that all data is represented correctly and most efficiently. These transformations are explained in detail in [11].

2.2   Arrays and pointers

The C language supports operators that obtain the address of (&) almost any data item and dereference an address (*) to access the value stored there. A

---

[1] Cepheus is a five-star constellation that is near to but does not include the North Star (Polaris).

naïve way to translate these operators into Fortran would be to provide external functions that mimic these operations. By doing so, a translator would introduce a great deal of overhead to a ubiquitous C programming idiom. It would also make data flow analysis on simple pointer operations nearly impossible due to the inability of the back-end FORTRAN compiler to analyze externally compiled functions.

Cepheus avoids these problems by representing each pointer as an index into a single array. When a pointer is used to refer to elements in more than one array or when it refers to dynamically-allocated storage, the corresponding array for that pointer is forced to be represented as a *type-specific universal array.*

For each C type and for each field of each structure, a type-specific universal array is allocated. Each of these arrays starts at address zero and is used to alias the entire logical address space. This effectively provides an efficient alternative to using an external function to dereference a pointer of a specified type. Universal arrays are not defined in the FORTRAN77 code but are, instead, created by special contract with the linker. Presently, we assume a fixed name for each array. For instance, the universal array corresponding to the C float type is called U_FLOAT.

Figure 1 shows the in-memory layout of several universal arrays that exist for an application containing a two element structure. Each universal array starts at address zero. The decl array occurs at some arbitrary location in memory, and its position is shown by the shaded regions of memory. The U_XYZ_I and U_XYZ_C entries are also considered to be disjoint despite their contiguity in the structure definition. Furthermore, note that the alignment, padding and field offsets are expected to be similar to those in C.

```
struct {
    int  i[3];
    char c;
} decl[2];
```

Fig. 1. Overlapping universal arrays.

When Cepheus must obtain the address of a variable it uses an external function called ADDROF that accepts the variable as an argument–which, by FORTRAN77 convention, is always passed by address–and returns its address to the caller. We can then obtain the address of any variable in the program and refer to its contents by accessing the universal array that corresponds to its type.

Cepheus attempts to represent all pointers as indices into local or global arrays and to avoid referencing universal arrays whenever possible. In doing so, it maximizes the possibilities for optimization by the FORTRAN back-end compiler. Therefore, universal arrays are only used when other representation will not suffice. However, we note that the reference to arbitrary variables through universal arrays is not a panacea for all pointer representation issues. Primarily, it introduces aliases that cannot easily be resolved by the transcriber. Rather than attempting to analyze and detect this problem, we simply allow the introduction of aliases so long as the transcription of the program would remain semantically correct for an execution model with sequential consistency and assume that our VSPM will handle the detection and correction at runtime. This is a situation where further analysis can provide an indication to our execution environment as to whether an alias definitely does, definitely does not or may include a potential alias. To do so, we expect that the ADDROF will eventually be incorporated into our target intermediate representation in order to assist the analysis of the cases where using a universal array is inevitable.

Figure 2 shows the transcription of a code segment that adds the elements of two arrays–one consisting of integers and the other of double precision values– and stores them into another array. Since the pointers in the add() routine do not refer to local arrays, they are treated as pointers into universal arrays that correspond to types int and double. The main() function allocates the arrays from the heap and Cepheus translates the resulting address into the appropriate index of the universal array of that type. Even though the allocation of the universal arrays overlap with each other and with every local and global variable in the application, we make the legitimate assumption that only one type of data at a time will exist at a given address. The FORTRAN compiler can treat accesses to these heap-allocated items as being independent as would normally happen with disjoint arrays. For instance, in the example, accesses to the U_INT array are known not to be aliased to the U_DOUBLE array. Furthermore, the elements pointed to by DP1 and DP2 can be determined not to be aliased to each other by range analysis and interprocedural analysis. Therefore, a typical FORTRAN compiler can fully parallelize the add() routine.

Cepheus can perform its analysis on *well-behaved* C applications that do not arbitrarily cast between incompatible pointer types. A cast from one pointer type to another effectively *unifies* the two types. If the types have different sizes, the unification is defined to be incompatible. However, if the cast is from a void* to another pointer type, no unification is considered and the pointer is simply re-typed. The cases where multiple possible alternative types exist in the same context is beyond the scope of our current consideration.

To perform pointer-to-array-index conversions, the transformation phases in Cepheus check each statement that causes a value assignment to occur either by a traditional variable assignment (=), a return or as a passed parameter. If the type of the assignment is a pointer, the base address of the value provider is registered in the Cepheus data structure that represents the assignment target. For example, in the piece of code in Figure 3(a), the base address for the value provider of the first assignment (&arr[15]) is simply arr. The second assignment, since we know that the base address of p is arr, has the same base address. The third assignment is not a pointer type and does not record a base address for

```c
void add(double *dp1, double *result, int *ip) {
    double *dp2;
    for(dp2=result; dp2<&result[1000]; dp2++) {
        *dp2 = *dp1 + *ip;
        *dp1++; *ip++;
    }
}
void main() {
    int    *ip;
    double *dp;
    ip = (int*)    malloc(1000*sizeof(int));
    dp = (double*)malloc(2000*sizeof(double));
    add(dp, &dp[1000], ip);
}
```

```fortran
      SUBROUTINE ADD(DP1_ARG,RESULT_ARG,IP_ARG)
      DOUBLE PRECISION DP1_ARG(0:0)
      DOUBLE PRECISION RESULT_ARG(0:0)
      INTEGER IP_ARG(0:0)
      INTEGER DP2, DP1, RESULT, IP

      DP1=0
      RESULT=0
      IP=0
      DO DP2=RESULT,RESULT+1000-1,1
         RESULT_ARG(DP2)=DP1_ARG(DP1)+DBLE(IP_ARG(IP))
         DP1=DP1+1
         IP=IP+1
      END DO
      END

      SUBROUTINE MAIN()
      INTEGER DP
      INTEGER U_INT(0:0)
      COMMON /U_INT/U_INT
      INTEGER MALLOC
      INTEGER IP
      DOUBLE PRECISION U_DOUBLE(0:0)
      COMMON /U_DOUBLE/U_DOUBLE

      IP=ISHFT(MALLOC(1000*4),-2)
      DP=ISHFT(MALLOC(2000*8),-3)
      CALL ADD(U_DOUBLE(DP),U_DOUBLE(DP+1000),U_INT(IP))
      END
```

Fig. 2. C program to add two arrays and its Cepheus-FORTRAN77 transcription.

the representation of x. In Figure 3(b), similarly, all pointer assignments involve
the base address arr and can be represented as index offsets into arr.

A different scenario is present in Figure 3(c), where a single pointer points to
two different arrays. In the resulting FORTRAN output, p will be represented as
an index into the universal array of integers. This shows a shortcoming of using
a simple transcriber: in each of the assignments, it is clear from the context of
the program which array p is pointing to at which times. It would be possible to
avoid upgrading it to universal status if the transcriber could keep track of which
point in the procedure the assignment took place. However, in more complicated
control-flow this would be more difficult to ascertain, and, in general, such a
representation would require the use of a full data-flow analysis in order to be
realized.

```
void ex_a() {          void ex_b()            void ex_d() {
    int arr[100];          int arr[100];          int arr1[10];
    int *p;                int *p, *q;            int arr2[20];
    int x;                                        int *p;
                          p = arr;               int x;
                          q = p;
    p = &arr[15];         q = &arr[10];          p = arr1;
    p = p + 1;            x = q[5];              x = *p;
    x = *p;              }                       p = arr2;
}                                                x = *p;
                                                }

        (a)                    (b)                    (c)
```

Fig. 3. Pointer assignments.

Cepheus also supports the translation of multi-dimensional arrays and multi-
level pointers. This is an area of representation that, despite its generality of
manipulation in a typical C compiler, was difficult to establish properly in the
FORTRAN domain. The problem revolves around the disparity between pointers
and arrays in C. For instance, Figure 4 shows proper FORTRAN transcriptions
of C subroutines that contain two-dimensional arrays. In each case, the last
statement assigns, to x, the value of a two-dimensional array reference. In the
first case, this is a straightforward two dimensional array reference. The array
indices are swapped as per the row-major/column-major differences between C
and FORTRAN. The second example shows a slightly more detailed situation
where a pointer is used to reference the element of the array. Here the pointer is
represented by a composite index into the array and is broken apart at the time
of access. Note that in some implementations, the array might also be referenced
with simply x=arr2(p,0).

Figure 4(c) shows the somewhat surprising result of a reference to an array
of pointers. Here, Cepheus records the base address for arrp[] as being arr.
Therefore, a double dereference of arrp constitutes a reference to arr.

```
void ex_a() {                      subroutine ex_a()
    int arr2[10][8];                   integer arr2(0:7,0:9)
    int x;                             integer x
    x = arr[3][4];                     x=arr(4,3)
}                                  end
```

(a) Manipulation of a two-dimensional array.

```
void ex_b() {                      subroutine ex_b()
    int arr2[10][8];                   integer arr2(0:7,0:9)
    int *p;                            integer p
    int x;                             integer x
    p = &arr[3][4];                    p = 3*10+4
    x = *p;                            x = arr(p/10,mod(p,10))
}                                  end
```

(b) Manipulation of a two-dimensional array with pointer.

```
void ex_c() {                      subroutine ex_c()
    int *arrp[10];                     integer arrp(0:9)
    int arr[8];                        integer arr(0:7)
    int *p;                            integer p
    int x;                             integer x
    arr[6] = 27;                       arr(6) = 27
    arrp[3] = &arr[2];                 arrp(3) = 2
    p = arrp[3][4];                    p = arrp(3) + 4
    x = *p;                            x=arr(p)
}                                  end
```

(c) Manipulation of an array of pointers.

Fig. 4. Various forms of manipulation of a two-dimensional reference.

2.3   Expression simplification

The C language supports several complex operators that have side-effects or
multiple effects. For instance the pre-increment operator (++) first increments
the contents of an element of storage, then supplies its value to the enclosing
expression. Compound expressions cause a sequence of expressions to be evaluated and only the value of the last one is returned to the enclosing expression.
For each of these and other cases, Cepheus supports transformations to split
and rearrange the expression in a manner that preserves the original execution
semantics. In some cases, this requires temporary variable creation, code block
duplication and control-flow induction by generation of if-then-else nests to
represent the original expression.

2.4   Flow control statement manipulation

In addition to expression simplification, Cepheus performs control-flow statement modification to support proper transcription to FORTRAN77. It is able to recognize a C canonical for loop and turn it into a FORTRAN DO loop. In all cases where irregular control flow makes this impossible, the loop is represented using GOTO statements. For instance, by using GOTOs and labels, FORTRAN can naturally support the break and continue semantics available in every type of C loop and switch construct.

A FORTRAN compiler, such as Polaris, changes control-flow of an application using only high-level transformations such as inlining, loop reordering, merging, splitting and unrolling. Here, the potential for parallelism is clearly defined by FORTRAN77 loops and the task of Polaris is to express this parallelism using a specified directive language. Any other parallelism present in the application but not expressed in canonical DO loop syntax is not considered. Situations where clearly bounded iteration takes place as a result of jumps to labels, recursive invocation of subroutines, or other irregular control-flow are not uncommon in C programs. Since such an example would represent a parallelizable entity, some means of control-flow normalization is appropriate. Ammarguellat [2] describes a general method for normalization of irregular control-flow. We are considering the implementation of a similar method in Cepheus, however, implementation of this or any other control flow normalization would also require the ability for full data-flow analysis, which will be implemented in a later integration step with a FORTRAN back-end compiler.

2.5   Recursion

Early FORTRAN77 compilers had no support for recursive subroutines because they did not create stack-allocated variables. However, stack-allocated variables are a necessary requirement for modern FORTRAN77 compilers that generate parallel code (where multiple invocations of the same subroutine may be running simultaneously). We make the assumption that this feature is available in the back-end compiler that will be used with code produced by Cepheus.

The FORTRAN77 language also prohibits a function from calling itself since the function name represents a variable to which the return value is assigned. Cepheus generates a helper function for each recursive function that simply calls back to the original function.

2.6   Semantic emulation

We assume that Cepheus and Polaris will be operating under a closed-world model implying that subroutines do not have unknown side-effects. Therefore, the more that is known about any C support functions that are called, the more complete the program analysis can be. The ANSI-C standard includes the specification of several well-known library functions for tasks such as string manipulation, mathematical operations and format conversion operations. The semantics of many of these functions can be matched by the FORTRAN77 intrinsic functions. For instance, Cepheus supports the translation of calls to `printf()` into FORTRAN's `FORMAT` and `WRITE` intrinsics.

2.7 Data types

The C type system allows the automatic promotion of one type to another in an arbitrary expression. Cepheus recognizes where this occurs in a circumstance where it would not be valid in the resulting FORTRAN representation and inserts a conversion intrinsic. This sometimes involves multiple tiers of intrinsics due to the heterogeneity of FORTRAN types. For instance the assignment of a logical comparison to a float in C would require the generation of an IF-ELSE construct to operate correctly.

ANSI-C also supports several types that are not included in the FORTRAN77 specification: `short` integers, `unsigned` integers (of any size) and bitfields within structures. Each of these types can be represented by the standard integer type—albeit at the expense of storage waste and potentially lower performance. Unsigned integers require the use of intrinsic functions to ensure that non-circular numeric operations such as right-shift work properly. We further note that by using integers to represent specially packed structures, we cannot guarantee compatibility with an existing library's Application Binary Interface (ABI). Furthermore, although ANSI-C does not mandate a size for short and allows it to be potentially as large as an `int` or as small as a `char` it would also be necessary to match the size used by a particular implementation to support an ABI. We again make the assumption that the transcribed application will be subject to a closed-world constraint where all procedures (except, perhaps, for elements of the C standard library) will be compiled together and will not be linked with any foreign objects other than those meant to provide support for the Cepheus execution environment.

2.8 Other conversion issues

We note a few other matters regarding symbol names that are relevant to proper transcription of ANSI-C into FORTRAN77 that are not handled by Cepheus. First, the traditional matter of FORTRAN77 mandating variable and function names that are case-insensitive and unique in the first six-characters is not addressed. Instead, we take advantage of the ability of most modern FORTRAN77 compilers to handle symbols of arbitrary length. We currently make a manual check that there are no symbol collisions due to case-insensitivity. Also, Cepheus sometimes generates symbols for special symbols that are assumed to be unique but are not strictly enforced as being so. Indeed, many translation issues (e.g. static local variables) are simply a matter of resolving a proper symbol name to use and finding methods of doing so automatically.

3 Related Work

Although there has been a great deal of research in the direct parallelization of C and translation of other languages into C, we know of no prior research in translating C into a more restrictive language. The most distinguishing aspect of our work is that it takes advantage of an existing parallelizer for a language other than C. Our model of pointer analysis is similar in many respects to the Type-Based Alias Analysis described by Diwan, McKinley and Moss [7] for use with Modula-3. Their analysis is more general since it accommodates inherited types. However, instead of combining this work with parallelization, they demonstrate the capacity for redundant load elimination and the resulting improvement in instruction level parallelism.

Ghiya and Hendren [9] noted the efficiency realized in treating (named) local variable pointers and (unnamed) heap-allocated pointers differently for purposes of alias analysis in the McCAT optimizing/parallelizing compiler. This is similar to our treatment of pointers that reference either local/global arrays or are hoisted by the ADDROF operator to reference a universal array. However, McCAT's connection analysis does not use type analysis to further subdivide the potential alias space as Cepheus does.

We note the implementation of the restrict keyword in recent optimizing C compilers as a means of explicitly specifying the absence of aliases between pointers in a subroutine [1]. Experimental evidence [5] shows that it can make a great difference in the runtime of array-based scientific code. However, the programmer must take care to correctly specify which formal arguments of a function are immune from aliasing and then make sure that the function is never called with aliased pointers. In the case of more random pointer-chasing codes, the restrict keyword may not make a difference since it is difficult to express such irregular parallelism.

In contrast to this approach, Cepheus and Polaris analyze the situations where the restrict keyword could have been inserted automatically. This is less error prone and, for regular numerical applications, can be equally powerful.

4 Performance Results

To illustrate the potential performance improvements that can be realized by using Cepheus, we have constructed an example of a C program that is not easily optimized. The code in Figure 5 is a contrived way of implementing the formula

$$\overrightarrow{results} = e^{\overrightarrow{vec1}} + e^{\overrightarrow{vec2}}$$

Note that several transformations are possible in this code:

- The pow() function can be transcribed as the native FORTRAN77 ** operator.
- The declaration for variables fact and f can be moved out of the inner loop.
- The outer loop of calc() can be parallelized.

```
#include <math.h>

void calc(double *vec1, double *vec2, double *result)
{
    double *p1, *p2, *pr;
    int i;

    p2=vec2;
    pr=result;

    for(p1=vec1; p1<&vec1[10000]; p1++) {
        for(i=0; i<1000; i++) {
            double fact=1.0;
            int f;
            for(f=1; f<i; f++)
                fact=fact*f;
            *pr += (pow(*p1,0.0+i) + pow(*p2,0.0+i))/fact;
        }
        p2++; pr++;
    }
}

int main()
{
    double vec1[10000], vec2[10000], result[10000];
    double *p1, *p2, *pr;
    int i;

    i=1;
    for(p1=vec1; p1<&vec1[10000]; p1++) {
        *p1=i/20.0;
        i++;
    }
    calc(vec1, vec2, result);
    return 0;
}
```

Fig. 5. Computation on vectors of numbers.

We first compiled this program with the Sun WorkShop Pro C compiler (v4.2) with the best generic (-O5) and architecture-specific (-fast) optimization flags and ran the executables on a five processor Sun Enterprise Server. The results are shown in Figure 6. Neither of these compilers supports automatic parallelization of pointer codes so their performance results only demonstrate scalar optimization. Next, we used Cepheus to transcribe the program to FORTRAN77 and compiled the resulting program with the Sun FORTRAN compiler (v4.2) with the best generic (-O5) and architecture-specific (-fast) flags and ran

the executables. Finally, we compiled the FORTRAN code with Polaris in order
to generate explicit Sun FORTRAN directives and then compiled the resulting
code with the Sun FORTRAN compiler. The results for Polaris show the use of
between 1 and 5 processors.

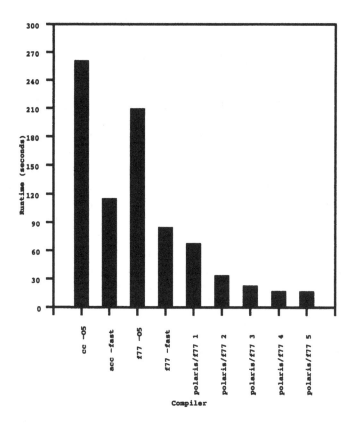

Fig. 6. Performance results using different forms of compilation.

Polaris recognizes the available parallelism and is able to describe it explicitly,
allowing the Sun FORTRAN compiler to further optimize the application. The
five-processor trial represents an almost seven-fold improvement in runtime over
the best possible C-compiled trial.

Even without parallelization, the FORTRAN compiler does better than the
C compiler at scalar optimization not only for trivial codes such as Figure 5
but also for real applications. For instance, the serial version of the Integer
Sort (IS) benchmark from the NAS Parallel Benchmark Suite is written in C.
The Cepheus-transcribed FORTRAN77 version runs 2% faster than the best
C-compiled version on the same architecture.

5   Conclusion

By being able to reduce ANSI-C code to FORTRAN77 with Cepheus, we have demonstrated that existing parallelizing compiler technology can be applied to new or disparate languages by means of transcription. Control-flow normalization and pointer representation and aggregate data structure decomposition are examples where the transcriber can express constructs that are difficult to optimize in a manner that facilitates their parallelization. The task of creating the transcriber was accomplished with considerably less complexity than building a new C parallelizer while benefiting from all of the existing and future abilities of a FORTRAN77 parallelizer. Specifically Cepheus allows us to take advantage of the Polaris translator, which is one of the most powerful parallelizers.

We have presented a proof of concept in the form of a simple example, for which the Cepheus-Polaris translated version substantially outperforms the original C code. We are presently working on improving Cepheus to the point where it is able to analyze and transcribe large applications and also investigating the possibility of transcription of other languages into FORTRAN. Furthermore, while language transcription at the source level is an adequate means for our studies, the ultimate goal is to express C programs in the Polaris intermediate representation directly. In doing so, we will keep modifications to the IR as small as possible. Extensions will only be made where the Cepheus transcription is unable to generate a program that can be successfully parallelized by Polaris.

We expect Cepheus+Polaris to detect parallelism in many C programs. However there will also be many codes whose pointer arithmetic, complex control flow and data structures will make it very difficult to prove parallelism sufficiently for exploiting current parallel computers. To overcome this problem. we have described our vision of a virtual speculative parallel architecture as the target machine. It will allow compilers to apply optimizations in the most aggressive way and to avoid conservative assumptions, which would severely limit the feasible performance goals. The combination of advanced Fortran optimization technology, C program translation, and a speculative target machine puts our ultimate goal of automatically parallelizing a broad range of both C and Fortran computer applications within reach.

References

1. Restricted Pointers in C. Numerical C Extensions Group / ANSI X3J11/94-019, Aliasing Subcommittee, June 1993.
2. A Control-Flow Normalization Algorithm and Its Complexity. *IEEE Transactions on Software Engineering*, Volume 18(3), pages 237-251, 1992.
3. Compiler-Directed Page Coloring for Multiprocessors. E. Bugnion, J. M. Anderson, T. C. Mowry, M. Rosenblum and M. S. Lam. In *Proceedings of the Seventh International Conference on Architectural Support for Programming Languages and Operating Systems*, October 1996.

4. William Blume, Ramon Doallo, Rudolf Eigenmann, John Grout, Jay Hoeflinger, Thomas Lawrence, Jaejin Lee, David Padua, Yunheung Paek, Bill Pottenger, Lawrence Rauchwerger, and Peng Tu. Advanced program restructuring for high-performance computers with Polaris. *IEEE Computer*, December 1996.

5. Doug Cook. Performance Implications of Pointer Aliasing (Whitepaper). Silicon Graphics, Inc. http://reality.sgi.com/cook/audio.apps/dev/aliasing.html August, 1997.

6. David R. Chase, Mark Wegman, and F. Kenneth Zadeck. Analysis of pointers and structures. In *Proceedings of the ACM SIGPLAN '90 Conference on Programming Language Design and Implementation*, pages 296-310, 1990.

7. Amer Diwan, Kathryn S. McKinley, and J. Eliot B. Moss. Type-Based Alias Analysis. In *Proceedings of the ACM SIGPLAN '98 Conference on Programming Language Design and Implementation*, 1998.

8. Rudolf Eigenmann, Insung Park and Michael J. Voss. Are Parallel Workstations the Right Target for Parallelizing Compilers? In *Proceedings of the 10th Workshop on Languages and Compilers for Parallel Computing, August 1997.*

9. Rakesh Ghiya and Laurie J. Hendren. Connection Analysis: A Practical Interprocedural Heap Analysis for C. In *Proceedings of the 8th Workshop on Languages and Compilers for Parallel Computing*, August 1995.

10. Sridhar Gopal, T.N. Vijaykumar, James E. Smith and Gurindar S. Sohi. Speculative Versioning Cache. In *Proceedings of the Symposium on High-Performance Computer Architecture*. January 1998.

11. Richard L. Kennell. The Cepheus Transcriber. *Technical Report, Purdue University, School of ECE, #ECE-HPCLab-98213*. 1998.

12. OpenMP. OpenMP: A Proposed Industry Standard API for Shared Memory Programming (Whitepaper). http://www.openmp.org/openmp/mp-documents/ paper/paper.html. November 1997.

13. J. Oplinger et al. Software and Hardware for Exploiting Speculative Parallelism in Multiprocessors. *Stanford University Technical Report CSL-TR-97-715*. 1997.

14. Sun Microsystems, Inc., *FORTRAN 4.0 User's Guide*, 1996.

Improving Compiler and Run-Time Support for Irregular Reductions Using Local Writes *

Hwansoo Han and Chau-Wen Tseng

Department of Computer Science, University of Maryland
College Park, MD 20742, USA

Abstract. Current compilers for distributed-memory multiprocessors parallelize irregular reductions either by generating calls to sophisticated run-time systems (CHAOS) or by relying on replicated buffers and the shared-memory interface supported by software DSMs (TreadMarks). We introduce LOCALWRITE, a new technique for parallelizing irregular reductions based on the *owner-computes* rule. It eliminates the need for buffers or synchronized writes, but may replicate computation. We investigate the impact of *connectivity* (node/edge ratio), *locality* (accesses to local data) and *adaptivity* (edge modifications) on their relative performance. LOCALWRITE improves performance by 50–150% compared to using replicated buffers, and can match or exceed gather/scatter for applications with low locality or high adaptivity.

1 Introduction

Science is being transformed by the emergence of computation as a vital research tool. As scientists and engineers begin to tackle larger and more complex problems, they are increasingly beginning to exploit parallel computation to provide the computing power they need for research and development. Compilers can make the benefits of parallelism easier to obtain by efficiently mapping applications onto the complexities of high-performance architectures. Experiences show compilers for software DSMs running on distributed-memory multiprocessors can be quite efficient for dense-matrix computations with regular access patterns [6,11]. However, the ability of compilers to efficiently support scientific applications with irregular access patterns is less established.

Irregular data accesses are performed by scientific applications in order to solve increasingly complex problems. The core of these applications is frequently comprised of *reductions*, associative computations (e.g., SUM, MAX) which may be reordered and parallelized. These irregular computations are frequently run on distributed-memory multiprocessors due to their scalability and performance.

Researchers have previously proposed several methods to provide support for irregular reductions on distributed-memory multiprocessors. One approach

---

* This research was supported by NSF CAREER Development Award #ASC9625531 in New Technologies. The IBM SP-2 and DEC Alpha Cluster were provided by NSF CISE Institutional Infrastructure Award #CDA9401151 and grants from IBM and DEC.

S. Chatterjee (Ed.): LCPC'98, LNCS 1656, pp. 181–196, 1999.

is to rely on sophisticated run-time systems (e.g., CHAOS [4], PILAR [15]) which can identify and gather nonlocal data. A second approach is to combine shared-memory compilers (e.g., SUIF [6]) with software distributed shared-memory (DSM) systems (e.g., CVM [13], TreadMarks [17]), which provide a shared-memory interface. Software DSMs are less efficient than explicit messages, but are much simpler compilation targets [3,14].

In this paper, we introduce LOCALWRITE, a new compiler and run-time parallelization technique which can improve performance for certain classes of irregular reductions. We evaluate the performance of different parallelization approaches as we vary application characteristics, in order to identify areas in which software DSMs can match or even exceed the efficiency of explicit messages. Experiments are conducted in a prototype system [7,14] using the CVM [13] software distributed-shared-memory (DSM) as a compilation target for the SUIF [6] shared-memory compiler. Our paper makes the following contributions:

– develop and evaluate LOCALWRITE, a new compiler and run-time technique for parallelizing irregular reductions based on the owner-computes rule
– evaluate the impact of *connectivity*, *locality*, and *adaptivity* on techniques for parallelizing irregular reductions on both shared and distributed-memory multiprocessors

The remainder of the paper begins with background material on existing parallelization techniques for reductions, followed by a description of LOCALWRITE. We present experimental results and conclude with a discussion of related work.

2   Background

2.1   Irregular Reductions

We begin by examining the example irregular reduction shown in Figure 1. The computation loops over the edges of an irregular graph, computes a value, and applies it to both endpoints of the edge. The process repeats for many time steps. Occasionally the edges in the graph are modified. The computation is irregular because accesses to array y are determined by the *index arrays* idx1 and idx2, preventing the compiler from analyzing accesses exactly at compile time.

The example also demonstrates two important features of scientific applications. First, most computations are *iterative*, where the same code is executed many times. The example code is iterative since the main computation is inside a *time-step* loop t with many repetitions. The number of time steps executed is a function of the application, but is usually quite large. Iterative computations are a boon to software DSMs, which can take advantage of repeated communication patterns to predict prefetches to nonlocal data [14].

Second, many irregular scientific computations are *adaptive*, where the data access pattern may change over time as the computation adapts to data. The example in Figure 1 is adaptive because condition **change** may be satisfied on some iterations of the time-step loop, modifying elements of the index array idx1 and changing overall data access patterns as a result.

GatherScatter Compilers currently parallelize irregular reductions using either of two approaches, GATHERSCATTER or REPLICATEBUFS, depending on the target architecture. We start by examining GATHERSCATTER. Data-parallel compilers for distributed-memory multiprocessors (e.g., IBM SP-2, network of PCs) can generate explicit messages between processors [11]. Reductions with regular accesses can be converted directly to collective communication [16].

Irregular reductions may be parallelized by generating an *inspector* to identify nonlocal data needed by each processor. Inspectors are expensive, but their cost can be amortized over many time steps. On each time step an executor *gathers* nonlocal data using the communication schedule, performs the computation using local buffers, and *scatters* nonlocal results to the appropriate processors. This approach was pioneered by the CHAOS run-time system [4].

An example of GATHERSCATTER is displayed in Figure 2. The inspector is invoked outside the time-step loop t, along with a routine *localize()* to convert nonlocal indices in idx1 and idx2 into local buffer indices. Inside the time-step loop, *gather()* is first invoked to actually collect the nonlocal data. The computation then uses local buffer indices stored in idx1 and idx2. Each processor only performs a portion of the reduction. Results of local reductions are then accumulated globally with the *scatter_with_add()* CHAOS library routine.

GATHERSCATTER is very precise, but incurs significant overhead caused by the inspector and mapping nonlocal indices into local buffers (i.e., address translation). The cost of the inspector is proportional to the number of edges and may be amortized for iterative computations [4]. If the computation is adaptive, the inspector must be re-executed each time the access pattern changes, as shown in Figure 2, because communication and mapping may need to change as well.

ReplicateBufs Compilers for shared-memory multiprocessors (e.g., DEC Sable, SGI Origin2000) also detect parallelism and partition computation between processors. Shared-memory compilers parallelize irregular reductions by having each processor compute a portion of the reduction, storing results in a local *replicated buffer* the same size as the array holding reduction results. Results from all replicated buffers are then combined with the original global data, using synchronization to ensure mutual exclusion [6]. If large replicated buffers are to be combined, the compiler can avoid serialization by directing the run-time system to perform global accumulations in sections using a pipelined, round-robin algorithm [6]. Unfortunately, REPLICATEBUFS is inefficient when the reduction is to an array, since the entire array is replicated.

An example of REPLICATEBUFS is displayed in Figure 3. The buffer ybuf is used to store partial reductions results for y. Each processor only performs a portion of the overall computation, but since the compiler does not know which elements of y will be accessed, it must make the buffer as large as the original array. Not only does this waste memory, it increases overhead because the entire buffer must be first initialized, then used to update the actual array at the end with *reduce_sum()*, even if not all elements of the buffer are used during the reduction.

```
x[nodes],y[nodes]    // data in nodes
do t =               // time-step loop
  if (change)        // change accesses
    idx1[] =
  do i = 1, edges    // work on edges
    n = idx1[i]
    m = idx2[i]
    force = f(x[m], x[n]) // computation
    y[n] += force          // update edge
    y[m] += -force         // endpoints
```

Fig. 1. Irregular Reduction Example

```
x[nodes+buf1],y[nodes+buf2]
inspect(idx1,idx2)       // inspector
localize(idx1,idx2)      // translate addrs
do t =
  if (change)            // adaptive code
    idx1[] =
    inspect(idx1,idx2)   // inspector
    localize(idx1,idx2)  // translate addrs

                         // executor
  gather(x)              // get nonlocal data
  do i = my-edges        // local computation
    n = idx1[i]
    m = idx2[i]
    force = f(x[m], x[n]) // computation
    y[n] += force          // update local
    y[m] += -force
  scatter_with_add(y)    // update nonlocal
```

Fig. 2. GATHERSCATTER Example

```
x[nodes],y[nodes],ybuf[nodes]
do t =
  if (change)
    idx1[] =
  ybuf[] = 0               // initalize buffer
  do i = 1, my-edges       // local computation
    n = idx1[i]
    m = idx2[i]
    force = f(x[m], x[n])
    ybuf[n] += force        // updates stored in
    ybuf[m] += -force       // replicated ybuf
  reduce_sum(y, ybuf)      // combine buffers
```

Fig. 3. REPLICATEBUFS Example

```
inspect(idx1, idx2)  // calc my-edges
do t =
  do i = my-edges    // only local LHS
    n = idx1[i]
    m = idx2[i]
    force = f(x[m], x[n])
    y[n] += force
    y[m] += -force
```

Fig. 4. LOCALWRITE Inspector Example

```
inspect(idx1, idx2)  // calc my-edges
do t =
  do i = my-edges    // if some local LHS
    n = idx1[i]
    m = idx2[i]
    force = f(x[m], x[n])  // replicated
    if (own(y[n]))
      y[n] += force
    if (own(y[m]))
      y[m] += -force
```

Fig. 5. LOCALWRITE Cut Edge Example

```
inspect(idx1, idx2)    // calc my-edges
do t =
  if (change)
    idx1[] =              // access changed
    inspect(idx1, idx2)  // recalc my-edges
  do i = my-edges
    ...
```

Fig. 6. LOCALWRITE Adaptive Code Example

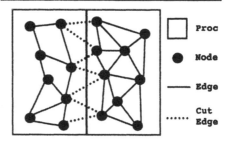

Proc

Node

Edge

Cut
Edge

Fig. 7. Cut Edges Example

2.2   Compiling for Software DSMs

One approach for eliminating the overhead of mapping nonlocal data on distributed-memory multiprocessors is to combine shared-memory parallelizing compilers with software distributed-shared-memory (DSM) systems which emulate global address space in software. Relying on software DSMs simplifies compilation, but is inherently less efficient than sending explicit messages.

Compilers for software DSMs have adopted a number of techniques for improving efficiency. One approach relies on precise communication analysis to insert explicit messages when analysis exactly identifies interprocessor communication [2,3,5]. A second approach exploits customized coherence protocols for reductions and nonlocal updates [13,14,18]. In addition, compilers can also eliminate unnecessary synchronization based on communication analysis [7,14].

TreadMarks is one of the most efficient software DSMs currently available. It relies on an invalidate coherence protocol, and parallelizes irregular reductions using REPLICATEBUFS. Performance is improved relying on a combination of compile-time and run-time support [17]. First, the compiler identifies the section of index array used by each processor, then prefetches it to reduce latency. At run time, the contents of the index array are analyzed and nonlocal data requests are aggregated. Reduction results are stored in a local buffer, then globally updated in parallel in a pipelined manner. Experiments show performance on an SP-2 is comparable to that achieved by CHAOS [4], which supports irregular reductions using GATHERSCATTER [17].

3   Improving Irregular Reductions

Now that we have seen how irregular reductions are parallelized by existing approaches, we consider LOCALWRITE, a new compiler and run-time technique for parallelizing irregular reductions.

3.1   LocalWrite

Two sources of inefficiency in REPLICATEBUFS are large local buffers and mutual exclusion during global accumulation of buffers. Eliminating these overhead provides the motivation for LOCALWRITE, a new technique for parallelizing irregular reductions. LOCALWRITE attempts to improve locality and reduce overhead for reductions by partitioning computation so that each processor only computes new values for locally-owned data. LOCALWRITE is an application of the *owner-computes* rule used in distributed-memory compilers [10]. By assigning only to local data, LOCALWRITE avoids the need for either buffers or mutual exclusion synchronization. The tradeoff is possibly replicated computation.

Consider how we can apply LOCALWRITE to the irregular reduction example in Figure 1. LOCALWRITE consists of two parts: selection of local iterations and execution of local iterations. Compiler analysis can recognize irregular reductions and identify which array variables (idx1, idx2) are used as index arrays [17], as well as which part of each index array is accessed by a processor at each point of the program [7,10]. Based on this information, we insert calls to inspectors to select a partial iteration space where each iteration only writes to the local portion of each variable. The inspector then examines the values of index arrays at run time to build a list of loop iterations which modify local data. The resulting code is shown in Figure 4.

The code generated to implement LOCALWRITE is complicated by the presence of *cut edges*, edges whose endpoints are on different processors. Figure 7 shows examples of cut edges for a sparse computation whose nodes are partitioned between two processors. Cut edges are problematic because for many scientific codes the computation needs to update both endpoints of an edge.

Iterations computing values for cut edges would then need to update data on two processors. To ensure each processor only updates the local portions of an array, LOCALWRITE will need to replicate the computation for the iteration on both processors. In comparison, GATHERSCATTER and REPLICATEBUFS would perform the iteration on one processor, and combine results with updates at the end of the reduction.

An example of computation replication in LOCALWRITE is shown in Figure 5. The inspector must assign to a processor any iteration which writes to data owned by a processor. Iterations representing cut edges are then assigned to two processors. When the iteration for the cut edge is executed, both processors perform the force computation, then use the result to update local data. In Figure 5 we use guarded assignment statements for simplicity. In our experiments we actually create a separate copy of the loop for cut edges, in order to avoid computing guards at run time. The inspector for LOCALWRITE must then generate two computation partitions, one for local edges and one for cut edges.

LOCALWRITE has two sources of overhead, the inspector and replicated computation. During each iteration of the time-step loop, each processor executes only the necessary iteration space using the stored information calculated by the inspector. As with GATHERSCATTER, the cost of the inspector can be amortized over many iterations of the time-step loop. However, the inspector needed for LOCALWRITE is less expensive than the inspector needed for GATHERSCATTER. The difference is because LOCALWRITE only partitions computation, whereas the GATHERSCATTER inspector must also build a communication schedule and perform address translation.

LOCALWRITE faces one additional issue: load balancing. Both REPLICATE-BUFS and GATHERSCATTER can partition computation evenly among processors by assigning equal numbers of edges to each processor. In contrast, LOCALWRITE assigns equal numbers of nodes to each processor. If connections between edges are not uniformly distributed, load imbalance may result if the numbers of edges assigned to each processor vary greatly. In particular, scientific applications may have access patterns which are clustered, as in astrophysical or molecular dynamics n-body computations. In such cases, LOCALWRITE will need to assign nodes to processors in a way which preserves load balance. An algorithm such as recursive coordinate bisection (RCB) may need to be applied, rather than simply using a simple block partition. Such an approach would reduce the efficiency of LOCALWRITE for adaptive computations. However, the overhead for LOCALWRITE should still be less than for GATHERSCATTER, because the LO-CALWRITE inspector does not build communication schedules or perform address translation.

3.2   Compiler Analysis

We have now presented three techniques (REPLICATEBUFS, LOCALWRITE, and GATHERSCATTER) for parallelizing irregular reductions. REPLICATEBUFS and LOCALWRITE can be used by shared-memory compilers, whereas distributed-memory compilers will need to apply GATHERSCATTER. REPLICATEBUFS is the simplest to implement, while GATHERSCATTER requires both complex compiler and run-time support. The implementation effort required for LOCALWRITE is in between.

To use LOCALWRITE, the compiler must insert inspectors both to calculate computation partitions based on local iterations, and compute updates when access patterns change. Otherwise the application will no longer produce correct results, because multiple processors may update the same array elements in an unsynchronized manner. To avoid these problems, we implemented in SUIF compiler analysis to detect adaptive computations.

Analysis is fairly straightforward, and similar to a simplified form of *glacial* variable analysis [1]. We examine global arrays accessed in parallelized loops. Array subscripts containing index arrays are found and the index arrays are marked. We also record whether the index array is read or written. The compiler then examines the program to determine whether index arrays are modified within the time-step loop. If no index arrays are modified, the computation is not adaptive. Otherwise it is adaptive.

We must then generate inspectors for LOCALWRITE. Fortunately, they are simpler than those for GATHERSCATTER, since it only needs to partition computation. The inspector thus only needs to examine the LHS of global assignments in parallel computations, not all global references. Communication schedules and address translation tables are not needed. An example of LOCALWRITE for an adaptive code is shown in Figure 6.

Previous research on data-parallel compilers such as the Fortran D compiler have discussed compiler techniques for automatically generating inspectors and executors for CHAOS [8,9,12]. Simplified versions of those techniques should be directly applicable to generating inspectors and executors for LOCALWRITE. We are in the process of implementing automatic generation of inspectors in SUIF.

4   Experimental Evaluation

4.1   Experimental Platform

We evaluated our optimizations on an IBM SP-2 with 66MHz RS/6000 Power2 processors operating AIX 4.1. Nodes are connected by a 120 Mbit/sec bi-directional Omega switch. We also evaluated the performance of irregular reductions on a DEC Sable multiprocessor with four 275MHz Alpha 21064 processors and 256 megabytes of memory, using Digital Unix V4.0.

Our experiments were conducted by combining the SUIF compiler with the CVM software DSM. We used SUIF to generate pthreads programs (DEC Sable) and CVM programs (IBM SP-2). We have implemented automatic change detection in SUIF, but are still in the process of implementing automatic inspector generation. For our experiments, we currently generate inspectors for LOCAL-WRITE by modifying SUIF output by hand.

CVM is a software DSM that supports coherent shared memory for multiple protocols and consistency models [13]. Performance was improved by adding

	Description	Problem Size	Time Steps	Connectivity	Cut Edges
IRREG	Irregular CFD Mesh	10000 Nodes	50	1–100	10–70%
NBF	Non-Bonded Force (GROMOS)	32000 Nodes	50	1–100	10–70%
MOLDYN	Molecular Dynamics (CHARMM)	16384 Molecules	50	6–124	31–72%

Table 1. Characteristics of Scientific Applications

customized protocol support for reductions, as well as a *flush-update* protocol that at barriers automatically sends updates to processors possessing copies of recently modified shared data [14]. To compare results, we also wrote explicitly parallel programs using a version of the CHAOS run-time system implemented on top of MPI (for the IBM SP-2) [4].

4.2   Applications

We evaluated the performance of our compiler/software DSM interface with three sample applications, IRREG, NBF, and MOLDYN. Application parameters are presented in Table 1. These applications contain an initialization section followed by the main computation enclosed in an sequential time-step loop. The main computation is thus repeated on each iteration of the time-step loop. Statistics and timings are collected after the initialization section and the first few iterations of the time-step loop, in order to more closely match steady-state execution.

IRREG is representative of iterative partial differential equation (PDE) solvers found in computational fluid dynamics (CFD) applications. In such codes, unstructured meshes are used to model physical structures. The mesh is represented by nodes and edges. The main computation kernel iterates over the edges of the mesh, computing modifications to its end points. IRREG computes a force which is applied to both endpoints of an edge. Modifications to the value of all nodes is in the form an irregular reduction.

NBF is a kernel abstracted from the GROMOS molecular dynamics code [8]. Instead of an edge list as in IRREG, it maintains a list of partners for each molecule. Partner lists are more compact than edge lists, but are fragmented and difficult to manage. NBF computes a force which is applied to both a molecule and its partner. Compared to IRREG, the force computation is more expensive.

MOLDYN is abstracted from the non-bonded force calculation in CHARMM, a key molecular dynamics application used at NIH to model macromolecular systems. A list of interactions (edges) is maintained between pairs of molecules. Since the strength of interactions between molecules drops with increasing distance, only molecules within a cutoff distance of each other are assumed to interact. The main computation kernel iterates over all interactions between molecules, computing a single force which is applied to both interacting molecules.

4.3   Application Characteristics

Because of the complexity of the parallelization process, we believe performance will be significantly affected by the application. We describe three important application characteristics, connectivity, locality, and adaptivity. If we view irregular accesses as edges in a graph, we can classify the irregular accesses according its *connectivity*, the edges/nodes ratio. If the ratio of edges to nodes is high, we consider the graph *densely* connected. A low ratio indicates a *sparsely* connected graph. *Locality* is the proportion of data accesses which are to data located on the processor. Another way of measuring locality is by the percentage of edges which are cut edges. Finally, *adaptivity* is the rate at which data access patterns change during program execution. *Static* applications have fixed data access and communication patterns. *Adaptive* applications change dynamically and are less well understood.

For our experiments, we need a standard baseline version of each program to perform comparisons. We chose for the base version of each application connectivity of 100, locality of 30%, and adaptivity set to none. Connectivity of 100 represents a moderately dense graph, and is similar to the connectivity reported by other researchers [17]. Locality of 30% cut edges represents codes with good partitions, as calculated by algorithms such as RCB. For instance, both applications in Mukherjee *et al* achieved locality of around 30% with RCB [18]. We chose to use the static, non-adaptive version of each program as the baseline in order to separate issues of adaptivity, particularly the high cost of inspectors in GATHERSCATTER.

4.4   Shared-Memory Speedups

We begin by examining performance on a four-processor DEC Alpha multiprocessor. Interprocessor communication is relatively inexpensive due to shared memory, so we expect overhead to be the main factor impacting performance. Figure 8 presents 4 processor speedups for REPLICATEBUFS and LOCALWRITE as the connectivity (edges/node ratio) varies while the adaptivity is held static (no updates). Speedups is measured along the y-axis. The x-axis displays connectivity measured as the edge/node ratio. Speedups for REPLICATEBUFS and LOCALWRITE, the two parallelization techniques, are presented as bars of different shades.

Since the amount of work is proportional to the number of edges, speedups generally increase as graphs become denser (i.e., the edge/node ratio increases), since we hold the number of nodes fixed. We see that LOCALWRITE enjoys an advantage for sparsely connected meshes. However, REPLICATEBUFS speedups improve more quickly, since more edges also increases the proportion of useful elements in replicated buffers. In comparison, LOCALWRITE pays a penalty for extra replicated computation for cut edges.

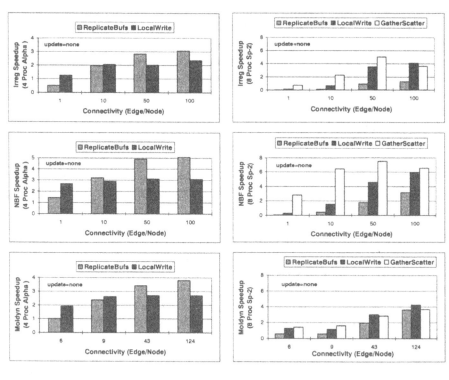

Fig. 8. Speedup vs Connectivity (Alpha)   **Fig. 9.** Speedup vs Connectivity (SP-2)

After the edge/node ratio passes 10 on a 4 processor Alpha multiprocessor, REPLICATEBUFS outperforms LOCALWRITE. It thus appears communication costs are low enough on shared-memory multiprocessors that replicating computation is not profitable unless the graph is sufficiently sparse that REPLICATEBUFS performs significant amounts of wasted work for replicated buffers.

4.5   Distributed-Memory Speedups

Performance results are quite different on the IBM SP-2, since communication is expensive for distributed-memory multiprocessors. We examine the performance of each techniques under different conditions.

Impact of Connectivity Figure 9 presents 8 processor speedups for REPLICATEBUFS, LOCALWRITE, and GATHERSCATTER as connectivity varies for the static version of each application (no connectivity updates). Unlike on the Alpha multiprocessor, results are different for each application. The difference is due to the fact communication costs are high relative to a a shared-memory multiprocessor, so performance is more dependent on the balance between communication and computation.

We begin with IRREG. The cost of the force computation for IRREG is inexpensive, so replicating computation to reduce communication is a major win. We see LOCALWRITE achieves significantly better speedups than REPLICATEBUFS, since the cost of interprocessor communication to accumulate local results into global data is expensive even with customized reduction protocols. The performance of REPLICATEBUFS improves for denser graphs since unused buffer elements are reduced, but LOCALWRITE improves even more quickly.

In IRREG, GATHERSCATTER achieves better speedups than LOCALWRITE for less connected meshes due to its more efficient communication, but the gap narrows as connectivity increases since the computation/communication ratio increases and communication becomes less important. Performance improves for GATHERSCATTER as connectivity increases, probably because the communication/computation ratio is reduced. Speedups drop for GATHERSCATTER going from connectivity of 50 to 100, possibly because of large buffer requirements. In comparison, LOCALWRITE continues to improve with higher connectivity. As a result, when the edge/node ratio reaches 100 LOCALWRITE actually outperforms GATHERSCATTER for IRREG.

For NBF, results are similar. LOCALWRITE again achieves better speedups than REPLICATEBUFS. Overall REPLICATEBUFS speedups are higher, since the force computation is more expensive than in IRREG. GATHERSCATTER outperforms LOCALWRITE, though the disparity again narrows for denser graphs.

For MOLDYN, LOCALWRITE still achieves better speedups than REPLICATE-BUFS, especially for sparse graphs. However, the force computation in MOLDYN is the most expensive of all, so the difference between LOCALWRITE and REPLICATEBUFS is reduced. Once again, GATHERSCATTER achieves the best performance for sparse graphs due to its precise messages, though the difference decreases as connectivity increases.

Overall, we see that LOCALWRITE always outperforms REPLICATEBUFS for distributed-memory multiprocessors. GATHERSCATTER generally achieves the highest speedups because of its more efficient communication. However, as connectivity rises, increasing inefficiencies in GATHERSCATTER allows LOCAL-WRITE to achieve comparable or even better performance.

Impact of Locality Figure 10 presents 8 processor speedups for REPLICATE-BUFS, LOCALWRITE, and GATHERSCATTER as locality varies for each application. Locality, measured as the percentage of cut edges, is measured along the y-axis. We vary locality in IRREG and NBF by changing the initial mesh, whereas for MOLDYN we change the molecule partition from block-wise to recursive coordinate bisection (RCB).

We see that the performance of REPLICATEBUFS is not significantly affected by locality in any application, and performance for LOCALWRITE only declines slightly. We believe speedup for LOCALWRITE turns out to be relatively insensitive to locality because coherence in CVM is maintained at page level (8K),

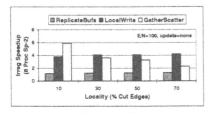

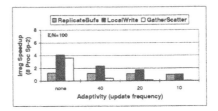

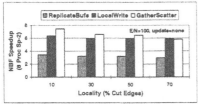

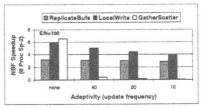

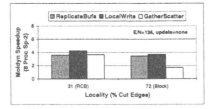

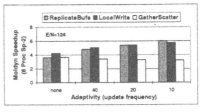

Fig. 10. Speedup vs Locality (SP-2)   **Fig. 11.** Speedup vs Adaptivity (SP-2)

and communication is aggregated and sent as individual messages by the flush-update protocol. As a result, the total amount of data communicated is less important unless it varies significantly. For IRREG and NBF the total amount of data communicated does not appear to vary sufficiently to cause a significant change in performance. The impact of computation replication for cut edges on LOCALWRITE also appears to be less than feared, and does not appear to be a significant source of overhead in IRREG or NBF.

In comparison, we see that the speedups of GATHERSCATTER drop significantly as locality decreases and more cut edges appear. When cut edges are around 30%, GATHERSCATTER speedups are comparable to LOCALWRITE. For IRREG and MOLDYN, GATHERSCATTER performance degrades significantly when cut edges reach 70%. The decrease is less for NBF, possibly because GATHERSCATTER is more efficient for partner lists than edge lists. Work performed by GATHERSCATTER increases in proportion to the number of nonlocal nodes accessed. Experimentally we find it to be more sensitive to locality than either REPLICATEBUFS or LOCALWRITE.

Impact of Adaptivity Figure 11 presents 8 processor SP-2 speedups for REPLICATEBUFS, LOCALWRITE, and GATHERSCATTER as adaptivity varies for each application. Adaptivity, measured as the number of time-step iterations between changes in the graph, is displayed along the x-axis. Versions range from none (no change) to 10 (graph is modified every ten time steps).

For both IRREG and NBF, we see REPLICATEBUFS is unaffected, LOCAL-WRITE gradually degrades, but still outperforms REPLICATEBUFS at each point. GATHERSCATTER degrades so quickly speedups become negligible. The results are mostly expected. Possible excess communication due to the flush-update protocol does not appear to be significant. LOCALWRITE incurs moderate overhead, because it must reanalyze the graph to partition computation between processors. In comparison, GATHERSCATTER faces the most overhead because it has to rebuild (either incrementally or completely) its local address buffers and communication schedule.

In comparison, for MOLDYN speedups of REPLICATEBUFS and LOCALWRITE actually increase as the underlying graph is changed. This is because recalculating the molecular interaction list is computationally intensive and provides additional opportunities to exploit parallelism. Speedups increase because of longer sequential times, even though actual parallel execution times lengthen as well. Similarly, the speedups for GATHERSCATTER do not drop as precipitously because longer sequential times partially compensate for the higher inspector overhead for adaptive codes. Speedups for LOCALWRITE grow more slowly due to inspector overhead. When access patterns change most frequently (every ten iterations), REPLICATEBUFS finally outperforms LOCALWRITE.

4.6   Discussion

Our experimental results show LOCALWRITE is definitely useful as a new technique for parallelizing irregular reductions. On a 4-processor shared-memory multiprocessor LOCALWRITE outperforms REPLICATEBUFS only for very sparse graphs. However, we expect it to be more profitable for larger numbers of processors, as it requires less communication and synchronization. On distributed-memory multiprocessors LOCALWRITE achieves higher speedups in nearly all conditions, improving performance roughly from 50–150% under a variety of conditions. When compared to GATHERSCATTER, experimental results show LO-CALWRITE can be the better choice under certain conditions. GATHERSCATTER generally provides better performance, but the gap can be small. There are conditions under which LOCALWRITE is the appropriate technique for parallelizing irregular reductions. LOCALWRITE outperforms GATHERSCATTER under conditions of low locality or high adaptivity.

5   Related Work

The importance of identifying and parallelizing reductions in scientific applications is well established [11,16]. Irregular reductions have been recognized as being particularly vital. Researchers have investigated both efficient run-time [4,12] and compiler [2,8,17] support.

Most research has been based on the CHAOS run-time system, a library written to support the needs of parallel irregular applications which incorporates the

GATHERSCATTER algorithm. CHAOS has been show to scale well for adaptive computations [12]. Compilers can also automatically generate calls to CHAOS run-time routines [8,9]. PILAR improves performance by tracking nonlocal access as *intervals* instead of individual elements [15].

Several research groups have examined combining compilers and software DSMs, usually with enhancements based on combining explicit messages with underlying mechanisms for supporting nonlocal accesses [2,5,3]. Analysis of nonlocal accesses and communication is used to help the runtime system aggregate communication and synchronization. In some cases the iterative nature of an application is used to predict nonlocal accesses and presend data to eliminate misses [14]. Special coherence protocols to aid reductions also help [14,18]. Reducing synchronization in software DSMs can improve performance, including nearest-neighbor synchronization [7].

Lu *et al.* found that software DSMs can efficiently support irregular applications when using compile-time analysis to prefetch index arrays at run time [17]. In comparison, we achieve comparable performance based on LOCALWRITE.

6   Conclusions

In this paper we investigate improving compiler and run-time support for irregular reductions, the key computation for many sparse scientific computations. We present LOCALWRITE, a new technique for parallelizing sparse reductions. *Inspectors* partition computation according to ownership, potentially replicating computation but eliminating the need for synchronized writes. Experiments on both shared and distributed-memory multiprocessors indicate LOCALWRITE can significantly improves performance for some irregular applications. We also vary the connectivity, locality, and adaptivity of the applications to gain a better understanding of the advantages of different reduction parallelization techniques. By improving compiler support for irregular reductions, we are contributing to our long-term goal: making it easier for scientists and engineers to take advantage of the benefits of parallel computing.

Acknowledgements

The authors are grateful to Pete Keleher for providing CVM and valuable assistance on this paper. We wish to thank Honghui Lu for providing several benchmark codes, and our referees for their helpful comments.

References

1. T. Autrey and M. Wolfe. Initial results for glacial variable analysis. In D. Sehr, U. Banerjee, D. Gelernter, A. Nicolau, and D. Padua, editors, *Languages and Compilers for Parallel Computing, Ninth International Workshop (LCPC'96)*, volume 1239 of *Lecture Notes in Computer Science*. Springer-Verlag, Santa Clara, CA, 1996.

2. S. Chandra and J.R. Larus. Optimizing communication in HPF programs for fine-grain distributed shared memory. In *Proceedings of the Sixth ACM SIGPLAN Symposium on Principles and Practice of Parallel Programming*, Las Vegas, NV, June 1997.

3. A. Cox, S. Dwarkadas, H. Lu, and W. Zwaenepoel. Evaluating the performance of software distributed shared memory as a target for parallelizing compilers. In *Proceedings of the 11th International Parallel Processing Symposium*, Geneva, Switzerland, April 1997.

4. R. Das, M. Uysal, J. Saltz, and Y.-S. Hwang. Communication optimizations for irregular scientific computations on distributed memory architectures. *Journal of Parallel and Distributed Computing*, 22(3):462–479, September 1994.

5. S. Dwarkadas, A. Cox, and W. Zwaenepoel. An integrated compile-time/run-time software distributed shared memory system. In *Proceedings of the Eighth International Conference on Architectural Support for Programming Languages and Operating Systems (ASPLOS-VIII)*, Boston, MA, October 1996.

6. M. Hall, S. Amarasinghe, B. Murphy, S. Liao, and M. Lam. Detecting coarse-grain parallelism using an interprocedural parallelizing compiler. In *Proceedings of Supercomputing '95*, San Diego, CA, December 1995.

7. H. Han and C.-W. Tseng. Compile-time synchronization optimizations for software DSMs. In *Proceedings of the 12th International Parallel Processing Symposium*, Orlando, FL, April 1998.

8. R. v. Hanxleden. Handling irregular problems with Fortran D — A preliminary report. In *Proceedings of the Fourth Workshop on Compilers for Parallel Computers*, Delft, The Netherlands, December 1993.

9. R. v. Hanxleden and K. Kennedy. Give-N-Take — A balanced code placement framework. In *Proceedings of the SIGPLAN '94 Conference on Programming Language Design and Implementation*, Orlando, FL, June 1994.

10. S. Hiranandani, K. Kennedy, and C.-W. Tseng. Compiling Fortran D for MIMD distributed-memory machines. *Communications of the ACM*, 35(8):66–80, August 1992.

11. S. Hiranandani, K. Kennedy, and C.-W. Tseng. Preliminary experiences with the Fortran D compiler. In *Proceedings of Supercomputing '93*, Portland, OR, November 1993.

12. Y.-S. Hwang, B. Moon, S. Sharma, R. Ponnusamy, R. Das, and J. Saltz. Runtime and language support for compiling adaptive irregular programs on distributed memory machines. *Software—Practice and Experience*, 25(6):597–621, June 1995.

13. P. Keleher. Update protocols and iterative scientific applications. In *Proceedings of the 12th International Parallel Processing Symposium*, Orlando, FL, April 1998.

14. P. Keleher and C.-W. Tseng. Enhancing software DSM for compiler-parallelized applications. In *Proceedings of the 11th International Parallel Processing Symposium*, Geneva, Switzerland, April 1997.

15. A. Lain and P. Banerjee. Exploiting spatial regularity in irregular iterative applications. In *Proceedings of the 9th International Parallel Processing Symposium*, Santa Barbara, CA, April 1995.

16. B. Lu and J. Mellor-Crummey. Compiler optimization of implicit reductions for distributed memory multiprocessors. In *Proceedings of the 12th International Parallel Processing Symposium*, Orlando, FL, April 1998.

17. H. Lu, A. Cox, S. Dwarkadas, R. Rajamony, and W. Zwaenepoel. Compiler and software distributed shared memory support for irregular applications. In *Proceedings of the Sixth ACM SIGPLAN Symposium on Principles and Practice of Parallel Programming*, Las Vegas, NV, June 1997.

18. S. Mukherjee, S. Sharma, M. Hill, J. Larus, A. Rogers, and J. Saltz. Efficient support for irregular applications on distributed-memory machines. In *Proceedings of the Fifth ACM SIGPLAN Symposium on Principles and Practice of Parallel Programming*, Santa Barbara, CA, July 1995.

Beyond Arrays — A Container-Centric Approach for Parallelization of Real-World Symbolic Applications

Peng Wu and David Padua

Department of Computer Science, University of Illinois at Urbana-Champaign
Urbana, IL 61801, USA
pengwu, padua@cs.uiuc.edu

Abstract. Parallelization of symbolic applications is difficult and a systematic approach has yet to be developed. In this paper, we introduce the concept **container**, which refers to any general-purpose aggregate data type, such as matrices, lists, tables, graphs and I/O streams. We propose the container-centric approach, in which containers are treated by the compiler as built-in types. Containers become the target of data-parallelism and the focus of program analysis and transformations.

1 Introduction

The last decade has witnessed extensive researches on automatic parallelization of numerical array-based applications. State-of-the-art parallelizing compilers now can parallelize some large and real scientific benchmarks[1] [2] [3][5][4]. However, there is a large set of non-numerical applications, some of which are fairly simple, that still cannot be parallelized by current techniques. The reasons, we believe, are our limited understanding of the characteristics of such applications and the consequent lack of effective parallelization techniques designed accordingly.

In this paper, we introduce the concept **container**, which refers to any general-purpose aggregate data type, such as matrices, lists, tables, graphs and I/O streams. Containers, as the major data storage media, are at the center of program data-flow and manipulations of their elements are the primary source of data-parallelism in real applications. We propose the container-centric approach in which containers are treated as intrinsic types during the parallelization. Not only should the compiler recognize containers, but containers are the target of data-parallelism and the focus of program analysis and transformations.

In the discussion of the container-centric approach, we start by providing abstractions of containers, **abstract container operations**. Our study of real-world applications shows that containers, even with different implementations or across programming languages, behave surprisingly similar, therefore highly amiable for abstraction. Then, we propose several key transformation and analysis techniques for the containers we are targeting. We apply by hand these techniques to parallelize a few real-world applications; among them are *javac, jar,*

S. Chatterjee (Ed.): LCPC'98, LNCS 1656, pp. 197–212, 1999.

javap and *javadoc*[1]. Parallelism is exploited at a very coarse granularity, almost all of the major loops of the four applications are parallelizable. The experimental results are very encouraging. To the best of our knowledge, this is the first work that characterizes real-world symbolic applications in terms of their underlying aggregate data structures and addresses their parallelization in a pragmatic way.

The paper is structured as follows. Section 2 gives an overview of containers and the container-centric approach. Section 3 proposes the abstract container operations and the concrete container description technique. Sections 4 and 5 introduce several compiler transformation and analysis techniques. Experimental results are given in section 6. Section 7 compares our work with others. And section 8 summarizes and presents a conclusion.

2   The Container-Centric Approach

2.1   Concept of container

We define any general-purpose aggregate data type as a **container**[6]. Examples of containers are matrices, lists, stacks, trees, graphs, I/O streams and hash tables. In the paper we focus on two types of containers:

- A **linear container** is a container whose elements are accessed by positions in an ordered manner. Commonly seen linear containers are lists, stacks and queues. Linear containers can be addressed through *iterators*[7], which allows container elements to be accessed in a way similar to how arrays are accessed through indices.
- In a **associate container**, elements are accessed by keys. Keys could be numerical (index-key), alpha-numerical (name-key) or pointers (pointer-key). Examples of associate containers are hash tables, sets and maps.

2.2   Motivation

Traditionally programmers work directly with intrinsic data types and language constructs. With the thriving of object-oriented programming and the wide availability of general-purpose libraries, modern applications are composed from a much higher abstraction level. Containers such as lists, stacks, hash tables, and I/O streams are common components of today's real-world symbolic applications and are treated by most programmers as if they were intrinsic data types. Common containers are provided by almost every object-oriented language as part of the core class libraries, such as *standard template library (STL)* for C++ and *java foundation classes (JFC)* for java.

```
for(e=list.getHead();list.hasMore();e=list.next()){
        do something on e...;
}
```

---

[1] the standard utility applications from *Java Developer's Toolkit (JDK)* package

Containers, sitting at the center of program data-flow and serving as primary source of data parallelism, play the same role in symbolic applications as arrays in numerical ones. Linear-containers such as lists, for instance, are one of the major sources of data parallelism for symbolic applications. The above example shows a very common loop that iterates a list. However, conventional compilers treat list the same as any other common object. Such unawareness of the container in program analysis and parallelization eliminates further possibilities to exploit parallelism on the example.

We believe that containers should be made distinguishable to parallelizing compilers, their characteristics studied, manipulation patterns identified, and basic operations reflected in the parallelization algorithms.

2.3   About the container-centric approach

In a container-centric approach, parallelizing compilers are designed with full knowledge of containers. We extend the compiler with new data types **abstract containers** which are specified by their operations **abstract container operations**. Abstract containers are "meaningful" entities to the compiler and are treated with no less importance and attention as any other intrinsic data type. Similar to the way we handle arrays, common manipulation patterns of abstract containers are studied, target loop patterns are identified, fundamental parallelization techniques are re-designed to be container-specific. For example, in our work on linear containers and associate containers, we have provided the dependence test for linear containers, commutativity analysis for associate containers, container privatization, etc. Figure 1 illustrates the compilation steps

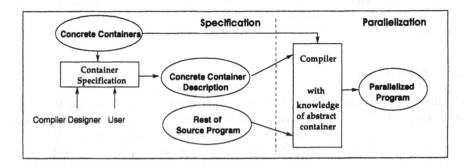

Fig. 1. Program parallelization using a container-aware compiler

with a container-aware compiler. Concrete containers[2] are first "described" using abstract container operations, and then fed into the compiler, together with the rest of the source program, as the inputs. The compiler then takes the abstract-container-based program, performs the container-specific analysis and transformations, identifies parallelizable sections and finally generates parallel codes.

---

[2] real-world containers are referred to as **concrete** as opposed to the abstract ones

The feasibility of such an approach, however, lies in greatly the generality of abstract containers. So that compilers based on them can benefit a reasonable large set of applications. Upon such consideration, abstract containers specifies only the very core container operations. Containers with more complicated semantics can be described through composition. Moreover, we intend to study containers that are more standardly and more commonly used, such as linear containers and associate containers. We also note that, in general, human efforts are necessary in describing concrete containers in terms of abstract ones. However, the process is fairly intuitive and localized. Description of the container can be fully decoupled from the source program using it and are highly reusable. Furthermore, by providing descriptions for *STL* containers or *JFC* containers once, all the applications use these standard container libraries, which fortunately is the trend, can benefit.

3 Container Specification

3.1 Abstract containers

Abstract containers are used by the compiler to represent internally concrete containers. There are several properties that we assume for abstract containers of any type.

- The structure of the container is fully encapsulated in method interfaces. The **structure of the container** is defined as any internal state of the container other than the elements inside. Since the structure of the container is mostly implementation-dependent, assuming such property, generality of abstract containers will not be compromised by the diversities in concrete container implementations.
- Abstract container operations change only the structure of the container. This property reflects the nature of containers as storage media, and keeps the semantics of abstract containers simple.
- Except for primitive data types, elements into or out of the container are passed by reference. Concrete containers vary in the definition of such an alias relation. Some use pass-by-value semantics, while others use pass-by-reference. Still others leave the choice to the programmer. We choose pass-by-reference semantics since it most closely reflects the nature of the store operation of containers and can easily describe other semantics as well.

3.2 Abstract container operations

Abstract container operations specify the syntax and semantics of abstract containers, As shown in Figure 2, each operation is composed of a name, a return value, and a set of parameters. Both the return value and the parameters are declared by **abstract types**. There are four abstract types that are general for all kinds of abstract containers. ABS_void, ABS_bool, and ABS_int stand for void-type, boolean-type and integer-type respectively. ABS_element represents the element of the abstract container, and it is of reference type.

```
ABS_void abs_push_back(ABS_element)     ABS_element abs_access(ABS_void)
ABS_void abs_push_front(ABS_element)    ABS_iterator abs_next(ABS_void)
ABS_element abs_pop_back(ABS_void)      ABS_iterator abs_prev(ABS_void)
ABS_element abs_pop_front(ABS_void)     ABS_bool abs_hasMore(ABS_void)

ABS_element abs_get_back(ABS_void)      (ii) abstract iterator operations
ABS_element abs_get_front(ABS_void)

ABS_iterator abs_begin(ABS_void)     ABS_bool abs_put(ABS_key,ABS_element)
ABS_iterator abs_end(ABS_void)       ABS_element abs_get(ABS_key)
                                     ABS_bool abs_remove(ABS_key)
ABS_int abs_size(ABS_void)           ABS_bool abs_contains(ABS_key)
ABS_bool abs_empty(ABS_void)

(i) abstract linear              (iii) abstract associate
    container operations               container operations
```

Fig. 2. Abstract container operations

Abstract linear container operations An abstract linear container can be viewed as a linear discrete space with two special positions: *begin* and *end*. We define *front* and *back* to be the element at position *begin* and *end* respectively. Position of a abstract linear container is represented by abstract iterators. There are two special values of abstract iterators, **abs_begin_iterator** and **abs_end_iterator**, which point to the *begin* and *end* of the container, respectively.

Abstract iterator operations Abstract iterator operations provide abstractions of concrete iterators. Each abstract iterator is associated with an abstract linear container . **Abs_access()** gets the container element at the position pointed to by the iterator. The call **Abs_hasMore()** checks whether the iterator has traversed to the end of the container, while the call **abs_next()**(**abs_prev()**) will evolve the current iterator to point to the next (previous) position of the container.

Abstract associate container operations Abstract associate container operations specify the basic update and access behaviors of a associate container. Keys of a associate container are unique. They are represented by abstract type **ABS_key**, which can be of three kinds: **ABS_index_key**, **ABS_name_key** and **ABS_pointer_key**.

3.3   Concrete container description

Abstract container operations provide the compiler with only the core container operations. Concrete containers, which usually have much more complicated semantics, will be described in terms of the abstract ones. Each abstract operations specifies a data-flow relation between the associated concrete container, the return instance and the actual parameters bound. In describing the concrete containers, abstract operations are to be "instantiated", by "invoking" the abstract operation on a receiver object, "binding" actual parameters to formal ones, and "assigning" the return value to other instance. During instantiation, the receiver object, actual parameters, and the return value can be concrete if declared by concrete data types, or abstract if declared by abstract types. In certain context, concrete types can be bound to abstract ones. For example, type int, void, and boolean of the target language can be bound to abstract type ABS_int, ABS_void, and ABS_bool, respectively.

```
void List::<Element>::append(List<Element>* list2) {
    for(ABS_iterator iterator=list2.abs_get_begin();
                     iterator.abs_hasMore();
         iterator=iterator.abs_next()) {
        abs_push_back(iterator.abs_access());
    }
}
```

The above shows the concrete container description of append() of class *List*, which appends elements (by reference) of *list2* to itself. The concrete container description "describes" the data-flow semantics of method append() by a set of abstract container operations. Moreover, in a concrete container description we can use any concrete variable visible in the scope, declare instances either as concrete or as abstract, or even invoke abstract operations on concrete instances. In the example, the new abstract instance *iterator* is declared and the abstract operation abs_get_begin() is invoked on the concrete instance *list2*.

4   Container-Based Transformation Techniques

4.1   Data dependences and loop-level parallelism

Target loops for exploiting parallelism Linear containers are amiable for exploiting loop-level parallelism. Figure 3 [3] shows two common iterative loops of linear containers: *iterator-based loop*, which iterates the linear container through an iterator; and *pop-based loop*, which iterates the container through the operation abs_pop_back(). Both are our target loop patterns for exploiting loop-level parallelism.

Container structural dependences Manipulating containers introduces new dependences. For example, in Figure 3(i), the three operations i.abs_next(), i.abs_hasMore(), and i.abs_access() introduce dependences. We define **container structural dependence** as dependences due to change upon the structure of the container. There are two basic container structural dependences:

---

[3] We'll use abstract container operations directly in the examples to illustrate exact semantics and patterns we are targeting.

```
for(ABS_iterator i=list.abs_begin();        for(;list.abs_empty();
    i.abs_hasMore(); i.abs_next()) {            list.abs_pop_back()) {
    Object o = i.abs_access();                  object o=list.abs_back();
    ...                                         ...
}                                           }
```

(i) iterator-based iterative loop   (ii) pop-based iterative loop

Fig. 3. Common loop patterns of container-based applications

1. of any two computations, if at least one of them adds or removes elements from the container, there is an **update structural dependence**;
2. if two computations access different elements of the container through the same iterator, there is an **access structural dependence**.

In Figure 3, loop (i) has access structural dependence and loop (ii) has update structural dependence. Structure dependences are inherent to many container manipulations, such as the sequential accessing of a list or an I/O stream and the recursive accessing of a tree. It explains, to some extent, why parallelization of container-based applications is much harder than that of array-based ones. Since conventional dependence test which is mostly based on memory dependence, is too restrictive to tolerate structural dependences. In most of the cases, detection of structural dependences is trivial; the difficulties, however, lie in program transformations to eliminate such dependences. Transformation techniques proposed in this section will focus on the elimination of structural dependences.

4.2   Loop parallelization

The loop parallelization techniques we discuss here are pattern-aware. We aim at handling dependences introduced by operations inside the loop header in the two loops in Figure 3. Such dependences are inherent to the loop pattern and very similar to those introduced by loop index in array-based loops. We assume in the examples that there are only two threads for parallel execution and that elements can be distributed evenly. The most general method of loop parallelization is to distribute container elements into several local containers and then have each parallel thread work on its own data. Figure 4(i) shows the container distribution for the loop in Figure 3(ii), in which elements of *stack* are distributed into two stacks, *s1* and *s2*.

Container distribution introduces the overhead of data copying even if only references are copied. Loop parallelization can be made more efficient taking consideration of the special feature of the concrete container. For instance, the java class *Vector* supports random element access through method elementAt(). The iterative loop can be parallelized in a way similar to that for arrays.

4.3   Container privatization

Containers observe different patterns from arrays in terms of privatization. Most linear containers observe the define-use-reset pattern. *Define-use-reset* is also

```
Stack s1, s2;                        Enumeration e=v.elements();
for(; stack.abs_empty();){           if(threadId==1)
    s1.push(stack.pop());                e.nextElement();
    if(stack.empty())                for(;e.hasMore();e.nextElement())
        break;                       {  ...
    s2.push(stack.pop());                Object o=e.nextElement();
}                                        ...
                                     }
(i) Through container distribution   (ii) With concrete iterator
```

Fig. 4. Loop parallelization

common in the manipulations of common objects. After "use" of the object (mostly involving complicated computations to change its internal states), states of the object are "reset" to the original states before the "use". This is because most objects are aggregate so that re-definition of the object depends on its previous states. *Reset* is a clean way of *killing* all the previous definitions of the object.

A container is **privatizable** if, in the end of any iteration, states of the container are "reset" to the states before it enters the iteration. In real applications, we see two common scenarios, shown in Figure 5, that can lead to a privatizable container.

```
list.abs_push_back(element);      list.abs_push_back(element1);
...                               list.abs_push_back(element2);
list.abs_pop_back();              ...
                                  while(!list.abs_empty()) {
                                      list.abs_pop_back();
                                  }

(i) "paired" operations           (ii) clean-up condition
```

Fig. 5. Two privatizable scenarios

In Figure 5(i), every call to abs_push_back() is "paired" with a call to abs_pop_back(), with the latter recovering the effect of the former. The concept of "paired" is recursively defined. For instance, the above two operations are "paired" if all the other appearances of calls to abs_push_back() and abs_pop_back() in between them are paired as well. In this example, *define-use-reset* is not just feasible, it is necessary. This is because, here, only computations that "define" (abs_push_back()) the list know how to "reset" (abs_pop_back()) it.

In Figure 5(ii), the container is reset to be empty after the use. One thing worth mentioned is that the reset is done through a loop whose termination is controlled by a test operation abs_empty(). Abs_empty() implies the state of the container after the loop, which can be illustrated more clearly by presenting the reset-loop in a program control graph as shown below.

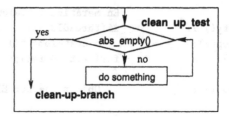

Fig. 6. Control flow graph of clean-up-condition and clean-up-branch

We define `abs_empty()` as the *clean-up-condition* and the yes-branch of the *clean-up-condition* as *clean-up-branch*. It is clear that the control-flow that follows the *clean-up-branch* will no longer see previous definitions of the container. The privatization algorithm can take advantage of such test operations. `Abs_empty()` is not the only *clean-up-condition* we have seen in programs. For example, the boolean expression `abs_size() == 0` is a *clean-up-condition* as well.

4.4 Exploiting associativity

We exploit associativity on operations, such as `abs_push_back` and `abs_push_front`, to eliminate update structural dependences. For example, in the loop shown in Figure 7(i), since the container is updated by operation `abs_push_back()` only, the structural dependences can be eliminated by letting each thread update its local container and joining the local containers together later. This is very similar to our handling of simple recurrences of scalars. Figure 7(ii) shows a more general case where we can exploit associativity; in the example the container is both accessed and updated in the loop.

```
for(int i=0; i<n; i++) {          for (int i=0; i < n; i++) {
    ...                               list.abs_push_back(element);
    list.abs_push_back(element);      ...
    ...                               list.abs_back();
}                                 }

(i)                               (ii)
```

Fig. 7. Scenarios of exploiting associativity on linear containers

We define that an access is **localized** to an iteration if it accesses only elements that are "structurally defined" in the same iteration. Any add operation **structurally defines** the container operations that access the elements it adds. In the above example, `list.abs_back()` is localized since `list.abs_push_back()` structurally defines `list.abs_back()`. Computations on the container within a loop are **associative** if there is an add operation, such as `abs_push_back()` or `abs_push_front()`, and the access operations of the container are localized.

5   Container-Based Dependence Test

Several factors can lead to data dependences in container manipulations, such as structural dependences, overlapped accesses of container elements, and aliasing between container elements. Detection of structural dependences is trivial. Dependences arising from aliasing are mostly not container-specific, and are addressed by alias analysis of[11][12]. Therefore, our discussion here focuses on only detection of dependences due to overlapped accesses of elements.

5.1   Data dependence test for linear containers

The Data dependence test for linear containers aims at detection of dependences due to overlapped accesses of elements. Since linear containers are mostly addressed by iterators, we first need a good way to summarize accesses of a linear container. We use the term **range** to represent the accesses of a container. A *range* is associated with a sequence of computations and is denoted as $[low, up]$, where *low* and *up* can be any iterator that is not defined inside the sequence of computations with which the range is associated. For example, the range associated with the loop in Figure 3(i) is $[abs\_begin\_iterator, abs\_end\_iterator]$. And, for fix-position accesses, such as abs_push_back(), the associated range is $[abs\_end\_iterator, abs\_end\_iterator]$.

Similar to the *range test* [14] for arrays, dependence tests for linear containers are based on the detection of possible overlapping between the ranges of any two iterations. Two relations on iterators are defined to compare iterators. Given two iterators $i1$ and $i2$, we define "<" as that $i1 < i2$ if $i1$ points to a position that is closer to *front* than $i2$ does; and we say $i1 == s2$ if both point to the same position of the container. The comparison of iterators is based on the following rules:

(1) $abs\_begin\_iterator \leq abs\_end\_iterator$
(2) $\forall i\ abs\_begin\_iterator \leq i \leq abs\_end\_iterator$
(3) $\forall i\ i < i.abs\_next()$
(4) $\forall i\ i.abs\_prev() < i$

The overlap of two iterator-based ranges can be detected, in a way similar to that of integer-based ranges: by comparing the lower-bound and upper-bound iterators of the ranges.

5.2   Commutativity analysis — dependence test for associate containers

Manipulation of associate containers is one of the major causes of loop-carried dependences in real-world symbolic applications. Traditionally parallelizable loops are detected by proving independent computation between iterations. Though sufficient, such a constraint is not necessary and too restricted for operations on associate container. A loop is parallelizable if computations across iterations are commutable[16]. We exploit commutativity on associate containers.

Commutativity analysis by disjoint key accesses Basic update and access operations of associate containers are commutable if they use different keys. The two operations in the following example, for instance, are commutable if *key*1 and *key*2 are different.

```
hashtable.abs_put(key1, element1);
hashtable.abs_put(key2, element2);
```

Commutativity analysis by disjoint key accesses is an extension of the array-based data dependence test in the sense that arrays are associate containers with indexes as their keys. The difference lies in the fact that equivalence of the keys (indexes) for arrays implies not only commutativity but also memory independence; whereas for most other containers, memory independence may not be observed. Therefore, when parallelizing loops that contain such commutable operations, critical sections are necessary to enforce the memory consistence. The rest of the loop, however, can be executed fully concurrently.

Commutativity analysis by disjoint keys is conducted according to the type of key. Keys of different types vary in their interpretations of equivalence: equivalence of pointer-keys is identity-based (based on memory equivalence), whereas that of name-keys is non-identity-based (based on the value). Traditional analysis techniques can be applied to test commutativity according to the key types, such as, array-based dependence test for index-keys, alias analysis for pointer-keys and run-time test for keys of any type.

Commutativity analysis with overlapped key accesses Key accesses of associate containers are more likely to be overlapped, since such containers are geared mainly to enable fast element retrieval with potentially large data sets and high access frequencies. Although proving commutativity in the case of overlapped key accesses in general is very difficult, we found an important manipulation pattern, *search-otherwise-insert*, which might be proven commutable.

Figure 8(i) shows an example of *search-otherwise-insert*, where *List* is a associate container with pointer-keys and the element itself serves as the key. In put(), an element is added into the container only if no element with the same key is already in the container. The intuition behind this pattern is that insertion of any new element into a associate container should keep keys of the container distinct, which is enforced by *search-otherwise-insert*. Operation put() in the example is commutable. To prove it informally, first consider the case $key1 \neq key2$: operations list.put(key1) and list.put(key2) are commutable due to disjoint key accesses. Then, when $key1 == key2$, any reordering of the above two operations will lead *list* to the same states.

It is easy to prove commutativity in the above example since elements of the container serve as the keys as well. However, it is more common for the elements and their keys to be separate. Figure 8(ii) shows a more realistic example of the *search-otherwise-insert* pattern taken from *javac*. *Classes* is a associate container with pointer-keys, which contains all the class declarations of the currently compiled file. Method getClassDeclaration() gets the class declaration from

```
void put(Object obj) {        hashtable classes;
if(!list.abs_contains(obj))   ClassDeclaration getClassDeclaration(Type t){
  list.abs_push_back(obj));    ClassDeclaration c=classes.get(t);
}                              if (c == null) {
                                 c = new ClassDeclaration(t.getClassName());
                                 classes.put(t,c);
                               }
                               return c;
                             }
```

(i) put()   (ii) getClassDeclaration()

Fig. 8. Two examples of search-otherwise-insert

classes and will add newly declared classes into *classes* if necessary. Considering the case where $key1 == key2$, if control follows into the yes-branch of the if-statement, regardless of the execution order, it is always the newly created instance c that is added into *classes*. Therefore, method getClassDeclaration() is commutable; recall that we assume $key1 == key2$, and c dependence on the key only.

6 Experimental Results

We have hand-parallelized several applications from the benchmark suite using the techniques we proposed in the previous sections. Four of them, *javac, jar, javap* and *javadoc*, are standard applications from JDK1.1.5 package, and another one is *calculator*. We changed the type checking algorithm of java, which is used by *javac* and *javadoc*. Since the original algorithm compiles not only user specified source files but also those of any class encountered during the compilation, it leads to the true flow-dependence during compilations of multiple function units and consequently makes *javac* and *javadoc* sequential. The algorithm is modified to parse user specified source files only. For other classes encountered during the compilation, their class files are loaded directly. We consider such a modification tolerable since most java code compilations can not see any difference of the modified algorithm from the original one. Furthermore, the modified algorithm is common in the compilations of programs coded in other programming languages, such as C and C++, which does not do source-parsing of any codes other than those specified by the user, and type information is loaded by header files.

   Table 1 summarizes, for each application, the major parallelizable loops, the percentage of execution time of the loops, and the analysis and transformation techniques applied to parallelize the loop. DD_{lc} stands for dependence test for linear containers, $DD_{disjoint}$ for dependence test with disjoint keys, $DD_{overlap}$ for dependence test with overlapped keys, *Assoc.* for exploiting associativity, *I-loop* for parallelization of iterator-based loops, and *Priv.* for container privatization. Parallelism has been exploited at a very coarse granularity, mostly from the file level. All of the parallelizable loops are outer-most. They are major loops of the applications, taking up 80% or more of the total execution time.

Program-loop	$\%T_{seq}$	DD_{lc}	$DD_{disjoint}$	$DD_{overlap}$	Assoc.	I-loop	Priv.
javac-parse	14%	X	X	X	X	X	
javac-check	14%	X	X	X		X	
javac-compile	70%	X	X	X	X	X	
javap-disassemble	77%	X	X			X	
javadoc-parse	23%	X	X	X	X	X	
javadoc-genclass	11%	X	X	X	X	X	
javadoc-genpack	53%	X	X	X	X	X	
jar-manifest	86%	X	X	X	X	X	
jar-add	8%	X			X	X	X
calc-main	90%	X				X	X

Table 1. Summary of Parallelizable Loop

Since the parallelism we exploited was of a very coarse granularity, and all of them were outer-most loops, the overhead from forking and joining of threads was trivial; the effect of load-imbalancing, however, was particularly significant. Moreover, the class-loading of java runtime more heavily burdened the first thread of the parallel execution, and the garbage collection complicated the measurement of workload.

7   Related Work

Previous work on the parallelization of non-array-based applications focuses primarily on the analysis of dynamic, pointer-based data structures, known as pointer analysis or alias analysis. Basic approaches of pointer analysis fall into two categories:(1) a fully automatic approach, in which the compiler discovers the shape[23][12][21] or alias properties[22] of the data structure; and (2) a data annotation approach, in which information of the data structure is provided by the user based on a pre-defined description language[24][18][19]. Hummel, Hendren, and Nicolau proposed two description languages, ADDS[18] and ASAP[19], by which users can describe the shape and traversal properties of the data structures. Based on the work of ASAP, which uses regular expressions to convey the alias property of the data structure, the authors later proposed a dependence test algorithm using theorem proving[17]. The difference between the data annotation approach and our approach is that the former requires program analysis information (e.g., alias properties of the data structure), which is static and context-sensitive whereas the latter requires only data type operation information, from which program analysis information can be derived automatically by the compiler. As a consequence, most of pointer analysis can deal only with data structures that do not change structurally.

Notable work has been done by Harrison[9][10] on the parallelization of Scheme programs, which we consider to be the work most similar to ours. Lists/trees are built-in data type of Scheme. Manipulations of lists in Scheme are through recursive functions, which, according to our definition, is the structural dependence of the container type. In his work, Harrison identified such a manipulation pattern and developed the technique *recursive splitting* to transform recursive functions into loops and exploit parallelism on the loops. Moreover, implementation of lists in the scheme run-time was enhanced with auxiliary access pointers to facilitate fast accesses of lists.

8 Conclusions

In this paper, we identified and exploited the roles of *containers* in parallelization of symbolic applications. By introducing the concept of container, a much broader and exploitable field is presented to parallelizing compilers. Although we targeted linear containers and content-addressable containers, the benefits are not limited to applications based on containers of these two types. For example, sparse codes and molecular dynamics have their own containers, and it is highly possible to characterize and generalize their underlying containers and to design container-specific analysis and transformation techniques for them. We believe that the container-centric approach will have a potential impact on the parallelization of applications based on any container type.

References

1. W.Blume, R.Eigenmann, J.Hoeflinger, D.Padua, P.Petersen and L.Rauchwerger. Automatic Detection of Parallelism: A Grand Challenge for High-Performance Computing. *IEEE Parallel and Distributed Technology*, 2(3):37–47, fall 1994.
2. U.Banerjee, R.Eigenmann, A.Nicolau, D.A.Padua. Automatic Program Parallelization. *Proceedings of of IEEE*, Vol.81.No.2, Feb.1993.
3. W.Blume, R.Eigenmann, K.Faigin, J.Grout, T.Lawrence, J.Hoeflinger, D.Padua, Y.Paek, P.Petersen, W.Pottenger, L.Rauchwerger, P.Tu, and S.Weatherford. Restructuring Programs for High-Speed Computers with Polaris. *Proceedings of the 1996 ICPP Workshop on Challendes for Parallel Processing.* August, 1996. pp.149-161.1996.
4. M.W.Hallm, J.M.Anderson, S.P.Amarasinghe, B.R.Murphy, S.-W.Liao, E.Bugnion and M.S.Lam. Maximizing Multiprocessor Performance with the SUIF Compiler. *IEEE Computer*, December 1996.
5. R.Eigenmann, J.Hoeflinger, Z.Li, and D.Padua. Experience in the automatic parallelization of four Perfect-Benchmark programs. *Proceedings of 4th Workshop on Programming Languages and Compilers for Parallel Computing.* Pitman/MIT Press, August 1991.
6. E. Gamma, R.Helm, R.Johnson, and J.Vlissides. Design Patterns, Elements of Reusable Object-Oriented Software. Addison-Wesley, 1994.
7. David R. Musser and Atul Saini. STL tutorial & reference guide : C++ programming with the standard template library. Addison-Wesley, 1996.

8. W.Blume, R.Doallo, R.Eigenmann, J.Grout, J.Hoeflinger, T.Lawrence, J.Lee, D.Padua, Y.Paek, W.Pottenger, L.Rauchwerger, and P.Tu. Parallel Programming with Polaris. *IEEE Computer*, 29(12):78–82, December 1996.

9. W.L.Harrison III. The interprocedural analysis and automatic parallelization of scheme programs. *Lisp and Symbolic Computation*, 2(3/4):179-396, 1989.

10. W.L.Harrison III. Generalized iteration space and the parallelization of symbolic programs. In Ian Foster and Evan Tick, editors, *Proceedings of the Workshop on Computation of Symbolic Languages for Parallel Computers*. Argonne National Laboratory, October 1991.

11. Evelyn Duesterwald, Rajiv Gupta, Mary Lou Soffa. A Practical Data Flow Framework for Array Reference Analysis and its Use in Optimizations. *the proceedings of the SIGPLAN '93 Conference on Programming Language Design and Implementation*, pp. 68-76, June. 1993.

12. James R. Larus and Paul N. Hilfinger. Detecting conflicts between structure accesses. *Proceedings of the SIGPLAN '88 COnference on Programming Language Design and Implementation*, pp. 21-34, June 1988.

13. D. E. Maydan, S. P. Amarasinghe, and M. S. Lam. Data dependence and data flow analysis of arrays. *Proceedings of 5th Workshop on Programming Languages and Compilers for Parallel Computing*, August 1992.

14. William Blume and Rudolf Eigenmann. The Range Test: A Dependence Test for Symboli, Non-linear Expressions. TR 1345, Univ. of Illinois Urbana-Champaign, Center for Supercomputing Research & Development, April 1994.

15. Peng Tu and David Padua. Automatic Array Privatization. *Proceedings of Sixth Workshop on Languages and Compilers for Parallel Computing, Portland, OR. Lecture Notes in Computer Science*, vol. 768, pp. 500–521, August 12-14, 1993.

16. Martin C. Rinard, Pedro C.Diniz. Commutativity Analysis: A New Analysis Technique for Parallelizing Compilers. *ACM Transactions on Programming Lanugages and Systems*, Volume 19, pages 942–991, November 1997.

17. J. Hummel and L. Hendren and A. Nicolau. A General Data Dependence Test for Dynamic, Pointer-Based Data Structures, *Proceedings of the ACM SIGPLAN Conference on Programming Language Design and Implementation*, pp. 218–229, June 1994.

18. L. Hendren and J. Hummel and A. Nicolau. Abstractions for Recursive Pointer Data Structures: Improving the Analysis and Transformation of Imperative programs, *Proceedings of the ACM SIGPLAN '92 Conference on Programming Language Design and Implementation*, pp. 249–260, June 1992.

19. J.Hummel, L.Hendren and A.Nicolau. A Language for Conveying the Alising Properties of Dynamic, Poiinter-Based Data Structures, *Proceedings of the 8th Inthernational Parallel Processing Symposium*, pp.208–216, April 1994.

20. Laurie J.Hendren, Guang R. Gao. Designing Programming Languages for Analyzability: a Fresh Look at Pointer Data Structures. *Proceedings of the International Conference on Computer Lanugaes*, pp. 242-251, Oakland, CA, April 1992.

21. D.R.Chase, M.Wegman, and F.K.Zadek. Analysis of pointers and structures. *Proceedings of the SIGPLAN '90 Conference on Programming Language Design and Implementation*, pp. 296-310, 1990.

22. Laurie J.Hendren and Alexandru Nicolau. Parallelizing programs with recursive data structures. *IEEE Thans. on Parallel and Distributed Computing*, Jan. 1990.

23. James R. Larus and Paul N. Hilfinger. Restructuring LISP programs for concurrent execution. *Proceedings of the ACM/SIGPLAN PPEALS 1988 – Parallel Programming: Experience with applications, Languages and Systems*, pp. 100-110, July 1988.
24. James R. Larus, Restructuring Symbolic Programs for Concurrent Execution on Multiprocessors. PhD thesis, University of California, Berkeley, 1989.

SIPR: A New Framework for Generating Efficient Code for Sparse Matrix Computations

William Pugh and Tatiana Shpeisman

Department of Computer Science, University of Maryland
College Park, MD 20742, USA
{pugh,murka}@cs.umd.edu

Abstract. Developing computational codes that compute with sparse matrices is a difficult and error-prone process. Automatic generation of sparse code from the corresponding dense version would simplify the programmer's task, provided that a compiler-generated code is fast enough to be used instead of a hand-written code. We propose a new Sparse Intermediate Program Representation (SIPR) that separates the issue of maintaining complicated data structures from the actual matrix computations to be performed. Cost analysis of SIPR allows for the prediction of the program efficiency, and provides a solid basis for choosing *efficient* sparse implementations among many possible ones. The SIPR framework allows the use of techniques that are frequently used in the hand-written codes but previously were not considered for compiler-generated codes due to their complexity. We have developed tools that allow the automatic generation of efficient C++ implementations from SIPR, and describe experimental results on the performance of those implementations.

1 Introduction

Matrix computation occurs in many domains of science and engineering. For example, any physical problem modeled by partial differential equations requires matrix computation. The matrices are typically large, having thousands to hundreds of thousands of rows and columns, and sparse, where the great majority of elements are zero. Generally, fewer than 1% of the elements are nonzero. Storing such a matrix as a full two-dimensional array is prohibitively expensive in terms of space and processing time. Instead, various special purpose data structures are used to store only the nonzero elements. As a result, developing sparse matrix code is a difficult and error-prone process.

Automatically converting a dense code into a sparse code could simplify the programmer's task. Yet, the compiler support is of little practical use, unless compiler-generated code performs at least as well as an average hand-written code. Generating an efficient sparse code is complicated. The specialized data structures for sparse arrays do not support efficient random access. Efficient access requires enumerating the nonzero array elements in a particular order, or

S. Chatterjee (Ed.): LCPC'98, LNCS 1656, pp. 213–229, 1999.

preprocessing. For example, in a Compressed Column Storage format, we can efficiently enumerate the nonzero elements in any column. We can also expand the column so as to allow efficient random access to any row of the column (expanding the entire array would require too much space). Expanding a column is not cheap, so once the column is expanded, we want to perform all computations that require that expanded column before we perform computations that require a different column to be expanded. In some cases, complicated auxiliary data structures need to be created and maintained in order to allow efficient access to the nonzero elements in the order desired.

Even when sparse matrix codes are written by hand, one of the difficult issues is determining when a solution is a good one. For dense matrix codes, the asymptotic complexity is fixed, and changing the asymptotic complexity requires a completely different algorithm. Optimization is mainly a matter of constant terms and the memory hierarchy. Such a straightforward analysis is useless for sparse codes; instead, the actual sparsity pattern of the matrix must be taken into account. For some matrices (e.g., banded matrices), the parameters of the sparsity can be used in asymptotic analysis. For general sparse matrices, no such simple analysis is possible. Instead, work-sensitive measurements are used. One such measurement is the number of required floating point operations. If an algorithm runs in time proportional to the number of required floating point operations, it is said to be asymptotically optimal.

Our goal is to develop a sparse compiler that is able to automatically generate close to optimal sparse matrix code. Such a compiler needs to have a reliable way to predict the performance of the generated code and find computation reorderings and data structures that allow for efficient computation. It should be able to represent a possibly extendible set of complicated data structures and techniques commonly used in hand-written codes.

In this paper we propose new *Sparse Intermediate Program Representation* (SIPR) that is intended as an internal representation for a sparse compiler. SIPR separates the complications of maintaining sparse matrix data structures from the actual matrix computations. It allows to represent variety of techniques for accessing and enumerating sparse matrix elements, as well, as changing the matrix storage format during the program execution. To predict the program efficiency, it uses a cost model based on estimation of the program asymptotic complexity.

Previous approaches have focused on a more uniform and homogeneous set of data structures and transformations. With these, it was sufficient to simply "improve" the code; there was no need to worry about comparing alternative implementations. We know of no previous work that utilizes a cost model as sophisticated as the ones used by numerical analysts and our own work.

2   Basic Sparse Matrix Programming Techniques

In this section, we describe basic data structures that have been used in implementing sparse matrix codes, and some of the basic techniques that have been used in previous work on automatic generation of sparse matrix codes. We need to (and are able to) incorporate all of these techniques into programs represented in our intermediate form.

Sparse matrix storage formats. General sparse matrices (that is, sparse matrices for which no particular information about their nonzero structure is available) are usually stored as set of packed vectors corresponding to matrix columns or rows. The corresponding sparse matrix storage formats are known as *Compressed Column Storage (CCS) format* and *Compressed Row Storage (CRS) format*. In general, a sparse matrix can be stored as a set of the packed vectors of any direction (e.g., compressed diagonal storage). We shall refer to this general format as *Compressed Stripe Storage*.

A packed vector is represented as two parallel arrays containing values and indices of the nonzero elements. Depending on the application, the nonzeros within each vector may be ordered according to their indices or stored in an arbitrary order.

In many FORTRAN codes, the vectors for each matrix are densely packed. If we use a more general memory model with each vector allocated its own chunk of memory, then we can create additional nonzeros in a vector without rearranging the storage for the whole matrix.

Guard encapsulation. Replacing a loop whose iterations are executed only when a corresponding element of the sparse vector is nonzero by the enumeration over the nonzero elements of the vector is central for sparse matrix programming. As an example, consider adding a sparse vector to a dense vector, as shown in Fig. 1a.

```
                      for i=1  to n
                        if x(i) <> 0              for nonzeros e in x
for i=1 to n                y(i)  += x(i)            i=index(e)
  y(i) += x(i)             endif                     y(i) += e
endfor                    endfor                    endfor

a) dense              b) sparse with a conditional   c) sparse
```

Fig. 1. Performing sparse vector addition

The addition does not change the value of $y(i)$ unless $x(i) \neq 0$. One way to avoid performing unnecessary operations is to check this condition at the run-time (Fig. 1b). Yet, on most computers the check is almost as expensive as the addition itself (perhaps slower). A better way is to replace the i-loop by the enumeration of the nonzero elements of x (Fig. 1c).

The techniques of performing such a transformation automatically have been developed by Bik and Wijshoff [3,2] and used by Stodghill, Pingali, and Kotlyar [14,17]. Using their terminology, we call the conditions of the form $A(i, j) \neq 0$ *guards* and the technique itself guard encapsulation.

When due to the loop-carried dependencies reordering loop iterations is illegal, guard encapsulation does not change the program semantics only if the enumeration of the nonzero elements is performed in order corresponding to the original order of loop iterations.

Permutations. Permuting matrix columns or rows is often used in sparse matrix computing. For a matrix in CCS form, directly swapping two columns is easy but directly swapping two rows requires time proportional to the number of nonzeros in the matrix (less if the nonzeros in each vector are sorted). Instead, an indirection vector called *permutation vector* is used to record permutations, and the underlying data structure is not changed. A permutation vector is simply a mapping from "current index" to "original index". Generally, an inverse mapping from "original index" to "current index" is also maintained.

Changing compression directions and sorting. There is an efficient algorithm to convert a matrix in CCS format into a matrix in CRS format, and viseversa [6]. This algorithm has the nice property that it doesn't care if the vectors in the source matrix are sorted according to their index, but always generates sorted vectors in the result matrix. This algorithm runs in time $O(q + n)$, where q is the number of nonzeros in the matrix and n is the number of rows/columns in the matrix. This also gives a fairly efficient method to sort the nonzero entries in each vector according to their index (e.g., by converting from CCS to CRS and then back to CCS).

Auxiliary data structures. The data structures described here are *not* used to store an entire sparse matrix. Rather, they are used to support efficient access to a single row or column of a matrix, or to allow the elements in another data structure to be enumerated efficiently.

Sparse Accumulator (SPA). A *Sparse Accumulator (SPA)* [9] is a representation for a sparse vector that includes a dense array of the vector elements, a parallel array of flags indicating whether an element is zero or not, and an unordered list of nonzero elements. A sparse accumulator allows for both enumeration of vector nonzero elements and access to an arbitrary element in amortized constant time.

Ordered SPA enumerator. An *Ordered SPA* [11] is a variation of SPA with the list of remaining nonzero elements stored in a heap. This representation is useful for performing an ordered enumeration of the sparse vector while modifying its nonzero structure.

Alternate enumerator. A technique described in [8] can be used to scan a matrix along a direction different from the direction of its packed vectors. For a matrix with n columns/rows all these data structures require only $O(n)$ space, and advancing over q elements requires only $O(q)$ time.

3   A New Framework for Sparse Code Generation

We propose a new framework, *Sparse Intermediate Program Representation*, or *SIPR*, for sparse code generation. This framework is intended as an internal representation for a compiler that automatically generates sparse matrix code from a dense one.

In our framework a sparse matrix is represented through the set of the data structures that are used to store its elements. We refer to these data structures as element stores. We start from describing static SIPR in which the relationship between the matrix elements and element stores is fixed throughout the program execution. Then, we introduce dynamic SIPR that allows the matrix elements to move from one element store into another. We present the techniques for cost analysis of SIPR programs and generating executable code from the SIPR programs. We finish this section with several examples.

3.1   Static SIPR

A program in SIPR consists of loops, guards, assignment statements and simple conditionals. Array references are simple references to elements of entire arrays (e.g., A(i,j)). There is also a collection of element stores for representing the arrays of the program. Each element store represents a region of one array (e.g, the area below the diagonal). In static SIPR, the region represented by each element store is invariant over time. Two element stores can overlap in the regions of an array they represent, although this is somewhat unusual. When this does occur, the two element stores must be consistent with regards to the values of the common elements.

Loops can encapsulate guards that restrict iterations to only those corresponding to nonzero elements of an array. In Figure 2, both the k and j loops have encapsulated guards.

```
      for i = 2 do n do
        for k = 1 to i-1 if A(i,k) != 0 do
S1:   A(i,k) /= A(k,k)
          forany j = k+1 to n if A(k,j) != 0 do
S2:       A(i,j) -= A(k,j) * A(i,k)
```

Fig. 2. Program Fragment

Attached to each element store can be a number of enumerators and accessors. An enumerator is an auxiliary data structure that enumerates the nonzero elements contained in a element store in some particular order. An enumerator can be used only for an array reference that is encapsulated as a guard. For example, in Fig. 2, we can use an enumerator for the A(i,k) reference. An accessor is an auxiliary data structure that facilitates certain accesses to array elements.

An accessor is attached to an array reference that is not encapsulated as a guard. In this context, we treat all instances of a loop invariant array reference as a single reference. For example, in Fig. 2, all of the occurrences of A(i,k) should be attached to the same enumerator.

Also, a permutation vector can be attached to a direction of an array (typically, rows or columns). Each element store for that array must either understand or incorporate the permutation vector.

One requirement of our framework is that each static (i.e., textual) array reference can be attached to exactly one enumerator/accessor, which can be attached to exactly one element store. Iteration set splitting [2] could be used when this is a problem.

3.2   A Sparse Data Structure Library

Element stores together with their enumerators and accessors constitute a Sparse Data Structure Library. Currently, we consider two element stores: Compressed Stripe Storage (CXS) and Sparse Accumulator (SPA). Some of accessors and enumerators for these element stores are shown in Tables 1 and 2. These element stores and enumerators/accessors are just some possible data structures and methods that are used in sparse matrix computing. It is our intention that this library could be extended, perhaps even by a user.

Table 1. Enumerators/accessors for Compressed Stripe Storage (CXS)

Enumerator/Accessor	Attribute Constraints	Cost
SE: Standard enumerator – iterates through a packed vector	E.direction = ES.direction E.ordered=ES.ordered	v
AE: Alternate enumerator – Sect. 2	E.direction $\neq$ ES.direction $\neg$ E.ordered $\wedge$ ES.ordered	$v + qs$
LSA: Linear search accessor – search through a packed vector	$\neg$ ES.ordered	vc
BSA: Binary search accessor – binary search through a packed vector	ES.ordered $\wedge$ A.modification = no_fill	$v \log c$

Both element stores and their enumerators/accessors have a set of optional attributes, and there are constraints between the attributes of an enumerator/accessor and the attributes of the underlying element store. For example, *Stripe Direction* attribute specifies the direction along which the elements are stored or traversed, and *Ordered* attribute specifies whether the elements are stored or generated in order of their indices.

Table 2. Enumerators/accessors for Spare Accumulator (SPA)

Enumerator/Accessor	Attribute Constraints	Cost
SE: Standard enumerator – traverses list of nonzero elements	¬ E.ordered	v
OE: Ordered enumerator – traverses list of nonzero elements (Sect. 2).	E.ordered	$v \log c$
DA: Direct accessor		v

Each enumerator/accessor has a cost function that is a measure of the work it performs during the program execution. The cost is expressed in terms of the following variables:

- A v variable that denotes number of elements (not necessary unique) referenced by the enumerator/accessor
- A q variable that denotes number of elements in the element store.
- A c variable that denotes maximum number of elements in a stored stripe.
- An s variable that describes the number of times an array is being "swept through".

3.3 Dynamic SIPR

Although Static SIPR is adequate for representing a number of sparse matrix algorithms, it is not for others. For example, a common technique used in sparse matrix programming is to scatter a compressed vector into a SPA before modifying it and to gather it back afterwards. In order to handle this, we extend SIPR to allow element stores to contain a dynamic set of elements. As time passes, the set of elements represented in each element store may change.

The dynamic mapping of array elements to element stores is described as a relation between the elements of the array, the moment(s) at which the element store becomes responsible for the element, and the moment at which each occurrence of responsibility ends. Note that an element store might be responsible for an element of an array, become no longer responsible for it, and then become responsible for it again.

To specify how elements move from one element store to another we use a set of *obtain* operations. A specification of an obtain operation gives the source and destination element stores, the time(s) at which it occurs, and the set of elements copied. Also, at the time an element store becomes no longer responsible for some elements, there must be a *discard* operation. The em discard operation can free up memory resources and restore data structures to a "pristine" state so that they can be ready to obtain more elements. Obtain and discard operations are included into the Sparse Data Structure Library. Similar to enumerators and accessors, obtain operations have attribute constraints and cost functions. The library does not include all possible obtain operations, thus, restricting kind of data moves that can be used in the program. For example, we do not include an operation that would obtain a new row for a compressed ordered column storage, as this expensive operation is not used in the efficient codes.

The obtain/discard operations are placed between the statements. To simplify things, we allow the time at which an element store becomes responsible for an element to be identical to the time the element store it obtains the value from stops being responsible for it. To make this valid, at each place where obtain/discard operations occur, we perform all obtain operations before we perform any discard operations.

To represent a moment of time at which an element store obtains or discards an element we use a global time index, similar to that described by Wayne Kelley and William Pugh [12]. A moment of global time is specified as a tuple in which the odd positions correspond to the statement number within the loop and the even positions correspond to the loop iterations. The statements are numbered using the odd numbers, while the even numbers indicate the places between the statements where the obtain/discard operations can be performed. For example, for the program fragment in Fig. 2 the tuple $[1, 3, 1, 2, 1]$ corresponds the instance of the statement S1 executed at the 3rd iteration of loop i and second iteration of loop k, while tuple $[1, 3, 0]$ corresponds to an obtain/discard operation that may be executed at the 3rd iteration of loop i before executing the loop k.

3.4   Cost Analysis of SIPR Programs

Since we want to consider a rich and extendible set of data structures for implementing sparse matrix algorithms, there is no one, obviously, best solution. Therefore, as a basis for comparing different implementations, we need to be able to automatically generate a good cost analysis of a SIPR program. Simply calculating the cost in terms of n is useless—we must perform an output sensitive analysis.

Our cost analysis will be in terms of the following variables:

- n_X denotes a scalar variable X, typically the number of rows/columns of some matrix.
- q_r denotes the number of distinct array elements referenced by a particular array reference r.
- w_i denotes the number of iterations of statement i that must be executed, given that all possible guards have been encapsulated.
- c_r denotes the maximum number of nonzeros that occur in a stripe of reference r.

Because of the number of variables and the difficulty in comparing the costs of two different programs, we typically drop the subscripts of all but the w_i variables. The additional information the subscripts provide is rather hard to use and interpret.

First step of the cost analysis is to label each loop (or guard) L with the number of times the body of that loop will execute in terms of the variables

Loop/Stmt Code						Count/Cost
k	forany i=1 to n					n
i	forany j=1 to n st. A(i,j)!=0					q
S_1	y(i) += A(i,j) * x(j)					w_1
	endfor					
	endfor					

| Element | | | | Enum/Acc Cost | |
Store	Format	Region	Reference	Kind	Func	Cost
A	CRS	[*,*]	A(i,j)	SE	v	q

Total cost: $O(w_1 + q + n)$

Fig. 3. Static SIPR for matrix-vector multiplication

above. If possible, we want an exact answer in terms of n and q. If that isn't possible, we shall allow an exact answer that also involves w_i terms. If that is also not possible, we shall allow an inexact upper bound that also involves c variables. Then we find the costs of enumerators/accessors and obtain operations by substituting variables used in their cost functions by the appropriate values for the particular program.

The cost of a program is the sum of the cost of all the accessors/enumerators, the cost of all the *obtain* operations, the cost of all the statements, and the cost of all the loops/guards. A simple example of static SIPR together with its cost calculation is shown in Fig. 3.

3.5 Generating Executable Code for SIPR Programs

Each element store, accessor and enumerator corresponds to and is implemented as a C++ class. Operations such as enumerating non-zero elements and accessing/updating elements are invoked as methods. Obtain/discard operations are also translated into element store method calls. An enumerator/accessor might also have a support code that is executed once for several enumerated/accessed elements. For example, an alternate enumerator has a *set_stripe*() method that is called whenever the processed stripe changes.

An enumerator might generate the elements that correspond to the loop iterations that are beyond the loop bounds. We have described techniques [15] that allow us to check to see if a run-time test will be needed (if the underlying element store only contains elements below the diagonal, then we do not need to check to see that enumerated elements are below the diagonal). When loop bounds are to be enforced at run-time we either surround a loop body by a conditional or pass the loop bounds to a "smart" enumerator so that it generates only the required elements. For example, a standard enumerator for the ordered compressed stripe storage may use a binary search to find a position from which it starts enumerating a stripe.

In order to get efficient code from this approach, we need a sophisticated and powerful optimizing C++ compiler. For example, it needs to take the fields of a class object and keep them in registers throughout the execution of a loop. While the Gnu and Sun C++ compilers fell short, the Dec cxx compiler, version 6.0, performs the optimizations we need.

3.6 Examples of Dynamic SIPR

Dynamic SIPR allows to represent many efficient sparse implementations that previously could not be generated automatically, such as matrix matrix multiplication with transposed arguments, LU decomposition with partial pivoting and Cholesky factorization. Below we present two examples: Matrix-Matrix Multiplication $C+ = A^T B$ and LU decomposition with partial pivoting.

Matrix-Matrix Multiplication: $C+ = A^T B$. In Fig. 4, we give the SIPR representation for an efficient algorithm for matrix-matrix multiplication $C+ = A^T B$.

Loop/Stmt Code						Count/Cost
j	forany j=1 to n					n
k	forany k=1 to n st. B(k,j)!=0					q
i	forany i=1 to n st. A(k,i)!=0					w_1
S_1	C(i,j) += A(k,i) * B(k,j)					w_1
	endfor					
	endfor					
	endfor					

Element Store	Format	Lifetime $[r, c] \to$	Reference	Enum/Acc Kind	Cost Func	Cost
A_0	CCS	$[-\infty] : [0]$				
A_1	CRS	$[0] : [+\infty]$	A(k,i)	SE	v	w_1
B	CCS	$[-\infty] : [+\infty]$	B(k,j)	SE	v	q
C_0	CCS	$[-\infty] : [1, c, 0]$ $[1, c, 2] : [+\infty]$				
C_1	SPA	$[1, c, 0] : [1, c, 2]$	C(i,j)	DA	v	w_1

Element Store	Operation	Time	Elements	Imple- mentation	Cost Func	Cost
A_1	obtain from A_0	$[0]$	$[*, *]$	2D-TranspCopy	v	q
A_0	discard	$[0]$	$[*, *]$			
C_1	obtain from C_0	$[1, j, 0]$	$[*, j]$	1D-SimpleCopy	v	q
C_0	discard	$[1, j, 0]$	$[*, j]$			
C_0	obtain from C_1	$[1, j, 2]$	$[*, j]$	1D-SimpleCopy	v	q
C_1	discard	$[1, j, 2]$	$[*, j]$			

Total cost: $O(w_1 + q + n)$

Fig. 4. Dynamic SIPR for matrix-matrix multiplication $C+ = A^T B$

We have assumed that A, B and C are all stored in CCS format. In actuality, it is difficult to efficiently calculate $C+ = A^T B$ with all three matrices stored in CCS format. That matrix A is accessed along the rows suggests that it would be worthwhile to transform A into CRS format to perform the calculations. After making the copy of A in CRS, we can either preserve the version of A in CCS format (someone else might have a use for it), or we can free it and the memory consumed by it. The representation in Fig. 4 assumes that we discarded the original copy of A, but this has no effect other than on memory consumption. Otherwise, the code is pretty straightforward; in each iteration of the j loop, column j of C is moved into a SPA, updated, and then moved out.

When we calculate the performance of program in Fig. 4, we find that the code will run in time $O(w_1 + q + n)$, that is, optimal. Performing the initial rearrangement of A has allowed us to use an efficient algorithm, and the cost of performing the initial rearrangement is small compared to the cost of performing the multiplication (for all but rather unusual and uninteresting cases). An experimental comparison of the performance with the codes generated by Bik's Sparse Compiler and Bernoulli Compiler is provided in Sect. 4.

Loop/Stmt	Code		Count/Cost
j	`for j=1 to n`		n
k	`  for k=1 to j-1 st A(k,j)!=0`		q
i	`    forany i=k+1 to n st A(i,k)!=0`		w_1
S_1	`      A(i,j) -= A(i,k) * A(k,j)`		w_1
	`    endfor`		
	`  endfor`		
S_2	`  piv=0; piv_val=0`		n
ii	`  forany ii=j to n st A(ii,j)!=0`		q
S_3	`    val=abs(A(ii,j))`		q
.	`    if (val > piv_val) then`		
.	`      piv=ii; piv_val=val`		
.	`    endif`		
.	`  endfor`		
S_4	`  call swap_rows(A,j,piv,j,n)`		n
l	`  forany l=k+1 to n st A(l,j)!=0`		q
S_5	`    A(l,j) /= A(j,j)`		q
	`  endfor`		
	`endfor`		

Element Store	Perm. Format Vector		Lifetime $[r,c] \to$	Reference	Enum/Acc Kind	Cost Func	Cost
A_0	CCS	p_1	$[-\infty] : [1, c, 0]$				
A_1	SPA	p_1	$[1, c, 0] : [1, c, 10]$	A(i,j)	DA	v	w_1
				A(k,j)	OE	$v \log c$	$q \log c$
				A(ii,j)	SE	v	q
				A(l,j)	SE	v	q
				A(j,j)	DA	v	n
A_2	CCS	p_1	$[1, c, 10] : [+\infty]\|r > c$ A(i,k)		SE	v	w_1
A_3	CCS	p_1	$[1, c, 10] : [+\infty]\|r \leq c$				

Element Store	Operation	Time	Elements	Imple- mentation	Cost Func	Cost
A_1	obtain from A_0	$[1, j, 0]$	$[*, j]$	1D-SimpleCopy	v	q
A_0	discard	$[1, j, 0]$	$[*, j]$			
A_2	obtain from A_1	$[1, j, 10]$	$[j+1 : n, j]$	1D-SimpleCopy	v	q
A_3	obtain from A_1	$[1, j, 10]$	$[1 : j, j]$	1D-SimpleCopy	v	q
A_1	discard	$[1, j, 10]$	$[*, j]$			

Total cost: $O(w_1 + q \log c + n)$

Fig. 5. Dynamic SIPR for LU decomposition with partial pivoting

LU decomposition with partial pivoting. Dynamic SIPR for an efficient algorithm for LU decomposition with partial pivoting is shown in Fig. 5. We have assumed that matrix A is stored in CCS format. At the beginning of each iteration of j loop column j of A is moved into SPA. After the column is processed, its part above and on the main diagonal is moved into a storage for the upper triangular factor, its part below the diagonal is moved into a storage for the lower triangular factor.

We use an ordered enumerator for reference $A(k, j)$, as loop k both encapsulates a guard with this reference and should be executed in the original order.

As a result the cost of the code differs from the optimal by $q \log c$ term. This term is usually insignificant compared to the cost of executing statement S_1. In Section 4.2 we give the experimental results that show that the code for SIPR representation shown in Fig. 5 performs better than GPLU code [10] that is theoretically optimal.

Bik's code for LU decomposition [2] solves the problem of executing k loop in the original order by disabling guard encapsulation for loop k. This is not a good solution, as it leads to n^2 complexity.

Swapping of the rows j and piv of A is implemented through the permutation vector. All element stores are effected by the same permutation vector p_1, so the enumerator for reference $A(i, k)$ and accessor for reference $A(i, j)$ in statement S_1 avoid extra indirection by using unpermuted value of row index i. The two last parameters of the swap operation $swap\_rows(A, j, piv, j, n)$ specify the range of the rows being swapped, that is, we are guaranteed that $j \leq j \leq n$ and $j \leq piv \leq n$. This is necessary to verify that row swap does not lead to the redistribution of the elements between the element stores.

4 Analytical and Experimental Results

In this section, we compare implementations generated from SIPR programs for sparse matrix-matrix multiplication and LU factorization (with and without pivoting) against the programs generated by Bik's MT compiler and the Bernoulli compiler, as well as against some hand-written programs used by numerical analysts.

First we present analytical results comparing the asymptotic complexity of different implementations. The asymptotic complexity of the programs has been computed from their SIPR representations by our SIPR compiler. To perform these computations for MT and Bernoulli codes, we first translated them into SIPR form. These SIPR forms perform essentially the same computations as the original codes, but use slightly different implementations of the data structures.

For experimental results, we used the codes as provided by the MT and Bernoulli programs. The matrix-matrix multiplication codes from Bik's MT compiler were generated by revision 5.1 of the MT compiler [4]. The three LU codes generated by Bik were taken from his Ph.D. thesis. The matrix-matrix multiplication codes from the Bernoulli compiler were provided by Paul Stodghill. Our codes has been translated from their SIPR representations into C++ by our SIPR compiler.

4.1 Analytical results

The asymptotic complexities of the programs are given in Table 3. The w, q, c and n variables have been described in Sect. 3.4. These results may be used to compare the program efficiency and determine how close a particular implementation is to the optimal one.

Table 3. Analytical performance of sparse matrix codes

Source	Problem	Variant	Time	Notes
MT compiler	Matrix-Matrix	$C+ = AB$	$O(w + q)$	
rev 5.1	multiplication	$C+ = A^T B$	$O(qn + w)$	
		$C+ = AB^T$	$O(qc + w)$	
		$C+ = A^T B^T$	$O(qnc + w)$	Dense result
Bik's	LU Decomposition	Sparse1	$O(qn + w)$	
Ph.D. thesis	without pivoting	Sparse2	$O(w + n^2 + qc)$	Requires hints
		LDU	$O(w + qc)$	Requires hints and
				transformations
Bernoulli	Matrix-Matrix	$C+ = AB$	$O(w \log c + q)$	All Bernoulli
compiler	multiplication	$C+ = AB^T$	$O(qc \log c)$	codes require
		$C+ = A^T B$	$O(w \log c + q)$	precomputed fill
		$C+ = A^T B^T$	$O(qc \log c)$	
	Cholesky Decomposition		$O((w + n) \log c + q)$	[13]
Hand-written	Matrix-Matrix	$C+ = AB$	$O(w + q)$	
SIPR	multiplication	$C+ = A^T B$	$O(w + q)$	Fig. 4
		$C+ = AB^T$	$O(w + q)$	
		$C+ = A^T B^T$	$O(w + q)$	
	LU decomposition with partial pivoting		$O(w + q \log c)$	Fig. 5
	Cholesky Decomposition		$O(w + q \log c)$	

Under reasonable assumptions (any row or column have at least one nonzero element, *etc.*), we know that $c \leq n \leq q \leq w \leq qc$. An optimal implementation would have a complexity of $O(w)$. Thus, in many cases we know that we have a near optimal code (hand-written SIPR, Bik's $C+ = AB$ code, Bernoulli's $C+ = AB$ and $C+ = A^T B$ codes). In some cases, the cost includes qn or n^2 component. For large, very sparse matrices, these are going to dominate the costs and make the algorithms impractical. In a couple of cases (Bik's $C+ = AB^T$, code, Bik's LDU code, Bernoulli code for $C+ = AB^T$ and $C+ = A^T B^T$), it is hard to tell how close the code comes to optimal, since it depends on how close qc is to w, and how tight an inexact bound of qc is, which is unknown at the compile time.

In general, asymptotic costs can be used to automatically identify a small set of promising implementations. Extending the cost model to include constant factors (rather than just asymptotic complexity) can provide further assistance. However, human judgment and/or experimental results are likely to be needed to find the best implementation among the good ones.

4.2 Experimental results

All the experiments have been run on AlphaStation 200 4/166. Following [16], we report some test results on DNC grid matrices. The test matrices have been obtained by applying a first-order stencil to a regular d-dimensional grid, with n points in each dimension and c component variables at each grid point. Following [2], we also consider $E(n, 5)$ matrices, that have nonzero elements in positions (r, c) such that $|r-c| \leq 1$ or $|r-c| = 5$. Also following [16], we report MegaFLOP rates rather than speed. In computing MegaFLOP rates, we use an optimal, algorithm-invariant calculation of the number of flops absolutely required by the program, rather than the flops actually performed.

Matrix matrix multiplication. We compare the performance of MT rev 5.1 code for matrix matrix multiplication $C+ = A^T B$ [4], Bernoulli's code provided by Paul Stodghill, and a code generated by a SIPR compiler from the representation shown in Fig. 4. The results in MFLOPS are shown in Fig. 6. Poor performance of Bik's code agrees with our analytical results. Bik's code becomes much worse on large matrices, reflecting the qn term. The Bernoulli code is not much slower than the code generated from Fig. 4 when there are not many non-zeros in each column. However, as the number of non-zeros in each column goes up, the Bernoulli code slows down (reflecting the $w \log c$ term), while the performance of Fig. 4 goes up (as the w term dominates the q term).

Grids			Rows	NZs	MFLOPS		
d	n	c	/Cols	/Col	Fig. 4	Bernoulli	Bik
2	10	1	100	5	2.2	2.2	0.210
2	17	1	289	5	3.4	2.7	0.078
2	25	1	625	5	3.0	2.7	0.033
3	10	1	1000	7	3.3	2.6	0.029
3	17	1	4913	7	2.9	2.2	0.005
3	25	1	15625	7	2.8	2.1	0.001
2	10	3	300	9	5.9	2.5	0.271

Grids			Rows/	NZs/	MFLOPS		
d	n	c	Cols	Col	Fig. 4	Bernoulli	Bik
2	17	3	867	9	6.0	2.4	0.101
2	25	3	1875	9	6.1	2.3	0.041
2	10	5	500	15	7.7	2.2	0.293
2	17	5	1445	15	8.0	2.2	0.079
2	10	7	700	21	8.7	2.1	0.246
2	17	7	2023	21	8.2	2.0	0.074
2	5	20	500	60	9.5	1.8	0.813

Fig. 6. Matrix matrix multiplication $C+ = A^T B$

LU decomposition without pivoting. We compare performance of several codes for LU decomposition without pivoting. Bik's sparse2 and LDU codes are the codes generated by Bik's Sparse Compiler [2, p.217-223] for matrices stored in compressed column format and LDU format, correspondingly. The SIPR representation that we used to generate our version of LU decomposition is similar to the one shown in Fig. 5 except that it does not include pivoting. GPLU is a hand-written code due to Gilbert and Perlis [10] that is guaranteed to run in time proportional to the number of floating point operations and until [5] was one of the fastest codes for sparse LU factorization.

Grids			MFLOPS			
d	n	c	Bik's sparse2	Bik's LDU	Fig. 5 w/o pivoting	GPLU
2	10	1	2.3	1.5	3.8	3.8
2	10	3	3.9	2.4	8.1	6.6
2	10	5	4.1	2.5	8.7	6.8
2	10	7	4.1	2.5	9.3	6.9
2	17	1	3.3	2.2	6.0	5.6
2	17	3	4.0	2.6	8.8	6.8
2	17	5	4.0	2.5	9.4	6.9
2	17	7	4.0	2.5	9.7	7.0

a) Regular grids

Matrix size	MFLOPS			
n	Bik's sparse2	Bik's LDU	Fig. 5 w/o pivoting	GPLU
1000	0.9	1.4	2.2	2.7
2000	0.5	1.5	2.2	2.7
3000	0.3	1.4	2.3	2.7
6000	0.21	1.4	2.2	2.6
9000	0.14	1.5	2.3	2.6
12000	0.10	1.4	2.3	2.5
15000	0.08	1.5	2.3	2.5

b) $E(n, 5)$ class matrices

Fig. 7. LU decomposition without pivoting

We ran the experiments on matrices generated from the regular (d, n, c) grids and the $E(n, 5)$ matrices. These matrices are symmetric positive-definite, so LU decomposition without pivoting is stable.

The MFLOPS rates for the above codes are shown in Fig. 7. The code derived from Fig. 5 outperforms all other versions except for the hand-written GPLU code for $E(n, 5)$ matrices where it is slightly slower. For the DNC matrices, the amount of work required is $O(n^2)$, so the n^2 term in the cost of Bik's sparse2 code is not much of a problem. However, for the $E(n, 5)$ matrices, the work required for LU factorization is $O(n)$, so Bik's sparse2 code performs very poorly as n grows. Note that for most realistic problems, sparse LU decomposition requires less than $O(n^2)$ flops, so Bik's sparse2 code is impractical.

LU decomposition with partial pivoting. We compare the code generated from Fig. 5 with the GPLU code [10] discussed above, and the SuperLU code [5] that uses a specially developed algorithm that provides much better cache performance and reduces indirection. Neither Bik's compiler nor the Bernoulli compiler is capable of handling LU decomposition with partial pivoting.

As a test suite we used several matrices from the Harwell-Boeing collection [7]. The columns of all the matrices have been permuted by Matlab's minimum degree ordering of $A^T A$ [9]. This is a standard technique used to increase the sparsity of the factors.

The characteristics of the test matrices and the performance results are shown in Table 4. The code generated from SIPR in Fig. 5 performs better than GPLU for almost all the examples. The SuperLU code [5] performs up to four times better than either GPLU or Fig. 5.

Table 4. LU decomposition with partial pivoting

Matrix	Size	Number of nonzeros	Density	MFLOPS Fig. 5	GPLU	SuperLU
west1505	1505	5414	0.002	1.8	2.2	2.3
gre343	343	1310	0.011	7.1	5.9	12.8
gemat11	4929	33108	0.001	4.4	4.7	5.1
mcfe	765	24382	0.041	7.8	6.5	13.1
orani678	2529	90158	0.014	6.7	5.9	9.1
sherman5	3312	20793	0.002	7.3	5.7	16.8
lns3937	3937	25407	0.002	7.1	5.5	14.8
orsreg1	2205	14133	0.003	6.4	5.1	18.1
saylr4	3564	22316	0.002	6.1	4.8	18.1

5   Previous Work

Previous work by Bik [2,1,3] and the Bernoulli project team [14,17,13,16] have focused a great deal of effort on automatic techniques to derive the one, right loop structure for a sparse computation that would provide for a particular program property. Bik's sparse compiler strives to generate the code that accesses a matrix along the specified preferred access direction [2,1]. The Bernoulli compiler, which uses relational algebra approach, looks for the join ordering that is consistent with the matrix format index hierarchy [14]. Even if the loop structure that satisfies these criteria exists it does not guarantee that the generated code is efficient, as we have seen in Sect. 4. For example, the code generated by Bik's sparse compiler for LU decomposition without pivoting is $O(n^2+qc)$ and $\Omega(n^2)$. Such complexity is considered unacceptable by numerical analysts:

> One of the subtleties in writing sparse matrix software lies in avoiding $O(n^2)$ or more operations. [6]

Our framework provides a reliable way to predict a program performance by estimating the program asymptotic complexity – the same criteria that is used by numerical analysts.

Both Bik's sparse compiler and Bernoulli compiler allow for only small set of the techniques to be used in the generated code. These techniques are sufficient for simple programs, such as matrix vector multiplication, or matrix matrix multiplication $C+ = AB$, but not for more complicated programs, such as matrix factorizations. The applicability of Bernoulli compiler is severely limited by its inability to handle fill-in. We propose a flexible framework with an extendible sparse data structure library that can accommodate the variety of techniques used in the hand-written sparse matrix codes.

6   Conclusions and Future Work

Previous work by Bik [2,1,3] and the Bernoulli project [14,17,13,16] have been hindered by its inability to accommodate complicated techniques used in hand-written sparse codes and lack of reliable criteria for prediction of the performance of the generated code.

In this paper we have presented a framework that does not have these limitations. Our framework incorporates many techniques that have been previously ignored due to their complexity. As a result, it allows to represent efficient code for such programs as LU decomposition with partial pivoting and Cholesky factorization that could not been satisfactory handled before. The cost analysis of sparse intermediate program representations allows us to predict and compare the performance of different sparse implementations.

In the future, we want to extend the SIPR form and our compiler to handle more complicated sparse matrix algorithms, such as the SuperLU algorithm. Another issue of research is that SIPR is not primarily designed as a user-level programming language; we shall look at ways of having the user specify sparse matrix algorithms that can be converted into a SIPR representation.

References

1. Peter M. W. Knijnenburg Aart J. C. Bik and Harry Wijshoff. Reshaping access patterns for generating sparse codes. In *Seventh Annual Workshop on Languages and Compilers for Parallel Computing*, August 1994.

2. A. J. C. Bik. *Compiler Support for Sparse Matrix Computations.* PhD thesis, Leiden University, May 1996.

3. Aart J.C. Bik and Harry A.G. Wijshoff. Compilation techniques for sparse matrix computations. In *ICS93*, July 1993.

4. P. Brinkhaus, A. Bik, and H. Wijshoff. Subrountine on demand-service. http://hp137a.wi.leidenuniv.nl/blas-service/blas.html.

5. Demmel, Eisenstat, Gilbert, Li, and Liu. A supernodal approach to sparse partial pivoting. Technical Report 95-883, Computer Science Dept., U. of California at Berkeley, Berkeley, CA, September 1995.

6. I. S. Duff, A. M. Erisman, and J. K. Reid. *Direct Methods for Sparse Matrices.* Oxford Science Publications, 1992.

7. I. S. Duff, R. Grimes, and J. Lewis. Sparse matrix test problems. *ACM Trans. on Mathematical Software*, 15:1–14, 1989.

8. A. George and J. W. H. Liu. *Computer Solution of Large Sparse Positive-definite Systems.* Prentice-Hall, 1981.

9. J.R. Gilbert, C.Moler, and R.Schreiber. Sparse matrices in matlab: Design and implementation. *SIAM J. on Matrix Analysis and Applications*, 13(1):333–356, 1992.

10. J.R. Gilbert and T. Peirls. Sparse partial pivoting in time proportional to arithmetic operations. *SIAM J. on Scientific and Statistical Computing*, 9:862–874, 1988.

11. J. Irwin, J.-M. Loingtier, J. Gilbert, G. Kiczales, J. Lamping, A. Mendhekar, and T. Shpeisman. Aspect-oriented programming of sparse matrix code. In *International Scientific Computing in Object-Oriented Parallel Environments*, December 1997. Marina del Rey, CA.

12. Wayne Kelly and William Pugh. Minimizing communication while preserving parallelism. In *Proceedings of the 1996 International Conference on Supercomputing*, May 1996.

13. V. Kotlyar and K. Pingali. Sparse code generation for imperfectly nested loops with dependences. In *Proceedings of the 1997 International Conference on Supercomputing*, July 1997.

14. V. Kotlyar, K. Pingali, and P. Stodghill. A relational approach to the compilation of sparse matrix programs. In *EuroPar 97*, 1997.

15. Tatiana Shpeisman. Generation of the efficient code for sparse matrix computations. Ph.D. Thesis Proposal, Dept. of Computer Science, University of Maryland, College Park, January 1998.

16. P. Stodghill. *A Relational Approach to the Automatic Generation of Sequential Sparse Matrix Codes.* PhD thesis, Dept. of Computer Science, Cornell U., 1997.

17. K. Pingali V. Kotlyar and P. Stodghill. Compiling parallel sparse code for user-defined data structures. In *"Eighth SIAM Conference on Parallel Processing for Scientific Computing"*, March 1997.

HPF-2 Support for Dynamic Sparse Computations*

R. Asenjo[1], O. Plata[1], J. Touriño[2], R. Doallo[2], and E.L. Zapata[1]

[1] Dept. Computer Architecture, University of Málaga, Spain
{asenjo,oscar,ezapata}@ac.uma.es
[2] Dept. Electronics and Systems, University of La Coruña, Spain
{juan,doallo}@udc.es

Abstract. There is a class of sparse matrix computations, such as direct solvers of systems of linear equations, that change the fill-in (nonzero entries) of the coefficient matrix, and involve row and column operations (pivoting). This paper addresses the problem of the parallelization of these sparse computations from the point of view of the parallel language and the compiler. Dynamic data structures for sparse matrix storage are analyzed, permitting to efficiently deal with fill-in and pivoting issues. Any of the data representations considered enforces the handling of indirections for data accesses, pointer referencing and dynamic data creation. All of these elements go beyond current data-parallel compilation technology. We propose a small set of new extensions to HPF-2 to parallelize these codes, supporting part of the new capabilities on a runtime library. This approach has been evaluated on a Cray T3E, implementing, in particular, the sparse LU factorization.

1 Introduction

Irregular computations, where data-access patterns and workload are not known at compile time, appear profusely on scientific and engineering applications. An approach to handle such computations is based on extending a data-parallel language with new constructs suitable to express non-structured parallelism. With this information, the compiler can perform at compile time a number of optimizations, usually embedding the rest of them into a runtime library. In Fortran D [12], the programmer can specify a mapping of array elements to processors using another array. Vienna-Fortran [22] lets programmers define functions to specify irregular distributions. HPF-2 [15,16] provides a generalized block distribution (GEN-BLOCK), where the contiguous array partitions may be of different sizes,

* This work was supported by the Ministry of Education and Science (CICYT) of Spain (TIC96-1125-C03), by the Xunta de Galicia (XUGA20605B96), by the European Union (BRITE-EURAM III BE95-1564), by the Human Capital and Mobility programme of the European Union (ERB4050P1921660), and by the Training and Research on Advanced Computing Systems (TRACS) at the Edinburgh Parallel Computing Centre (EPCC).

S. Chatterjee (Ed.): LCPC'98, LNCS 1656, pp. 230–246, 1999.

and an indirect distribution (INDIRECT), where a mapping array is defined to specify an arbitrary assignment of array elements to processors.

A different approach is based on runtime techniques, that is, the non-structured parallelism is captured and managed fully at runtime. These techniques automatically manage programmer-defined data distributions, partition loop iterations, remap data and generate optimized communication schedules. Most of these solutions are based on the inspector-executor paradigm [18,7].

Current language constructs and the supportive runtime libraries are insufficiently developed, leading to low efficiencies when they are applied to a wide set of irregular codes. In the context of sparse computations, we found useful to inform the compiler not only about the data distribution, but also about how these data are stored in memory. We will call *distribution scheme* the combination of these two aspects (data structure + data distribution). We have developed and extensively tested a number of pseudo-regular distribution schemes for sparse problems, which combines natural extensions of regular data distributions with compressed data storages [2,19,20,21]. These distribution schemes can be incorporated to a data-parallel language (HPF) in a simple way.

The above mentioned distribution schemes are faced to static sparse problems. In this paper we discuss data structures and distributions in the context of dynamic sparse matrix computations, involving fill-in and pivoting operations. Direct methods for solving sparse systems of linear equations, for instance, present this kind of computations. Factorization of the coefficient matrix may produce new nonzero values (fill-in), so that data structures must consider the inclusion of new elements at runtime. Also, row and/or column permutations of the coefficient matrix are usually accomplished to assure numerical stability and limit fill-in. All these features make such sparse computations hard to parallelize.

The rest of the paper is organized as follows. Section 2 discusses the dynamic data distributions schemes we have tested to implement efficient parallel sparse codes involving pivoting and fill-in. Specifically, a direct method for the LU factorization is taken as a working example. Section 3 describes our proposal to extend HPF-2 for considering the above dynamic distributions. Experimental results validating our approach are presented in Section 4.

2   Sparse Data Structures and Distributions

2.1   Sparse Data Structures

Two different approaches may be considered to represent a sparse matrix: static and dynamic data structures. Static data structures are the most used in Fortran codes. Common examples are Compressed Row and Column Storages (CRS and CCS) [4]. If the computation includes fill-in and/or pivoting operations, it may be preferably to use some more complex and flexible data structures (dynamic). We have experimented with linked lists and hybrid (semi-)dynamic data structures, depending on the type of data accesses we have to deal with.

To simplify the discussion, hereafter we will consider as a working example the LU factorization of a sparse matrix, computed using a general method [1,10].

```
do k = 1, n
     Find pivot=A_{ij}
     if (i ≠ k)
          swap A(k, 1 : n) and A(i, 1 : n)
     endif
     if (j ≠ k)
          swap A(1 : n, k) and A(1 : n, j)
     endif
     A(k + 1 : n, k) = A(k + 1 : n, k)/A(k, k)
     do j = k + 1, n
          do i = k + 1, n
               A(i, j) = A(i, j) − A(i, k)A(k, j)
          enddo
     enddo
enddo
```

Fig. 1. LU algorithm (General approach, right-looking version)

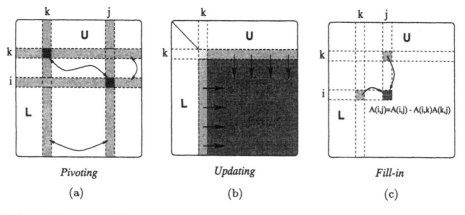

Pivoting	*Updating*	*Fill-in*
(a)	(b)	(c)

Fig. 2. Pivoting (a) and updating (b) operations, and fill-in (c) in right-looking LU

Fig. 1 shows an in-place code for the direct right-looking LU algorithm, where an n-by-n matrix A is factorized. The code includes a row and column pivoting operation (full pivoting) to provide numerical stability and preserve sparsity. Fig. 2 depicts the access patterns for the pivoting and updating operations on both matrices, L and U, and the generation of new entries. Note that efficient data accesses both by rows and columns are required.

The sparse coefficient matrix may be structured as a two-dimensional doubly linked list (see Fig. 3 (c)), to make efficient data accesses both by rows and columns. Each item in such a dynamic structure stores not only the value and the local row and column indices, but also pointers to the previous and next nonzero element in its row and column.

The complexity of this list can be reduced if full pivoting is replaced by partial pivoting, where only columns (or rows) are swapped. This may imply large memory and computation savings as we can use a simple list of packed vectors, or a one-dimensional doubly linked list structure, to store the sparse

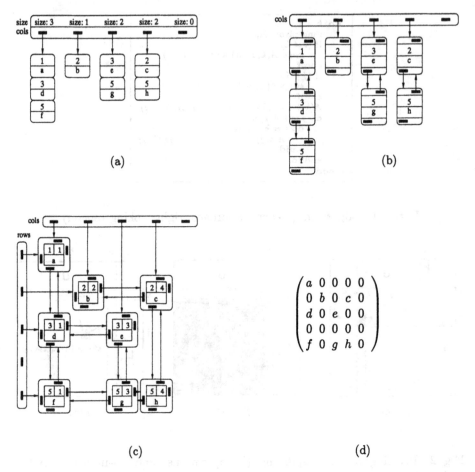

Fig. 3. Packed vectors and linked lists as efficient data structures for direct methods: (a) List of packed vectors; (b) one-dimensional doubly linked list; (c) two-dimensional doubly linked list; (d) local sparse matrix

matrix. As depicted in Fig. 3 (b), each linked list represents one column of the sparse matrix, where its nonzero entries are arranged in growing order of the row index. Each item of the list stores the row index, the matrix entry and two pointers. A simplification of the linked list is shown in Fig. 3 (a), where columns are stored as packed vectors, and they are referenced by means of an array of pointers. The list of packed vectors do not have pointers and, therefore, this mixed structure requires much less memory space than the doubly linked list.

Compressed formats and lists of packed vectors are very compact and allow fast accesses by rows or by columns to the matrix entries (but not both at the same time). Linked lists are useful when more flexible data accesses are needed. Two-dimensional lists, for instance, allow accesses to both rows and columns with the same overhead. The fill-in and pivoting issues are easily managed when doubly linked lists are used, as they make easy the entry insertion and dele-

```
!Doubly LLRS, LLCS (one-dimensional)          TYPE ptr
TYPE entry                                       TYPE (entry), POINTER:: p
  INTEGER:: index                             END TYPE ptr
  REAL:: value
  TYPE (entry), POINTER:: prev, next          TYPE (ptr), DIMENSION(n):: pex
END TYPE entry

!Doubly LLRCS (two-dimensional)
TYPE entry
  INTEGER:: indexi, indexj
  REAL:: value
  TYPE (entry), POINTER:: previ, prevj
  TYPE (entry), POINTER:: nexti, nextj
END TYPE entry
```

Fig. 4. Fortran 90 derived types for the items of LLRS, LLCS and LLRCS storage schemes, and a definition of an array of pointers (pex) to these items

tion operations. In the case of compressed formats (CRS, CCS ...) or a list of packed vectors, the fill-in problem is more difficult to solve. Compressed formats also have the inconvenience of not allowing the pivoting operation (column/row swapping) in an easy way. This can be overcome by using some mixed data structure, such as the list of packed vectors, or a linked list structure. Column pivoting is then implemented by just interchanging pointer values.

Albeit their flexibility, linked lists may have some drawbacks. The dynamic memory allocation for each new entry, as well as the list traversing, are time-consuming operations. Additionally, they consume more space memory than packed vectors. Finally, memory fragmentation due to allocation/deallocation of items may arise, as well as spatial data locality loss.

2.2 Dynamic Sparse Distribution Schemes

Four data storage schemes will be considered: LLCS (Linked List Column Storage), LLRS (Linked List Row Storage), LLRCS (Linked List Row-Column Storage) and CVS (Compressed Vector Storage), the first three schemes to represent sparse matrices, and the last one to represent sparse (one-dimensional) arrays. The LLCS storage scheme corresponds to the structure shown in Fig. 3 (b). In this figure the lists are doubly linked, but it can also be defined as singly linked, in order to save memory overhead. The LLRS storage scheme is similar to the LLCS scheme but considering linking by rows instead of columns. A combination of compressed columns and rows representation, interlinked among themselves, can be declared using the LLRCS storage scheme, as shown in Fig. 3 (c). As well as with the other two schemes, the entries can be singly or doubly linked. Finally, CVS scheme represents a sparse vector as two arrays and one scalar: the index array, containing the indices of the nonzero entries of the sparse array; the value array, containing the nonzero entries themselves; and the size scalar, containing the number of nonzero entries.

Fig. 4 displays the Fortran 90 derived types which may define the items of each kind of linked list. The first type corresponds to the LLRS and LLCS schemes

```
<sparse-directive>::= <datatype>, SPARSE (<sparse-content>) :: <array-objects>
<datatype>::= REAL | INTEGER
<sparse-content>::= LLRS (<ll-spec>)
                  | LLCS (<ll-spec>)
                  | LLRCS (<ll2-spec>)
                  | CVS (<cvs-spec>)
<ll-spec>::= <pointer-array-name>, <pointer-array-name>,
             <size-array-name>,
             <link-spec>
<ll2-spec>::= <pointer-array-name>, <pointer-array-name>,
              <pointer-array-name>, <pointer-array-name>,
              <size-array-name>, <size-array-name>,
              <link-spec>
<cvs-spec>::= <index-array-name>, <value-array-name>, <size-scalar-name>
<link-spec>::= SINGLY | DOUBLY
<array-objects>::= <sized-array>{,<sized-array>}
<sized-array>::= <array-name>(<subscript>[,<subscript>])
```

Fig. 5. Syntax for the proposed HPF-2 SPARSE directive with dynamic data structures

(doubly linked), indistinctly, and the second one to the LLRCS scheme, doubly linked. The singly linked versions for these data types are equivalent but without the *prev* pointers. The list itself is declared also through a derived type, **pex**, which defines an array (or two) of pointers to the above items.

Once storage schemes have been defined, we can use the SPARSE directive to specify that a sparse matrix (or sparse array) is stored using a particular linked list scheme. This directive was previously introduced [2,19] in the context of static sparse applications. Fig. 5 shows the BNF syntax for the dynamic SPARSE directive. The first two data structures, LLRS and LLCS, are defined by two arrays of pointers (<*pointer-array-name*>), which point to the beginning and to the end, respectively, of each row (or column) list, and a third array (<*size-array-name*>), containing the number of elements per row (for LLRS) or per column (for LLCS). The option <*link-spec*> specifies the type of linking of the list data structure (singly or doubly). Regarding the LLRCS data structure, we have four arrays of pointers which point to the beginning and to the end of each row and each column of the sparse matrix, and two additional arrays storing the number of elements per row and per column, respectively.

As an example, the following statement,

```
!HPF$ REAL, DYNAMIC, SPARSE (CVS(vi, vv, sz)):: V(10)
```

declares V as a sparse vector compressed using the CVS format. V will work in the code as a place holder of the sparse vector, which occupies no storage. What is really stored are the nonzero entries of the sparse array in vv, the corresponding array indices in vi, and the number of nonzero entries in sz. The place holder V actually provides an abstract object with which other data objects can be aligned and which can then be distributed. The DYNAMIC keyword means that the contents of the three arrays, vi, vv and sz, are determined dynamically, as a result of executing a DISTRIBUTE statement.

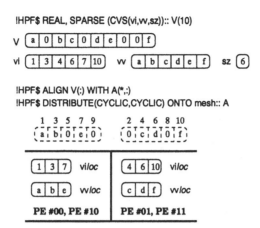

Fig. 6. Alignment and distribution of a sparse array on a 2×2 processor mesh

The HPF directives DISTRIBUTE and ALIGN can be applied to sparse place holders with the same syntax as in the standard. Distributing a sparse place holder is equivalent to distributing it as if it was a dense array (matrix). For instance, the statement,

```
!HPF$ DISTRIBUTE(CYCLIC) ONTO mesh:: V
```

considers V as a dense array (not compressed), mapping this array on the processors using the standard CYCLIC data distribution, and representing the distributed (local) sparse arrays using the CVS compressed format.

In the case of the ALIGN directive, however, the semantics is slightly different. From the next example code,

```
REAL, DIMENSION(10,10):: A
INTEGER, DIMENSION(10):: vi
REAL, DIMENSION(10):: vv
INTEGER:: sz
!HPF$ PROCESSORS, DIMENSION(2,2):: mesh
!HPF$ REAL, DYNAMIC, SPARSE (CVS(vi, vv, sz)):: V(10)
!HPF$ ALIGN V(:) WITH A(*,:)
!HPF$ DISTRIBUTE(CYCLIC,CYCLIC) ONTO mesh:: A
```

the (nonzero) entries of V (that is, vv) are aligned with the columns of A depending on the positions stored in the array vi, and not in the corresponding positions in their own vv array (which is the standard semantics). Now, the DISTRIBUTE directive replicates the V array over the first dimension of the processor array mesh, and distributes it over the second dimension in the same way as the second dimension of the A matrix. Observe that in this distribution operation, vi is taken as the index array for the entries stored in vv. Fig. 6 shows the combined effect of alignment/distribution for a particular case.

The combination of the directives SPARSE and DISTRIBUTE defines the distribution scheme of a sparse matrix. The variable V in the example code above

```
INTEGER, PARAMETER:: n=1000, dim=8
INTEGER:: k, i, j
REAL:: maxpiv, pivot, amul, product
INTEGER:: actpiv, pivcol
TYPE (entry), POINTER:: aux

TYPE (ptr), DIMENSION(n):: first, last, vpiv
INTEGER, DIMENSION(n):: vsize

REAL, DIMENSION(n):: vcolv, vmaxval
INTEGER, DIMENSION(n):: vcoli
INTEGER:: size

!HPF$ PROCESSORS, DIMENSION(dim):: linear
!HPF$ REAL, DYNAMIC, SPARSE(LLCS(first, last, vsize, DOUBLY)):: A(n,n)
!HPF$ REAL, DYNAMIC, SPARSE(CVS(vcoli, vcolv, size)):: VCOL(n)
!HPF$ ALIGN iq(:) WITH A(*,:)
!HPF$ ALIGN vpiv(:) WITH A(*,:)
!HPF$ ALIGN vmaxval(:) WITH A(*,:)
!HPF$ ALIGN VCOL(:) WITH A(:,*)
!HPF$ DISTRIBUTE (*,CYCLIC) ONTO linear:: A
```

Fig. 7. Declarative section of the extended HPF-2 parallel sparse LU code

really works as a place holder for the sparse array. The SPARSE directive establishes the connection between the logical entity V and its actual representation (compressed format). The benefit of this approach is that we can use the standard HPF DISTRIBUTE and ALIGN directives applied to the array V and, at the same time, store the array itself using a compressed format. In the rest of the code, the sparse matrix is operated using directly its compressed format.

3 Parallel Dynamic Sparse Computations

The SPARSE directive establishes a link between the sparse matrix (or array) and its storage structure. From this point on, we can choose to hide the storage scheme to programmers, and allow them to write the parallel sparse code using dense matrix notations. The compiler will be in charge of translating these dense notations into parallel sparse codes taking into account the storage schemes specified. However, this approach supposes a great effort in compiler implementation, as well as the possibility of mixing in the same code place holders (dense notations) with *real* arrays. Bik and Wijshoff [6] and Kotlyar and Pingaly [17] propose a similar approach, based on the automatic transformation of a dense program, annotated with sparse directives, into a semantically equivalent sparse code. The design of such compiler is, however, very complex, in such a way that no implementation of it is available for general and real problems.

A different approach is based on forcing programmers to use explicitly the compressed storage structures common in sparse codes, and allow them to use the place holders (dense notations) only for aligning and distributing purposes. Parallelism is constrained to the directives. If the parallel code is sequentially compiled, the resulting code would run properly.

3.1 Parallel Sparse LU Code

A direct right-looking LU factorization with partial pivoting (column swapping) will be considered in this section. In most cases, partial pivoting leads to similar numerical error results than full pivoting, but at a lower cost. However, a matrix reordering stage (*analyze* stage) should be added before the factorization. This is in charge of updating the permutation vectors so as sparsity and numerical stability are preserved in the subsequent factorization stage. A partial numerical pivoting is however retained in the factorization stage to cover the case that the selected pivot in the analyze stage turns to be unstable during factorization.

Despite pivoting, the sparsity of the matrix usually decreases during the factorization. In such case, a switch to a dense LU factorization may be advantageous at some point of the computation. This dense code is based on Level 2 BLAS, and includes numerical partial pivoting. At the switch point, the reduced sparse submatrix is scattered to a dense array. The overhead of the switch operation is negligible (as the analyze stage) and the reduced dense submatrix appears distributed in a regular cyclic manner. A 15% sparsity threshold value was used in our experiments to switch from the sparse to the dense code.

Fig. 7 shows the declarative section of the parallel sparse LU code, using the proposed extensions to HPF-2. Matrix A is defined as sparse and stored using the LLCS data structure. The arrays of pointers `first` and `last` indicate the first and the last nonzero entry, respectively, of each column of A The array `vsize` stores the number of nonzero entries on each column of A. The sparse array VCOL is also defined, stored using the CVS format. This array contains the normalized pivot column of A, calculated in each outer iteration of the algorithm.

The last sentence in the declaration section distributes the columns of the sparse matrix A cyclically over a one-dimensional arrangement of abstract processors (the one-dimensional characteristic is not essential). Previously, three dense arrays, iq, vpiv and vmaxval, were aligned with the columns of A, while VCOL was aligned with the rows of A. Hence, after distributing A, VCOL is replicated over all the processors. At each iteration of the main loop of the algorithm (loop k in Fig. 1), the owner of the column k of A selects and updates on VCOL the pivot column, which is consistently broadcast to the rest of processors to enable the subsequent parallel submatrix update. Fig. 8 shows an example of this declaration.

Fig. 9 presents the rest of the parallel LU code. The first action corresponds to the initialization of the array vpiv, which should point to the row that includes the pivot. This loop is parallel and no communications are required, as both arrays, vpiv and `first`, were aligned. Next, loop k starts. SwitchIter was calculated by the analyze stage, value from which the sparse code switches to an equivalent dense one.

The first action inside the main loop corresponds to column pivoting pivoting, in which we look for a stable pivot and, if possible, in agreement with the recommended permutation vector iq (obtained in the analyze stage). To fulfill the first condition, the pivot should be greater than the maximum absolute value of the pivot row times an input parameter called u ($0 \leq u \leq 1$). The maximum absolute value is calculated using the Fortran 90 MAXVAL() intrinsic funtion, evaluated over vmaxval vector. The update of vmaxval takes place on the second INDEPENDENT loop which traverses the pivot row storing the absolute

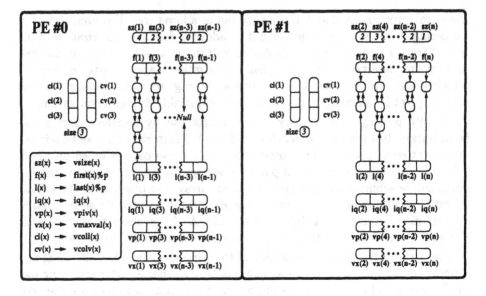

Fig. 8. Partitioning of most LU arrays/matrices on two processors, according to the HPF declaration of Fig. 7 (an even number of columns for A, and that the outer loop of the LU algorithm is in the fourth iteration, are assumed)

value of each entry on **vmaxval**. These entries are candidates for pivot. The ON HOME (vpiv(j)) directive tells the compiler that the processor owning vpiv(j) will be encharged of iteration j. The RESIDENT annotation points out to the compiler that all variables referenced inside the directive's body are local. Thus, the compiler analysis is simplified and more optimized code may be generated.

Once the threshold **maxpiv** is obtained, the pivot is chosen in such a way that its value is greater than the above threshold, and, on the other hand, sparsity is preserved by following the iq recommendations. This computation is, in fact, a reduction operation, and consequently we annotate the corresponding INDEPENDENT loop with such directive. This user-defined reduction operation is indeed not considered by the HPF-2 standard, but its inclusion would not add any significant complexity to the compiler implementation. Finally, after selecting the pivot, the **swap()** routine is called to perform the permutation of the current column k and the pivot column of matrix A.

After the pivoting operation, the pivot column is updated and packed into the sparse VCOL array. This is computed by the owner of such column (ON HOME directive). As VCOL is a replicated array, any update made on it is communicated to the rest of processors. Finally, the submatrix $(k + 1 : n, k + 1 : n)$ of A is updated. Loop j runs over the columns of the matrix, and it is parallel. The NEW directive prevents the compiler from considering inexistent data dependences due to variables that are actually private to each iteration.

The code also contains the user-defined routines **append()** and **insert()** for list management, which are included in a Fortran 90 module. The append()

```
! --> Initialization
!HPF$ INDEPENDENT
      DO j = 1, n
         vpiv(j)%p => first(j)%p
      END DO

! --> Main loop LU
main: DO k = 1, SwitchIter

! --> Pivoting
! --> Candidates for pivot are selected and ...
!HPF$ INDEPENDENT
      DO j = k, n
!HPF$ ON HOME (vpiv(j)), RESIDENT BEGIN
         IF (.NOT.ASSOCIATED(vpiv(j)%p)) CYCLE
         IF (vpiv(j)%p%index /= k) CYCLE
         vmaxval(j) = ABS(vpiv(j)%p%value)
!HPF$ END ON
      END DO

! --> ... the maximum value is calculated
      maxpiv = MAXVAL(vmaxval(k:n))
      maxpiv = maxpiv*u

! --> The pivot is chosen from the candidates
! --> (reduction operation)
      actpiv = 0
      pivcol = 0
!HPF$ INDEPENDENT, REDUCTION(actpiv,pivcol)
      DO j = k, n
         IF (vmaxval(j) > maxpiv .AND.
            iq(pivcol) > iq(j)) THEN
            actpiv = vmaxval(j)
            pivcol = j
         END IF
      END DO
      IF(pivcol == 0) pivcol=k
      IF(pivcol /= k) THEN
! ----> Columns are swapped
         CALL swap(k,pivcol,first,last,vpiv,vsize,iq)
      END IF

! --> Pivot column is updated and packed
!HPF ON HOME (vpiv(k)), RESIDENT BEGIN
      aux => vpiv(k)%p
      pivot = 1/(aux%value)
      aux%value = pivot
      aux => aux%next
      size = vsize(k)-1

      DO i = 1, size
         aux%value = aux%value*pivot
         vcolv(i) = aux%value
         vcoli(i) = aux%index
         aux => aux%next
      END DO
!HPF END ON
                              •
                              •
                              •
```

Fig. 9. Outline of an extended HPF-2 specification of the parallel right-looking partial pivoting LU algorithm (first part)

routine adds an entry at the end of a list, while the insert() routine adds an element at the beginning or in the middle of a list.

4   Evaluating Results

A parallel sparse right-looking partial pivoting LU algorithm was implemented using the Cray T3E Fortran 90 and the SHMEM library [5]. The columns of

```
                              •
                              •
                              •
! --> Submatrix of A is Updated
!HPF$ INDEPENDENT, NEW (aux,i,amul,product)
loopj:  DO j = k+1, n
!HPF$ ON HOME (vpiv(j)), RESIDENT BEGIN
            aux => vpiv(j)%p
            IF (.NOT.ASSOCIATED(aux)) CYCLE
            IF (aux%index /= k) CYCLE
            amul = aux%value
            vsize(j) = vsize(j)-1
            vpiv(j)%p => aux%next
            aux => aux%next
loopi:      DO i = 1, size
              product = -amul*vcolv(i)
              DO
                IF (.NOT.ASSOCIATED(aux)) EXIT
                IF (aux%index >= vcoli(i)) EXIT
                aux => aux%next
              END DO
outer_if:     IF (ASSOCIATED(aux)) THEN
                IF (aux%index == vcoli(i)) THEN
                   aux%value = aux%value + product
                ELSE
! ----> First or middle position insertion
                   CALL insert(aux,vcoli(i),product,first(j)%p,
                               vsize(j))
                   IF (vpiv(j)%p%index >= aux%prev%index)
                       vpiv(j)%p => aux%prev
                END IF
              ELSE outer_if
! ----> End position insertion
                CALL append(vcoli(i),product,first(j)%p,last(j)%p,
                            vsize(j))
                IF (.NOT.ASSOCIATED(vpiv(j)%p)) vpiv(j)%p => last(j)%p
              END IF outer_if
            END DO loopi
!HPF$ END ON
          END DO loopj
        END DO main
```

Fig. 9 (cont.). Outline for an extended HPF-2 specification of the parallel right-looking partial pivoting LU algorithm (last part)

the sparse matrix A were cyclically distributed over the processors (linearly arranged), and stored in the local memories using one-dimensional doubly linked lists. This parallel algorithm is similar to the sequential version, but with local indices instead of the global ones, and Cray SHMEM routines performing communication/synchronization operations. All these operations were encapsulated into calls to the DDLY (Data Distribution Layer) runtime library [20]. The parallel code was designed in such a way that it could be the output of a hypothetic extended HPF-2 compiler (extended with the directives for the proposed distribution schemes). That is, it should be not considered as an optimized hand-coded program.

Fig. 10 shows execution times and speed-up for the parallel LU algorithm. Test sparse matrices were taken from the Harwell-Boeing suite and University of Florida Sparse Matrix Collection [8] (see Table 1). The efficiency of the parallel code is high when the size of the input matrix is significantly large. We also carried out experiments considering meshes of processors instead of linear arrays, but the best times were obtained in the latter case and when the matrices were distributed by columns. Load imbalances due to fill-in (cyclic distribution) were not a problem for any matrix (see Fig. 11).

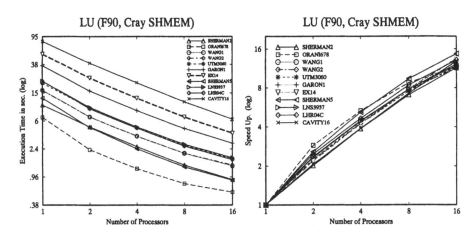

Fig. 10. Parallel sparse LU execution times and speed-up for different sparse matrices, using F90 linked lists and Cray T3E SHMEM

Table 1. Harwell-Boeing and Univ. of Florida test matrices

Matrix	Origin	n	# entries	sparsity
STEAM2	Oil reservoir simulation	600	13760	3.82%
JPWH991	Circuit physics modeling	991	6027	0.61%
SHERMAN1	Oil reservoir modeling	1000	3750	0.37%
SHERMAN2	Oil reservoir modeling	1080	23094	1.98%
ORANI678	Economic modeling	2529	90158	1.41%
WANG1	Discretized electron continuity	2903	19093	0.22%
WANG2	Discretized electron continuity	2903	19093	0.22%
UTM3060	Uedge test matrix	3060	42211	0.45%
GARON1	2D FEM, Navier-Stokes, CFD	3175	88927	0.88%
EX14	2D isothermal seepage flow	3251	66775	0.63%
SHERMAN5	Oil reservoir modeling	3312	20793	0.19%
LNS3937	Compressible fluid flow	3937	25407	0.16%
LHR04C	Light hydrocarbon recovery	4101	82682	0.49%
CAVITY16	Driven cavity problem	4562	138187	0.66%

The sequential efficiency of the Fortran 90 implementation of the sparse LU algorithm was also tested. Table 2 presents comparison results from this implementation and the Fortran 77 MA48 routine [10]. We observe that the MA48 routine is significantly faster than our algorithm for many matrices, but it should be considered the fact that the Cray Fortran 90 compiler is not efficient generating code for managing lists. However, the resulting computing errors are practically the same for both algorithms. The main advantage of our approach is its ease to be parallelized, as opposite to the MA48 routine, which is inherently sequential, as corresponds to a left-looking algorithm.

The analyze and solve (forward and backward substitution) stages of the LU algorithm were also implemented, but they are not presented here as no

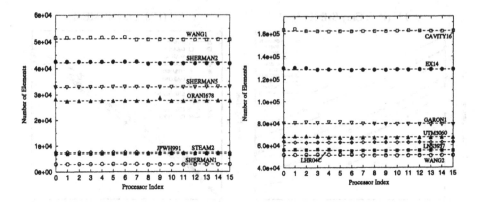

Fig. 11. Workload (non-null matrix values) on each processor after executing the parallel sparse LU factorization on a 16-processor system

Table 2. Comparison between Fortran 90 LU and MA48 (times in sec.)

	Times		Errors
Matrix	**F90 – MA48 ratio**		**F90 – MA48**
STEAM2	.572 – .373	1.53	.15E-11 – .13E-11
JPWH991	1.039 – .563	1.84	.44E-13 – .82E-13
SHERMAN1	.574 – .148	3.87	.14E-12 – .16E-12
SHERMAN2	10.05 – 9.77	1.02	.14E-05 – .15E-05
ORANI678	6.74 – 3.52	1.91	.70E-13 – .74E-13
WANG1	16.33 – 18.76	0.87	.11E-12 – .97E-13
WANG2	16.19 – 16.54	0.97	.53E-13 – .52E-13
UTM3060	20.57 – 22.68	0.90	.53E-08 – .58E-08
GARON1	36.39 – 28.80	1.26	.53E-09 – .21E-08
EX14	53.68 – 62.78	0.85	.28E+01 – .93E+01
SHERMAN5	12.58 – 6.09	2.06	.75E-12 – .59E-12
LNS3937	21.88 – 15.09	1.44	.15E-02 – .13E-02
LHR04C	22.15 – 10.42	2.12	.22E-03 – .10E-03
CAVITY16	81.23 – 88.48	0.91	.39E-09 – .49E-09

additional relevant aspect is contributed. Both execution time and fill-in are comparable with those of the MA48 routine (they do not differ more than 10%).

5   Related Work

There are many parallel sparse LU factorization designs in the literature. From the loop-level parallelism point of view, the parallel pivot approach allows the extraction of an additional parallelism due to the sparsity of the matrix, besides the obvious one coming from the independences on the loops traversing rows and columns [3]. Coarser parallelism level can be exploited thanks to the elimination tree, which can be used to schedule parallel tasks in a multifrontal [11] code. It is also possible to use a coarse matrix decomposition to obtain an ordering to bordered block triangular form, as is done in the MCSPARSE package [14]. The supernodal [9] approach is also a parallelizable code [13].

Some of the above parallel solutions can be implemented using the approach described in this paper. Loop-level LU approaches can be implemented using the LLRCS data storage (in addition to LLCS), and some other complex reductions to choose a good parallel pivot set, but loosing some of the performance due to the semi-automatic implementation. The multifrontal approach, however, is not suitable to the linked list sparse directive, due to the use of different data storage schemes. However, they could be implemented using the basic BCS or BRS sparse distributions [2,19]. The implementation of the supernodal code in [9] uses some sort of column compressed storage, but it would be necessary to simplify the memory management and the data access patterns to consider a data-parallel implementation of this code.

6   Conclusions

This paper presented a solution to the parallelization of dynamic sparse matrix computations (applications suffering from fill-in and/or involving pivoting operations) in a HPF-2 environment. The programmer is allowed to specify a particular sparse data storage representation, in addition to a standard data distribution. Sparse computations are specified by means of the storage representation constructs, while the (dense) matrix notation is reserved to declare alignments and distributions. Our experiments (a parallel sparse direct LU solver, *emulating* the output of an extended HPF-2 compiler) show that we can obtain high efficiencies using that strategy.

The research discussed in this paper gives new in-depth understanding in the semi-automatic parallelization of irregular codes dealing with dynamic data structures (list based), in such a way that the parallel code becomes a generalization of the original sequential code. An efficient parallel sparse code can be obtained by annotating the corresponding sequential version with a few number of HPF-like directives. The techniques described in this paper are not only useful to deal with the fill-in and pivoting problems, but they can also be applied to many other applications where the same or similar data structures are in use.

Acknowledgements

We gratefully thank Iain Duff and all members in the parallel algorithm team at CERFACS, Toulouse (France), for their kindly help and collaboration. We also thank the CIEMAT (Centro de Investigaciones Energéticas, Medioambientales y Tecnológicas), Spain, for giving us access to the Cray T3E multiprocessor.

References

1. R. Asenjo. Sparse LU Factorization in Multiprocessors. Ph.D. Dissertation, Dept. Computer Architecture, Univ. of Málaga, Spain, 1997.

2. R. Asenjo, L.F. Romero, M. Ujaldón and E.L. Zapata. Sparse Block and Cyclic Data Distributions for Matrix Computations. in *NATO Adv. Res. Works. on High Performance Computing: Technology, Methods and Applications*, Cetraro, Italy, 1994. (Elsevier Science B.V., The Netherlands, pp. 359–377, 1995).

3. R. Asenjo and E.L. Zapata. Sparse LU Factorization on the Cray T3D. *Int'l. Conf. on High-Performance Computing and Networking (HPCN'95)*, Milan, Italy, pp. 690–696, 1995.

4. R. Barret, M. Berry, T. Chan, J. Demmel, J. Donato, J. Dongarra, V. Eijkhout, R. Pozo, C. Romine and H. van der Vorst. *Templates for the Solution of Linear Systems: Building Blocks for Iterative Methods*. Siam Press, 1994.

5. R. Barriuso, A. Knies. SHMEM User's Guide for Fortran, Rev. 2.2. Cray Research, Inc, 1994.

6. A. Bik. Compiler Support for Sparse Matrix Computations. Ph.D. Dissertation, University of Leiden, The Netherlands, 1996.

7. P. Brezany, K. Sanjari, O. Cheron and E. Van Konijnenburg. Processing Irregular Codes Containing Arrays with Multi-Dimensional Distributions by the PREPARE HPF Compiler. *Int'l. Conf. on High-Performance Computing and Networking (HPCN'95)*, Milan, Italy, pp. 526–531, 1995.

8. T. Davis, University of Florida Sparse Matrix Collection. *NA Digest*, 92(42), 1994, 96(28), 1996, 97(23), 1997. See http://www.cise.ufl.edu/~davis/sparse/.

9. J.W. Demmel, S.C. Eisenstat, J.R. Gilbert, X.S. Li and J.W.H. Liu. A Supernodal Approach to Sparse Partial Pivoting. Tech. Report UCB/CSD-95-883, Computer Science Division, Univ. of California at Berkeley, CA, 1995.

10. I.S. Duff and J.K. Reid. MA48, a Fortran Code for Direct Solution of Sparse Unsymmetric Linear Systems of Equations. Tech. Report RAL-93-072, Rutherford Appleton Lab., UK, 1993.

11. I.S. Duff and J.A. Scott. The Design of a New Frontal Code of Solving Sparse Unsymmetric Systems. *ACM Trans. on Mathematical Software*, 22(1):30–45, 1996.

12. G. Fox, S. Hiranandani, K. Kennedy, C. Koelbel, U. Kremer, C-W. Tseng and M. Wu. Fortran D Language Specification. Tech. Report COMP TR90-141, Computer Science Dept., Rice University, 1990.

13. C. Fu and T. Yang,. Run-time Compilation for Parallel Sparse Matrix Computations. *10th ACM Int'l Conf. on Supercomputing*, Philadelphia, pp. 237–244, May 1996.

14. K. Gallivan, B.A. Marsolf and H.A.G. Wijshoff. Solving Large Nonsymmetric Sparse Linear Systems Using MCSPARSE. *Parallel Computing*, 22(10):1291–1333, 1996.

15. High Performance Fortran Forum. High Performance Language Specification, Ver. 1.0. *Scientific Programming*, 2(1–2):1–170, 1993.

16. High Performance Fortran Forum. High Performance Language Specification, Ver. 2.0". Rice University, Houston, TX, February 1997.

17. V. Kotlyar and K. Pingali. Sparse Code Generation for Imperfectly Nested Loops with Dependences. *11th ACM Int'l Conf. on Supercomputing*, Vienna, Austria, 188–195, July 1997.

18. R. Ponnusamy, Y.-S. Hwang, R. Das, J. Saltz, A. Choudhary and G. Fox. Supporting Irregular Distributions Using Data-Parallel Language. *IEEE Parallel and Distributed Technology: Systems and Applications*, 3(1):12–24, 1995.

19. L.F. Romero and E.L. Zapata. Data Distributions for Sparse Matrix Vector Multiplication. *Parallel Computing*, 21(4):583–605, 1995.

20. G.P. Trabado and E.L. Zapata. Exploiting Locality on Parallel Sparse Matrix Computations. *3rd EUROMICRO Works. on Parallel and Distributed Processing*, San Remo, Italy, pp. 2–9, 1995.
21. M. Ujaldón, E.L. Zapata, B. Chapman and H.P. Zima. Vienna-Fortran/HPF Extensions for Sparse and Irregular Problems and their Compilation. *IEEE Trans. on Parallel and Distributed Systems*, 8(10):1068–1083, 1997.
22. H. Zima, P. Brezany, B. Chapman, P. Mehrotra and A. Schwald. Vienna Fortran – A Language Specification. Tech. Report ACPC–TR92–4, Austrian Center for Parallel Computation, University of Vienna, Austria, 1992.

Integrated Instruction Scheduling and Register Allocation Techniques*

David A. Berson[1], Rajiv Gupta[2], and Mary Lou Soffa[2]

[1] Intel Corporation, Microcomputer Research Lab
2200 Mission College Blvd., Santa Clara, CA 95052, USA
[2] Dept. of Computer Science, University of Pittsburgh
Pittsburgh, PA 15260, USA

Abstract. An algorithm for integrating instruction scheduling and register allocation must support mechanisms for **detecting excessive** register and functional unit demands and **applying reductions** for lessening these demands. The excessive demands for functional units can be detected by identifying the instructions that can execute in parallel, and can be reduced by scheduling some of these instructions sequentially. The excessive demands for registers can be detected on-the-fly while scheduling by maintaining register pressure values or may be detected prior to scheduling using an appropriate representation such as parallel interference graphs or register reuse dags. Reductions in excessive register demands can be achieved by live range spilling or live range splitting. However, existing integrated algorithms that are based upon mechanisms other than register reuse dags do not employ live range splitting. In this paper, we demonstrate that for integrated algorithms, register reuse dags are more effective than either on-the-fly computation of register pressure or interference graphs and that live range splitting is more effective than live range spilling. Moreover the choice of mechanisms greatly impacts on the performance of an integrated algorithm.

1 Introduction

The interaction of instruction scheduling and register allocation is an important issue for VLIW and superscalar architectures that exploit significant degrees of instruction level parallelism (ILP). Register allocation and instruction scheduling have somewhat conflicting goals. In order to keep the functional units busy, an instruction scheduler exploits ILP and thus requires that a large number of operand values be available in registers. On the other hand, a register allocator attempts to keep the register pressure low by maintaining fewer values in registers so as to minimize the need for generating spill code.

If register allocation is performed first, it limits the amount of ILP available by introducing additional dependences between the instructions based on the temporal sharing of registers. If instruction scheduling is performed first, it can

---

* Supported in part by NSF Grants CCR-9402226 and CCR-9808590 to the Univ. of Pittsburgh.

S. Chatterjee (Ed.): LCPC'98, LNCS 1656, pp. 247–262, 1999.
© Springer-Verlag Berlin Heidelberg 1999

create a schedule demanding more registers than are available, causing more work for the register allocator. In addition, the spill code subsequently generated must be placed in the schedule by a post-pass cleanup scheduler, degrading the performance of the schedule. Thus, an effective solution should integrate register allocation and instruction scheduling.

An integrated approach must provide mechanisms for *detecting* excess demands for both functional unit and register resources and for *reducing* the resource demands to the level supported by the architecture. Excessive demands for functional units due to a high degree of ILP are reduced by the instruction scheduler by scheduling the execution of independent, and thus potentially parallel, instructions sequentially. Excessive demands for registers cannot always be reduced through sequentialization alone and may further require the saving of register values in memory through live range spilling or live range splitting.

In this paper we demonstrate that the performance of an integrated algorithm is greatly impacted by the mechanism it uses to determine excessive register demands and the manner in which it reduces the register demands. Excessive register demands can be determined by maintaining register pressure during scheduling, constructing a parallel interference graph, or by constructing register reuse dags. Reduction can be achieved through live range spilling or live range splitting. Our results show that excessive register demands can be best determined using register reuse dags and reduction is best achieved through live range splitting. However, none of the existing integrated algorithms are based upon these mechanisms. We implemented newly developed integrated algorithms as well as existing algorithms to obtain the above results as follows.

- The *on-the-fly* approach (IPS) developed by Goodman and Hsu [11] performs local register allocation within extended basic blocks during instruction scheduling. It tracks *register pressure* to detect excessive register demands and uses *live range spilling* to reduce register pressure. We extended this technique to incorporate *live range splitting* (ILS). Based upon the performances of the original and extended versions of the algorithm we conclude that live range splitting is far superior to live range spilling when developing an integrated resource allocator.
- The *parallel interference graph* approach developed by Norris and Pollock [14] uses an extended interference graph to detect excessive register demands and guide schedule sensitive register allocation (PIR). The reduction in register demands is achieved through *live range spilling*. We modified this technique to incorporate the use of the register reuse dag in place of the interference graphs for detecting excessive register demands (RRD). Variations of priority functions for selecting candidate live ranges for spilling are also considered. By comparing the performances of the above algorithms we conclude that register reuse dags are superior to interference graphs.
- The *unified resource allocation* (URSA) approach developed by us is based upon the *measure-and-reduce* paradigm for both registers and functional units [4]. Using the *reuse dags*, this approach identifies *excessive sets* that represent groups of instructions whose parallel scheduling requires more re-

sources than are available [1]. The excessive sets are then used to drive reductions of the excessive demands for resources. *Live range splitting* is used to reduce register demands. This algorithm performs better than the algorithms based upon the on-the-fly approach and interference graphs and also has the lowest compilation times.

The table given below summarizes the integrated algorithms implemented in this work.

Register Pressure Computation	Live Range Spilling	Live Range Splitting
On-the-fly	IPS	ILS
Parallel Interference Graph	PIR	-
Register Reuse DAG	RRD	URSA

The significance of integration is greatly increased in programs where the register pressure is high. Thus when compiling programs for VLIW architectures, or other types of multiple issue architectures, the need for integration is the greatest. In comparing the above algorithms, we experimentally evaluated the integrated algorithms using a 6 issue architecture. Previous studies have been limited to single issue pipelined machines and therefore do not reveal the true significance of integration. In our algorithms, both instruction scheduling and register allocation are performed hierarchically over the program dependence graph (PDG) [10]; that is, each algorithm traverses the control dependence graph in a bottom-up fashion, performing integrated instruction scheduling and register allocation in each region and then using the results at the next higher control dependence level.

In section 2 we provide an overview of important issues that an integrated algorithm for instruction scheduling and register allocation must address. In section 3 we describe algorithms that perform on-the-fly register allocation and study the effect of live range spilling and splitting on performance. In section 4 we evaluate an algorithm based upon a parallel interference graph approach and compare it with one that uses register reuse dags. In section 5 we describe algorithms based upon the unified resource allocation approach which employs both register reuse dags and live range splitting. We conclude by summarizing the main results of this work in section 6.

2   Issues in Integrating Register Allocation with Instruction Scheduling

Each of the integrated instruction scheduling and register allocation algorithms must support mechanisms for detecting excess requirements for functional units and registers as well as techniques for reducing these requirements to the levels supported by the architecture. In addition, the order in which reductions for functional units versus registers are applied may differ from one technique to another. We first discuss a variety of detection and reduction methods that have been proposed and then we briefly describe the specific choices made by algorithms implemented in this study.

Excessive requirements for *functional units* arise when the degree of parallelism identified in a program segment is found to be greater than the number of functional units available. The excess parallelism may be identified either *on-the-fly* while the schedule is being generated or *precomputed* prior to the start of instruction scheduling. An example of the former approach is a list scheduler which can, at any point in time during scheduling, identify excess parallelism by simply examining the ready list for the number of operations that are ready for scheduling. An example of the latter approach is one in which an acyclic data dependence graph is constructed for a code segment prior to scheduling and examined to identify the maximum degree of parallelism.

Reductions of functional unit resources are performed by sequentially scheduling some of the operations that are able to execute in parallel. Reductions can be performed either on-the-fly or prior to scheduling. A priority based list scheduler faced with excess parallelism may first on-the-fly choose the nodes with higher priority for scheduling while delaying the scheduling of other ready nodes. Reductions can also be performed prior to scheduling by introducing sequentialization edges in an acyclic data dependence graph to reduce the maximum degree of parallelism in the graph.

Excessive requirements for *registers* arise when the number of values that are live exceed the number of registers available. Similar to functional units, the excess register requirements for registers can be detected *on-the-fly* during scheduling or *precomputed* prior to scheduling. A list scheduler will identify excess register requirements when it tries to schedule an instruction and finds that no register is free to hold the result of the instruction. Excess register requirements can be precomputed using two different methods. The first method, used by register allocators based on graph coloring, identifies excessive register demands by finding uncolorable components in the *parallel interference graph*. Another method constructs a directed acyclic graph, called the *register reuse dag*, in which an edge is drawn from one instruction to another if the latter is able to reuse the register freed by the former. By finding the maximum number of independent instructions in the register reuse dag, the excessive register demands are identified. A set of instructions identified to require more registers than are available is said to form an *excessive set*.

There are a number of register reduction techniques available. The first is *sequentialization* which orders instructions that can be executed in parallel so that the instructions can use the same register. This reduction technique is not always applicable due to other dependences in the program. The second reduction technique is *live range spilling*, where a store instruction is inserted immediately after the definition of the value. A load instruction is then inserted before every use of the value. This approach results in a large number of loads from memory; however, it can always be performed and removes many interferences. The third reduction technique is *live range splitting*, which tries to reduce the number of load instructions by having several close uses of the value share a single load.

In determining the uses that should share a register, the register allocator must ensure that the register pressure does not exceed the limit imposed by the architecture. In the case where the instructions have not been scheduled yet, it is difficult for the register allocator to know how "close" several uses are, or if by sharing a load, they will result in competing with other live ranges. To our knowledge, none of the previously developed integrated techniques use live range splitting. Finally by combining the introduction of sequential dependences with live range splitting, a special form of live range splitting can be performed in cases where neither sequentialization nor live range splitting alone would be feasible or result in a reduction of register pressure.

In developing an algorithm that integrates instruction scheduling and register allocation, the selected register allocation and scheduling techniques to detect and reduce the requirements must cooperate in some way. No integration means that the heuristics for register allocation and scheduling are performed independently of one another in separate phases. One approach to integration is to allocate register allocation and functional units simultaneously in one phase, resulting in a fully integrated system. Another approach is to allocate the resources separately, but use information about the allocation of the other resource. There are various strategies that can be used to order the allocation phases. One strategy is to allocate all of resources of one type in one phase and then allocate the other resource in a subsequent phase, passing information from one phase to the other. Another ordering would be to interleave the allocation heuristics. Thus, some resources of one type are allocated and then some of the other type are allocated. The important component of either approach is the information about one resource that is used during the allocation of the other resource.

3   Live Range Spilling vs Live Range Splitting

Typically a list scheduler uses the *heights* of instructions in the dependence DAG to prioritize the scheduling. In this technique, to reduce excessive register demands, *register pressure* is continuously tracked during instruction scheduling and used in conjunction with instruction heights to guide scheduling. Thus, the excessive demands for both resources are reduced by the scheduler in the process of selecting instructions for scheduling. If register pressure exceeds the maximum number of registers available, register spilling is required.

The two algorithms based upon this approach that were implemented differ in their treatment of excessive register requirements. The IPS algorithm proposed by Goodman and Hsu [11] addresses the excessive requirements for registers through *live range spilling* which is carried out during a separate pass following the scheduling prepass using extended basic blocks. The ILS algorithm developed by us extends IPS by performing register allocation hierarchically on a PDG and eliminating a need for separate spilling pass by performing *live range splitting* during instruction scheduling. Next we describe the two algorithms in greater detail.

In IPS the list scheduler alternates between two states. In the first state, register pressure is low and the scheduler selects instructions to exploit ILP based upon their heights. When the register pressure crosses a threshold, the scheduler switches to a second state that gives preference to instructions that reduce register pressure, possibly sacrificing opportunities to exploit ILP in the process. Additionally, no spilling of values is performed. When register pressure falls back below the threshold, the first state is reentered. In this manner scheduling and allocation are integrated. IPS attempts to sequence live ranges to reduce live range interferences. This reduction is accomplished by giving preference to scheduling instructions that kill live ranges prior to ones that only start new ones when register pressure reaches a specified threshold. If the scheduler is unable to select instructions in a manner that keeps the register pressure below the maximum allowed by the architecture, then live range spilling is unavoidable. A postpass register allocation via coloring is performed to handle any register allocation problems that the scheduler is unable to address. This register allocator uses a traditional priority based coloring approach to select candidate live ranges for spilling [8].

The ILS algorithm eliminates the need for the spilling postpass by using *live range splitting* during instruction scheduling to ensure that the register pressure never exceeds the maximum allowable value. This approach requires that ILS be applied hierarchically in a bottom-up fashion so that the live ranges that extend across child regions are also considered in computing the register pressure. ILS maintains a list of all values that are alive in the cycle currently being scheduled. When ILS detects that register pressure is high, and there are no ready instructions that reduce the number of currently active live ranges, it selects a live range for splitting. ILS injects a store instruction into the ready list and a load instruction dependent on the store into the not-ready list. ILS then moves the dependencies of all unscheduled uses of the value from the original definition to the injected load. In this manner ILS essentially performs live range splitting. The priority function used for selecting a live range for splitting gives preference to the live range whose earliest subsequent use is farthest from the current instruction cycle being scheduled. To avoid useless loads of values the priority functions are designed to not schedule injected load instructions unless it can be guaranteed that at least one of the dependent uses can also be scheduled. The incorporation of live range splitting into ILS creates a powerful and complete single pass allocation algorithm for both registers and functional units.

Next we present results of experiments that compare the performances of ILS and IPS algorithms. Performances of all algorithms are presented in terms of the speedups they achieve for a 6 issue machine in comparison to a base algorithm for a single issue machine. The base algorithm was chosen to be the interference graph based algorithm since it performed the worst of all the algorithms. Since the objective of the experiments is to see how well various algorithms perform under high register pressure, the algorithms were executed for a machine with varying number of registers. In computing the speedups achieved by any algorithm over the base algorithm, the same number of registers were provided to both algorithms. By doing so the results that are obtained demonstrate the impact of integration capability of an algorithm on the effectiveness with which parallelism is exploited.

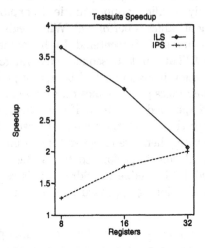

Fig. 1. Comparison of IPS and ILS for a 6 issue architecture.

The performances of IPS and ILS are shown in Figure 1. As we can see, our ILS algorithm performs much better than the IPS approach. After analyzing the code generated by the two algorithms we observed that this difference in performance was attributable to significantly greater amounts of spill code introduced by IPS. Thus, we conclude that an algorithm such as ILS that incorporates live range splitting performs better than an algorithm such as IPS that is based only on spilling. This result is not entirely unexpected as spilling can be viewed as a special case of splitting. The results also show that the difference in the performance of ILS and IPS decreases as greater numbers of registers are made available. This trend indicates that the effectiveness of integration strategy has a greater impact on performance for higher register pressures.

4 Parallel Interference Graphs vs Register Reuse Dags

A more sophisticated approach for global register allocation is based upon the coloring of interference graphs [9,8]. This approach was extended to make the process of register allocation schedule sensitive through the construction of a *parallel interference graph* [14,15]. The algorithm (PIR) we implemented is based on a parallel interference graph proposed by Norris and Pollock [14] and uses a Chaitin [8] style register allocator which relies upon live range spilling. The parallel interference graph represents all interferences that can occur in legal schedules.

The interference graph is constructed by adding interference edges between nodes representing live ranges that may overlap in the current region or in the child regions of the current region. The interference graph is simplified by removing all nodes that are incident on fewer edges than the number of registers available. The remaining nodes are then processed to reduce the register requirements. Reductions are achieved using both *sequentialization* and *spilling*. While *live range splitting* has been incorporated into traditional coloring based register allocators [9], it has not been incorporated in schedule sensitive allocators based upon parallel interference graphs due to the lack of a complete ordering of the instructions. Without a complete ordering, it cannot be guaranteed that a particular splitting of a live range will reduce the number of interferences. Therefore the *splitting* reduction is not used by existing algorithms.

The order in which nodes are considered for reduction is based upon cost functions that prioritize the nodes. After applying a reduction, the interference graph is recomputed and the process is repeated until no more reductions are required. At this point, all nodes can be successfully colored; that is, register allocation is now complete. In the process of coloring, the instructions are partially scheduled through the application of sequentialization reductions. A postpass list scheduler is run as a last step to produce the final code schedule. In our implementation of PIR, the ILS scheduler (with register allocation turned off) was used for this purpose.

The cost functions that prioritize the nodes compute the cost for both spilling the value and for sequentializing the live range after all uses of another live range. The costs are computed in terms of the effect of the transformations on the critical path length. The minimum of these two costs is used as the priority and the corresponding reduction method is recorded in case the node is selected for reduction.

Sequentialization of a live value defined by D_1 is performed by finding a second value D_2 which interferes with D_1 and then introducing temporal dependences from all uses of D_2 to definition D_1. The cost of sequentialization reduction is computed using the following formula:

$$Cost_{seq} = \frac{max_{u \in Uses(D_2)}(u.EST + D_1.LST) \ominus cpl}{NumInterferences}$$

where $u.EST$ is the earliest start time of the use instruction u, $D_1.LST$ is the latest start time of definition D_1, cpl is the critical path length of the region containing D_1, $Uses(D_2)$ is the set of uses of D_2, and the symbol $\ominus$ represents *floored subtraction* function ($a \ominus b = if\ a > b\ then\ a - b\ else\ 0$).

Two different functions were used to compute the cost of spilling, measured by the effect on the critical path lengths. The first cost function considers the increase in critical path length for a given region as the number of loads and stores that are required in the region. The total increase in critical path length was computed by summing together the product of the increase in length and the execution count of all relevant regions. The second priority function considers the slack time in scheduling spill code in computing the increase in critical path length. The slack time of an instruction is the difference between the earliest time and the latest time at which the instruction can be scheduled. The motivation behind this cost function is that high slack times reduce the likelihood of an increase in critical path length. The formulas for computing the spill costs based upon the above approaches are given below:

$$Cost_{spill} = \frac{StoreCost \times def.ExecCnt + \sum_{u \in uses} LoadCost \times u.ExecCnt}{NumInterferences}$$

$$SCost_{spill} = \frac{(StoreCost \ominus def.Slack) \times def.ExecCnt + \sum_{u \in uses} LoadCost \times (u.ExecCnt \ominus u.Slack)}{NumInterferences}$$

where $StoreCost/LoadCost$ is the cost in cycles to execute a store/load instruction, $i.ExecCnt$ is the execution count for the region containing instruction i, $i.Slack$ is the slack time of instruction i, the symbol $\ominus$ represents the *floored subtraction* function, and $NumInterferences$ is the number of other live ranges with which the spilled value interferes.

We evaluated the register coloring approach using both of the above cost functions. The algorithm PIR uses the first spill cost function and the algorithm $SPIR$ uses the second spill cost function that incorporates slack times. The results of these evaluations are shown in Figure 2.

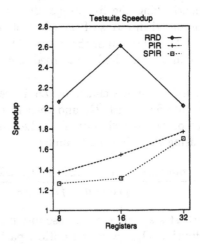

Fig. 2. Comparison of PIR and SPIR with RRD for a 6 issue architecture.

The results show that PIR performs consistently better than SPIR. We were surprised to find that the priority function that considers slack times tended to degrade performance rather than improve performance. Examination of several cases revealed that more spill code was generated because either some values were spilled prior to attempts to sequentialize live ranges, or values were selected that had less of an impact on reducing the size of the excessive requirements. The consideration of slack time tended to negate the effects of considering the number of interferences in the cost function.

PIR and SPIR identify excessive sets using a simplified interference graph. The excessive sets computed by register reuse dags are conceptually similar to those computed by PIR/SPIR. In both cases the sets represent the instructions that the respective heuristics believe will interfere and cause excessive demands. Thus, it is possible to substitute excessive sets for the simplified interference graphs used by PIR and then proceed using coloring's priority function and spill code generation.

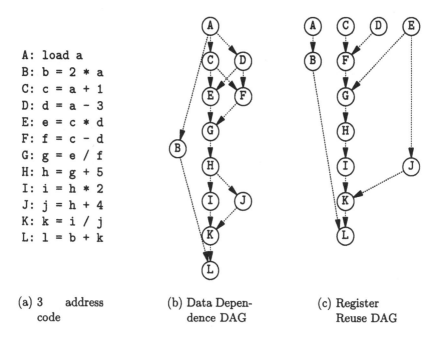

```
A: load a
B: b = 2 * a
C: c = a + 1
D: d = a - 3
E: e = c * d
F: f = c - d
G: g = e / f
H: h = g + 5
I: i = h * 2
J: j = h + 4
K: k = i / j
L: l = b + k
```

(a) 3   address   (b) Data Depen-   (c) Register
    code   dence DAG   Reuse DAG

Fig. 3. Example code and corresponding Reuse DAGs

In Figure 3(a) we show the 3 address code for a basic block, the data dependence dag using statement labels for the code in Figure 3(b), and the register reuse dag in Figure 3(c). The register reuse dag is used to determine the excessive sets of registers. The reuse dag chains those values that are not simultaneously live and can thus share a register under all schedules allowed for parallel execution. In the example, the values computed by statements A, C, D and E can all be alive at the same time and thus cannot share registers. Likewise, the values computed by B G and J cannot share registers since they are on separate chains. If the architecture does not have 4 registers, then the set A, C, D, E is an excessive set.

To compare the performance of excessive sets with the PDG-interference graph we implemented the above modification resulting in the register reuse dag (RRD) algorithm. The comparison of RRD and PIR determines the benefit of excessive sets over interference graphs. The results that were obtained show that the amount of spill code generated in RRD was significantly less than the amount generated in PIR (see Figure 2). We examined numerous cases to verify the results and found a common occurrence mentioned in Briggs' dissertation [5]. Although all nodes in the reduced interference graph interfere with at least K other values, those K values may not need all K colors. Excessive set measurement computations realize when such a situation occurs and count fewer interferences. The result of fewer interferences is that either a smaller excessive interference set is generated in comparison to the interference graph reduction, or no excessive interference set is generated while interference graph reduction does generate one. The better performance of RRD in comparison to PIR is directly due to this effect.

By comparing the results of PIR with the results in the previous section we observed that although PIR sometimes performs marginally better than IPS, in many situations IPS performs significantly better than PIR. Furthermore, PIR consistently performs significantly worse than ILS. This is because ILS makes use of live range splitting while PIR does not. In summary our experimentation shows that the overall performance of the on-the-fly approach is better than the interference graph approach. We also note that the difference in the performance of various algorithms is greater for higher register pressures. Once enough registers are available, the difference in the performances of the various algorithms is relatively small indicating that integration becomes less important.

5   Unified Resource Allocation Using Reuse Dags and Splitting

Finally we present an algorithm that uses register reuse dags and live range splitting. This algorithm is based upon an approach that provides a uniform view of instruction scheduling and register allocation by treating both of them as resource allocation problems. Instruction scheduling is viewed as the allocation of functional units in this approach. Integration is achieved by simultaneously allocating both functional unit and register resources to an instruction. Due to its unified treatment of resources, this approach is referred to as the unified resource allocation approach or URSA [1,3,2,4]. Algorithms that use the URSA approach are based upon the *measure-and-reduce* paradigm. In this approach the areas of the program with excessive resource requirements are located and reductions are performed by transforming the intermediate representation of the program. The selection of a reduction is based upon its effect on the critical path length.

The URSA framework provides a set of techniques to compute resource requirements. When compiling a program to exploit ILP, the dependencies in an acyclic segment of the program are used to represent the set of all semantically correct ways of scheduling the segment. Different schedules may result in different resource requirements. The approach taken in the measure-and-reduce paradigm is to remove from consideration all schedules that result in excessive resource demands using the reduction techniques. Any schedule selected from the remaining set of schedules is feasible with respect to the available resources. Thus, the measurement technique must consider the worst case schedule for each resource to compute the *maximum* resource requirements.

In addition to computing the maximum number of resources required, the measurement techniques must identify the locations in a program where there are excessive resource demands and the locations where a resource is underutilized and available for additional allocations. The areas of overutilization are referred to *excessive sets* and the areas of underutilization are called *resource holes*. The GURRR intermediate representation has been developed to explicitly incorporate maximum resource requirements, excessive sets and resource holes [2]. This representation used in URSA combines information about a program's requirements for both registers and functional units with scheduling information in a single DAG-based representation. In this manner, GURRR facilitates the determination of the impact of all scheduling and allocation decisions on the critical path length of the code affected. GURRR extends the instruction level PDG by the addition of resource hole nodes and reuse edges, which connect nodes that can temporally share an instance of a resource.

The URSA framework supports a set of techniques to perform the allocation of resources to instructions. The techniques utilize the resource holes in GURRR during this process. These techniques are referred to as *resource spackling* techniques because they perform allocations by trying to fill the resource holes with instructions [3]. Register holes represent the cases where a register can be assigned to hold a value. There are two such cases: when the register is unoccupied and when the register is occupied but the value in it is not currently being referenced, and so, the live range can be split. The spackling of an instruction may require live range splitting corresponding to one value in the former type of hole and of two values in the latter.

Instructions belonging to excessive sets are spackled to eliminate excessive resource requirements. The selection of nodes for spackling from excessive sets is based upon priority functions. We considered two different priority functions: the first, URSA-1, selects nodes with the most amount of slack first while the second, URSA-2, selects the same nodes as URSA-1 but spackles them in reverse order. Since instructions with greater slack time have a higher flexibility in their scheduling times, we expected the second priority function to perform better. Different options for spackling an instruction are evaluated by comparing the increases in estimated execution times that are expected as a result. This estimate is obtained as the product of increase in critical path and the execution count of the control dependence region under consideration.

First let us compare the performance of the URSA algorithms with ILS and IPS. As indicated by the results in Figure 4, URSA performs better than ILS on our architecture. Since the difference in the performance of URSA and ILS was lower than we expected, we decided to further investigate the behavior of URSA's reduction techniques. We examined the code generated by URSA for some of the benchmarks to determine if further improvements could be achieved. We found that through *handcoding* we were able to reduce the amount of spill code significantly. As shown in Table 1, the critical path length (CPL) and the number of instructions for loop2 and loop10 can be greatly used through handcoding.

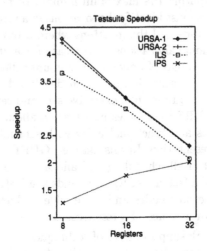

Fig. 4. Comparison of URSA with ILS and IPS for a 6 issue architecture.

Benchmark	CPL URSA-2	CPL Handcoding	Insts. URSA-2	Insts. Handcoding
loop2	95	22	79	40
loop10	181	42	150	71

Table 1. URSA-2 vs Handcoding

Further examination of the above benchmarks revealed the reason for URSA's inability to discover solutions with less spill code. In situations with high degree of ILP, it is beneficial to apply sequentialization reduction to *groups* of related instructions rather than applying reductions to *individual* instructions. In particular, if the dependence graph contains two relatively independent subdags which are parts of excessive sets, sequentialization of the entire subdags with respect to each other can greatly lower resource requirements without introducing spill code. On the other hand when URSA selected instructions for sequentialization one at a time, it tended to interleave the execution of the two subdags thus requiring spill code. The above observation clearly indicates that URSA's reductions can be enhanced to further improve performance. However, the same cannot be said for ILS since list scheduling uses a greedy approach rather than the measure-and-reduce paradigm.

We also found that the priority function which considers instructions with most slack time first (i.e., URSA-1) does consistently better than the one that considers instructions with least slack time first (i.e., URSA-2). This result was a bit unexpected due to the fact that Goodman and Hsu [11] recommend the scheduling of instructions with the least amount of slack time first. This experiment suggests that scheduling the instructions with the most slack first achieves better performance because these instructions are most likely to be moved beyond the range of the excessive set. Thus fewer reduction transformations are typically required.

The performance of RRD is worse in comparison to URSA because RRD uses live range spilling while URSA employs live range splitting (see Figure 5). Again the difference in the performance of various algorithms diminishes as larger number of registers are made available.

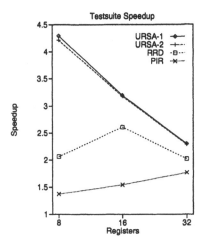

Fig. 5. Comparison of URSA with RRD and PIR for a 6 issue architecture.

Finally we compared the compile-time costs of the various approaches. As shown by the results in Figure 6, URSA based algorithms required the lowest compilation times and the ILS algorithm was the next best performer. The IPS algorithm is slower because it required a register coloring phase following the scheduling to carry out spilling. Finally, RRD ran slower than PIR due to the excessive set computations required by RRD. The interesting aspect of the results is that the algorithms that generated higher quality code also exhibited lower compile-time costs. It should be noted that heuristics implemented were prototypes and there are known areas of improvement for each.

6   Conclusion

In this paper, we presented various versions of algorithms that implement the integration of register allocation and instruction scheduling. From the experiments we conclude that URSA has the overall best performance in integrating register allocation and instruction scheduling. URSA exploits excessive sets that

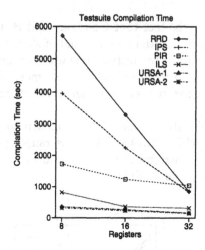

Fig. 6. Compile-time costs of various approaches.

are more accurate than interference graphs in determining the excessive register demands. It also uses live range splitting that performs better than live range spilling. Furthermore, URSA is also efficient in terms of its compilation time costs.

Our results indicate that the on-the-fly register allocation scheme when used with live range splitting always performed better than the interference graph approach. When only considering on-the-fly register allocation with scheduling technique, we show that the ILS technique proposed by us that uses live range splitting performs much better than Goodman and Hsu's IPS technique [11] that uses live range spilling.

Finally a general trend was observed in all the experiments. The difference in the performances of different heuristics grew smaller as greater numbers of registers were made available. This is because the higher the register pressure the greater is need for effective integration of register allocation and instruction scheduling.

Results of two additional studies that have considered the interaction between instruction scheduling and register allocation were reported by Bradlee et al. [6] and Norris et al. [13]. In contrast to these studies, our study shows a greater degree of variation in the performance of different algorithms and thus indicating a greater significance of the impact of integration on performance. We believe this is due to the fact that our study is the only one that consider an architecture with a high degree of ILP. Both of the earlier studies were performed in context of single issue pipelined machines capable of exploiting only low degrees of ILP.

References

1. David A. Berson, Unification of register allocation and instruction scheduling in compilers for fine grain architectures. *Ph.D. Thesis, Dept. of Computer Science, University of Pittsburgh, Pittsburgh, PA*, November 1996.

2. David A. Berson, Rajiv Gupta, and Mary Lou Soffa. GURRR: A global unified resource requirements representation. In *Proc. of ACM Workshop on Intermediate Representations, Sigplan Notices*, vol. 30, pages 23–34, April 1995.

3. David A. Berson, Rajiv Gupta, and Mary Lou Soffa. Resource Spackling: A framework for integrating register allocation in local and global schedulers. In *Proc. of IFIP WG 10.3 Working Conference on Parallel Architectures and Compilation Techniques*, pages 135–146, 1994.

4. David A. Berson, Rajiv Gupta, and Mary Lou Soffa. URSA: A Unified ReSource Allocator for registers and functional units in VLIW architectures. In *Proc. of IFIP WG 10.3 Working Conference on Architectures and Compilation Techniques for Fine and Medium Grain Parallelism*, pages 243–254, 1993.

5. Preston Briggs. Register allocation via graph coloring. *Ph.D. Thesis, Dept. of Computer Science, Rice University, Houston, TX*, April 1992.

6. David Bradlee, Susan Eggers, and Robert Henry. Integrating register allocation and instruction scheduling for riscs. In *Proceedings of ASPLOS*, April 1991.

7. Claude-Nicholas Fiechter, PDG C Compiler. Technical Report, Dept. of Computer Science, University of Pittsburgh, Pittsburgh, PA, 1993.

8. G. J. Chaitin, M. A. Auslander, A. K. Chandra, J. Cocke, M. E. Hopkins, and P. W. Markstein. Register allocation via coloring. *Computer Languages*, 6(1):47–58, 1981.

9. F. Chow and J. Hennessy. Register allocation by priority-based coloring. *ACM Trans. Prog. Lang. and Systems*, 12(4):501–536, 1990.

10. Jeanne Ferrante, Karl J. Ottenstein, and Joe D. Warren. The program dependence graph and its use in optimization. *ACM Trans. Prog. Lang. and Systems*, 9(3):319–349, 1987.

11. James R. Goodman and Wie-Chung Hsu. Code scheduling and register allocation in large basic blocks. In *Proc. of ACM Supercomputing Conf.*, pages 442–452, 1988.

12. Cindy Norris and Lori L. Pollock. Register allocation over the program dependence graph. In *Proc. of Sigplan '94 Conf. on Programming Language Design and Implementation*, pages 266–277, 1994.

13. Cindy Norris and Lori L. Pollock. An experimental study of several cooperative register allocation and instruction scheduling strategies. *Proceedings of MICRO-28*, Nov. 1995.

14. Cindy Norris and Lori L. Pollock. A scheduler-sensitive global register allocator. *Proceedings of Supercomputing'93*, pages 804–813, Portland, Oregon, 1993.

15. Shlomit S. Pinter. Register allocation with instruction scheduling: A new approach. In *Proc. of Sigplan '93 Conf. on Programming Language Design and Implementation*, pages 248–257, 1993.

A Spill Code Placement Framework for Code Scheduling

Dingchao Li[1], Yuji Iwahori[1], Tatsuya Hayashi[2], and Naohiro Ishii[3]

[1] Educational Center for Information Processing
[2] Department of Electrical and Computer Engineering
[3] Department of Intelligence and Computer Science, Nagoya Institute of Technology
Gokisocho Showaku, Nagoya, 466-8555, Japan

Abstract. Many of compiler optimization techniques either reply on or can benefit from the timing information associated with each instruction and each variable in a given program. Using such information, in this paper, we develop an analytical approach that helps the parallelizing compiler to determine whether to spill a variable or not, which variable to spill and the places where spill code needs to be added, when a register is needed for a computation but all available registers are in use. The preliminary experimental results show that this new approach produces better object code.

Keywords: Fine grain parallel architectures, compiler optimization, program behavior analysis, code scheduling, register spilling.

1 Introduction

Registers are a scarce resource on all modern high-performance computer architectures, and their need is further increased by scheduling optimizations that introduce temporaries that have to reside in registers. To best exploit available instruction-level parallelism, the code must be scheduled in the face of a bounded number of available registers.

Deciding which variables to keep in registers at each scheduling point is usually a difficult task, particularly when the total number of registers needed is greater than the number physically available. In this paper, we attempt to develop an efficient approach that helps the compiler to make decisions to spill variables for reducing register requirements during the scheduling process. Generally, three factors make register spilling difficult: the spill code's occupation of instruction slots, the need to hide the latency of spill code, and the scheduling restrictions caused by spilling [1]. This naturally brings the following questions: which variable should be spilled, when and where to insert spill code, and how long the execution delay takes.

To answer these questions, the algorithm described in this paper analyzes the execution timing of each instruction and the live range of each variable in a given program. Using this information, the algorithm dynamically compares register reuse cost and register spilling cost during the scheduling process in

S. Chatterjee (Ed.): LCPC'98, LNCS 1656, pp. 263–274, 1999.
© Springer-Verlag Berlin Heidelberg 1999

an attempt to determine whether to spill a variable to memory and when and where to insert store and load instructions to spill. This enables the compiler to intelligently hide latency of spill code from computation so that the program execution time (or the schedule length) is reduced as much as possible.

The remainder of this paper is organized as follows. Section 2 discusses related work. Section 3 establishes machine and program models. Section 4 evaluates the execution time of each instruction and live range of each variable. Section 5 discusses in detail how to estimate register reuse cost and register spilling cost, and then derives the condition for inserting spill code during the scheduling process. Section 6 provides an illustrative example and experimental results to support the theoretical result. Finally, Section 7 gives concluding remarks.

2   Related Work

Existing work on adding spill code has mainly focused on improving heuristics for graph coloring register allocation [2]-[7]. For example, Briggs et al. [3,4] presented an improvement for producing better colorings, with less spill code. Bradlee et al. [5] slightly modified the version of integrated prepass scheduling in which the scheduler is invoked after register allocation in order to better schedule spill code. They also developed a more integrated approach in which the scheduler is invoked twice in order to calculate cost estimates for guiding the register allocator. After the allocation, a final scheduler is run using the register limit from allocation and inserting spill code as it schedules. Pinter [6] introduced spill code in case of a need for spilling, by performing heuristics for both code scheduling and register allocation on an interference graph. Also, several algorithms have been developed which insert spill code to minimize register requirements for software pipelining [8,9]. Our approach is different from all of the above in that it does not attempt to find an optimal register allocation with minimum number of registers, while it aggressively makes use of spill code to produce faster code when the number of registers available is insufficient for scheduling.

3   Definitions and Notations

We consider that a target machine is a RISC type architecture [1] and consists of heterogeneous functional units (FUs) so as to more realistically model architectures with a variety of functional unit types, such as Integer, Load/Store, and Float Point. The functional units of different types may use separate register files, as did the Multiflow Trace architecture [11]. To simplify the discussion in this paper, we assume that this machine has a single set of identical general-purpose registers $R = \{r_1, \cdots, r_{|R|}\}$, where $|R|$ is the number of registers.

A program input is a possible sequence of instructions for a particular control path that forms a program trace [12,13]. Without loss of generality, the input is

---

[1] Memory reference instructions are only load and store while computations are done in registers.

also assumed to be in SSA form; i.e., a variable [2] only has a definition but may have more than one use. Such a program trace is formally a directed acyclic graph (DAG) $G = (\Gamma, A, \mu, \nu)$, where Γ is a finite set of vertices I_i $(i = 1, 2, \cdots, n)$ representing instructions, $A \subseteq \Gamma \times \Gamma$ is a finite set of directed arcs representing precedence constraints among instructions, μ is an execution time function whose value $\mu(I_i)$ (time units) is the execution time of instruction I_i, and ν is a type function indicating if $\nu(I_i) = k$ $(k = 1, 2, \cdots, s)$ then I_i must be executed by a functional unit of type k.

In a DAG, an arc (I_i, I_j) from I_i to I_j indicates the fact that executing I_j before I_i could alter the program's semantics because I_i and I_j may reference the same memory location with at least one of them writing to that location. Thus, I_i is an immediate predecessor of I_j and I_j is an immediate successor of I_i. Also, let $I_i \xrightarrow{+} I_j$ denote that there is a path from I_i to I_j. We define the set of predecessors and the set of successors for instruction I_i as $pred(I_i) = \{I_j | I_j \xrightarrow{+} I_i\}$ and $succ(I_i) = \{I_j | I_i \xrightarrow{+} I_j\}$, respectively.

4 Program Behavior

4.1 Execution Timing

Consider an instruction I_i in a given graph G. When the instruction is placed into an optimal schedule, it will in general have an earliest starting time and a latest starting time, due to predecessors and successors that have already been placed. Let $\tau_{es}(I_i)$ represent the earliest starting time of I_i which indicates the least time in which this instruction can be started, and $\tau_{ls}(I_i)$ represent the latest starting time of I_i which indicates how long the start of this instruction can be delayed without increasing the minimum execution time of the graph. The two points in time, thus, give the starting execution interval $[\tau_{es}(I_i), \tau_{ls}(I_i)]$ in which instruction I_i must start for execution without delaying any of its successors. Similarly, the finishing execution interval of I_i can be defined as $[\tau_{ef}(I_i), \tau_{lf}(I_i)]$, where $\tau_{ef}(I_i)(= \tau_{es}(I_i) + \mu(I_i))$ and $\tau_{lf}(I_i)(= \tau_{ls}(I_i) + \mu(I_i))$ represent the earliest and the latest finishing times of I_i, respectively. Let t_{cp} denote the length of critical paths in G, which is just the sum of all the instruction execution times along the longest path from I_1 to I_n. Mathematically, we are able to determine the interval $[\tau_{es}(I_i), \tau_{ls}(I_i)]$ as follows.

$$\tau_{es}(I_i) = \max_k \sum_{I_j \in \pi_k} \mu(I_j), \qquad (1)$$

$$\tau_{ls}(I_i) = \min_k \{t_{cp} - \sum_{I_j \in \hat{\pi}_k} \mu(I_j)\}, \qquad (2)$$

---

[2] The term *variable* will be used to include all such register-residing candidates. In RISC type machines, even a constant can be a register-residing candidate if the constant cannot be put in an instruction as an immediate value.

where π_k is the kth path from the entry instruction I_1 through instruction I_i, and $\hat{\pi}_k$ is the kth path from the exit instruction I_n to instruction I_i (reversing all arrows in the digraph).

4.2   Register Requirement

We now discuss how to evaluate the live range of each variable in G. Typically, the live range of a variable begins at the definition point of the variable and terminates at its last use. Let $\tau_s(v)$ denote the time at which v is defined and $\tau_f(v)$ denote the time at which the last use of v terminates. Also, assume that an instruction will require all the inputs before starting its execution and none of the outputs will be available until after its execution was over. Thus, we easily derive $\tau_{ef}(I_i) \leq \tau_s(v) \leq \tau_{lf}(I_i)$ and $\tau_{es}(I_j) \leq \tau_f(v) \leq \tau_{ls}(I_j)$, where I_i is the instruction that defines v and I_j is the last instruction that accesses v. As a result, the minimum live range of variable v can be defined as

$$range(v) = [\tau_{lf}(I_i), \tau_{es}(I_j)].$$

If two variables are live at some point, they cannot be assigned to the same physical register. In other words, when the value of a variable is stored in a register by an instruction, a new value cannot be inserted into the register until after all the instructions which access the current value have been executed. Thus, a lower bound on the number of registers required within a given time interval $[\tau_1, \tau_2]$ can be computed as follows.

$$register(\tau_1, \tau_2) = \max_{\tau_1 \leq \tau \leq \tau_2} |\{v | there\ is\ an\ overlap \quad \\ between\ range(v)\ and\ [\tau, \tau + 1]\}|. \tag{3}$$

Perhaps this bound is not achievable in practice because of a finite number of registers, but it can help us in the next section to determine if the current number of live variables has reached the register limit.

5   Condition for Register Spilling

This section discusses the condition for inserting spill code during the scheduling process. The scheduling algorithm used in this paper is a modified critical path method [14]. Conceptually, it works as follows: when a function unit finishes its local execution, it computes the mobility of each ready instruction I_i, which is defined as $\tau_{ls}(I_i) - \tau_{es}(I_i)$, and then selects the instruction with the smallest mobility value to assign it onto the idle function unit.

Let us now assume that instruction I_u has been selected for scheduling. The next work that the compiler must do is to assign a physical registers to the symbolic one. If all available registers are in use, the code scheduler has to reuse a register or store (spill) the contents of one of the used registers into a memory location in order to free up a register. In this case, we need to estimate two costs: the cost caused by reusing a register and the cost caused by adding spill code.

We first consider register reuse. Let $t_{free}(r_i)$ represent the time when a register r_i becomes free (see Fig. 1). The time in which instruction I_u can start execution is therefore

$$\tau_s^{reuse}(I_u) = \min_{r_i \in R}\{t_{free}(r_i)\} \tag{4}$$

Recall that $\tau_{ls}(I_u)$ is the latest starting time of instruction I_u without increasing program completion time. In other words, if the starting time of I_u becomes later than its latest starting time, the overall completion time of the whole graph will be increased. Thus, we can evaluate the cost due to register reuse as follows.

$$cost_{reuse} = \tau_s^{reuse}(I_u) - \tau_{ls}(I_u), \tag{5}$$

which indicates the increase over the minimum time required to execute G on a given target machine. A greater difference value implies larger increase in program completion time. To obtain a shorter schedule, we further estimate the cost possibly created by inserting spill code.

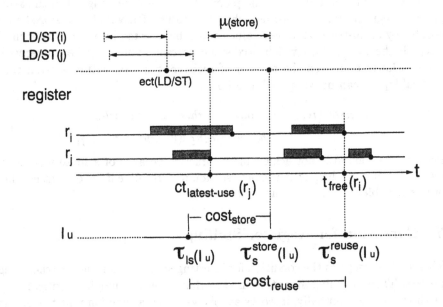

Fig. 1. Estimation of costs for register reuse and store instruction insertion.

When introducing spill code, a store instruction (spill-out) after the definition and a load instruction (spill-in) before the spilled use are inserted, and other uses still reference the value of the variable in a register [4]. Therefore, to guide the reasonable placement of spill code here, we compute the spill-out and spill-in costs for each register r_j ($\in R$), $j = 1, \cdots, |R|$.

Let $ct_{latest-use}(r_j)$ denote the completion time of the latest definition/use of register r_j. Also, let $ect(LD/ST)$ denote the earliest completion time at which Load/Store units finish execution, and $\mu(store)$ denote the execution time of a store instruction. It is easy to see from Fig. 1 that inserting a store instruction will postpone the starting time of instruction I_u to the time

$$\tau_s^{store}(I_u) = \max\{ect(LD/ST), ct_{latest-use}(r_j)\} + \mu(store) \tag{6}$$

The cost caused by the store instruction insertion is therefore

$$cost_{store}(r_j) = \tau_s^{store}(I_u) - \tau_{ls}(I_u). \tag{7}$$

Obviously, if $cost_{store}(r_j) \geq cost_{reuse}$, there is no benefit from the spilling of register r_j; in this case, we proceed to the estimation of cost for the remaining registers.

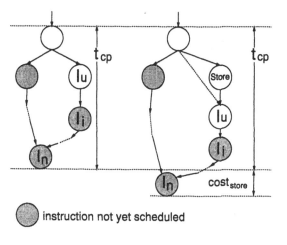

instruction not yet scheduled

Fig. 2. Recomputation of execution timing for instructions not yet scheduled.

Assume now that $cost_{store}(r_j) < cost_{reuse}$. Thus, we need further evaluate the cost incurred due to the load instruction insertion before the spilled use. To obtain a more accurate estimate, we first recompute the earliest and the latest starting times for each instruction not yet scheduled, since inserting a store instruction may generate several new critical paths; i.e., it may result in some non-critical instructions among them to become critical, as shown in Fig. 2. Let us use $\tau_{es}^{store}(I_i)$ and $\tau_{ls}^{store}(I_i)$ to represent the earliest and the latest starting times of instruction I_i after inserting the store instruction, respectively. Taking into account that $\tau_{es}^{store}(I_u) = \tau_s^{store}(I_u)$, we can recursively calculate them as follows.

$$\tau_{es}^{store}(I_i) = \begin{cases} \max_{(I_j,I_i)\in A} \{\tau_{es}(I_i), \tau_{es}^{store}(I_j) + \mu(I_j)\}, \\ \qquad\qquad \text{if } I_i \in succ(I_u), \\ \tau_{es}(I_i), \qquad \text{otherwise.} \end{cases} \tag{8}$$

$$\tau_{ls}^{store}(I_i) = \tau_{ls}(I_i) + cost_{store}(r_j). \tag{9}$$

According to both the new execution timing information and the results of our program behavior analysis, we easily find the instruction that will use the variable spilled to memory in the nearest future. Let I_v denote this instruction. A load instruction must be inserted before I_v starts execution. To hide the latency $\mu(load)$ of the load instruction, as shown in Fig. 3, we now consider a time interval $[\tau, \tau + \mu(load)]$ $(\subset [\tau_s(I_u) + \mu(I_u), \tau_{ls}^{store}(I_v)])$, within which if the instruction can be processed then no increase over the program execution time occurs. For convenience of the presentation, let $\tau_s = \tau$ and $\tau_f = \tau + \mu(load)$. Also, let $\Pi_{unscheduled}^{LD/ST}$ denote the set of the load/store instructions not yet scheduled. The increase possibly created by the load instruction insertion within this interval is thus given by

$$increase(\tau_s, \tau_f, load) = \lceil \frac{\sum_{I_i \in \Pi_{unscheduled}^{LD/ST}} \mu(\tau_s, \tau_f, I_i)}{number\ of\ Load/Store\ units} \rceil, \tag{10}$$

where $\mu(\tau_s, \tau_f, I_i)$ represents the time of instruction I_i that must be processed within $[\tau_s, \tau_f]$, and it can be easily calculated using the method in [15].

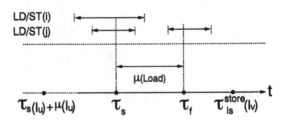

Fig. 3. Estimation of cost for load instruction insertion.

In order to avoid spilling registers repeatedly, we now assume that the load instruction does not produce a new register spilling. As a result, this suggests the algorithm shown in Fig. 4, which evaluates the cost $cost_{load}(r_j)$ created by inserting a load instruction.

Let $cost_{spill}(r_j) = |cost_{store}(r_j)| + |cost_{load}(r_j)|$ denote the cost created by both the store and load instructions used to spill register r_j. We finally derive the following condition: the compiler should select register r to spill such that

$$cost_{spill}(r) = \min\{cost_{spill}(r_j)|cost_{spill}(r_j) < cost_{reuse}, r_j \in R\}. \tag{11}$$

```
costload(rj) = ∞;
For τs from τls^store(Iv) − μ(load) to τs(Iu) + μ(Iu) Do
  If register(τs, τf) ≥ |R| Then Exit
  Else costload(rj) = min{costload(rj), increase(τs, τf, load)}
    If costload(rj) = 0 Then Exit
Endfor
```

Fig. 4. Algorithm to evaluate the cost due to the load operation insertion.

6 Discussion

This section first provides an example to illustrate the effectiveness of the proposed method. Consider Fig. 5, which represents the source program of Livermore kernel No.1 and its intermediate code to be scheduled. Assume that the target machine consists of one integer unit (IU) of latency 1, one floating point unit (FU) of latency 3, one Load/Store unit (LD/ST) of latency 2, and one branch unit (BU) of latency 1. Table 1 shows the results of our timing analysis. It is easy to see from this table that the critical path length is $t_{cp} = 16$ (time units).

Table 1. The results of timing analysis.

Execution Timing	Instructions														
	I_1	I_2	I_3	I_4	I_5	I_6	I_7	I_8	I_9	I_{10}	I_{11}	I_{12}	I_{13}	I_{14}	I_{15}
τ_{es}	0	1	3	0	1	3	6	0	7	10	0	11	13	14	15
τ_{ef}	1	3	6	1	3	6	7	2	10	11	1	13	14	15	16
τ_{ls}	0	1	3	0	1	3	6	5	7	10	12	11	13	14	15
τ_{lf}	1	3	6	1	3	6	7	7	10	11	13	13	14	15	16

Based on the above timing information, by Eq. (3) we easily obtain that the register requirement for executing the program is $register(0, t_{cp}) = 9$. Assume now that only 8 identical general-purpose registers can be used for executing the program. Thus, the compiler has to determine whether to spill a variable and which variable to spill during the scheduling process. As can be seen in Fig. 6, instruction I_3 is chosen for scheduling at time 3, but there are no available registers to save the result t7 of I_3. To solve this problem, by the proposed method we first evaluate register reuse cost. According to the results of live range analysis for variables in the program, the earliest time at which at least one register becomes free is that $t_{free}(r_6) = 5$. In other words, instruction I_3 must wait to use a register until register r_6 becomes free at time 5. Thus, by Eqs. (9) and (10) the time at which I_3 can start execution is that $\tau_s^{reuse}(I_3) = 5$ and the cost due to register reuse is

```
/*  Kernel 1 -- hydro fragment  */

    for ( l= 1 ; l <= loop; l++ ) {
        for ( k=0 ; k<N ; k++ ) {
            x[k] = q + y[k]*(r*z[k+10]+t*z[k+11]);
        }
    }

/*  Intermediate code */

t1:k , t2:q, t3:r, t4:t
I1  :  Loop addi   t1  , #10 , t5      t5 := k+10
I2  :       load   z(t5) , t6          t6 := z[k+10]
I3  :       mul    t3  , t6  , t7      t7 := r*z[k+10]
I4  :       addi   t1  , #11 , t8      t8 := k+11
I5  :       load   z(t8) , t9          t9 := Z[k+11]
I6  :       mul    t4  , t9  , t10     t10 := r*Z[k+11]
I7  :       add    t7  , t10 , t11     t11 := t7+t10
I8  :       load   x(r1) , t12         t12 := x[k]
I9  :       mul    t11 , t12 , t13     t13 := t11*t12
I10 :       add    t2  , t13 , t14     t14 := t2+t13
I11 :       addi   t1  , #1  , t15     t15 := k+1
I12 :       store  t14 , x(t15)        x[k+1] := t14
I13 :       addi   t1  , #1  , t1      k := k+1
I14 :       cmp    r1  , #n  , tf1     ( r1 <= N ) ?
I15 :       jmp    tf1 , Loop
```

Fig. 5. Livermore kernel No.1 and the intermediate code.

$$cost_{reuse} = \tau_s^{reuse}(I_3) - \tau_{ls}(I_3) = 5 - 3 = 2.$$

Next, we estimate the cost possibly created by spilling a register to execute I_3. For example, let us consider register r_1. As can be seen in Fig. 6, the completion time of the latest definition/use of register r_1 is that $ct_{latest-use}(r_1) = 3$, and the earliest completion time at which the Load/Store unit finishes execution is that $ect(LD/ST) = 3$. Thus, inserting a store instruction to spill the value $t1$ in register r_1 into memory will result in that $\tau_s^{store}(I_3) = 5$. By Eq. (11), the cost due to the store instruction insertion is therefore

$$cost_{store}(r_1) = \tau_s^{store}(I_3) - \tau_{ls}(I_3) = 5 - 3 = 2,$$

which is equal to $cost_{reuse}$. Using the same way, we obtain $cost_{store}(r_i) \geq cost_{reuse}, \forall r_i \in R$. Thus, instead of adding spill code in this scheduling point we should let I_3 wait for the reuse of register r_6.

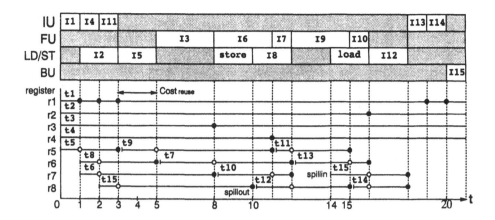

Fig. 6. The schedule obtained by the register spilling scheme.

Similarly, we can also solve the scheduling-time register assignment problem for instruction I_8 at time 5, in which the register assignment for the value $t12$ of I_8 fails to find a solution with the number of registers available. Firstly, by Eqs. (9) and (10) we easily obtain the cost due to register reuse as follows.

$$cost_{reuse} = \tau_s^{reuse}(I_8) - \tau_{ls}(I_8) = 11 - 5 = 6.$$

Secondly, we compute register spilling cost. As an example, let us consider register r_8. By Eq. (11), the cost due to the store operation used to spill register r_8 is

$$cost_{store}(r_8) = \tau_s^{store}(I_8) - \tau_{ls}(I_8) = 8 - 5 = 3.$$

Thus, we need further evaluate the cost caused by inserting a load instruction before the spilled use. The value of variable $t15$ stored in memory must be reloaded into a register before the execution of instruction I_{12}. The time interval in which the load instruction is processed is therefore $[\tau_s, \tau_f] \in [\tau_s^{store}(I_8) + \mu(I_8), \tau_{ls}^{store}(I_{12})]$; i.e., $[12, 16]$. By using the algorithm described in Fig. 4, we finally obtain the cost due to the load instruction insertion, which is

$$cost_{load}(r_8) = 0$$

in the time interval $[\tau_s, \tau_f] = [14, 16]$. Consequently, we have that

$$|cost_{store}(r_8)| + |cost_{load}(r_8)| < |cost_{reuse}|;$$

i.e., we should add spill code to ensure a register for the execution of I_8. Figure 6 shows the schedule obtained, which is 21 (time units).

We have implemented the proposed method in C on a SUN workstation running the Unix operating system. Five kernels in the Livermore benchmark was tested for our method and a non-aggressive spilling method. The non-aggressive spilling method used introduces spill code as less as possible. Because there is no method in literature, which considers both register reuse and register spilling when the compiler does instruction scheduling, we compared the aggressive and non-aggressive schemes to show the fact that the compiler does not need to avoid register spilling if the spilling cost is less than register reuse cost. Table 2 demonstrates the time units of scheduling results obtained. The results are encouraging. Our method either produces the same schedule as the non-aggressive spilling method, or it produces a better schedule.

Table 2. Experimental results for the aggressive and non-aggressive spilling strategies.

	$|R| = 8$		$|R| = 12$		$|R| = 16$	
	Aggr.	Non-aggr.	Aggr.	Non-aggr.	Aggr.	Non-aggr.
Kernel No. 2	21	24	16	19	13	13
Kernel No. 5	33	37	27	31	24	25
Kernel No. 7	56	60	41	47	35	37
Kernel No. 9	52	57	44	45	41	41
Kernel No. 18	67	76	55	69	51	51

7   Conclusions

In this paper we have presented a method to analyze the execution behavior of a given program for register assignment during the code scheduling process. Using this information, we have also developed a novel approach that computes register spill cost and register reuse cost when insufficient registers available in order to efficiently determine whether to spill or not, the least spill cost, and the places where spill code needs to be added. The preliminary experimental results have shown that this technique is promising. We are currently developing a programming environment that will permit much more extensive experimentation with the technique.

Acknowledgment

This work was supported in part by the Ministry of Education, Science and Culture under Grant No. 09780263, and by a Grant from the Artificial Intelligence Research Promotion Foundation under contract number 9AI252-9. We would like to thank Nobutoshi Onoda, who developed the initial version of the compiler and whose comments were helpful in the development of the algorithm. We would also like to thank the anonymous referees for both their careful reading and valuable comments.

References

1. T. Kiyohara and J.C.Gyllenhaal, "Code Scheduling for VLIW/Superscalar Processors with Limited Register Files", Proc. of the 1992 International Symposium on Microarchitecture, pp.197-201, 1992.
2. D.Bernstein, D.Goldin, M.Golumbic, H.Krawczyk, Y.Mansour, I.Nahshon, and R. Pinter, "Spill code minimization techniques for optimizing compilers", Proc. of the ACM SIGPLAN'89 Conf. Programming Languages Design and Implementation, pp. 258-263, 1989.
3. P.Briggs, K.Cooper, K.Kennedy, and L.Torczon, "Coloring heuristics for register allocation", Proc. of the ACM SIGPLAN'89 Conf. Programming Languages Design and Implementation, pp. 275-284, 1989.
4. P.Briggs, K.Cooper, and L.Torczon, "Improvements to graph coloring register allocation", ACM Trans. on Programming Languages and Systems, vol. 16, no. 3, pp. 428-455, May 1994.
5. D.G.Bradlee, S.J.Eggers, and R.R.Henry, "Integrating Register Allocation and Instruction Scheduling for RISCs," Proc. Fourth International Conference on Architectural Support for Programming Languages and Operating Systems, pp. 122-131, 1991.
6. S.S.Pinter, "Register Allocation with Instruction Scheduling: a New Approach, Proc. the SIGPLAN'93 Conference on Programming Language Design and Implementation, 1993.
7. C.Norris, and L.L.Pollock, "A Scheduler-Sensitive Global Register Allocator," Proc. Supercomputing'93, pp. 804-813, 1993.
8. J. Wang, A. Krall, M.A. Ertl and C. Eisenbeis, "Software Pipelining with Register Allocation and Spilling," Proc. of the 1994 International Symposium on Microarchitecture, pp. 95-99, 1994.
9. J. Llosa, M. Valero and E. Ayguade, "Heuristic for Register-constrained Software Pipelining," Proc. of the 1996 International Symposium on Microarchitecture, pp. 250-261, 1996.
10. B.Natarajan, and M.Schlansker, "Spill-Free Scheduling of Basic Blocks," Proc. the 28th International Symposium on Microarchitecture, pp. 119-124, 1995.
11. G.Lowney et al., "The Multiflow Trace Scheduling Compiler," J. of Supercomputing, vol. 7, pp. 51-142, 1993.
12. J.A.Fisher, "Trace Scheduling: A Technique for Global Microcode Compaction," IEEE Trans. on Comput., vol. C-30, no. 7, pp. 478-490, 1981.
13. J.Ellis, "Bulldog: A Compiler for VLIW Architectures," The MIT Press, Cambridge, Mass., 1986.
14. M.Y.Wu and D.Gajski, "Hypertool: A Programming Aid for Message-Passing Systems," IEEE Trans. on Parallel and Distributed Systems, vol.1, no.3, pp. 101-119, 1990.
15. E.B.Fernandez and B.Bussell,"Bounds on the Number of Processors and Time for Multiprocessor Optimal Schedules," IEEE Trans. on Comput., Vol.C-22, No.8, pp.745-751, 1973.

Copy Elimination for Parallelizing Compilers *

David J. Kolson, Alexandru Nicolau, and Nikil Dutt

Dept. of Information and Computer Science, University of California, Irvine
Irvine, CA 92697, USA

Abstract. Techniques for aggressive optimization and parallelization of applications can have the side-effect of introducing copy instructions, register-to-register move instructions, into the generated code. This preserves program correctness while avoiding the need for global search-and-update of registers. However, copy instructions only transfer data between registers while requiring the use of system resources (ALUs) and are essentially overhead operations which can potentially limit performance. Conventional copy propagation and copy removal techniques are not powerful enough to remove these copies as, during loop parallelization, the lifetimes of the values copied may span over loop boundaries. In this paper, we present a technique for copy removal that incrementally unrolls a loop body and re-allocates registers to values so that no copy operations are required. We also present a heuristic version that limits the amount of unrolling and present experimentation that demonstrates the necessity of copy removal in gaining improved code performance.

1 Introduction

Optimizing compilers can generate many copy instructions, register-to-register move instructions, both due to the aggressive application of program transformations as well as the compiler's internal representation. "Classic" optimizations such as common sub-expression elimination [1] and induction variable elimination [1] as well as more sophisticated techniques such as redundant load elimination [4,20], variable or register renaming [11,22] and variable lifetime splitting [10], add copy instructions into the code in order to control compiler complexity as the global search-and-replace of registers within instructions each time that an optimization is performed is too costly.

Also, compilers which utilize a static single assignment (SSA) [12] internal form, for instance, must honor the requirement that each variable be assigned exactly once. This has the effect of breaking a variable's lifetime into several (shorter) lifetimes. A consequence of this is that, at join points in program flow, intermittent values may need to be transferred from one temporary to another (via the ϕ-function), thus potentially generating copy instructions in the final code.

* This work supported in part by ONR grant N000149311348 and ARPA grant MDA904-96-C-1472.

In the generation of sequential code, copy propagation is typically applied as a post-pass process to reduce/eliminate the number of copy instructions present and, in some cases, may be implemented within a graph coloring register allocator as the coloring of the source and target temporaries with the same color allows the copy instruction to be removed. Compilers which seek to expose and to exploit instruction-level parallelism (ILP) typically employ some of the same optimizations. Copy removal is then crucial to an ILP compiler as copy instructions are essentially overhead instructions which require system resources (ALUs) to execute[1]. Thus, the presence of copy instructions in the schedule represents a negative impact to the attainable performance of parallel code. However, the solutions available to sequential optimizing compilers: standard copy propagation and node coalescing during graph coloring, are unavailable to an ILP compiler.

During scheduling [14,15,17,21] and software pipelining [2,13,18,24], when iterations of a loop are overlapped, copy instructions potentially keep values live over loop boundaries and serve to 'queue' values for future use. Thus, these copy instructions are not amenable to removal via conventional copy propagation as, in parallel code, multiple values generated by the same instruction (but from different loop iterations) may be simultaneously live due to copy instructions and simple copy propagation would lead to incorrect results.

Also, in the context of ILP compilers, where an integrated approach to instruction scheduling and register allocation [23,5,3] is necessary as: 1) an instruction scheduler requires accurate information on the resources required by each instruction, and 2) resource re-allocation is necessary to reduce resource contention, continually applying a graph coloring algorithm to the code is too costly. Thus, approaches which rely on graph coloring to remove copy instructions by coalescing the source and target temporaries via coloring the respective nodes the same color are inappropriate.

In this paper, a generalized technique for copy removal is presented. This technique removes copy instructions that keep values live over loop iterations by unrolling the loop code and re-allocating registers to instructions. As a result, copies which preserve values within an iteration—"traditional" copies—are also removed. Thus, this technique subsumes conventional copy propagation techniques while providing a method for removing more advanced forms of copy instruction chains. In the context of ILP compilers, this is particularly useful as the realization of available ILP can be greatly reduced by copy instruction occupation of system resources (ALUs).

2   Introductory Example

As an introductory example, consider the code in Figure 1(a) which will serve to demonstrate how parallelization inserts copy instructions into code. In this example, the value written into $R0$ in node M is used by the instruction $R5 = R0 + 10$

---

[1] Practically, a copy $R1 = R2$ would be performed by executing some instruction as $R1 = R2 + 0$ or $R1 = R2 << 0$.

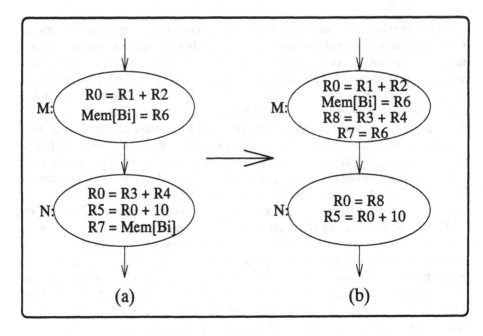

Fig. 1. Introducing copy instructions into the code.

in the next node[2]. During parallelization, the instruction $R0 = R3 + R4$ from node N may not be moved into (i.e., executed in parallel with the instructions of) node M as it redefines $R0$ and would cause incorrect values to be computed by the instruction $R5 = R0 + 10$ in node N. If a free register exists ($R8$ in this example), then the destination register of instruction $R0 = R3 + R4$ is renamed and the new instruction, $R8 = R3 + R4$, is moved into node M. To maintain correctness, a copy instruction $R0 = R8$ is necessary in node N to correctly move the value from $R8$ into $R0$, thereby compacting the code of (a) to that of (b).

Also, in node M, a value is stored[3] to the memory location B_i. In node N, this value is loaded from memory by the load instruction $R7 = Mem[B_i]$. Rather than re-loading the value from memory, the value stored to memory by instruction $Mem[Bi] = R6$ can be directly copied. Thus, the load is removed, resulting in the earlier availability of the value (i.e., the latency of the load is removed), and the copy instruction $R7 = R6$ is added to node M.

In the previous example, simple copy propagation may be used to eliminate the copies as the code is straight-line. However, during software pipelining when multiple iterations of a loop are overlapped and optimizations are performed, the

---

[2] Note that the value read by the instruction $R5 = R0 + 10$ is that produced by the instruction $R0 = R1 + R2$ in node M rather than the instruction $R0 = R3 + R4$ in node N as, due to the machine model, all operands are read before any results are written.

[3] For simplicity, loads and stores are shown here symbolically. Typically, the address is calculated into a register and analysis [4,20] is required to determine equivalency in memory references.

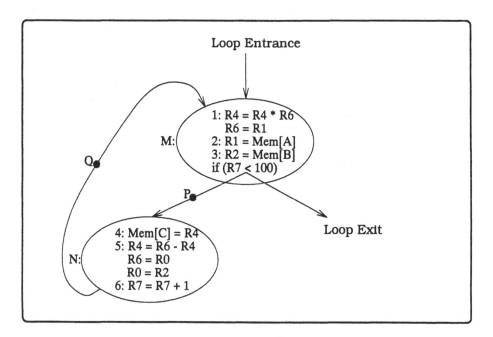

Fig. 2. Loop code with copy instructions.

uses of copied values can span across iteration boundaries. Thus, conventional copy propagation techniques [1] are not powerful enough to remove many of the copies introduced during loop parallelization.

As an example, in Figure 2, several optimizations were applied during the parallelization of a loop. As a result, several copy instructions are found in this code[4]. Conventional copy propagation cannot remove any of these copy instructions as those copies serve to keep values live over multiple iterations of the loop. For instance, the copy $R6 = R1$ in node M cannot be removed as it preserves a value loaded by $R1 = Mem[A]$ from the previous iteration (the previous execution of node M) and propagating $R1$ in place of $R6$ into the following node (into the instruction $R4 = R6 - R4$) would result in the use of an incorrect value (the newly loaded value from instruction #2 would be incorrectly used rather than the previously loaded value). Thus, conventional copy propagation is not adequate to remove these copies.

3   Related Work

Redundant memory instruction elimination [4,7,20] is a technique which minimizes the number of memory referencing instructions associated with array

---

[4] Note that four ALUs and two memory units are necessary to execute this parallel code, while, if copies were removed, only two ALUs and two memory units are necessary.

accessing. This technique will insert copy instructions into the schedule to eliminate a memory reference to a value which is already present in the register set.

Static renaming [11,22] is a method utilized during scheduling to allocate "on-the-fly" a currently unused memory location (register) when code optimization is prohibited due to false (anti- and output-) dependencies. A copy instruction is inserted to copy the generated value from the newly allocated register into the original register.

In the context of register allocation by graph coloring, several researchers [6,8,10,16] have addressed the problem of copy or move coalescing. Chaitin [8,9] proposes to combine the source and target nodes thereby producing a single node with the union of the interferences and removing the need for the move instruction. Since the degree of the new node is now higher, this can complicate the coloring process of the graph. Briggs *et al.* [6] have proposed a less aggressive, heuristic coalescing scheme which improves the colorability of the graph, but leaves copy instructions in the code. George and Appel [16] have extended Briggs' heuristic approach to improve coalescing in the SML/NJ compiler.

Chow and Hennessy [10] improve the quality of the spill code produced by a graph coloring allocator by splitting variable lifetimes at points in the code where register pressure is high. This allows a higher degree of freedom when coloring the graph, but requires move instructions when a variable's lifetime is not contained within the same register.

Another approach to register allocation for straight-line code is interval graph coloring. In [19], the interval graph coloring solution is extended to register allocation for loop graphs. In doing so, variable lifetimes are arbitrarily broken at loop boundaries and when the lifetime segments cannot be colored with the same color, copy instructions are necessary to transfer the value from one register to another.

4   Eliminating Copy Instructions

Copies generated during parallelization do not *produce* new values but, rather, *preserve* already computed values for future uses. In other words, multiple values produced in various iterations by an instruction are simultaneously live and transferred from definition to last use by chains of copy instructions. Copies related to a specific copy chain cannot be removed without affecting the 'queueing' of values for use. As depicted in the code of Figure 3, which has been compacted into one node, by unrolling the loop body sufficiently, the definition of a value and its last use become explicit thereby eliminating the need for the copy chain and, thus, enabling copy elimination[5]. In this example, the solution loop spans three iterations of the original loop.

---

[5] Once again, recall that, due to the machine model, all operands are read before any results are written. Therefore, in the first node, for instance, the value "X" used by A = X + B is that generated by the previous execution of that node.

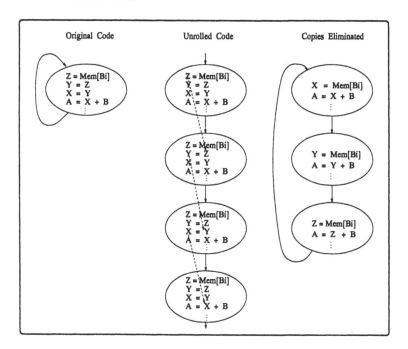

Fig. 3. Unrolling loop code to eliminate copies.

4.1   An Algorithm for Copy Elimination

Figure 4 contains an algorithm which performs copy elimination on a loop. As input, this algorithm takes a loop body or loop graph where each node contains instructions which are executed in parallel and produces a new loop without copy instructions which may span multiple iterations of the original (input) loop.

The first step of the algorithm is to compute the register mappings for each node in the graph. The register mapping for a node represents the contents of the registers *immediately preceding* the execution of that node and are derived similar to program data-flow analysis. (An algorithm for this is presented shortly.)

At this point, a loop template, or copy of the loop with its register mappings, is made and used for future reference. During copy elimination, the source registers of each instruction are looked up in this template to determine the tags for the values they use in the original loop. As values may be re-allocated to registers during copy elimination, it may become necessary to update or to change the source operands of some instructions. For instance, suppose the following is the register mapping for a node in the loop template:

$$(R0, 10.1)\ \ (R1, 9.0)\ \ (R2, 7.0)\ \ (R3, 10.0)$$

and the current instruction from that respective node in the current unrolling is $R2 = R0 - R3$ with a current register mapping of:

$$(R0, 9.0)\ \ (R1, 10.0)\ \ (R2, 7.0)\ \ (R3, 10.1)$$

In the original loop, this instruction uses values 10.1 for the first argument and 10.0 for the second. During copy elimination when considering the instruction

Procedure *copy_elimination*(L : loop)
Begin
      /* compute initial register maps for L */
      /* split nodes having multiple defs, recalc register maps */
      /* make loop template */
      /* add the header of L to the headers_list */
      /* add all backedges found in L to backedges_list */
      scan_and_reallocate (*header_of*(L));
      While (not empty backedges_list) {
           /* unroll along backedge b from backedges_list */
           /* add new iteration headers and backedges to respective lists */
           scan_and_reallocate (*header*);
           /* match backedges to header nodes */
      }
End *copy_elimination*

Fig. 4. An algorithm for copy elimination.

$R2 = R0 - R3$, these values (10.1 and 10.0) are looked up in the current register mapping to find the registers which contain them. If the registers currently containing those values are different from the source operands, the source operands are updated as appropriate, as is the case here where the first argument must be changed to $R2$ and the second argument becomes $R1$, thus, $R2 = R3 - R1$ is the instruction for the copy eliminated code.

Once the register mappings are calculated and the loop template is made, the header of the loop is added to a *headers_list* and all of the backedges of that loop are added to the *backedges_list*. The *headers_list* is used to keep track of all loop entry points to determine, after unrolling and copy elimination, if a backedge may be directed to any previous header that has an identical register mapping. The *backedges_list* is the list of loop iterative points along which an iteration of the loop is to be unrolled.

While there are backedges to unroll along, the algorithm iterates over the following steps: unroll the loop along that backedge; add the new header and backedges to the respective lists; *scan_and_reallocate*() (discussed further) and, finally, once copy elimination has been performed on the current unrolling, the backedges of this loop iteration are checked against all headers in the *headers_list*. Those backedges with register mappings that match the register mappings of an iteration header are directed to the respective matching header while those with no match are added to the *backedges_list*. The algorithm terminates once there are no more backedges left.

Computing Register Mappings

Figure 5 contains an algorithm patterned after dataflow analysis which computes the register mappings of a loop. To derive the mappings of a node, each instruction in the node is considered. If the instruction is a copy, then a new entry is made with the destination register and the value being copied.

```
Procedure compute_register_maps  (L : loop)
    /* initialize all register maps to φ */
    changes = true
    while (changes) {
        changes = false
        add loop header to l
        while (not empty l) {
            remove node, N, from l
            Rmaps = reg_map_of(N)
            new_maps = copy(Rmaps)
            Foreach operation, op, in N {
                if (op is a copy)
                    (value.age) = lookup src1_reg_of(op) in Rmaps
                    Add (dest_reg_of(op), value.age) to new_maps
                else
                    Foreach map in new_maps with same id_of(op)
                        increment age
                    Delete all maps from new_maps with dest_reg_of(op)
                    Add (dest_reg_of(op), op_id_of(op).0) to new_maps
                endif
            }
            For all successors, S, of N {
                if (new_maps != reg_map_of(S))
                    changes = true
                    reg_map_of(S) = copy(new_maps)
                endif
                Add S to l
            }
        }
    }
End compute_register_maps
```

Fig. 5. An algorithm for computing register mappings.

If the instruction is not a copy, it defines a new value. An entry is added to the register mapping annotated with the destination register of the instruction and a tag of instruction identifier and 0 (zero signifies the birth of a value). Any annotation in the mapping with the same instruction identifier will have its *age* field incremented, as this value has become "older" by the generation of the new value. Also, any entry with the destination register is now killed and deleted from the mapping.

As an example of deriving the register mappings of a loop, the register mappings for the example of Figure 2 are derived in Table 1.

Scan-and-Reallocate

Figure 6 contains an algorithm for scanning a loop. This algorithm is similar to the algorithm for computing register mappings as it is necessary when reallocating registers to instructions to keep track of the values in the registers.

Iteration of Algorithm

	Initially	1st	2nd	3rd	no changes
Maps At Point P	ϕ	$(R1, 2.0)$ $(R2, 3.0)$ $(R4, 1.0)$	$(R0, 3.1)$ $(R1, 2.0)$ $(R2, 3.0)$ $(R4, 1.0)$	$(R0, 3.1)$ $(R1, 2.0)$ $(R2, 3.0)$ $(R4, 1.0)$ $(R6, 2.1)$	$(R0, 3.1)$ $(R1, 2.0)$ $(R2, 3.0)$ $(R4, 1.0)$ $(R6, 2.1)$
Maps At Point Q	ϕ	$(R0, 3.0)$ $(R4, 5.0)$ $(R7, 6.0)$	$(R0, 3.0)$ $(R1, 2.0)$ $(R4, 5.0)$ $(R6, 3.1)$ $(R7, 6.0)$	$(R0, 3.0)$ $(R1, 2.0)$ $(R4, 5.0)$ $(R6, 3.1)$ $(R7, 6.0)$	$(R0, 3.0)$ $(R1, 2.0)$ $(R4, 5.0)$ $(R6, 3.1)$ $(R7, 6.0)$

Table 1. Register mappings for the code of Figure ??.

```
Procedure Scan_and_Reallocate(L : loop)
     /* initialize all register maps to φ */
     reg_map_of(header) = /* output map of backedge */
     add loop header to l
     while (not empty l) {
          remove node, N, from l
          Rmaps = reg_map_of(N)
          new_maps = copy(Rmaps)
          Foreach operation, op, in N
               if (op is a copy)
                    Remove op
               else
                    Update_Args(op)
                    if (dest_reg_of(op) ∈ Rmap and live)
                         dest_reg_of(op) = get free register
                    Delete all maps from new_maps with dest_reg_of(op)
                    Add (dest_reg_of(op), (op_id_of(op), 0)) to new_maps
               endif
          For all successors, S, of N {
               reg_map_of(S) = copy(new_maps)
               Add S to l
          }
     }
End scan_and_reallocate
```

Fig. 6. An algorithm for removing copies and updating register usages.

Initially, the register maps are initialized to ϕ and the entry register mapping to the loop is the register mapping found at the end of the previous iteration, or that found along the backedge unrolled upon. As the loop nodes are scanned, if an instruction is a copy, it is removed from the node. If not, the arguments to the instruction are updated as registers are re-allocated and the appropriate values may not still be in the used registers. Updating entails look-up of the sources in the loop template to determine the referenced values; those values are then found in the current mapping to obtain the register that currently contains the appropriate value(s). It might be necessary to re-allocate the destination of this instruction if that register contains a live value. Finally, values killed by this instruction are removed and an annotation is added for the processed instruction.

4.2   Heuristic Copy Elimination

Possibly the most noticeable feature of our copy elimination algorithm is that the final loop solution spans multiple iterations of the original loop in order to make value definitions and uses explicit. In some cases, it may not be desirable to unroll the loop for the necessary number of iterations. In this case, the algorithm may be parameterized with the maximal number of iterations to unroll. However, when this threshold value is reached, it is not guaranteed that the backedges for that unrolling depth will match any of the previous iteration headers. When the threshold is reached, a simple strategy may be employed to match backedges to headers so that a minimal number of copy instructions is introduced.

4.3   An Example

As an example, copy elimination is performed on the loop code of Figure 2 with the initial register mappings from Table 1.

The copy elimination algorithm applies the *scan_and_realloc()* procedure to the first iteration of the loop. As node M_0 is scanned, the first instruction considered is $R4 = R4 - R6$. The procedure *update_args()* looks up this instruction in the loop template and determines that argument one is the value (5.0) and argument two is the value (3.1). These values, (5.0) and (3.1), are looked up in the current register mapping (the register mapping found at point I in Figure 7) and are currently found in the registers $R4$ and $R6$, respectively. Since these values are already referenced in the appropriate registers, no changes to the instruction's operands are made. Since this is the last use of the value (5.0), contained in register $R4$, a new register is not needed for the destination register of the instruction. Lastly, an entry is made in the current register mapping of $(R4, (1.0))$.

The next instruction is the copy instruction $R6 = R1$ and is removed from the code. The next instruction, $R1 = Mem[A]$, is examined and is found to contain a live value (i.e., a value that is used beyond this node). Thus, a call to *get_free_register()* is necessary to re-allocate a register to the destination of this instruction. In this case, the function call returns the register $R2$ as the value

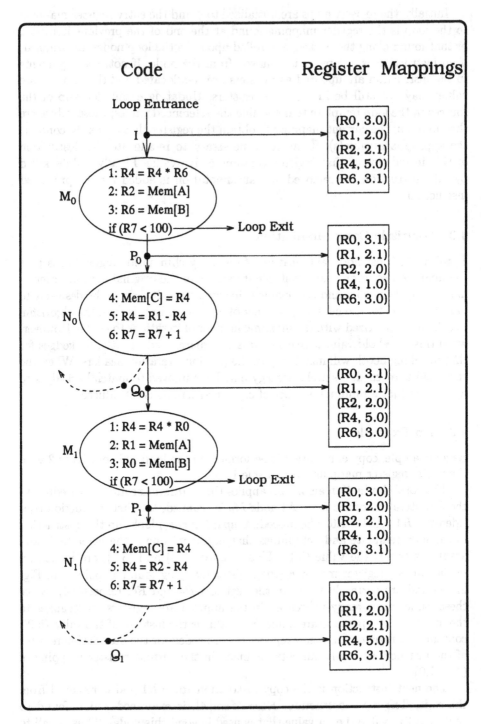

Fig. 7. Unrolling loop code to eliminate copies.

it contains, (2.1) becomes dead in this node[6]. Thus, $R1 = Mem[A]$ becomes $R2 = Mem[A]$.

When node N_0 is scanned, the argument to instruction $Mem[C] = R4$ is checked in the loop template. This instruction uses $R4$ which contains the value (1.0) at point P. In the current register mapping, $R4$ contains this value, so no updating takes place. The next instruction is $R4 = R6 - R4$ and uses the values (2.1) and (1.0), as source values, respectively. In the current mapping, those values are contained in $R1$ and $R4$, respectively. As the value (1.0) dies, the destination register of this instruction does not require updating. The next two instructions, $R6 = R0$ and $R0 = R2$, are copies and are removed. Finally, the last instruction requires no updating, leaving the code found in node N_0 of Figure 7.

This process continues and the derived mapping at Q_1 is found to match that at the loop top (point I), so the algorithm converges and the new loop spans two iterations of the original loop, containing no copies.

5   Experiments and Results

We conducted experiments on a suite of benchmarks which consisted of 11 numerical and scientific codes to study the effects of copy elimination on performance. Latencies given to our parameterized scheduler are one cycle for copy operations, two cycles for add/subtract operations, three cycles for multiply operations and three cycles for memory accessing operations. For functional unit constraints, two add/subtract units, one multiply and a single-ported memory which can handle only one request at a time, were used.

For each benchmark, three schedules were generated: the first schedule contained copy operations, the second schedule utilized our copy elimination algorithm and the third used a heuristic version with the maximum number of iterations, three. From these schedules performance measures were made. These performance improvement measures are with respect to sequential execution of the code and are measured as:

$$SU = \frac{cycles_{seq}}{cycles_{par}}$$

Thus, in our tables, columns labeled with "copies" refers to the speed-up of parallelized code which contains copy operations; "no copies" refers to the speed-up of parallelized code with copy elimination; and "heur" refers to the speed-up of parallelized code with the heuristic version of copy elimination. Percentage improvement (% Improvement) is the percentage improvement of the schedules

---

[6] When the instruction $R1 = Mem[A]$ generates a new value, it will cause all other values in the register mapping with the same identifier to become "older" (i.e., the age value increases). Thus, the value in $R1$, (2.0), will become (2.1) and the value in $R2$, (2.1), will become (2.2). As the value (2.2) is never used, the register containing that value is free for re-allocation in this node.

with copies eliminated versus the schedules that contain copies and is measured as:

$$Impr = \frac{SU_{nocopies} - SU_{copies}}{SU_{copies}} * 100$$

Our observed performance results on the benchmark suite are contained in Table 2 for codes with no copy elimination and codes where copies were removed. In all cases, copy elimination increased the performance of the parallelized code with percentage improvements ranging from 11% to 72%.

Table 2. Observed speed-up on benchmark suite.

Benchmark	copies	no copies	% Impr
2D-Hydro exerpt	1.27	1.99	57%
Cholesky Conj. Grad.	1.47	1.81	23%
Tri-diagonal Elim.	1.38	2.20	59%
GLR	1.61	1.79	11%
State Equations	1.11	1.91	72%
Partial Diff. Solver	1.48	1.99	34%
Integrator Pred.	1.05	1.56	49%
Difference Pred.	1.20	1.98	65%
Partial sum (scan)	1.80	2.25	25%
Difference sum	1.50	1.93	29%
2D Particle	1.70	1.90	12%

Table 3 contains the observed performance results on the benchmark suite for code with copy elimination and codes with heuristic copy elimination with an unrolling bound of three iterations. Also noted in the table is the number of iterations spanned by the optimal (i.e., no bounds on unrolling) copy elimination codes. In some cases, the heuristic version was able to derive the same solution as the optimal and in other cases derived solutions with results which are close to the optimal. It should be noted that, even though the optimal solutions span more iterations, the number of iterations spanned is not prohibitive.

6   Conclusion

Aggressive code motion and program optimization techniques, necessary for exploiting the parallelism inherent in application code, can have the side-effect of introducing many copy instructions—register-to-register move instructions, into the parallel code. These copies are necessary overhead for reducing compiler complexity, but their presence in the final code represents a hindrance to high performance as they consume functional resources, but perform no significant computation. In order to improve the attainable performance, copy elimination is necessary. This paper presents a technique which eliminates all copy instructions from parallel code by unrolling and remapping registers to values. As the

Table 3. Speed-up of copy elimination and heuristic.

Benchmark	no copies	heur	# Iters
2D-Hydro exerpt	1.99	1.89	4
Cholesky Conj. Grad.	1.81	1.81	3
Tri-diagonal Elim.	2.20	1.92	5
GLR	1.79	1.70	4
State Equations	1.91	1.91	3
Partial Diff. Solver	1.99	1.88	5
Integrator Pred.	1.56	1.56	3
Difference Pred.	1.98	1.98	3
Partial sum (scan)	2.25	1.99	4
Difference sum	1.93	1.80	4
2D Particle	1.90	1.83	4

increase in code size may be a consideration, a heuristic version is presented which bounds the amount of loop unrolling performed. Experimentation with a suite of benchmarks demonstrates that significant performance improvements are possible by eliminating copy instructions.

References

1. A. H. Aho, R. Sethi, and J. D. Ullman. *Compilers: Principles, Techniques and Tools.* Addison-Wesley,Reading,Massachusetts, 1986.
2. A. Aiken and A. Nicolau. Perfect Pipelining: A New Loop Parallelization Technique. *Proc. of the 1988 European Symp. on Programming*, March 1988.
3. D. A. Berson, P.Chang, R. Gupta, and M. L. Soffa. Integrating Program Optimizations and Transformations with the Scheduling of Instruction Level Parallelism. *Proceedings of the International Workshop on Languages and Compilers for Parallel Computing*, pages 207–221, August 1996. San Jose, California.
4. R. Bodik and R. Gupta. Array Data Flow Analysis for Load-Store Optimizations in Superscalar Architectures. *Proceedings of the International Workshop on Languages and Compilers for Parallel Computing*, August 1995.
5. D. G. Bradlee, S. J. Eggers, and R. R. Henry. Integrating Register Allocation and Instruction Scheduling for RISCs. *Proceedings of SIGPLAN Architectural Support for Programming Languages and Operating Systems*, 26(4), April 1991.
6. P. Briggs, K. D. Cooper, and L. Torczon. Improvements to Graph Coloring Register Allocation. *ACM Transactions on Programming Languages and Systems*, 16(3), May 1994.
7. D. Callahan, J. Cocke, and K. Kennedy. Estimating Interlock and Improving Balance for Pipelined Architectures. *Proceedings of the International Conference on Parallel Processing*, 1987.
8. G. Chaitin. Register Allocation and Spilling Via Graph Coloring. *Proc. of SIGPLAN Symp. on Comp. Const.*, 176, June 1982.
9. G. Chaitin, M. Auslander, A. Chandra, J. Cocke, M. Hopkins, and P. Markstein. Register Allocation Via Coloring. *Computer Languages*, 6:47–57, January 1981.

10. F. Chow and J. Hennessy. The Priority-Based Coloring Approach to Register Allocation. *ACM Transactions on Programming Languages and Systems*, 12(4):501–536, October 1990.

11. R. Cytron and J. Ferrante. What's in a name? The value of renaming for parallelism detection and storage allocation. *Proceedings of the Internation al Conference on Parallel Processing*, August 1987.

12. R. Cytron, J. Ferrante, B. K. Rosen, M. N. Wegman, and F. K. Zadeck. Efficiently Computing Static Single Assignment Form and the Control Dependence Graph. *ACM Transactions on Programming Languages and Systems*, 13(4):451–490, October 1991.

13. K. Ebcioglu. Compilation Technique for Software Pipelining of Loops with Conditional Jumps. *20th Annual Workshop on Microprogramming*, 1987.

14. J. R. Ellis. *Bulldog: A Compiler for VLIW Architectures.* PhD thesis, Yale University, 1985.

15. J. Fisher. Trace Scheduling: A Technique for Global Microcode Compaction. *IEEE Trans. on Comp.*, C-30(7), July 1981.

16. L. George and A. W. Appel. *Iterated Register Coalescing.* ACM Transactions on Programming Languages and Systems, 18(3):300–324, May 1996.

17. J. R. Goodman and W.-C. Hsu. Code Scheduling and Register Allocation in Large Basic Blocks. *International Conference on Supercomputing*, 1988.

18. T. Gross and M. S. Lam. Compilation for High-Performance Systolic Array. *Proceedings of the Symposium on Compiler Construction*, 1986.

19. L. J. Hendren, G. R. Gao, E. Altman, and C. Mukerji. A Register Allocation Framework Based on Heirarchical Cyclic Interval Graphs. *International Conference on Compiler Construction*, pages 176–191, April 1992. Paderborn, Germany.

20. D. J. Kolson, A. Nicolau, and N. Dutt. Elimination of Redundant Memory Traffic in High-Level Synthesis. *IEEE Transactions on the Computer Aided Design of Integrated Circuits and Systems*, pages 1354–1364, November 1996.

21. A. Nicolau. Uniform Parallelism Exploitation in Ordinary Programs. *Proceedings of ICPP*, August 1985.

22. A. Nicolau, R. Potasman, and H. Wang. Register Allocation, Renaming and Their Impact on Fine-Grain Parallelism. *4th Int. Wksp on Lang. and Comp. for Par. Comp.*, 1991.

23. S. S. Pinter. Register Allocation with Instruction Scheduling : A New Approach. *SIGPLAN PLDI*, 1993.

24. B. R. Rau and C. D. Glaeser. Some Scheduling Techniques and An Easily Schedulable Horizontal Architecture for High Performance Scientific Computing. *Micro-14*, June 1981.

Compiling for SIMD Within a Register

Randall J. Fisher and Henry G. Dietz

School of Electrical and Computer Engineering, Purdue University
West Lafayette, IN 47907-1285, USA
{rfisher,hankd}@ecn.purdue.edu

Abstract. Although SIMD (Single Instruction stream Multiple Data stream) parallel computers have existed for decades, it is only in the past few years that a new version of SIMD has evolved: SIMD Within A Register (SWAR). Unlike other styles of SIMD hardware, SWAR models are tuned to be integrated within conventional microprocessors, using their existing memory reference and instruction handling mechanisms, with the primary goal of improving the speed of specific multimedia operations.

Because the SWAR implementations for various microprocessors vary widely and each is missing instructions for some SWAR operations that are needed to support a more general, portable, high-level SIMD execution model, this paper focuses on how these missing operations can be implemented using either the existing SWAR hardware or even conventional 32-bit integer instructions. In addition, SWAR offers a few new challenges for compiler optimization, and these are briefly introduced.

1 Introduction

The SWAR model takes advantage of the fact that a wide data path within a processor also can be treated as multiple, thinner, SIMD-parallel data paths. Thus, each register is effectively partitioned into *fields* that can be operated on in parallel. Operations like partitioned field-by-field addition are easily implemented with minimal hardware enhancements. For example, to make a 64-bit adder function as eight 8-bit adders, one simply needs to modify the adder's carry logic so that carry from one 8-bit field to the next is suppressed. But what SWAR field sizes and operations should be supported?

Because the introduction of SWAR techniques was motivated by the need to improve multimedia application performance, it is not surprising that the field sizes supported in hardware tend to be those commonly associated with multimedia's "natural" data types. In particular, 8-bit pixel color channel values are used for most forms of video and image processing, so this data size becomes very important. Similarly, 16-bit audio samples are very commonly used, and this field size also can be used for intermediate results when computations on 8-bit values need more than 8-bit precision. Other data sizes are common in other applications yet not directly supported by any of the SWAR hardware extensions in current microprocessors, for example: 1-bit fields hold boolean values, 2-bit

S. Chatterjee (Ed.): LCPC'98, LNCS 1656, pp. 290–304, 1999.

fields hold either 0/1/X values for a logic simulator or a base-pair value for operating on a gene database, and 10-bit or 12-bit values are used for a wide range of digitizing devices. A high-level SWAR language can and should allow users to specify the precise number of bits needed for each datum.

The operations implemented in SWAR hardware also are strongly biased in favor of specific multimedia applications and algorithms. Addition, subtraction, and various other integer operations are commonly supported. Because adding two bright pixel values should not result in a dark pixel, there are a variety of *saturation arithmetic* operations supported (e.g., overflow in saturation arithmetic yields the maximum representable value rather than the low bits of a larger value). 32-bit floating-point operations are also supported (e.g. by AMD's 3DNow! [10] which Cyrix and WinChip [9] will also support and soon by Cyrix's MMFP), although all current SWAR hardware supports only integer field operations.

Unfortunately, at least from the point of view of building high-level language compilers, current SWAR hardware support is limited to just a few field sizes and operations. Even worse, the supported operations and partitioning reflect the designers' expectations of the needs of multimedia programmers and the internal structures within the particular processor architectures, and are therefore inconsistent across architecture families. Table 1 illustrates this point by showing the partitioning supported by each of five enhanced architecture families for typical arithmetic operations.

In this table, the columns represent the multimedia extension set families. The extension families included are Digital Equipment Corporation extensions for the Alpha [3]; Hewlett-Packard PA-RISC MAX v2.0 [5,6]; Intel [4], Advanced Micro Devices [1], and Cyrix [2] versions of MMX; Silicon Graphics MIPS MDMX [7]; and Sun SPARC V9 VIS [8].

The first few rows of the table describe the basic characteristics of the multimedia (MM) registers used for SWAR: How many registers are there? How wide is each register? Are these registers the processor's integer registers or are they overlaid on the floating-point register file? The remaining rows sample various parallel arithmetic operations which one or more of the families support. "Part" is used to identify operations using partitioned register operands, with the notation $a \times b$u specifying that the register holds a fields, each containing a b-bit value, with the u suffix indicating that the field values are unsigned. "Single" refers to a single, scalar, operand value; "Immed" refers to an immediate value.

The many differences between these SWAR extension implementations are significantly more complex to manage than the variations in the base instruction sets of these processors. A number of instructions are conspicuously absent — for example, instructions to help implement SIMD-style conditional branches based on ANY or ALL condition tests. To support a high-level language, these problems must be efficiently managed by the compiler.

One obvious shortcoming of the SWAR hardware support is that it generally provides operations for just a few field sizes. Fortunately, we are not limited to the set of partitionings directly supported by the hardware. Logically, partitioning is

Table 1. Comparison Of Multimedia Instruction Set Extensions

	DEC Alpha	HP PA-RISC MAX	SGI MIPS MDMX	Intel, AMD,& Cyrix MMX	Sun Sparc V9 VIS
# MM Registers	32	31	32 (1 Acc.)	8 (+ Mem.)	32
# Bits/ MM Reg.	64	32 or 64	64 (192 Acc.)	64	64
Which Registers?	Integer	Integer	Float	Float	Float
Modular Add					
Part/Part	-	4x16,4x16u	8x8u,4x16	8x8,8x8u, 4x16, 4x16u, 2x32,2x32u	2x16,4x16, 1x32,2x32
Single/Part	-	-	8x8u,4x16	-	-
Immed/Part	-	-	8x8u,4x16	-	-
Saturation Add					
Part/Part	-	4x16,4x16u	8x8u,4x16	8x8,8x8u, 4x16, 4x16u	-
Single/Part	-	-	8x8u,4x16	-	-
Immed/Part	-	-	8x8u,4x16	-	-
Sum of Abs. Diffs	8x8→4x16, 8x8u→4x16u	-	-	-	-
Modular Mul					
Part/Part	-	-	8x8u,4x16	(4x16)x(4x16) →(4x16 high), (4x16)x(4x16) →(4x16 low)	(4x16)x(4x8) →(4x16)
Single/Part	-	-	8x8u,4x16	-	-
Immed/Part	-	-	8x8u,4x16	-	-
Saturation Mul					
Part/Part	-	-	8x8u,4x16	-	-
Single/Part	-	-	8x8u,4x16	-	-
Immed/Part	-	-	8x8u,4x16	-	-
Mul by Sign(-,0,+)					
Part/Part	-	-	4x16	-	-
Single/Part	-	-	4x16	-	-
Immed/Part	-	-	4x16	-	-
Mul/Add	-	-	-	2-(4x16)→ 2-(2x32)→ (2x32)	-
Average	-	4x16,4x16u	-	-	-
Shift Left/Right					
Part/Part	-	-	8x8u,4x16	-	-
Single/Part	-	-	8x8u,4x16	4x16,2x32, 1x64	-
Immed/Part	-	4x16,4x16u	8x8u,4x16	4x16,2x32, 1x64	-
Signed Shift Right					
Part/Part	-	-	4x16	-	-
Single/Part	-	-	4x16	4x16,2x32, 1x64	-
Immed/Part	-	4x16	4x16	4x16,2x32	-
Shift and Add (1,2,3, or 4-bit Immed)	-	4x16,4x16u	-	-	-
Scale (various forms)	-	-	8x8u,4x16	-	-
Maximum					
Part/Part	8x8,8x8u, 4x16,4x16u	-	8x8u,4x16	-	-
Single/Part	-	-	8x8u,4x16	-	-
Immed/Part	-	-	8x8u,4x16	-	-

not a property of "partitioned registers," but of an operation applied to the data in one or more registers. In other words, the data path through the function units may be partitioned in various ways, but the registers really are not partitioned; for example, there is nothing to prevent the programmer from treating a register's contents as having 8-bit fields in one operation and 16-bit fields in the next. It is even possible, and sometimes desirable, for operations to treat a register as though it is partitioned into field sizes which are not supported directly by the enhanced hardware. In fact, the partitioning need not even keep all fields within a register the same size, although managing irregular field sizes is too complex to be discussed in detail in this paper.

In summary, the fact that multimedia registers do not store partitioning information offers great flexibility. In a traditional SIMD execution model, data storage is allocated to each processing element, thus fixing both the number of data that can be operated on in parallel and the boundaries between values in different processors. Using SWAR, we can explicitly trade precision for parallelism width, using only as many bits for each operation as is algorithmically required. Further, the penalty for data crossing these imaginary inter-processing-element boundaries is zero for a SWAR system, which gives SWAR interesting new abilities for operations like reductions.

Our approach to making use of SWAR is based on creating a SWAR module language and compilers, so that users can write **portable SIMD programs** that will be compiled into efficient SWAR modules and interface code that allows these modules to be used within ordinary C programs. It is not particularly difficult to build an optimizing SIMD module compiler supporting only those operations directly provided by a particular SWAR hardware implementation, but portability across all flavors of SWAR-capable hardware makes basic coding of constructs an interesting problem. Section 2 discusses the basic coding techniques needed to achieve efficient execution of general SIMD constructs on any type of SWAR hardware support — including 32-bit integer instruction sets that have no explicit support for SWAR. Beyond the basic coding of SWAR constructs, the SWAR execution model makes it appropriate to consider several new types of compiler optimizations, which are briefly discussed in section 3. The work is summarized, and pointers to the support code that we have developed are given, in section 4.

2   Basic SIMD-to-SWAR Compilation

In determining how to code high-level SIMD constructs using SWAR instructions, it is useful to distinguish several different classes of SIMD operations based on how they can be implemented using SWAR:

- A *polymorphic* operation is a SIMD operation for which the same instruction(s) can be used to implement the operation, independent of the field partitioning. For example, bitwise operations like NOT, AND, OR, and XOR are polymorphic, as is the classical SIMD conditional test ANY (which returns "true" if any bit in any field is a 1).

- A *partitioned* operation is a SIMD operation in which the value computed by each processing element is a function only of data that also resides in that processing element. In a SWAR implementation, a partitioned operation requires corresponding operand fields to be manipulated without interfering with adjacent fields. However, no current SWAR hardware implements fully general partitioning for all operations, so software techniques to construct appropriate partitioned operations are critical.
- A *communication* operation logically transmits data across processing elements in an arbitrary pattern. For example, the MasPar MPL construct router[a].b accesses the value of the variable b on processing element a. Unfortunately, except for HP PA-RISC MAX, current SWAR extensions do not allow such general communication patterns to be used in rearranging field values, and even MAX only allows this rearrangement within a single register (thus not solving the problem when SIMD vector lengths exceed one register). In fact, most SWAR hardware does not explicitly provide any communication operations; instead, they must be constructed using operations that can cross field boundaries, such as unpartitioned shifts.
- A *type conversion* operation converts SIMD data of one type into another. This becomes complicated in SWAR systems because data types that have different sizes yield different parallelism widths (numbers of fields per register). However, current SWAR hardware supports a variety of type conversion operations, and others can be constructed easily using communication and partitioned operations.
- A *reduction* operation recursively combines field values into a single value. In a traditional SIMD architecture, this involves communication between a shrinking set of processing elements working on values slowly growing in precision; this is a much more natural procedure for SWAR, and is thus worth exploring.
- A *masking* operation allows some processing elements to disable themselves. Obviously, for SWAR, there is no way to disable part of a register; however, there are arithmetic techniques that can be used to achieve the same result.
- A *control flow* operation is essentially a branch instruction that is executed by the SIMD control unit. Although SWAR systems do not have a control unit per se, the ordinary processor instruction set can be viewed as providing this functionality. In order to simplify pipeline structure, most SWAR hardware does not directly allow branching based on the contents of a partitioned SWAR register; it is thus necessary to move the SWAR fields into an ordinary register and test them there.

The following sections describe the basic coding of each of the more interesting classes: partitioned, communication, reduction, and masking operations.

2.1   Partitioned Operations

Partitioned operations are the primary focus of most of the hardware support for SWAR. In particular, most of the speedup claims for SWAR are based on

partitioned additions of 8-bit fields, etc. However, not all important field sizes
are handled by all SWAR hardware, and many partitioned instructions are simply omitted. We describe three different methods for implementing partitioned
operations.

Hardware-Partitioned Operations In an ideal partitioned operation, the
operation is applied both concurrently and independently to the entire set of
register fields. Thus, where SWAR hardware supports this, the SWAR code
looks just like a single pure SIMD instruction. For example, consider adding two
4x8 values, A and B (each stored in a 32-bit register), using SWAR partitioned
unsigned modular addition as shown in Figure 1.

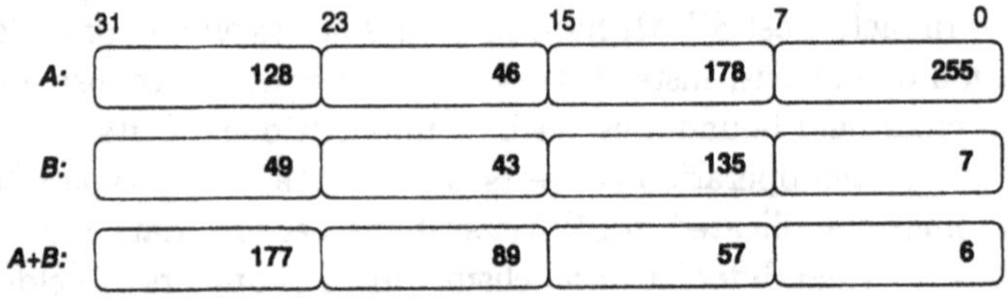

Fig. 1. Hardware-partitioned 4x8u modular addition

Numbering the fields from right to left, the addition performed in field 3 is
128+49 and yields the field result 177. Because this value is storable in an 8-bit
field, it is not modified for storage. In contrast, the addition performed in field 1
is 178+135 and yields 313. This value requires nine bits for proper storage, thus
it is modularized to fit in the eight bits which are available. The result stored
for field 1 is then $313\%(2^8)$, or 57. Note that the overflow bit is lost and does
not interfere with the operation as performed in field 2.

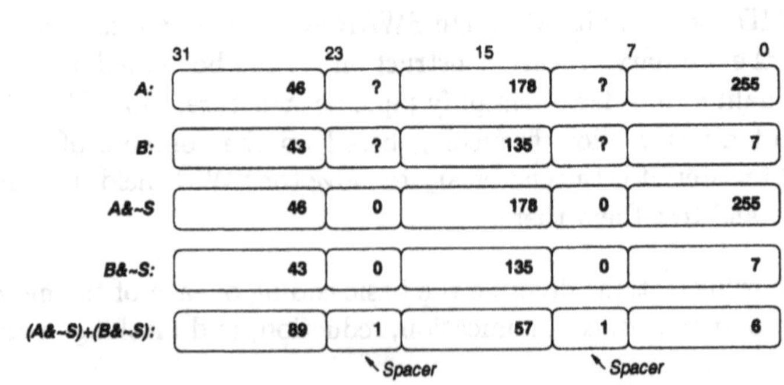

Fig. 2. 3x8u modular addition using spacers

Partitioned Operations Using Spacer Bits When an ideal partitioned addition is not supported by the hardware, spacer bits may be used to allow the field operations to be applied concurrently and independently as shown in Figure 2. These spacer bits are used as buffer zones between data fields, so that overflow and/or borrow can occur without interfering with adjacent fields. The spacer bit technique may be used not only to implement additional field sizes for SWAR hardware, but also to implement SWAR partitioned operations on architectures providing only conventional 32-bit integer operations.

The example shown is essentially the same as the previous one, but use of spacer bits allows only 3x8 values to fit in each register. At the start of the operation, the spacer values are unknown. This is indicated by a question mark (?) in each spacer field. To ensure that none of the field additions will overflow into the next field, the spacer bits of the addends are preset, or normalized, to zero before the addition is performed. This is done by ANDing the addends with a mask S, which has 1 bits only in the spacer positions.

The addition performed in field 2 occurs just as for an ideal partitioned addition, with no overflow and no modification of the stored result. The addition performed in field 1 is 178+135, yielding 313. This value requires nine bits for storage, and is stored with its lower eight bits in field 1, and its ninth bit carried into the spacer between fields 1 and 2. Only the part of the result stored in field 1 is considered to be valid. Thus, the valid result stored is $313\%(2^8)$ or 57. Note that the overflow bit does not interfere with the operation as performed in field 2. Similarly, the addition in field 0 results in a carry to the spacer between fields 0 and 1, and the storage of the result 6.

Only one spacer bit is needed between fields for addition or subtraction, but use of multiple spacer bits between the fields may allow multiple partitioned operations to be performed before re-normalizing the spacer bits. This static optimization simply requires tracking the range of possible values of the spacer bits to determine when re-normalization would be required.

Software-Partitioned Operations Although the spacer-based partitioned operation code is fast, it only allows 3x8 values in each 32-bit register — not the 4x8 that could be used with hardware partitioning. With a few more instructions, the full densely-packed partitioned operation can be implemented.

The trick is simply to consider each field as being one or more bits smaller than it truly is, replacing the most significant bit of each field by a "virtual" spacer bit. After performing the spacer-partitioned operation on the modified register value, the most significant bits of each field are computed and inserted in the result. Thus, adding two 4x8 values is done as shown in Figure 3.

At the start of the operation, the two addends are each split into two partitioned registers. C and D contain the data — with the virtual spacer bit positions cleared in preparation for the partitioned addition. The resulting value for E is the correct 4x8 value, except in that the most significant bits of fields in A and B have not been added in. Fortunately, the bitwise XOR operation implements a one-bit add with no carry; thus, we can compute the addition of the most significant bits of each field by XORing the most significant bits of A, B, and E (with appropriate masking of the other bits).

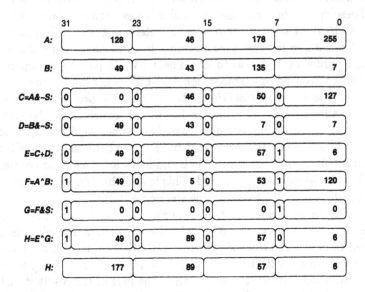

Fig. 3. 4x8u modular addition using virtual spacers

Note that the result field values in H are the same as those for ideal partitioned addition.

2.2   Inter-Processing-Element Communication

	31	23	15	7	0
A0:	3	2	1	0	
A1:	7	6	5	4	
B=A0>>8:	0	3	2	1	
C=A1<<24:	4	0	0	0	
A0'=B|C:	4	3	2	1	
A1'=A1>>8:	0	7	6	5	

Fig. 4. Toroidal communication on 8x8 in two 4x8 registers

Partitioned registers may allow mesh and toroidal communication to be performed by applying shift and rotate instructions to the register. In Figure 4,

A1 and A0 are, respectively, the upper and lower halves of an 8x8 vector layed out across two 4x8 partitioned registers. Although the numbering of fields is somewhat arbitrary, consider a right-neighbor communication as each processing element sending its value one field to the right.

Notice that the new value A0' was harder to compute than A1' because the datum from processing element 0 logically fell off the right side of the machine. If the right-neighbor communication had included a wrap-around (toroidal) link, the computation of A1' would have been much more similar to that of A0'.

Unfortunately, more complex communication patterns are not directly supported by most of the SWAR implementations. Implementations of more general communication patterns can be built using the PACK and UNPACK operations of SWAR extensions like MMX to implement shuffle and inverse-shuffle communication patterns that can be composed to simulate a multistage interconnection network; however, even this is not particularly efficient. Thus, SWAR programs should avoid the use of complex communication patterns.

2.3   Reductions

Reductions are operations in which the values stored in the fields of a register are combined into a single result value by successively applying an operation to an intermediate result and each of the field values. The final value may be stored in one or all of the fields of the result register.

For example, if a 4x8 partitioned register contains the values { 3, 4, 9, 18 }, we may store the result of a reduceAdd (3+4+9+18=34) in each of the fields to form the single result 34. In Figure 5, we perform an unsigned reduceAdd of the fields of the 4x8 partitioned register A containing the values { 4, 3, 2, 1 } to form the single result value 10.

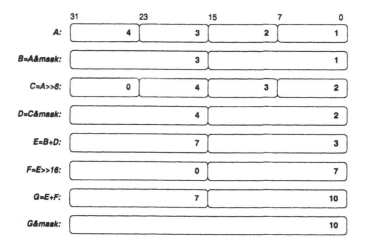

Fig. 5. 4x8u reduceAdd

This operation is performed recursively. First, the register is split into the even (multiples of two) and odd (non-multiples of two) fields using masking operations. Then, using an unpartitioned shift, the fields are aligned and added. The result is a register with half as many fields, but each is twice as large — conveniently ensuring that overflow will not occur, even if no spacers are used. This process is repeated until only one field remains.

2.4 Enable Masking

```
            31            23            15             7             0
        A:  |     4     |      3     |      2     |      1     |
        B:  |     8     |      7     |      6     |      5     |
        C:  |     0     |     27     |    148     |      0     |
   D=C>>4:  | 0 | 0 | 0 | 1 | 11 |  9 |  4 |  0 |
    E=C|D:  | 0 | 0 | 1 | 11 | 11 | 13 |  4 |  0 |
   F=E>>2:  |0|0|0|0|0|0|1|2|3|2|3|3|1|1|0|0|
    G=E|F:  |0|0|0|0|0|1|3|3|3|3|3|3|1|1|0|0|
   H=G>>1:  |0|0|0|0|0|0|0|0|0|0|0|0|1|1|1|1|1|1|1|1|1|1|1|1|1|0|1|0|1|0|0|0|
    I=G|H:  |0|0|0|0|0|0|0|0|0|0|0|0|1|1|1|1|1|1|1|1|1|1|1|1|1|1|1|1|1|0|0|0|
  J=I&LSBs: |     0     |      1     |      1     |      0     |
  K=MSBs-J: |    128    |    127     |    127     |    128     |
  L=K^MSBs: |     0     |    255     |    255     |      0     |
    M=B&L:  |     0     |      7     |      6     |      0     |
   N=A&~L:  |     4     |      0     |      0     |      1     |
      M|N:  |     4     |      7     |      6     |      1     |
```

Fig. 6. 4x8 where(C) A=B

One of the distinguishing characteristics of SIMD computation is the ability to disable processing elements for portions of a computation. Unfortunately, SWAR hardware does not allow fields to be disabled per se; instead, a form of arithmetic nulling must be used. Consider the simple SIMD code fragment:

```
WHERE (C) A=B
```

In this code, A, B, and C are all vectors of the same length. Where the corresponding field of C is true (non-zero), that field within A should be replaced with the value from the corresponding field from B. Other elements of A should be unaltered. If it were possible to disable fields, the above statement could be executed very straightforwardly by disabling fields corresponding to 0 values within C and then simply having the enabled processing elements execute A=B.

Without the ability to disable fields, we will need to arithmetically nullify the undesired computations. The first step is to make the SIMD code fragment symmetric:

WHERE (C) A=B ELSEWHERE A=A

This looks strange, but accurately reflects the fact that the fields of A that are to be unaffected by the WHERE must literally be actively read and pasted-together with the fields taken from B.

There are a variety of techniques that can be used to arithmetically merge the appropriate fields taken from A and B, but by far the cheapest is to use bitwise AND to mask the undesired field and then use bitwise OR to merge the masked results. Indeed, this is the approach used in the example in Figure 6.

First C must be converted into an appropriate mask, which has a field full of 0s where C was 0 and a field full of 1s where C was non-zero. A log-length sequence of unpartitioned shifts and bitwise OR operations is used to convert C into a usable mask, L. This mask is then used to select the appropriate fields of A and B. In terms of scalar C code:

```
if (c) a=b; else a=a;
```

Essentially became:

```
l = -(c != 0);
a = ((b & l) | (a & ~l));
```

Although the SWAR code looks somewhat strange, this arithmetic masking is actually an old trick borrowed from various early SIMD machines. For example, the Thinking Machines CM-2 used this approach.

3   Compiler Optimizations for SWAR

Optimizations that have been devised for SIMD programming often apply in a natural way to SWAR programming. However, the unique features of SWAR execution also motivate a variety of new compiler technologies. Three such technologies are briefly discussed here: promotion of field sizes, SWAR value tracking, and enable masking optimizations.

3.1   Promotion of Field Sizes

Just because a high-level language program stated that a value needed only k bits does not mean that *precisely* k bits worth of hardware must be used. For example, 16 bit values are handled very well by HP's PA-RISC MAX, but smaller sizes are not. Thus, a vector that was declared as containing 14-bit values will yield more efficient code sequences if the array's object type is promoted to 16-bit fields. This promotion is particularly favorable because the number of 16-bit fields that fit in a 64-bit register is precisely the same as the number of 14-bit fields that would fit — using 14-bit fields would not add any parallelism. Not all hardware-unsupported field sizes are inefficient; for example, 2-bit fields are not directly supported by any of the SWAR hardware, but for all the SWAR implementations described, the extra parallelism width makes operations on 2-bit fields far more effective than promoting these fields to 8-bits. In general, for each SWAR implementation, there are certain field sizes that are less efficient than a somewhat larger field size, and thus none of these inefficient field sizes should be directly used.

Notice that this promotion of field sizes, and even the use of spacer bits, can result in different data layouts for the same vector on different computers, and the user-specified field sizes do not imply any particular field layout. However, by using a separate SWAR module compiler that communicates only through C code interfaces that it generates, we can ensure that non-obvious machine-dependent layouts are not visible outside the SWAR modules.

3.2   SWAR Value Tracking

Nearly all traditional compiler optimizations are based on tracking which values are available where and when. For example, common subexpression elimination (CSE) depends on this analysis. The interesting question that SWAR technology raises is what constitutes the basic unit of SWAR data that we wish to track?

Fundamentally, one would like to track the values of all the fields within a SWAR register or vector. However, as we have discussed, the compiler's treatment of SWAR coding often results in code sequences that dynamically change the apparent partitioning, and this would have the effect of destroying the field-based value tracking information. Similarly, as discussed in section 2.1, it is often desirable to use spacer bits between fields to allow ordinary instructions to function as partitioned operations, and these spacer bits are by definition not part of the fields they separate. To optimize spacer manipulations, we need to be able to track spacer values as well as field values. In fact, unpartitioned operations manipulate both field and spacer values alike, and operations such as shifts can transform one into the other.

To support aggressive SWAR optimizations, a new value tracking method is necessary. We suggest that symbolic tracking of values for arbitrary masked-bit-patterns within a register is appropriate. The following two subsections give brief examples of the benefits of such tracking.

Bitwise Value Tracking It is not surprising that SWAR code often uses many bitwise masking (AND and OR) operations and unpartitioned shifts using constant-valued masks and shift distances. Consider a simple C code example:

```
x = (( (x & 0x00ff) << 4 ) & 0xff00);
```

By tracking how arbitrary masked-bit-patterns are shifted in this sequence, this code can be converted to the equivalent, but simpler, form:

```
x = (( x << 4 ) & 0x0f00);
```

In general, this type of tracking can merge multiple AND or OR operations through shifts, as well as merging shifts.

Simplification Of Spacer Manipulation It is not unusual that the manipulations of spacer bits will become a significant fraction of all the instructions executed. Thus, any optimization technique that can reduce the frequency of spacer manipulations is highly desirable.

In preparation for a partitioned operation, the spacer bits may have to be set to particular values which depend on the operation. For example, if the operation is an addition, the spacer bits should be set to 0 in both operand registers. After a partitioned operation, a carry or borrow may alter these spacer bit values. Thus, it may be necessary to zero all the spacer bits to correctly isolate the fields.

Actually, most operations can alter the values of spacer bits. The interesting fact is that even though most polymorphic instructions, such as bitwise operations, can alter spacer bit values, they produce field values without being affected by the values of spacer bits. Thus, these instructions offer the opportunity to set spacer bits to the next desired value at no cost. For example, consider computing e=((a+b)-(c+d)); using a SWAR representation employing spacer bits identified by the mask s:

```
e = (((((a & ~s) + (b & ~s)) & ~s) | s) -
        ((((c & ~s) + (d & ~s)) & ~s) & ~s)) & ~s;
```

We would expect conventional compiler optimizations to eliminate the redundant AND of the subtrahend with the one's complement of the spacer mask required by the field isolation stage of the addition and the normalization stage of the subtraction. This would save one operation, and change the calculation of the subtrahend from

```
((((c & ~s) + (d & ~s)) & ~s) & ~s)
```

To:

```
(((c & ~s) + (d & ~s)) & ~s)
```

By using spacer value tracking, we may be able to make significantly larger reductions in the number of spacer manipulations needed. Suppose that the spacer bits for each of a, b, c, and d were already known by the compiler to be zeros. The normalizations for the additions would not be required, and the original code could be compacted to the following:

```
e = ((((a + b) & ~s) | s) -
     (((c + d) & ~s) & ~s)) & ~s;
```

Further inspection reveals that the isolation stages following the additions are unnecessary because they are immediately followed by the normalization stage of the subtraction, which overwrites the spacer values just written. This last observation reduces the original 12 operations to its final form, with just 6 operations (given that s and ~s are constants):

```
e = (((a + b) | s) |
     ((c + d) & ~s)) & ~s;
```

It is also interesting to note that by the same analysis, computing $e = ((a+b) - ((c+d)\&M))$; where M is a constant-valued mask, could be accomplished in the same number of instructions:

```
e = (((a + b) | s) |
     ((c + d) & (M & ~s)) & ~s;
```

This is because (M & ~s) is also a constant. In general, the bitwise operations and unpartitioned shifts discussed in the previous section can be optimized at the same time as the spacer manipulation.

3.3 Enable Masking Optimizations

Because SWAR hardware does not allow fields to be disabled, there is a significant cost associated with the arithmetic nulling of undesired field computations. However, this cost need not be incurred if the compiler's static analysis can prove that *all* fields are active, or if the compiler can generate code that allows all fields to be active later correcting the should-have-been-inactive field values.

For "virtualized" processing elements, a single vector may span the fields of multiple words (registers). Thus, enable masking would have to be performed on each of the words. This allows the compiler to generate three different versions of the word-wide SWAR code, and to select among them by examining each word worth of enable mask:

- If the enable mask word is entirely enabled, then no masking is done; the corresponding word of the result is directly computed.
- If the enable mask word is entirely disabled, then the corresponding word of the result is copied from the original value — no computation is done.
- If the enable mask word is partially enabled, then the usual masking is used in computing the result.

4 Conclusion

The latest processors from DEC, HP, MIPS, Intel, AMD, Cyrix, and Sun (and also the soon-to-be-announced next generation of the PowerPC) have proven that hardware support for SWAR, SIMD Within A Register, is easily and efficiently added to a conventional microprocessor. However, more than year after most of these processors became available, there are still no general-purpose high-level languages that allow them to be programmed using a portable SIMD model. Essentially by design, these SWAR hardware implementations are tuned for hand-coding of specific algorithms, with sparse coverage of SWAR functionality driven by the need to minimize disturbance of the base processor instruction set and architecture.

In this paper, we have shown that these flaws can be largely overcome by the combination of clever coding sequences and a few new types of compiler analysis and optimization. Only the lack of random inter-field communication is an unsolvable problem, but these operations have been avoided in many SIMD algorithms because many traditional SIMD machines also lacked the necessary hardware support.

For more information about the SWAR model, libraries, and module compilers, see:

$$\text{http://shay.ecn.purdue.edu/~swar/}$$

References

1. Advanced Micro Devices, Inc.: *AMD-K6 Processor Multimedia Extensions*, Advanced Micro Devices, Inc., Sunnyvale, California, March 1997.
2. Cyrix Corporation, *Multimedia Instruction Set Extensions for a Sixth-Generation x86 Processor*, Cyrix Corporation, ftp://ftp.cyrix.com/developr/hc-mmx4.pdf, August 1996.
3. Digital Equipment Corporation, *Alpha Architecture Handbook, Version 3*, Digital Equipment Corporation, Maynard, Massachusetts, October 1996.
4. Intel Corporation, *Intel Architecture MMX Technology: Programmer's Reference Manual*, Intel Corporation, http://developer.intel.com/drg/mmx/Manuals/prm/prm_covr.htm, Mar. 1996.
5. Ruby B. Lee, Accelerating Multimedia with Enhanced Microprocessors, *IEEE Micro*, 15(2):22-32, April 1995.
6. Ruby Lee and Jerry Huck, *HP Technical Computing — 64-bit and Multimedia in the PA-RISC 2.0 Architecture*, Hewlett-Packard Company, http://hpcc997.external.hp.com:80/wsg/strategies/pa2go3/pa2go3.html, June 1996.
7. Silicon Graphics, Inc., *MIPS Digital Media Extension*, Silicon Graphics, Inc., http://www.sgi.com/MIPS/arch/ISA5/, 1996.
8. Sun Microsystems, Inc., *The VIS Instruction Set*, Sun Microelectronics, Sun Microsystems Corporation, http://www.sun.com/sparc/vis/index.html, April 1997.
9. Integrated Device Technology, Inc., *IDT WinChip Home Page*, Integrated Device Technology, Inc., http://www.winchip.com/, 1998.
10. Advanced Micro Devices, Inc.: *3DNow! Technology Manual*, Advanced Micro Devices, Inc., http://www.amd.com/K6/k6docs/pdf/21928c.pdf, 1998.

Automatic Analysis of Loops to Exploit Operator Parallelism on Reconfigurable Systems *

Narasimhan Ramasubramanian, Ram Subramanian, and Santosh Pande**

Dept. of ECECS, University of Cincinnati
Cincinnati, OH 45221, USA
{lnarasim,rsubrama,santosh}@ececs.uc.edu

1   Introduction

With rapid advances in FPGA and other hardware technologies, architectures based on configurable computing engines, in which the Arithmetic Logic Unit (ALU) can be modified on-the-fly during computation, are becoming popular. Configurable architectures offer an opportunity for adapting the underlying hardware to the computation for efficiency. Typically, the need for configuration arises due to the fact that a given hardware ALU configuration is better suited for execution of a given algorithmic step. Since a program is an abstraction of a sequence of algorithmic steps, the need for such a reconfiguration (i.e., changing from one configuration to another), would thus, arise at different program points corresponding to these algorithmic steps. The problem of identifying the optimal configurations at different steps in a program is a very complex issue but allows the power of these architectures to be maximally used if solved. The success of these architectures critically depends on the effectiveness of the compiler and the research in this area is just beginning. The purpose of this paper is to specifically focus on an *automatic* compilation framework developed to effectively exploit operator parallelism.

For example, consider the following loop nest to be executed on a configurable ALU:

```
for i := 1 to 100
  A[i] = B[i] * C[i]   \\S1
  D[i] = A[i] + B[i]   \\S2
end for
```

This loop is split into two for-all loops preserving forward dependence due to A[i]. The reconfigurable ALU is configured to 100 multipliers at the entry point of the first for-all loop, so that all instances of S1 can execute in parallel. The ALU is then reconfigured at the entry point of the next loop to 100 adders to execute all instances of S2. Configuring the hardware at the entry point of a loop

---

* This work is supported by the DARPA contract ARMY DABT63–97–C–0029
** Responsible for all communication.

S. Chatterjee (Ed.): LCPC'98, LNCS 1656, pp. 305–322, 1999.
© Springer-Verlag Berlin Heidelberg 1999

nest has an overhead associated with it. Thus, the success of the above scheme depends on the trade-off between performance gain due to operator parallelism exploited through configuration and the overheads of generating configurations. This trade-off is the focal point of the automatic compiler analysis and transformation framework presented in this paper.

The paper is organized as follows: Section 2 discusses related work, section 3 discusses the overall approach of our work, section 4 discusses the framework for loop and operator transformations. Section 5 discusses analysis of trade-offs between gains and overheads of reconfiguration. The motivation is first illustrated through an example and then our algorithms for automatic reconfiguration analysis and loop transformations are presented. Results are discussed in section 6, conclusions in section 7. The appendix gives the pseudo codes of the algorithm developed in this framework.

2   Related Work

There has been a considerable amount of work done on loop optimizations in parallel computing especially focusing on issues of loop transformations [3]. Most works deal with the optimizations of loops focusing on data locality [10,11,12,4], and on data and loop alignment [6] and redistribution [7]. High Performance Fortran [8] is an important attempt to exploit data parallelism in loops. Vectorization was an early attempt in exploiting vector parallelism in many codes. Randy Allen and Ken Kennedy [1] discuss a comprehensive framework for translating FORTRAN programs to vector form. M. Gokhale and W. Carlson [9] have discussed compilation issues for parallel machines. However, none of the above approaches assume a configurable ALU. A configurable ALU could support varying demands for operator parallelism, thus opening important issues to be analyzed by the compiler.

Developing efficient mapping techniques for reconfigurable architectures has been the focus of recent research [2,5]. Hardware libraries [16], synthesis of efficient hardware [15], exploiting instruction level parallelism (ILP) [14,17,5] have been the different approaches. Many approaches have focused on effectively utilizing the power of reconfigurable ALUs by proposing variable instruction-sets like the PRISM-I and II [2] and Brigham Young University's Dynamic Instruction Set Computer (DISC) [17]. Recently, Weinhardt [15] developed a framework to synthesize an efficient hardware pipeline that can be configured to suit the computation. One of the important compiler driven approaches undertaken recently is the Raw Project [14]. The Raw compilation framework tries to exploit ILP through asynchronous instruction streams across basic blocks. This approach gives excellent speedups for custom ALUs (such as [14]) but its applicability to general purpose reconfigurable engines such as FPGAs is limited due to very high overheads of reconfiguration. This motivates our approach of analyzing loops to determine trade-offs at a macro level for achieving performance enhancement. Our goal is to determine program points where reconfiguration is most beneficial; where the overhead of reconfiguration is incurred only once across loop nests but benefits gained are as many times as the trip count.

3   Overall Approach

We first introduce some notations and definitions that we have used - **Configuration:** A set of operators, and the number of each operator that are implemented on the hardware to support computation at a given time. A configuration is expressed as a set of tuples. For example, a configuration comprising 100 multipliers and 50 adders is represented as $\{< *, 100 >, < +, 50 >\}$. **Cutset:** A group of statements, represented as a set, that execute under a particular configuration. Fo r example, if statements $S1, S2$, and $S3$ execute under the configuration $\{< *, 100 >, < +, 50 >\}$, they are denoted as cutset $\{S1, S2, S3\}$. We now present an overall approach of the automatic reconfiguration analysis.

1. **Loop and Operator Transformations:** This is the first phase which takes a PDG as an input and performs loop transformations such as loop splitting, statement reordering, etc. within loops. It also undertakes operator transformations for reconfiguration elimination by configuration reuse. Section 4 explains the specific optimizations undertaken in detail.
2. **Reconfiguration Analysis:** This phase analyzes the trade-offs between the costs of reconfiguration and performance gains due to reconfiguration for exploiting operator parallelism within loop nests. Space-time cost models of operators are used for compile time analysis by this phase. The phase uses a two-pass solution and generates a PDG annotated with reconfiguration directives.
3. **Machine Dependent Optimizations:** This phase performs architecture specific optimizations targetted towards the specific reconfigurable system and is our future work.
4. **Code Generation:** This phase generates code for execution on reconfigurable hardware and will be implemented in the near future.

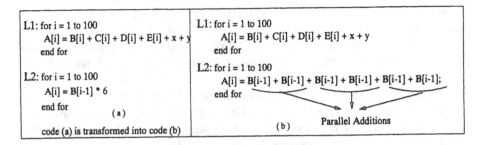

Fig. 1. Example codes

Depending on the computational demands of a loop, a given set of statements within a loop may demand a certain hardware configuration for their best execution. The problem of determining a set of statements that prefer a certain configuration is highly combinatorial due to enormous number of possibilities involved. Also, once the statements are grouped in terms of their preferred configurations, the next goal is to analyze whether or not they should be assigned to two different configurations. This is a hard graph partitioning problem. We have developed heuristics to efficiently solve these problems.

In practice, the costs of reconfiguration for current generation of FPGAs are quite high. Thus, the performance gains on these systems are greatly increased if the number of reconfigurations are kept to a minimum. In order for the heuristics to be effective, program transformations should be done to expose more opportunities for configuration reuse. The focus of the next section is on operator and loop transformations targetted towards configuration reuse. These transformations are done as a preprocessing step to configuration analysis.

4   Framework for Operator and Loop Transformations

Initially, loop transformations are performed to expose parallelism in statements to optimally utilize the hardware space for parallel execution of operations. A very useful transformation is a for-all loop conversion, where a given loop is split into a sequence of for-all loops. Each for-all loop therefore, would exhibit maximum operator parallelism, and each boundary between the for-all loops could be a potential reconfiguration point. Certain loop transformations such as loop peeling, scalar expansion [18,3,4], etc are performed to remove some of these dependencies so that the resulting loop could be split into a sequence of for-all loops.

4.1   Operator Transformation

The motivation for operator transformation is the reuse of previous configurations generated in order to reduce reconfigurations. Consider the code given in Figure 1 (a), that has to be implemented on hardware for execution. Loop nest L1 consists of 3 parallel additions per iteration and thus, the configuration for L1 would be $\{< +, 300 >\}$. Loop nest L2, on the other hand, contains a multiplication operation and its configuration would be $\{< *, 100 >\}$. A reconfiguration would have to be done between the two loop nests. If we can transform the multiplication operator into a series of additions as shown in Figure 1 (b), we can avoid the reconfiguration since the configuration demand of L2 is now $\{< +, 300 >\}$.

Although the cost of implementing a multiplication through a series of additions is higher, such a transformation could reuse previous configurations, saving reconfiguration overheads. Each complex operation can thus be broken down into simpler constituent operations that can be executed in parallel. Since the hardware can support a higher multiplicity of simple operations, and such operations can span a range of complex operations, we can eliminate redundant reconfigurations by operator transformations.

4.2   Statement re-ordering for configuration reuse

Since each configuration consists of a set of operators along with their multiplicities, one may attempt a transformation where statements with "similar" operators are moved together through statement re-ordering. In doing so the dependencies of the program must be preserved. Consider the statements given in the loop below,

```
for i = 1 to 100              Cutset      Configuration
  a[i] = b[i] + c[i]   //S1    {S1, S2}   {<+,100>,<-,100>}
  d[i] = a[i] - b[i]   //S2    {S3, S4}   {<*,100>,<-,100>}
  e[i] = d[i] * a[i]   //S3    {S5}       {<+,100>}
  f[i] = e[i] - a[i]   //S4
  g[i] = a[i] + b[i]   //S5
end for
```

Due to limited hardware space, the compiler may attempt to generate three configurations as shown above. But as one can see, statements S1 and S5 share the same operator $< + >$, and statements S2 and S4 share the same operator $< - >$. We note that by moving S5 before S2 and after S1, we maintain the dependency and increase configuration locality. The custets and configurations are now reduced to $\{S1, S5\}$ executing in $\{< +, 100 >\}$ and $\{S2, S3, S4\}$ executing in $\{< *, 100 >, < -, 100 >\}$. Thus, operator locality results in fewer number of configurations.

5   Framework for Reconfiguration Analysis

Once the above transformations are done, the next phase of the compiler focuses on analyzing the Program Dependency Graph (PDG) to determine cut-sets and the corresponding configurations. This phase is split into two passes (Figure 2). The input to the first pass is a PDG and a cost model of the reconfigurable ALU which includes execution time of operators, RPU (Reconfigurable Processing Unit) space occupied, total reconfigurable space and reconfiguration time [1]. The algorithm generates cut-sets and corresponding configurations for loops. The problem of generating optimal cut-sets and corresponding configurations is NP-hard. This problem can be shown to be equivalent to a 0/1 knapsack problem, the idea being to pack as many statements as possible in one configuration to minimize reconfiguration subject to constraint of hardware space. We use two heuristics to make the analysis more tractable. The heuristics are described in the next subsection. In the second pass, analysis to reduce the number of reconfigurations is undertaken. In this pass, the total cost of execution for two consecutive cut-sets along with the reconfiguration overheads is compared with the total time to execute when the two cut-sets are merged into a single configuration. If the latter cost is lesser than the former, the cut-sets are merged eliminating reconfiguration between the cut-sets.

---

[1] A detailed description of the cost model for Xilinx 6200 family used for compile time analysis is given in the implementation section.

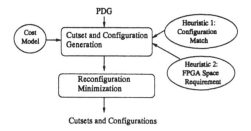

Fig. 2. Cutset and configuration generation

5.1 Motivating Example

We now explain the motivation behind our approach through an example.

```
for i = 0 to 100                    Cutset          Configuration
  A[i] = A[i] * a + b;    // S1     {S1, S2}        {<*,100>,<+,100>} Config-1
  B[i] = A[i] + B[i] * b; // S2     {S3,S5,S6}      {</,100>,<+,100>} Config-2
  C[i] = A[i] / c + a;    // S3     {S4}            {<*,100>,<+,100>} Config-3
  D[i] = B[i] * c + D[i]; // S4
  E[i] = B[i] + C[i] / c; // S5
  F[i] = F[i] + C[i];     // S6
end for
```

In the given example, there are only forward dependencies among the statements in the loop. The loop can be split into sequence of for-all loops. A PDG (Figure 3(a)) is generated for the loop and the statements are analyzed in the topological order. The statements in *level 1 (S1)* require multiplication and addition operations and each statement in the loop is executed 100 times. Thus, if there are 100 multipliers and 100 adders, all instances of S1 can be executed in parallel. Similarly, in *level 2* there are two statements - *S2*, and *S3*, and in *level 3* there are 3 statements - *S4*, *S5*, and *S6*. Statements in the same level can be executed in any order since there are no data dependencies among them. If all the operators required by the statement for all the instances can be generated on the hardware, they can be executed in parallel. However, each statement may need a different support for concurrent execution of its instances. Given limited hardware, the problem is to group statements that need similar operator support together to form cut-sets. We use two heuristics to find cut-sets, *Configuration Match* and *FPGA space requirement*, which are explained in the next subsection. The cut-sets, along with the associated hardware configuration found by the *Configuration Match* heuristic for the above loop are tabulated beside the example. As can be seen the loop can be split into a sequence of for-all loops. Each for-all loop is a cutset, executing under the configuration of that cutset. Reconfiguration is needed between two for-all loop nests since their configuration requirements are different. The transformed loop is given in Figure 3(b).

5.2 Cut-set and Configuration Generation

Our approach involves analysis of the program using a PDG constructed at loop nest level. The nodes of the PDG are annotated with the data (array and scalar)

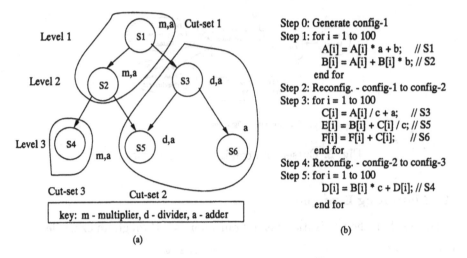

(a)

(b)

Fig. 3. PDG for the given loop

elements referenced, and the operations involved on these data elements. Each node of the PDG corresponds to a given statement. The directed edges in the PDG represent the data dependence from one node to another in the direction of the edge. The nodes in the PDG are given level numbers. Level number represents the depth of the node in the PDG. A node has level number 1 if it is not data dependent on any of the statements in the loop. A level of node n is thus given by: $level(n) = 1 + max_{p \in predecessor(n)}(level(p))$. The nodes with the same level number are can be executed in any order.

The PDG of the loop is traversed level by level in the order of the *flow-dependence* in the program. From the annotated node, the operators required for each statement (such as multipliers, adders, etc) are determined. The amount of space required by each statement is given by the multiplicity of each of its operators given by the surrounding loop trip count and the space needed for its implementation. For example, if a statement involves one multiplication and one addition, and the loop count is 100, we will require 100 multipliers and 100 adders to execute all instances of the statement in parallel. If the underlying hard-ware can be configured to support 100 multipliers and 100 adders, all 100 instances of the statement will execute in parallel in one step. Our algorithm for generating cut-sets uses the space constraint to determine which statements should be grouped into one configuration.

The following factors affecting program execution motivate the development of our two heuristic approaches to generate cut-sets.

1. **Number of reconfigurations performed:** Since reconfiguration overhead is significant, reconfigurations have to be kept a minimum. This motivates grouping of statements with similar operator requirements.
2. **FPGA space utilization:** The FPGA space should be utilized to the maximum extent to fully exploit available parallelism within each configuration.

The algorithm traverses the PDG in topological order and generates cut-sets and configurations incrementally. At every level, the algorithm invokes the selected heuristic to determine the ordering on the statements at that level for inclusion in the current cutset being incremented. Once the statements are ordered, the algorithm uses space constraints to decide whether to include the statement in the current cutset or whether to start a new cutset. In case the algorithm decides to include the statement in the current cutset, the corresponding configuration may or may not have to be incremented. We give a formal description of the algorithm in the appendix.

The heuristics developed to generate cut-sets are as follows:

Configuration Match: This heuristic selects a statement for inclusion in the current cutset if there is a maximal match between the operator support available in the current configuration and the operator support required by the statement. Assume that the heuristic is in the process of selecting the next statement for inclusion in the current cutset. Let the current configuration comprise of operators O_i and, O_j. Let there be 3 statements S_1, S_2 and S_3 which are candidates for inclusion in the current cutset for the above configuration. Let S_1 require operators O_k, O_i; S_2 require operators O_i, O_j; and S_3 require operators O_m, O_n. For statement S_1, one of the required operators O_i is available in the current configuration (a *match*), and the other is not (an *unmatch*). For S_2, both the operators are available (two matches), and for S_3 none match (two unmatches). We then perform ordering ($>$) on statements using their match and unmatch counts. Statement $S_i > S_j$ (S_i is placed before S_j) if unmatch count of S_i is lower than that of S_j. If the unmatch count is equal, then $S_i > S_j$ if match count of S_i is greater than that of S_j. Based on this criteria, the given statements will be ordered as $S_2 > S_1 > S_3$. Thus, S_2 is a better candidate for inclusion in the current cutset than both S_1 and S_3.

In the above heuristic, the motivation behind ordering statements is to enforce maximal overlap between the new configuration and the old configuration to maximally utilize partial reconfiguration when space constraint is not met. For example, in the above illustration, for the candidate S_1 if the space constraint is not met, one would start a new cutset and a new configuration $< O_k, O_i >$. One can see that this new configuration has a good amount of overlap with the previous configuration $< O_i, O_j >$. Thus, reconfiguration would be partial resulting in minimal reconfiguration overheads.

FPGA Space Requirement: The second heuristic orders statements such that those which require higher FPGA space for generating their configuration are placed before those which need lesser space. The cutset and the corresponding configuration are then generated until the space constraint is met. A new cutset and configuration is generated when the space constraint is not met. This will enable maximum utilization of FPGA space, and would give better performance of the loop nest. The ideas given above are formally presented in the algorithms detailed in the appendix.

5.3 Reconfiguration Minimization

Once the PDG has been completely traversed and cut-sets generated, we make another pass over the cut-sets. In this pass the cut-sets are analyzed taking two adjacent ones at a time. Let C1 denote the sum of the execution cost of cut-sets under their respective configurations, along with the reconfiguration cost. Let C2 denote the total execution cost of the two cut-sets under a common configuration. If C2 is lesser than C1, this phase will merge the cut-sets and generate a common configuration. Otherwise, the cut-sets and configurations are left unchanged.

The common configuration would comprise all the operators that are present in the configuration of the given two cut-sets. For example, if configuration of cutset-1 is $\{< *, 100 >, < +, 100 >\}$, and that of cutset-2 is $\{< /, 100 >, < -, 100 >\}$, then the common configuration would comprise $\{*, /, +, -\}$. The multiplicity of each operator is computed based on the total FPGA chip space. For example, if the available space enables us to generate 50 of each operator, then the common configuration would be $\{< *, 50 >, < +, 50 >, < /, 50 >, < -, 50 >\}$.

6 Implementation and Results

6.1 Implementation

Our framework is implemented using the SUIF [13] compilation system. The framework has been tested using loops taken from standard benchmarks, such as the *Perfect benchmarks*, a suite of scientific and engineering programs such as NASI, WSSI and SRSI; and the *Livermore* loops, a set of loops extracted from operational codes used at the Lawrence Livermore National Laboratory. Some scalar variables in the loop were scalar expanded to arrays. For loops with unknown loop bounds, three cases of loop counts are considered: small (100), medium (1000) and large (10000). The benchmark loop structures are shown in Figure 4

6.2 Results

The cost model for Xilinx 6200 family of FPGAs was developed and used by the compiler for analysis. The cost model provides the cost (time) of executing an operator, the space an operator takes on the reconfigurable system, and partial reconfiguration costs. In this work, we first developed a parametric model for Xilinx 6200 family of processors for different operator implementations. We have used the models for XC6216 and XC6264 to measure and characterize the performance of our approach. The relative space-time costs (derived from detailed space-time cost model of each operator) of some common operators that are involved in the benchmark programs are shown below:

Perfect benchmark loops :		Livermore loops :

Perfect benchmark loops :

Loop-2 taken from SRSI

```
for ( J = 1; J <= JMAX; J++ ) {
    RHO = Q[J][K][1] * XYJ[J][K];
    U[J] = Q[J][K][2] / Q[J][K][1];
    V[J] = Q[J][K][3] / Q[J][K][1];
    UVSQ[J] = U[J]*U[J] + V[J]*V[J];
    ENERGY = Q[J][K][4] * XYJ[J][K];
    PPP[J] = PRESS[J][K] * XYJ[J][K];
    CPC[J] = 2 / (GAMMA * FSMACH *
                  FSMACH);
    CP = (PPP[J] * GAMMA - 1) * CPC[J];
    EMACH = UVSQ[J] / SNDSP[J][K];
}
```

Loop-1 taken from WSSI

```
for ( i = 1; i <= N; i++ ) {
    DUP[i] = P1[i] * TG[LO][i+1] - TG[LO][i];
    DVP[i] = CI[i+1] * CB[12] - CB[i];
}
```

Loop-4 taken from NASI

```
for ( I = 1; I <= NBF; I++ ) {
    AC[I] = A[I] * EFACT;
    BC[I] = B[I] * RFACT;
    AD[I] = AC[I] / UNITE;
    BD[I] = BC[I] * UNITL;
    A[I] = AD[I];
    B[I] = BD[I];
}
```

Loop-3 taken from WSSI

```
for ( I = 0; I < LOT; I+= 96 ) {
    W[I] = G[I] + G[I+32] + G[I+64];
    W[I+1] = G[I+1] + G[I+33] + G[I+65];
    W[I+2] = ( G[I] + HM*(G[I+32]+G[I+64]))
             - (SIN60*(G[I+33]-G[I+65]));
    W[I+4] = (G[I]+HM*(G[I+32]+G[I+64]))
             + (SIN60*(G[I+33]-G[I+65]));
    W[I+3] = (G[I+1]+HM*(G[I+33]+G[I+65]))
             + (SIN60*(G[I+32]-G[I+64]));
    W[I+5] = (G[I+1]+HM*(G[I+33]+G[I+65]))
             - (SIN60*(G[I+32]-G[I+64]));
}
```

Livermore loops :

Loop-1 (Hydro fragment) :

```
for ( l = 1; l <= loop; l++) {
    for (k = 0; k < n; k++) {
        a[k] = r * z[k+10] + t* z[k+11];
        x[k] = q + y[k] * a[k];
    }
}
```

Loop-2 (Equation of state fragment)

```
for ( l = 1; l <= loop; l++) {
    for (k = 0; k < n; k++) {
        a[k] = r * (z[k] + r * y[k]);
        b[k] = r * (u[k+2] + r * u[k+1]);
        c[k] = r * (u[k+5] + r * u[k+4]);
        d[k] = t * (u[k+6] + c[k]);
        e[k] = t * (u[k+3] + b[k] + d[k]);
        x[k] = u[k] + a[k] + e[k];
    }
}
```

Loop-3 (Discrete ordinates transport,
        conditional recurrence on xx)

```
for ( l = 1; l <= loop; l++) {
    for (k = 0; k < n; k++) {
        di[k] = (y[k] - g[k]) / (xx[k] + dk);
        dn[k] = z[k] / di[k];
        a[k] = (w[k]+v[k]*dn[k]) * xx[k];
        b[k] = (vx[k] + v[k]*dn[k]);
        x[k] = (a[k] + u[k])/ b[k];
        xx[k+1] = (x[k] - xx[k])*dn[k] + xx[k];
    }
}
```

Fig. 4. Benchmark Loops

Operator	ADD	SUB	MUL	DIV
Time	1	1	3	3.5
Space	1	1	4	10

The loops are partitioned into cut-sets and corresponding configurations are generated. The total execution time including reconfiguration overhead is computed for each loop. For determining speed-ups, the loop completion time on a reconfigurable processor, such as XC6264, is compared with the time taken on a non-reconfigurable processor. We assume that the reconfigurable system is a *co-processor* type of environment, with a reconfigurable FPGA and memory local to the system. In our experiments, we assume that the corresponding data needed by the loops is locally available in the memory through a pre-fetch by overlapping the DMA cycles with the CPU during execution. The speed-up is defined as the ratio of sequential execution time on a non-reconfigurable processor to the execution time on a reconfigurable processor. We illustrate the speed-up calculation through an example loop, loop-4 taken from NASI (Figure 4). Statements are denoted as S1, S2, ..., S6 in the order in which they appear in the loop. On a non-reconfigurable processor, the loop is executed sequentially. There are 3 multiplications and 1 division operation in the loop. The loop count is 1000. Based on our cost model, the loop completion time = 1000 * (3 + 3 + 3 + 3.5) = 12500 time units. The cut-sets and the configuration obtained by our algorithm is given below.

Type	Loop	Livermore Loops				Perfect Benchmarks			
		Conf match		FPGA Space		Conf match		FPGA Space	
		Pass1 Spd	Pass2 Spd	Pass1 Spd	Pass2 Spd	Pass1 Spd	Pass2 Spd	Pass1 Spd	Pass2 Spd
Small	1	20	20	20	20	16.67	16.67	16.67	16.67
	2	20	20	20	20	4.51	5.77	5.65	5.77
	3	5.28	5.39	5.28	5.39	17.01	18.98	19.43	19.43
	4					7.31	7.31	4.61	6.67
Medium	1	20.84	20.84	20.84	20.84	16.95	16.95	16.95	16.95
	2	20.92	20.92	20.92	20.92	10.59	10.59	9.17	9.17
	3	10.67	10.67	10.67	10.67	21.25	21.25	19.91	19.91
	4					15.60	15.60	13.87	13.87
Large	1	20.96	20.96	20.96	20.96	16.97	16.97	16.97	16.97
	2	21.06	21.06	21.06	21.06	12.35	12.35	9.76	9.76
	3	11.87	11.87	11.87	11.87	21.83	21.83	19.96	19.96
	4					17.69	17.69	17.44	17.44

Table 1. Speed-ups obtained for the benchmarks for XC6216 processor

Type	Loop	Livermore Loops				Perfect Benchmarks			
		Conf match		FPGA Space		Conf match		FPGA Space	
		Pass1 Spd	Pass2 Spd	Pass1 Spd	Pass2 Spd	Pass1 Spd	Pass2 Spd	Pass1 Spd	Pass2 Spd
Small	1	50	50	50	50	50	50	50	50
	2	50	50	50	50	1.72	25	3.72	25
	3	2.31	24.18	2.31	24.18	15.47	60.29	56.94	56.94
	4					2.98	25	1.53	25
Medium	1	83.33	83.33	83.33	83.33	66.67	66.67	66.67	66.67
	2	83.33	83.33	83.33	83.33	13.3	25.64	18.69	25.64
	3	16.35	24.8	16.35	24.8	60.29	75.92	76.63	76.63
	4					21.77	29.41	12.83	29.41
Large	1	84.74	84.74	84.74	84.74	70.92	70.92	70.92	70.92
	2	84.89	84.89	84.89	84.89	40.64	40.94	35.78	36.01
	3	41.51	41.51	41.51	41.51	87.4	87.4	81.01	81.01
	4					60.02	60.02	50.35	50.35

Table 2. Speed-ups obtained for the benchmarks for XC6264 processor

Cut-set	Config	Steps	Time
{S1, S2, S4}	{<*, 26>}	39*(3 mul)=117	117*3 = 351
{S3, S5, S6}	{</, 10>}	100*(1 div)=100	100*3.5 = 350

Reconfiguration time for reconfiguring XC6216 chip from $\{<*, 26>\}$ to $\{</, 10>\}$ is 100 time units. The loop completion time for medium loop, including reconfiguration overhead, is 351 (for multiplication) + 100 (1 reconf) + 350 (for division) = 801 time units. Speedup = 12500/801 = 15.60.

In the above speed-up computation, the clock speeds of the reconfigurable and non-reconfigurable processors are assumed to be the same. In practice, however, the FPGA based reconfigurable processors are slower than the traditional non-reconfigurable processors such as RISC, by a factor of 10 or so in terms of clock speeds. However, non-reconfigurable instruction set based processors need memory accesses for instruction fetch, and incur overheads for instruction decode. These overheads are absent in hardware based approaches using reconfigurable processors. Considering this trade-off, the speed-ups shown could degrade by a factor of 6. The resulting speed-up values are still quite attractive.

| Type | Loop | Livermore Loops | | | | Perfect Benchmarks | | | |
| | | XC6216 | | XC6264 | | XC6216 | | XC6264 | |
		RS_{cm}	RS_{fs}	RS_{cm}	RS_{fs}	RS_{cm}	RS_{fs}	RS_{cm}	RS_{fs}
Small	1	1.86	1.86	0.71	0.71	4.67	4.67	0.46	0.46
	2	0	0	0	0	1.86	1.86	2.8	2.8
	3	4.36	4.36	2.8	2.8	4.67	0	0.46	0
	4					4.67	8.4	1.87	1.87
Medium	1	1.86	1.86	0.71	0.71	4.67	4.67	0.46	0.46
	2	0	0	0	0	4.41	2.8	2.8	2.8
	3	3.74	3.74	2.8	2.8	2.33	0	0.46	0
	4					4.67	4.04	1.87	1.87
Large	1	1.86	1.86	0.71	0.71	4.67	4.67	0.46	0.46
	2	0	0	0	0	4.4	2.8	1.01	0.77
	3	3.74	3.74	1.34	1.34	2.33	0	0.23	0
	4					4.67	4.04	0.93	0.62

Table 3. Average remnant space (% of total) on FPGA for the benchmarks

Table 3 gives the average remnant space on the FPGA processor after the required configurations have been generated. RS_{cm} refers to remnant space when Config Match heuristic was applied, and RS_{fs} refers to remnant space when FPGA Space heuristic was applied. The average remnant space is given as a percentage of total hardware space.

The speedup results for small, medium and large size benchmark loops for the XC6216 reconfigurable chip are computed as above and are given in Table 1. For the XC6264 chip, the results are given in Table 2. Cut-sets and their corresponding configurations are generated in Pass 1. In Pass 2, a merging of cut-sets is performed when reconfiguration overheads outweigh the performance benefits obtained through reconfiguration. In the tables, *Spd* refers to Speed-Up obtained as a factor of the execution times. In the next subsection, we summarize the discussion of these results.

6.3   Discussion of Results

Comparison of Speed-ups:

The speed-ups obtained are substantial in all cases (ranging from 5.39 to 87.4). As noted earlier, the actual speed-up could be 5-6 times lesser accounting for slow clock speeds of current FPGAs.

Across the two heuristics: In most cases, the speed-ups using both heuristics are comparable, but in the case of Loop 2 and Loop 4 in the Perfect Benchmarks suite, the Configuration Match heuristic has performed significantly better for medium and large sized loops (Tables 1 and 2). As can be seen from the loop structures, these loops have complex operations such as multiplications and divisions, which have a wide disparity in their space- time costs. This suggests that a better configuration match would reduce execution time even though it tends to waste some FPGA space. As the loop bounds are increased, the parallelism also increases, and Config Match algorithm tends to utilize more FPGA space, reducing the wastage. Hence it is able to perform better for loops with a large diversity in operators and for large loop bounds.

Across loop sizes: As loop sizes increase, operator parallelism increases, and in all cases, the speed-ups also increase. Since the FPGA space is limited, an increase in parallelism beyond the space limitation does not help in improving performance. This is because for large loop sizes, the execution becomes sequential once the FPGA space constraint limit is reached. For example, for loop 2 in Livermore, loop 2 in Perfect and loop 4 in Perfect, there is a considerable change in speed-up from small loop bounds to medium loop bounds, but a small change in speed-up from medium to large.

Improvement after optimizing second pass: The second pass resulted in significantly improved speed-ups in case of small loops. The speed-up improvements are almost 4 times in some cases.

Comparison of Remnant FPGA Space

In all cases, the two heuristics are very efficient in using the FPGA space, with only a small fraction of the space left unused. It is quite obvious that the second heuristic would perform better in terms of FPGA space utilization, and this is evident in the case of some loops with medium and large loop bounds (refer Table 3). In most cases, as the loop bounds increase, the unused FPGA space decreases as the two heuristics effectively use the FPGA space.

7   Conclusion

This paper presents a framework for automatic compilation analysis for loops targetted towards reconfigurable systems. We have also presented methods for improving effectiveness of analysis through configuration reuse, loop and operator transformations. The key focus of the framework is on identifying the program points where reconfiguration is most beneficial by analyzing trade-offs between costs and benefits due to reconfiguration. The framework proposes a two pass solution to the problem and is implemented in SUIF compilation system.

This work shows that lot of operator parallelism exists within loops and can be exploited by performing the right analysis to utilize the power of reconfigurable ALUs. A reconfigurable system based on commercially available FPGAs is a very cost-effective method of exploiting such parallelism. With the advent of larger and faster FPGAs these solutions could thus provide a powerful mechanism for exploiting operator parallelism.

References

1. Randy Allen and Ken Kennedy. Automatric tranlation of FORTRAN programs to vector form. *ACM Transactions on Programming Languages and Systems*, 9(4):491–542, Oct 1987.
2. Peter M. Athanas and Harvey F. Silverman. Processor reconfiguration through instruction-set metamorphosis. *IEEE Computer*, 26(3):11–18, March 1993.
3. Utpal Banerjee. *Loop Parallelization*. Loop transformations for restructuring compilers. Boston : Kluwer Academic, 1994.
4. G. E. Blelloch, S. Chatterjee, and M. Zagha. Solving linear recurrences with loop raking. *Journal of Parallel and Distributed Computing*, 25(1):91–97, Feb 1995.
5. D.A. Clark and B.L. Hutchings. Supporting FPGA microprocessors through re-targettable software tools. In *Proceedings of the IEEE Workshop on FPGAs for Custom Computing Machines.*, pages 195–203, April 1996.

6. Bau D., Kodukula I., Kotlyar V., Pingali K., and Stodghill P. Solving alignment using elementary linear algebra. In *Proceedings of 7th International Workshop on Languages and Compilers for Parallel Computing*, pages 46–60, June 1994. LNCS 892.
7. Kaushik S. D., Huang C.-H., Johnson R. W., and Sadayappan P. An approach to communication-efficient data redistribution. In *Proceedings of the 1994 ACM International Conference on Supercomputing*, pages 364–373, June 1994.
8. High Performance Fortran Forum. High performance fortran language specification, version 1.0. Technical Report CRPC–TR92225, Center for Research on Parallel Computation, Rice University, Houston, TX, 1992. Revised January 1993.
9. M. Gokhale and W. Carlson. An introduction to compilation issues for parallel machines. *Journal of Supercomputing*, 6(3-4):283–314, Dec 1992.
10. Anderson J. and Lam M. Global optimizations for parallelism and locality on scalable paralle machines. In *Proceedings of SIGPLAN '93 conference on Programming Language Design and Implementation*, pages 112–125, 1993.
11. Tu P. and Padua D. Automatic array privatization. In *Proceedings of the Sixth Workshop on Language and Compilers for Parallel Computing*, August 1993.
12. Pande S. S. A compile time partitioning method for doall loops on distributed memory systems. In *Proceedings of the 1996 International Conference on Parallel Processing*, pages 35–44, August 1996.
13. Stanford University. *The SUIF Library*, 1994. This manual is a part of the SUIF compiler documentation set, http://suif.stanford.edu/.
14. Elliot Waingold, Michael Taylor, Devabhaktuni Srikrishna, Vivek Sarkar, Walter Lee, Victor Lee, Jang Kim, Matthew Frank, Peter Finch, Rajeev Barua, Jonathan Babb, Saman Amarasinghe, and Anant Agarwal. Baring it all to software : Raw machines. *IEEE Computer*, 30(9):86–93, September 1997.
15. M. Weinhardt. Compilation and pipeline synthesis for reconfigurable architectures. In *"Reconfigurable Architectures - High Performance by Configware" (Proceedings of the RAW'97)*, April 1997.
16. A. Wenben and G. Brown. A software development system for FPGA-based data acqusition system. In *Proceedings of the IEEE Workshop Custom Computing Machines*, pages 28–37, April 1996.
17. Michael J. Wirthlin and Brad L. Hutchings. A dynamic instruction set computer. In *Proceedings of the IEEE Workshop on FPGAs for Custom Computing Machines*, pages 99–107, April 1995.
18. Michael Wolfe. *High Performance Compilers for Parallel Computing*. Addison-Wesley Publishing Company, 1996.

Appendix

Notations used in the algorithm:

config_tuple: The operator field of the configuration tuple *(config_tuple)* is denoted by *config_tuple(oper)* and its multiplicity is denoted by *config_tuple(oper_count)*.

space_req$_j$ denotes space required to implement the operator O_j on hardware.

space_req(s_i) denotes space required to implement all the operators needed for statement s_i.

Note: In the following algorithm, the variable *TotalCutsetConfig* is used to store the configuration of the current cutset. This is copied to the variable *CurrentConfig* when we go to a new level in the PDG. *CurrentConfig* is used for processing. Whenever new operators are added, and/or operator multiplicity is changed, *TotalCutsetConfig* is updated.

Algorithms

Algorithm I : GenerateCutsetsAndCongurations

Input: PDG for the loop body.
          Heuristic chosen /* Config Match or FPGA Space Requirement
Output: Cut-Sets, comprising the group of statements, and the edges between the cut-sets annotated with reconfiguration directives.

1. $AvailableFPGASpace \leftarrow TotalFPGASpace$
2. $TotalCutsetConfig \leftarrow \emptyset$
3. $CutsetList \leftarrow \emptyset$
   /* This list will be used to store the Cut-sets and the corresponding
   /* Configurations. The list will consist of nodes, where each node will
   /* have the cutset, and the corresponding configuration.
4. $CurrentLevelInPDG \leftarrow 1$
5. $CurrentCutset \leftarrow \emptyset$
6. Traverse the PDG in *topological order* (In the order of flow dependence in the program) and perform the following:
   a. Group all the statements in the PDG that are at level $CurrentLevelInPDG$.
   b. Call *RearrangeStatements*
       /* Returns the ordered set of statements at $CurrentLevelInPDG$ as
       /* per chosen heuristic.
   c. Copy all the tuples in $TotalCutsetConfig$ to $CurrentConfig$.
   d. **for** each statement s_i in the sorted order **do**
       • Determine the operators required for s_i.
       • $ConfigReq \leftarrow \emptyset$
       • **for** each operator O_i in s_i **do**
          ○ $config\_tuple(oper) \leftarrow O_i$
          ○ $config\_tuple(oper\_count) \leftarrow loop\_count$.
          ○ $ConfigReq \leftarrow ConfigReq \cup config\_tuple$
       • **if** $\forall config\_tuple \in ConfigReq, \exists currconfig\_tuple \in CurrentConfig$
         $such\ that(config\_tuple(oper) = currconfig\_tuple(oper))$ **then**
         $Is\_Subset \leftarrow TRUE$ **else** $Is\_Subset \leftarrow FALSE$
       • **if** $\forall config\_tuple \in ConfigReq, \exists currconfig\_tuple \in CurrentConfig$
         $such\ that\ ((config\_tuple(oper) = currconfig\_tuple(oper))$ **AND**
         $((config\_tuple(oper\_count) \leq currconfig\_tuple(oper\_count))$ **then**
            $Is\_Less \leftarrow FALSE$
         else $Is\_Less \leftarrow TRUE$
       • **if** $Is\_Subset = TRUE$ **AND** $Is\_Less = FALSE$ **then**
         /* All the required operators and their required number are
         /* available in $CurrentConfig$. So, we can support parallel
         /* execution of all the instances of statement s_i.

○ $CurrentCutset \leftarrow CurrentCutset \cup \{s_i\}$
/* For each operator that'll be used from $CurrentConfig$,
/* subtract the count of the operator in $ConfigReq$ from the
/* corresponding operator count in $CurrentConfig$
○ for each $currconfig\_tuple \in CurrentConfig$, $config\_tuple \in ConfigReq$
   do
    if $\exists(currconfig\_tuple(oper), config\_tuple(oper))$ such that
    $currconfig\_tuple(oper) = config\_tuple(oper)$ then
      $currconfig\_tuple(oper\_count) \leftarrow currconfig\_tuple(oper\_count) -$
      $config\_tuple(oper\_count)$

else
/* We need to support new operators or more number of existing
/* operators in $CurrentConfig$. Check if we can satisfy the
/* requirement.
- $space\_req(s_i) \leftarrow 0$
- for each $config\_tuple \in ConfigReq$, $currconfig\_tuple \in CurrentConfig$
   do
    if $\exists(currconfig\_tuple(oper), config\_tuple(oper))$ such that
    $(config\_tuple(oper) = currconfig\_tuple(oper)$ then
     $diff \leftarrow config\_tuple(oper\_count) - currconfig\_tuple(oper\_count)$
    else
     $diff \leftarrow config\_tuple(oper\_count)$
    $space\_req(s_i) \leftarrow space\_req(s_i) + diff \times space\_req(config\_tuple(oper))$
- if $AvailableFPGASpace \geq space\_req(s_i)$ then
  /* We have FPGA space to generate the required operators. We
  /* update the configuration to include newly generated
  /* operators and/or update the multiplicity of operators
  /* already existing in $CurrentConfig$.
  ○ $CurrentCutset \leftarrow CurrentCutset \cup \{s_i\}$
  ○ $AvailableFPGASpace \leftarrow (AvailableFPGASpace - space\_req(s_i))$
    /* For those operators in $ConfigReq$ that are also in
    /* $CurrentConfig$, we have to update the multiplicity in
    /* $TotalCutsetConfig$. For the new operators, we create a new
    /* tuple, set the fields of the tuple, and add it to
    /* $TotalCutsetConfig$.
  ○ for each $config\_tuple \in ConfigReq$,
      $currconfig\_tuple \in TotalCutsetConfig$ do
    if $\exists(currconfig\_tuple(oper), config\_tuple(oper))$ such that
    $(config\_tuple(oper) = currconfig\_tuple(oper)$
    then
     $currconfig\_tuple(oper\_count) \leftarrow currconfig\_tuple(oper\_count)+$
     $config\_tuple(oper\_count)$
    else
     $currconfig\_tuple(oper) \leftarrow config\_tuple(oper)$
     $currconfig\_tuple(oper\_count) \leftarrow config\_tuple(oper\_count)$
     $TotalCutsetConfig \leftarrow TotalCutsetConfig \cup \{currconfig\_tuple\}$
- else if (Is_Subset = TRUE) then
  /* The required operators are present in $CurrentConfig$, but
  /* their multiplicity is lower than the required number. No
  /* additional space available to increase multiplicity. So, we

/* cannot execute all instances of s_i in parallel.
/* We execute a set of instances of s_i in sequential steps.
- o $CurrentCutset \leftarrow CurrentCutset \cup \{s_i\}$
- o $min\_count \leftarrow$ The count of that operator in s_i whose multiplicity is minimum in $TotalCutsetConfig$.
  /* Among the operators required by s_i, we take the count of
  /* that operator whose multiplicity is min in
  /* $TotalCutsetConfig$. This many instances of s_i can execute
  /* in parallel. So, number of steps required is $\lceil \frac{loop\_count}{min\_count} \rceil$.
- o steps = $\lceil \frac{loop\_count}{min\_count} \rceil$

- **else**
  /* The required operators are not present in $CurrentConfig$,
  /* and there is no additional FPGA space to create them.
  /* So we need to reconfigure.
  - o Set the configuration of $CurrentCutset$ to $TotalCutsetConfig$.
  - o Add $CurrentCutset$ to $CutsetList$.
  - o $CurrentCutset \leftarrow$ new Cutset.
  - o $CurrentCutset \leftarrow \{s_i\}$
  - o $AvailableFPGASpace \leftarrow TotalFPGASpace$
  - o $space\_req(s_i) = \sum_{j \in operator\ in\ s_i} (space\_req_j)$
  - o $noof\_opers = min(\lfloor \frac{AvailableFPGASpace}{space\_req(s_i)} \rfloor, loop\_count)$
  - o $TotalCutsetConfig \leftarrow \emptyset$
    /* We update TotalCutsetConfig with newly created config.
    /* We also update CurrentConfig to the same, except that
    /* the operator multiplicities are 0. This is because all
    /* the generated operators are already used by s_i.
  - o for each operator O_i in s_i do
    $config\_tuple(oper) \leftarrow O_i$
    $config\_tuple(oper\_count) \leftarrow noof\_opers$
    $TotalCutsetConfig \leftarrow TotalCutsetConfig \cup \{config\_tuple\}$
    $currconfig\_tuple(oper) \leftarrow O_i$
    $currconfig\_tuple(oper\_count) \leftarrow 0$
    $CurrentConfig \leftarrow CurrentConfig \cup \{currconfig\_tuple\}$
  - o $AvailableFPGASpace \leftarrow (AvailableFPGASpace - space\_req(s_i))$

e. Increment $CurrentLevelInPDG$
f. Repeat statements **a, b, c, d** and **e** for all the statements in the PDG.

Procedure : RearrangeStatements

Input: CurrentConfig - Current FPGA configuration.
Heuristic chosen - "Configuration Match" or "FPGA Space Requirement"
Set of statements to be rearranged.
Output: Rearranged statements.

if heuristic is Configuration Match **then**
/* Statements are to be arranged such that those whose configuration
/* requirement closely matches $CurrentConfig$ are arranged first
/* followed by statements that have fewer match.

- Create a local array of size equal to number of statements in input. Each element of the array is a structure with 3 fields : $Match\_Count$, $Unmatch\_Count$, and an input statement.
- **for** each element e_i in local array **do**
  - $e_i.Match\_Count \leftarrow 0$
  - $e_i.Unmatch\_Count \leftarrow 0$
  - $e_i.statement \leftarrow s_i$. /* $s_i \in$ Input statements
- **for** each element e_i in the local array **do**
  - $s_i \leftarrow e_i.statement$
  - **for** each operator O_j in s_i **do**
    - **if** O_j is present in $CurrentConfig$ **then**
      Increment $e_i.Match\_Count$.
    - **else**
      Increment $e_i.Unmatch\_Count$.
- Arrange elements in the local array in decreasing sorted order based on the following criteria.
  /* Statement $e_i.s_i > e_j.s_j$ if $e_i.Unmatch\_Count < e_j.Unmatch\_Count$.
  /* If $e_i.Unmatch\_Count = e_j.Unmatch\_Count$, then $e_i.s_i > e_j.s_j$,
  /* if $e_i.Match\_Count > e_j.Match\_Count$. Otherwise, $e_i.s_i < e_j.s_j$.
- Return the sorted statements.

if heuristic is FPGA Space Requirement **then**
- **for** each statement s_i in the input **do**
  - $space\_req(s_i) = \sum_{j \in operator\ in\ s_i}(space\_req_j)$
- Arrange statements in the local array in decreasing order of FPGA space required.
- Return the sorted statements.

Principles of Speculative Run–Time Parallelization

Devang Patel and Lawrence Rauchwerger *

Dept. of Computer Science, Texas A&M University
College Station, TX 77843-3112, USA
{dpatel,rwerger}@cs.tamu.edu,
http://www.cs.tamu.edu/faculty/rwerger

Abstract. Current parallelizing compilers cannot identify a significant fraction of parallelizable loops because they have complex or statically insufficiently defined access patterns. We advocate a novel framework for the identification of parallel loops. It speculatively executes a loop as a doall and applies a fully parallel data dependence test to check for any unsatisfied data dependencies; if the test fails, then the loop is re–executed serially. We will present the principles of the design and implementation of a compiler that employs both run-time and static techniques to parallelize dynamic applications. Run-time optimizations always represent a tradeoff between a *speculated* potential benefit and a *certain* (sure) overhead that must be paid. We will introduce techniques that take advantage of classic compiler methods to reduce the cost of run-time optimization thus tilting the outcome of *speculation* in favor of significant performance gains. Experimental results from the PERFECT, SPEC and NCSA Benchmark suites show that these techniques yield speedups not obtainable by any other known method.

1   Run-Time Optimization Is Necessary

To achieve a high level of performance for a particular program on today's super-computers, software developers are often forced to tediously hand–code optimizations tailored to a specific machine. Such hand–coding is difficult, increases the possibility of error over sequential programming, and the resulting code may not be portable to other machines. Restructuring, or parallelizing, compilers address these problems by detecting and exploiting parallelism in sequential programs written in conventional languages. Although compiler techniques for the automatic detection of parallelism have been studied extensively over the last two decades, current parallelizing compilers cannot extract a significant fraction of the available parallelism in a loop if it has a complex and/or statically insufficiently defined access pattern. Typical examples are complex simulations such as SPICE [16], DYNA–3D [27], GAUSSIAN [14], CHARMM [1].

---

* Research supported in part by NSF CAREER Award CCR-9734471 and utilized the SGI systems at the NCSA, University of Illinois under grant#ASC980006N.

S. Chatterjee (Ed.): LCPC'98, LNCS 1656, pp. 323–337, 1999.
© Springer-Verlag Berlin Heidelberg 1999

It has become clear that static (compile–time) analysis must be comple-
mented by new methods capable of automatically extracting parallelism at *run–
time* [6]. Run–time techniques can succeed where static compilation fails because
they have access to the input data. For example, input dependent or dynamic
data distribution, memory accesses guarded by run–time dependent conditions,
and subscript expressions can all be analyzed unambiguously at run–time. In
contrast, at compile–time the access pattern of some programs cannot be determined, sometimes due to limitations in the current analysis algorithms but often
because the necessary information is just not available, i.e., the access pattern is
a function of the input data. For example, most dependence analysis algorithms
can only deal with subscript expressions that are affine in the loop indices. In the
presence of non–linear expressions, or of subscripted subscripts, compilers generally conservatively assume data dependences. Although more powerful analysis
techniques could remove this last limitation when the index arrays are computed
using only statically–known values, nothing can be done at compile–time when
the index arrays are a function of the input data [12,25,28].

We will present the principles of the design and implementation of a compiling system that employs run-time and classic techniques in tandem to automatically parallelize irregular, dynamic applications. We will show that run-time
optimizations always represent a tradeoff between a *speculated* potential benefit
and a *certain* (sure) overhead that must be paid. This work models the competing factors of this optimization technique and outlines a guiding strategy for
increasing performance. We will introduce techniques that take advantage of
classic compiler methods to reduce the cost of run-time optimization thus tilting
the outcome of *speculation* in favor of significant performance gains.

The scope of presented work will be initially limited to loop level parallelization and optimization of Fortran programs in a shared memory environment
using the SPMD programming paradigm. The run–time techniques described
here are designed to be used in the automatic parallelization of 'legacy' Fortran
applications as well as in explicit parallel coding of new, dynamic codes, where
concurrency is a function of the input data.

2   Run-Time Optimization

Maximizing the performance of an application executing on a specific parallel
system can be derived from three fundamental optimization principles: (i) maximizing parallelism while minimizing overhead and redundant computation, (ii)
minimizing wait-time due to load imbalance, and (iii) minimizing wait-time due
to memory latency.

Maximizing the parallelism in a program is probably the most important
factor affecting parallel, scalable performance. It allows full concurrent use of all
the resources of any given architecture without any idle (wait) time. At the limit,
full parallelism also allows perfect scalability with the number of processors and
can be efficiently used to improve memory latency and load balancing.

The most effective vehicle for improving multiprocessor performance has been the restructuring compiler [5,10,18,9]. Compilers have incorporated sophisticated data dependence analysis techniques(e.g., [3,19]) to detect intrinsic parallelism in codes and transform them for parallel execution. These techniques usually rely on a static (compile time) analysis of the memory access pattern (array subscripts in the case of Fortran programs) and on parallelism enabling transformations like privatization, reduction parallelization, induction variable substitution, etc. [7]. When static information is insufficient to safely perform an optimizing transformation the classic compiler emits conservative code. Alternatively it might delay the decision to execution time, when sufficient information becomes available. This strategy implies that a certain amount of code analysis has to be performed during the time which was initially allocated to useful data processing. This shift of activity will inherently account for *a priori* performance degradation. Only when the outcome of the run-time analysis is a safe optimization can we hope that the overall execution time will decrease. For example, if the parallelization of a loop depends on the value of a parameter that is statically unavailable the compiler can generate a two-version loop (one parallel and one sequential) and code that will test the parameter at run-time and decide which version to execute. While this is a very simple case it shows that time will be 'lost' testing the parameter and, depending on the outcome, may or may not lead to an optimization. Furthermore, even if the loop under question is executed in parallel, performance gains are not certain. All this implies that run-time optimizations always represent a tradeoff which needs a guiding strategy; they represent a *speculation* about a potential benefit for which a *certain* (sure) overhead will have to be paid.

2.1   Principles of Run-Time Optimization

Loop parallelization is the most effective and far reaching optimization for scientific applications. Briefly stated, a loop can be safely executed in parallel if and only if its later iterations do not use data computed in its earlier iterations, i.e., there are no flow dependences. The safety of this and other related transformations (e.g., privatization, reduction parallelization) is checked at compile time through data dependence analysis (i.e., analyzing array subscript functions). When static analysis is not possible the access pattern is analyzed at run-time through various techniques which we will shortly introduce and analyze.

Inspector/Executor vs. Speculative run-time testing. All run-time optimizations in general, and parallelization in particular, consist of at least two activities: *(a)* a test of a set of run-time values (e.g., the values taken by array subscripts) and *(b)* the execution of one of the compiler generated options (e.g., multi-version loops).

If the test phase is performed before the execution of the loop and has no side effects, i.e., it does not modify the state of the original program (shared) variables then this technique is called *inspector/executor* [4]. Its run-time overhead consists only of the time to execute the inspection phase.

If the test phase is done at the same time as the execution of the aggressively optimized loop and, in general, the state of the program is modified during this process, then the technique is called *speculative execution*. Its associated overhead consists at least of the test itself and the saving of the program state (checkpointing). If the optimization test fails, then extra overhead is paid during a program *ante loop* state restoration phase before the conservative version of the code can be executed. In this scenario the the initial optimized loop execution time becomes additional overhead too.

Although it might appear that the more 'sedate' *inspector/executor* method is a better overall strategy than the *speculative* technique, there is in fact a much more subtle trade-off between the two. An inspector loop represents a segment of code that must always be executed before any decision can be made and always adds to the program's critical path. However, if the test is executed concurrently with the actual computation (it is always quasi-independent of it – computation cannot possibly depend on the test) then some of the overhead may not add additional wall-clock time. The same is true if checkpointing is done 'on-the-fly', just before a variable is about to be modified. In other words *with respect to performance alone* the two methods are competitive.

A potential negative effect of speculative execution is that the optimization test's data structures are used concurrently with those of the original program, which could increase the working set of the loop and degrade its cache performance.

The previous comparison assumes an important principle: *any run-time parallelization technique must be fully parallel* to scale with the number of processors. For the speculative method this is always implicitly true – we test during a speculative parallel execution. Inspectors may be executed sequentially or in parallel – but, with the exception of simple cases, only parallel execution can lead to scalable performance. Inspector loops cannot always be parallelized. If there exists a data or control dependence cycle between shared data and its address computation then it is not possible to extract an address inspector that can be safely parallelized and/or that is side effect free. In fact the inspector would contain most of the original loop, in effect degenerating into a *speculative* technique (will need checkpointing) without its benefits.

In summary we conclude that both run-time techniques are generally competitive but that the speculative method is the only generally applicable one.

2.2   Obtaining Performance

Run-time optimization can produce performance gains only if the associated overhead for its validation is outweighed by the obtained speedup or,

$$Speedup = SuccessRate \times (Optimization\_Speedup - Testing\_Overhead) > 0$$

This *Speedup* function can be maximized by increasing the power of the intended optimization and decreasing the time it takes to validate it. Because run-time optimizations are speculative, their success is not guaranteed and therefore, their *SuccessRate*, needs to be maximized.

Performance through Run-time Overhead Reduction. The optimization representing the focus of this paper is loop parallelization within a SPMD computation. This transformation generally scales with data size and number of processors and its overall potential for speedup is unquestionable. Its general profitability (when and where to apply it) has been the topic of previous research and its conclusions remain valid in our context.

Thus, the task at hand is to decrease the second term of our performance objective function, the testing-overhead. Regardless of the adopted testing strategy (inspector/executor or aggressive speculation) this overhead can be broken down into (a) the time it takes to extract data dependence information about the statically un-analyzable access pattern, and (b) the time to perform an analysis of the collected data dependence information.

The first rule we have adopted is that all run-time processing (access tracing and analysis) must be performed in parallel — otherwise it may become the sequential bottleneck of the application. The access pattern tracing will be performed within a parallel region either before the loop in case of the inspector approach or during the speculative execution of the transformed loop. The amount of work can be upper bounded by the length of the trace but (see Section 5) can be further reduced (at times dramatically) through reference aggregation and elimination of duplicated (redundant) address records. This type of optimization can be achieved through the use of static, i.e., compile time information. Usually, when a compiler cannot prove independence for all referenced variables, the partial information obtained during static analysis is discarded. In such a case our run-time compiler phase will retrieve all previously considered useless, but valid information and complement it with only the really dynamic data. This tight integration of the run-time technique with the classic compiler methods is the key to the reduction of tracing overhead.

Another important tool in reducing overhead is the development of static heuristics for uncovering the algorithms and data structures used in the original program. For example, pattern matching a reduction can encourage the use of a run-time reduction validation technique. An inference about the use of structures may reduce the number of addresses shadowed.

Increasing the Success Rate of Speculation. Collecting the outcome of every speculation and using this data in the computation of a *statistic* could drastically alter the success rate of speculation. The use of *meaningful* statistics about the parallelism profile of dynamic programs will require some evidence that different experiments on one application with different input sets produces similar results (with respect to parallelism). Feeding back the results of speculative parallelization during the same execution of a code may be, for the moment, a more practical approach. For example, after failing speculation on loop several consecutive times a more conservative approach can adopted 'on-the-fly'.

A more difficult but more effective strategy in enhancing both the success rate of speculation as well as lowering run-time overhead is to find heuristics that can 'guess' the algorithmic approach and/or data structure used by the original program and drive the speculation in the right direction. A simple example is reduction recognition: if a statement 'looks' like a reduction then it can be verified by generating a speculative test for it – the chances of success are very high. Making the correct assumption at compile time whether an access pattern is sparse or dense or whether we use linked lists or arrays (regardless of their implementation) can go a long way in making run-time optimization profitable (see Section 5).

3   Foundational Work: Run-Time Parallelization

We have developed several techniques [20,21,22,23,24] that can detect and exploit loop level parallelism in various cases encountered in irregular applications: (i) a speculative method to detect fully parallel loops (The LRPD Test), (ii) an inspector/executor technique to compute wavefronts (sequences of mutually independent sets of iterations that can be executed in parallel) and (iii) a technique for parallelizing while loops (do loops with an unknown number of iterations and/or containing linked list traversals). We now briefly describe a simplified version of the speculative LRPD test (complete details can be found in [20,22]).

The LRPD Test. The LRPD test speculatively executes a loop in parallel and tests subsequently if any data dependences could have occurred. If the test fails, the loop is re–executed sequentially. To qualify more parallel loops, *array privatization* and *reduction parallelization* can be speculatively applied and their validity tested after loop termination.[1] For simplicity, reduction parallelization is not shown in the example below; it is tested in a similar manner as independence and privatization. The LRPD test is fully parallel and requires time $O(a/p + \log p)$, where p is the number of processors, and a is the total number of accesses made to A in the loop.

Consider a do loop for which the compiler cannot statically determine the access pattern of a shared array A (Fig. 1(a)). We allocate the shadow arrays for marking the write accesses, A_w, and the read accesses, A_r, and an array A_{np}, for flagging non-privatizable elements. The loop is augmented with code (Fig. 1(b)) that will mark during speculative execution the shadow arrays every time A is referenced (based on specific rules). The result of the marking can be seen in Fig. 1(c). The first time an element of A is written during an iteration, the corresponding element in the write shadow array A_w is marked. If, during any iteration, an element in A is read, but never written, then the corresponding element in the read shadow array A_r is marked. Another shadow array A_{np} is used to flag the elements of A that *cannot* be privatized: an element in A_{np} is

---

[1] *Privatization* creates, for each processor cooperating on the execution of the loop, private copies of the program variables. A shared variable is privatizable if it is always written in an iteration before it is read, e.g., many temporary variables. A *reduction variable* is a variable used in one operation of the form $x = x \otimes exp$, where $\otimes$ is an associative and commutative operator and x does not occur in exp or anywhere else in the loop. There are known transformations for implementing reductions in parallel [26,15,13].

marked if the corresponding element in A is both read and written, and is read first, in any iteration.

A post-execution analysis, illustrated in Fig. 1(c), determines whether there were any cross-iteration dependencies between statements referencing A as follows. If $\text{any}(A_w(:) \wedge A_r(:))^2$ is true, then there is at least one flow- or anti-dependence that was not removed by privatizing A (some element is read and written in different iterations). If $\text{any}(A_{np}(:))$ is true, then A is not privatizable (some element is read before being written in an iteration). If Atw, the total number of writes marked during the parallel execution, is not equal to Atm, the total number of marks computed after the parallel execution, then there is at least one output dependence (some element is overwritten); however, if A is privatizable (i.e., if $\text{any}(A_{np}(:))$ is false), then these dependencies were removed by privatizing A.

```
do i=1,5
  z = A(K(i))
  if (B1(i) .eq. .true.) then
    A(L(i)) = z + C(i)
  endif
enddo

B1(1:5) = (1 0 1 0 1)
K(1:5) = (1 2 3 4 1)
L(1:5) = (2 2 4 4 2)

        (a)
```

```
do i=1,5
  markread(K(i))
  z = A(K(i))
  if (B1(i) .eq. .true.) then
    markwrite(L(i))
    A(L(i)) = z + C(i)
  endif
enddo

        (b)
```

Operation	Value				
	1	2	3	4	5
Aw	0	1	0	1	0
Ar	1	1	1	1	0
Anp	1	1	1	1	0
Aw(:) ∧ Ar(:)	0	1	0	1	0
Aw(:) ∧ Anp(:)	0	1	0	1	0
Atw	3				
Atm	2				

(c)

Fig. 1. Do loop (a) transformed for speculative execution, (b) the markwrite and markread operations update the appropriate shadow arrays, (c) shadow arrays after loop execution. In this example, the test fails.

4   Variations of the LRPD Test

Static compilation can generate a wealth of incomplete information that, by itself, is insufficient to decide whether parallelization is safe but can be exploited to reduce run-time overhead. When we can establish statically that, for example, all iterations of a loop first read and then write a shared array (but nothing else) then we can conclude that privatization is not possible, and therefore should not test for it. This approach of using partial information has led to the development of simplified variants of the LRPD test. The overall purpose of the various specialized forms of the LRPD test presented in this section is (a) to reduce the overhead of run-time processing to the minimum necessary and sufficient to achieve safe parallelization (but without becoming conservative), and (b) to extend the number of access patterns that can be recognized as parallelizable. We will now enumerate some of the more frequently used variants of the LRPD test that we have developed and elaborate on those that have not been presented elsewhere [24,22]. Further refinements and related issues (such as choice of marking data structures) are discussed in Section 5.

---

2 any returns the "OR" of its vector operand's elements, i.e., $\text{any}(v(1:n)) = (v(1) \vee v(2) \vee \ldots \vee v(n))$.

- Processor–wise LRPD test for testing cross-processor instead of cross-iteration dependences, qualifying more parallel loops with less overhead.
- A test supporting copy-in of external values to allow loops that first read-in a value to be executed in parallel.
- Early failure detection test to reduce the overhead of failed speculation.
- Early success detection test with on-demand cross-processor analysis.
- A test that can distinguish between fully independent and privatizable accesses to reduce private storage replication for privatized arrays.
- An Aggregate LRPD test – aggregates individual memory the references in contiguous intervals or sets of points.

4.1   Early Failure Detection

Note that it can be detected *during* the execution of the LRPD test, almost without any additional cost, if a reference under test causes a failure condition (read and written in different iterations, or, within the same iteration, read before write or just referenced outside a reduction statement) among those iterations executing on the same processor. If this happens we can fail the test immediately without actually finishing the rest of the **un**-executed code and without any cross-processor analysis. Of course, if we decide to apply the processor-wise version of the test then cross-iteration dependences between iterations scheduled on the same processor may not necessarily cause failure. A more sophisticated approach is to establish a correlation between the number of cross-iteration dependences and the probability of finding cross-processor dependences after a complete loop execution. If a loop has dependences it is highly likely that these dependences will appear well before the last iteration is executed.

4.2   Faster Analysis and Early Success Detection

The analysis phase of the processor-wise version of the LRPD test can be reduced by maintaining a flag per processor (each representing an entire array with one scalar), per possible cause of failure (see Section 4.1). If, after loop execution, these flags have not been set on any processor then no further analysis is necessary and speculation was successful. If only some of the processors show a potential problem then only their shadows will be analyzed, thus reducing the overall work. If the flags show problems everywhere then classic parallel merge is performed. For example, we can keep a per-processor reduction flag (a bit) and mark any occurrence of an array reference outside the reduction statement. After loop execution only the processors with flags set will participate in the analysis phase because they are the only potential cause for dependences – if no processor has the flag set then the test passes without any further overhead.

We have modified the cross-processor analysis phase itself in an optimistic manner to reduce cross-processor communication in the following way: each processor traverses its own shadow array and 'looks' at the contents of the other ones only if it detects a cause for failure. If, for example, we test reduction and/or privatization the processor(s) that find the flag set will 'look' in the same position of the shadow across processors and merge their information. This technique could be named 'on demand merging'.

4.3   Fully Independent and Privatizable Accesses

Since privatization generally implies replication of program variables (i.e., an increase in memory requirements), this transformation should be avoided when there is no benefit to be gained. Instead of privatizing entire arrays, the LRPD test can identify and privatize only elements that are actually written. However, if an element is written only once in the loop, then there is no need for it to be privatized and replicated on multiple processors.

The LRPD test can easily be augmented to determine whether a element if written more than once. One simple approach is to use another shadow structure A_{mw}^p to flag the array elements which have been written multiple times. On a write to an element during the marking phase, the corresponding entry of A_{mw}^p is marked if the corresponding entry of A_w is already marked. The global shadow structure A_{mw} is now constructed from the processors' shadow structures A_{mw}^p and A_w. First, the marked elements in the processors' A_{mw}^p are transferred directly, without synchronization, into A_{mw}. If the private structures A_w are merged pairwise into the global shadow structure A_w, then during this process it can be determined if an element is marked in more than one A_w, i.e., if it was written more than once. Note that the pairwise merges can be eliminated if the accesses to the global shadow structure are placed in critical sections.

It is simple to see that the need for the additional structure A_{mw}^p can be eliminated by using three states for the structure A_{np}, e.g., negative values for multiple writes and privatizable, 0 for at most one write and privatizable (initial value), and positive values for not privatizable (once set, never reset).

If the processor–wise version of the LRPD test is used then the elements that are written more than once can be identified in essentially the same manner. Note that for the processor–wise version it is possible that the number of private variables could be reduced even more since only the processors that actually write the elements need copies, and the private structures identify these elements.

4.4   Aggregate LRPD test

The simple, and rather naive way to insert the marking code into a loop is to simply add a markwrite, markread, markredux macro for every occurrence of a write and read access to the shadowed array.

There are however many programs that although irregular in general have a specific 'local' or partial regularity. These types of access patterns can be classified in the following manner:

– Arrays in nested loops accessed by an index of the form (affine_fcn, ptr). The innermost loop index generates points for the affine function, and the outermost loop for the pointer. Generally the first dimension of the array

is relatively small and is often traversed in an innermost loop or, for very small loop bounds, completely unrolled. It usually represents the access to the components of an n-dimensional vector. The bounds of this inner loop never change throughout the program.
– Multi-dimensional access patterns described by complex but statically determined functions, but where one more of the inner dimensions are simple functions.

A commonality in these cases is the fact that they all perform portion-wise contiguous accesses. The length of this regular interval can be either fixed (vectors with n-components, structures) or of variable length (e.g., in sparse matrix solvers). This characteristic can be exploited by marking contiguous intervals rather than every element accessed. Depending on the actual length of the intervals this technique can lead to major performance improvements.

In the case of fixed-size intervals the information is kept implicitly (not stored in the shadow structures themselves) and the analysis phase needs only minor adjustment to the generic LRPD test. When intervals are variable in size within the context of the tested loop, their length will be kept explicitly and the shadow structures adapted accordingly into *shadow interval structures* (e.g., interval trees). The analysis phase will change to a more complex algorithm to reflect the parallel merge of complex data structures. While the asymptotic complexity increases the problem size can decrease dramatically (depending on the average length of intervals).

In our implementation the compile time detection of these types of semi-irregular access patterns is obtained using recently developed array region analysis techniques [17].

It important to mention here the possibility of applying the run-time test somewhat conservatively by always marking whole intervals even if only some of the addresses within the interval have actually been referenced during loop execution. This will reduce overhead and, in the case of fixed size intervals, rarely result in overly conservative loss of parallelism. For example, if a program is using 2 dimensional arrays to simulate structures we can map the *entire* structure into one shadow point. While there is the possibility that such a structure is accessed in more than one iteration at different offsets (and therefore would conservatively fail the test) we have not found such an occurrence.

5 Some Strategy and Implementation Issues

In this section we mention some techniques for optimizing the implementation of the LRPD test. Due to space constraints, complete details are omitted here.

Merging the Phases of LRPD Test. Some of the steps of a speculative execution can be merged, i.e., executed concurrently, thereby increasing fine grain parallelism without increasing the working set. For example, cross-processor last value assignment, merge-out and reduction can be done concurrently after the analysis phase, if necessary. Also, operations such as copy-in of shared values, checkpointing, or initialization of shadow structures can be performed *on–demand*, which decreases the critical path and also the total operations required (e.g., checkpointing only the modified elements of an array).

Choosing Shadow Structures. The choice of shadow structures is dictated by the characteristics of the access pattern and the data structures used (implicitly or explicitly) of the original program. If the access pattern is dense (inferred from the ratio of the number of references to the array size), we choose shadow arrays, and if it is sparse (regular or irregular) we choose specialized shadow structures such as hash-tables. If the application performs portion-wise contiguous regular accesses, then shadow arrays are used for fixed-size intervals, and interval trees are used if the intervals are loop variant. More sophisticated data structures such as linked lists are currently under development.

Schedule reuse, inspector decoupling, two-process solution. If the speculatively executed loop is re-executed during the program with the same data access pattern, then the results of the first LRPD test can be reused (this is an instance of *schedule reuse* [25]). If the defining parameters of an inspector loop are available well before the loop will be executed, then the test code can be executed early, perhaps during a portion of the program that does not have enough (or any) parallelism. A way to ensure that the program's critical path is never increased, is to fork two processes: one processor executes the original sequential loop and the remaining processors proceed on the more aggressive parallel path.

6   Current Implementation of Run-Time Pass in Polaris

Based on the previously presented techniques and the early work described in [22] and [11] we have implemented a first version of run-time parallelization in the Polaris compiler infrastructure [8]. Here is a very general overview of this 'run-time pass'.

Currently, candidate loops for run-time parallelization are marked by a a special directive in the Fortran source code. Alternatively, all loops that Polaris leaves sequential are run-time parallelized. As a statistical model of loop parallelism in irregular applications will be developed we will be able to automatically select the candidates which have the highest possibility of success.

The bulk of the run-time pass is placed after all other static analysis has been completed and just before the post-pass (code generation). It can therefore use all the information uncovered by the existing Polaris analysis.

7   Experimental Results of Run-Time Test in Polaris

We will now present experimental results obtained on several important loops from three applications that Polaris could not parallelize, namely, **TFFT2**, **P3M** and **TRACK**. After inserting run-time test directives before the loop, the codes have been automatically transformed by the compiler and executed in dedicated mode on an SGI Power Challenge with R10K processors at NCSA, University of Illinois. All test variant selections and other optimizations are automatic and no special, application specific compiler switches have been used.

TFFT2, a SPEC code has a fairly simple structure and all access patterns are statically defined, i.e., they are not dynamic or input dependent. Nevertheless, difficulties in its analysis arise due to (1) five levels of subroutine calls within a loop, (2) array reshaping between subroutine calls , (3) exponential relations between inner and outer loop bounds, and (4) array index offsets that depend on outer loop index. We have transformed all important loops of this program for speculative execution.

The speedups shown in Figure 3 reflect the application of the speculative LRPD test to the five most important loops of the program: CFFTZ_DO#1, CFFTZ_DO#2, CFFTZ_DO_#3, RCFFTZ_DO_110, and CRFFTZ_DO_100. While speedups are generally good Loop CFFTZ_DO_#2 performs poorly because we allocated a shadow array four times larger than the actual access region (allocation based on dimension rather than access region) and because the loop itself is relatively small. The overall speedup of the TFFT2 program is 2.2 on 8 processors.

From the **P3M**, NCSA benchmark, a N-body simulation we have considered the triply nested loop in subroutine pp which takes about 50% of the actual sequential execution time. For better load balancing we have coalesced the loop nest and then applied speculative parallelization to several arrays that could not be proven privatizable by Polaris. For the best result we have employed the processor-wise privatization test (with dynamic scheduling) with shadow arrays and early success detection. No checkpointing was necessary because all arrays are privatized and the final reduction is performed on private arrays that are merged after loop execution. Figure 4 shows good speedup and scalability. The obtained speedup is significantly less than the manually parallelized version because the initialization phase, though short, has a cache flushing effect, thus causing the speculative loop to slow down; misses are experienced on all read-only arrays.

TRACK, a PERFECT code that simulates missile tracking, is one of the more interesting programs we have encountered. The tested loop, NLFILT_DO_300, has cross-iteration dependences in some of its instantiations and their frequency is input dependent. For the data set presented in Figure 2 the loop fails the cross-iteration dependence once in its 60 instantiations. However, the processor-wise test 'hides' the dependences and passes every time. The checkpointing overhead is quite important when array sizes are large with respect to the actual work that the loops performs. We believe that an improved on-demand checkpointing scheme will reduce this overhead. Note: The hand-parallel speedup in Figure 2 is in fact an *ideal* speedup because the loop cannot be manually parallelized (because its parallelism is input dependent). The value shown is still correct because the hand-parallel version has been statically scheduled and there are no cross-processor dependences.

8 Conclusion

While the general LRPD algorithm has been extensively presented in [24] and briefly shown here for clarity of the presentation, this paper emphasizes the practical aspects of its application and integration in a compiler. In essence we advocate a very tight connection between static information obtained through classical compiler methods and the run-time system. This resulting optimized code will make use of all available static information and test only the necessary and sufficient conditions for safe parallelization. This interplay between compiler and run-time system results in testing methods that are tailored to a particular application (within limits) and that perform better.

A major source of optimization in speculative parallelization is the use of heuristics for inferring the data structure and access pattern characteristics of the program. Once a hypothesis is made, it can be tested at run-time much faster than a general method. For example, guessing the use of linked list or a structure and testing accordingly can improve performance dramatically.

Reducing run-time overhead may also require the speculative application of known code transformations, e.g., loop distribution, forward substitution. Their validity will be checked simultaneously with the previously presented run-time data dependence test, without incurring any additional overhead.

References

1. Charmm: A program for macromolecular energy, minimization, and dynamics calculations. *J. of Computational Chemistry*, 4(6), 1983.
2. Santosh Abraham. *Private Communication*. Hewlett Packard Laboratories, 1994.
3. Utpal Banerjee. *Loop Parallelization*. Norwell, MA: Kluwer Publishers, 1994.
4. H. Berryman and J. Saltz. A manual for PARTI runtime primitives. Interim Report 90-13, ICASE, 1990.
5. W. Blume, *et. al.* Advanced Program Restructuring for High-Performance Computers with Polaris. *IEEE Computer*, 29(12):78–82, December 1996.
6. W. Blume and R. Eigenmann. Performance Analysis of Parallelizing Compilers on the Perfect Benchmarks^{TM} Programs. *IEEE Trans. on Parallel and Distributed Systems*, 3(6):643–656, November 1992.
7. W. Blume et. al. Effective automatic parallelization with polaris. *Int. J. Paral. Prog.*, May 1995.
8. W. Blume et al. Polaris: The next generation in parallelizing compilers,. In *Proc. of the 7-th Workshop on Languages and Compilers for Parallel Computing*, 1994.
9. K. Cooper et al. The parascope parallel programming environment. *Proc. of IEEE*, pp. 84–89, February 1993.
10. M. Hall et. al. Maximizing multiprocessor performance with the suif compiler. *IEEE Computer*, 29(12):84–89, December 1996.
11. T. Lawrence. Implementation of run time techniques in the polaris fortran restructurer. TR 1501, CSRD, Univ. of Illinois at Urbana-Champaign, July 1995.
12. S. Leung and J. Zahorjan. Improving the performance of runtime parallelization. In *4th PPOPP*, pp. 83–91, May 1993.
13. Z. Li. Array privatization for parallel execution of loops. In *Proceedings of the 19th International Symposium on Computer Architecture*, pp. 313–322, 1992.

14. M. J. Frisch et. al. *Gaussian 94*. Gaussian, Inc., Pittsburgh PA, 1995.
15. D. E. Maydan, S. P. Amarasinghe, and M. S. Lam. Data dependence and data-flow analysis of arrays. In *Proc. 5th Workshop on Programming Languages and Compilers for Parallel Computing*, August 1992.
16. L. Nagel. *SPICE2: A Computer Program to Simulate Semiconductor Circuits.* PhD thesis, University of California, May 1975.
17. Y. Paek, J. Hoeflinger, and D. Padua. Simplification of Array Access Patterns for Compiler Optimizat ions. In *Proc. of the SIGPLAN 1998 Conf. on Programming Language Design and Implementation, Montreal, Canada*, June 1998.
18. C. Polychronopoulos et. al. Parafrase-2: A New Generation Parallelizing Compiler. *Proc. of 1989 Int. Conf. on Parallel Processing, St. Charles, IL*, II:39–48, August 1989.
19. W. Pugh. A practical algorithm for exact array dependence analysis. *Comm. of the ACM*, 35(8):102–114, August 1992.
20. L. Rauchwerger, N. Amato, and D. Padua. A scalable method for run-time loop parallelization. *IJPP*, 26(6):537–576, July 1995.
21. L. Rauchwerger and D. Padua. The privatizing doall test: A run-time technique for doall loop identification and array privatization. In *Proc. of the 1994 International Conf. on Supercomputing*, pp. 33–43, July 1994.
22. L. Rauchwerger. Run–time parallelization: A framework for parallel computation. TR UIUCDCS-R-95-1926, Dept. of Computer Science, University of Illinois, Urbana, IL, September 1995.
23. L. Rauchwerger and D. Padua. Parallelizing WHILE Loops for Multiprocessor Systems. In *Proc. of 9th International Parallel Processing Symposium*, April 1995.
24. L. Rauchwerger and D. Padua. The LRPD Test: Speculative Run-Time Parallelization of Loops with Privatization and Reduction Parallelization. In *Proc. of the SIGPLAN 1995 Conf. on Programming Language Design and Implementation, La Jolla, CA*, pp. 218–232, June 1995.
25. J. Saltz, R. Mirchandaney, and K. Crowley. Run-time parallelization and scheduling of loops. *IEEE Trans. Comput.*, 40(5), May 1991.
26. P. Tu and D. Padua. Array privatization for shared and distributed memory machines. In *Proc. 2nd Workshop on Languages, Compilers, and Run-Time Environments for Distributed Memory Machines*, September 1992.
27. R. Whirley and B. Engelmann. *DYNA3D: A Nonlinear, Explicit, Three-Dimensional Finite Element Code For Solid and Structural Mechanics.* Lawrence Livermore National Laboratory, Nov., 1993.
28. C. Zhu and P. C. Yew. A scheme to enforce data dependence on large multiprocessor systems. *IEEE Trans. Softw. Eng.*, 13(6):726–739, June 1987.

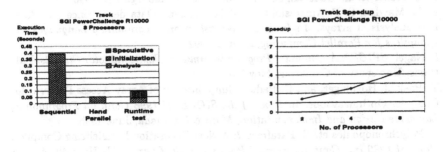

(a)   (b)

Fig. 2. Loop TRACK_NLFITL_DO_300: (a) Timing of test phases, (b) Speedup

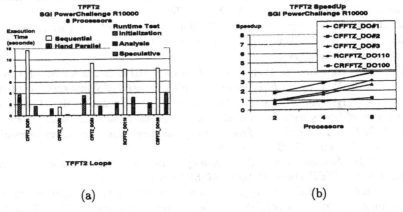

(a)   (b)

Fig. 3. Major Loops in TFFT2: (a) Timing of test phases, (b) Speedup

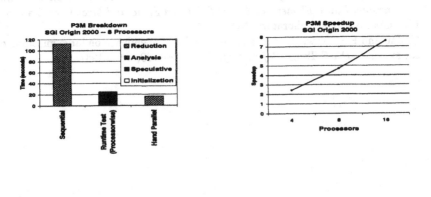

(a)   (b)

Fig. 4. Loop P3M_PP_DO_100: (a) Timing of test phases, (b) Speedup

The Advantages of Instance-Wise Reaching Definition Analyses in Array (S)SA

Jean-François Collard

CNRS & PR*i*SM-University of Versailles,
45 avenue des tats-Unis, 78035 Versailles, France
`Jean-Francois.Collard@prism.uvsq.fr`

Abstract. Several parallelizing or general-purpose compilers have been using intermediate representations based on some form of single-assignment. Extending these representations to arrays has been done in two ways: Array SA, and Array SSA, the extension of the widely-used Static Single Assignment (SSA). We formally define and compare Array SA and Array SSA, and show that (1) They both need instance-wise reaching-definition analyses to (a) be streamlined and (b) allow a parallelizing compiler to choose the most appropriate form, (2) The "same name - same value" property holds for Array SSA in a restricted way only.

1 Introduction

Single assignment is an important concept to reason about, and perhaps modify, imperative programs. Why? Because it allows to exhibit a fundamental property of the algorithm coded in a program: flows of values. In single assignment (SA), each scalar is assigned at most once. I.e., the dynamic, run-time instances of assignments in a program with loops assign to distinct variables. *Static Single Assignment* (SSA) is a slightly different form, defined as follows: There is only one assignment *statement* for each variable. Rosen et al. stress this difference from usual single assignment: In *static* SA, the unique statement assigning to a variable may have several instances writing successive values to the same variable. SSA has been widely used as an *intermediate representation* in compilers, because of its "same name - same value" property (to use an expression coined in [20]). Applications of SSA include constant propagation, global value numbering [21,2], register promotion [22], etc. Moreover, some researchers have been using SSA as a *concrete form in the generated code* because it eliminates all output- and anti-dependences (e.g., cf [7] page 160).

Several methods have been crafted to extend these intermediate representations to arrays. Array SSA, which extends SSA to arrays, has been introduced lately thanks to Knobe and Sarkar [18]. In Array SSA, each *array* is assigned to by one *statement*. On the other hand, Array SA is the extension of SA [15,16]: Each array *element* is written at most once, by a single statement *instance*. In both frameworks, ϕ-functions may be inserted to restore the flow of data when nondeterministic confluence points occur in the control flow.

S. Chatterjee (Ed.): LCPC'98, LNCS 1656, pp. 338–352, 1999.

However, several issues in Array SSA are still unclear.

1. Whereas formal definition of scalar SSA is well known, no formal definition exists for Array SSA. This in turn hampers the comparison with other related frameworks, such as its "sibling" Array SA.
2. Because of the lack of formal definition, it is unclear when and where properties on control flow should be taken into account in Array SSA, and what its relationship with reaching-definition analysis precisely is.
3. When parallelizing programs automatically, single-assignment is interesting not only as an intermediate representation but also as a concrete form for generated code. However, Array SSA does not eliminate all output- and anti-dependences, which in turn hampers from extracting all the parallelism from a program. For this reason, Knobe and Sarkar do not always parallelize using Array SSA in [18] (The reader may check that the loop in Figure 12 is different from the one in Figure 6 in [18]). As explained later, they use a special form of Array SA instead.
4. The *"same name - same value" property of SSA breaks down*, on most cases, for Array SSA. More precisely, two arrays with the same name store the same *set of* values. The "same name - same value" property, therefore, holds for the entire arrays ("Same array name - same array value"). Most programs, however, use arrays on a per-element basis, and the value equality of two elements is often what we are looking for. We show that Array SA solves this issue since it has the "same element name - same element value" property.

Issues 1, 2 and 3 are directly related to parallelizing compilers, and will be the core of this paper. Issue 4, hinting to extensions of classical algorithms based on (scalar) SSA, is addressed shortly in Section 8 and is left for future work. To sum things up, contributions of this paper include:

- Formal definitions of Array SSA and Array SA.
- An algorithm based on reaching definition analysis to translate to Array SA any program with reducible flow graph and with any array subscripts.
- Evidence that Array SSA fails to extract all the parallelism from programs.
- Evidence that Array SSA and Array SA without *instance-wise reaching definition analyses* (IRDA, to be formally defined later) introduce useless ϕ-functions and the associated run-time overhead. Thanks to an instance-wise reaching-definition analysis, ϕ functions need to be introduced only when the control flow is nondeterministic or when array subscripts cannot be analyzed at compile-time.
- Criteria, based on the output of the IRDA, to guide the compiler when choosing among the various expansion schemes. We compare the respective benefits of Array SA and Array SSA for parallelization and give preliminary experimental results on an SGI Origin 2000.

Section 2 motivates this work. Section 3 iteration-wise reaching definition analyses. Section 4 then defines Array SA and Array SSA in a unified way. The algorithm for Array SA conversion appears in Section 5. Related work are discussed in Section 6, before we report some preliminary experimental results.

2 Motivations

In the context of automatic parallelization, it is well known that expansion of data structures allow to eliminate some (if not all) output- and anti-dependences and some (if not all) spurious true dependences. Actually, the only dependences to be preserved are those carrying the flow of values.

However, when arrays come into play, this property is not preserved by the extension of reaching definition analyses and of SSA to arrays:

Consider example std in Figure 1. Its Array SSA in Figure 2 does not expand array a, and therefore fails to extract all possible parallelism. On the contrary, Array SA form in Figure 3 eliminates all anti- and output-dependences. (Array SA uses φ-functions. Intuitively, these functions are similar to ϕ-functions in Array SSA.) This does not prove, however, that parallel programs with Array SA perform better: the overhead due to φ-functions and to the management of bigger arrays may not pay off. This point is discussed in Section 7 and in the conclusion.

On the other hand, we now show that, whichever single-assignment form is chosen, an instance-wise reaching definition analysis is needed to avoid useless ϕ- or φ-functions.

```
      a[..] = ...
      for i = 1 to n
        if( P(i) ) then
          for j = 1 to n
S             a[i+j] = 1+a[i+j-1]
          end for
        end if
      end for
```

Fig. 1. Example std.

```
a[..] = ...
for i = 1 to n
   if( P(i) ) then
      for j = 1 to n
         AS[i+j] = 1+( @AS[ i+j − 1 ]== ⊥
            ?a[i+j-1]
            :AS[i+j-1])
         @AS[ i+j ]= max≪ (@AS[ i+j ],(i,j))
      end for
   end if
end for
```

Fig. 2. Array SSA form for example std. @A (introduced by Knobe and Sarkar) serves to restore the flow of data (which cannot be predicted at compile-time because of P). ⊥ conventionally denotes the undefined value.

```
for i = 1 to n
  if( P(i) ) then
    for j = 1 to n
      Last[i+j]= max≪ (Last[i+j],(i,j))
      A[i,j] = 1 + if j ≥ 2
                    then A[i,j-1]
                    else if i ≥ 2
                         then φ(i,j)
                         else a[i+j-1]
    end for
  end if
end for

int  φ (i,j) {  (j has to be equal to 1)
  return A[Last[i]] }
```

Fig. 3. Array SA form for example std. φ-functions in Array SA are similar to ϕ-functions in Array SSA, see Section 4. In the example, φ picks the last executed instance in $\{\langle S, i', j'\rangle : 1 \le i' < i, 1 \le j' \le n, i' + j' = i + j - 1 = i\}$, where $\langle S, i', j'\rangle$ denotes the instance of S for iteration vector (i', j').

Consider the examples in Figure 4. In both cases, an Array SSA without IRDA has spurious ϕ-nodes or ϕ-nodes with spurious arguments. (The corresponding codes translated to Array SSA appear in Figures 5 and 6.) For program isv, the value stored by S_2 is killed either by S_1 in the next iteration or, in the final iteration, by S_3. Therefore, whatever the value of foo, the only definitions reaching R are those of S_1 and S_3, array A2 is not used by R and does not need to appear as an argument to ϕ in R'.

Now consider program sjs; it has only affine loops and affine subscripts, but it needs an IRDA to see that S_2 cannot be the definition reaching any of its right-hand side expressions or, more precisely, that the definition reaching A3[i+j-1], for given i and j, is:

$$\begin{aligned} &\text{if } j \ge 2 \\ &\text{then } S_1\text{at iteration}(i, j - 1) \\ &\text{else if } i \ge 2 \\ &\quad\quad\text{then } S_1\text{at iteration}(i - 1, j) \\ &\quad\quad\text{else } S_0 \end{aligned} \tag{1}$$

Moreover, no run-time decision has to be taken about the identity of the reaching definition: this identity is exactly given by (1), and, thanks to IRDA, the Array SSA version of sjs is simply the code in Figure 6.(b).

This yields to a very important remark. In the code in Figure 6.(b), some run-time computation does occur to compute the array element that stores the correct value. However, there is only one such array element, i.e., a *single* reaching definition for a given read, and thus no run-time decision has to be made among several possible array elements. In other words, the IRDA has been able to take into account the static behavior of control to eliminate non-reaching definitions.

```
        for i = 1 to n do           S₀  a[1] = 0
S₁      a[i] = ...                       for i = 1 to n
S₂      if(..) a[i+1] = ...                  for j = 1 to n
        end for                     S₁          a[i+j] = ...
S₃  a[n+1] = ..                     S₂          a[i] = ... a[i+j-1]
R   .. = a[foo]                             end for
                                        end for
```

(a) Example isv   (b) Example sjs

Fig. 4. Two example programs isv and sjs.

```
        for i = 1 to n do
S₁      A1[i] = ...
S₂      if(..) A2[i+1] = ...
        end for
S₃  A3[n+1] = ..
R'  A4= φ(A1,A2,A3) (A2 spurious)
R   .. = A4[foo]
```

Fig. 5. Example isv from Figure 4 translated to Array SSA without IRDA, illustrating that spurious arguments may appear in φ-nodes.

3   Reaching Definition Analyses

Classical reaching-definition analyses compute, for every statement R with a reading reference to r, the set of all statements S defining r and such that there is a program path from S to R being free of any modification of r.

Let S be a statement in the program. Because of the surrounding control structures, S may execute several times. Our aim is to distinguish between these successive instances. The set of all the instances of S is denoted by $D(S)$. Therefore, a specific instance of S when its iteration vector is equal to w, $w \in D(S)$, is denoted by $\langle S, w \rangle$.

Let I be the set of all statements, and Ω and $W \subset \Omega$ be, respectively, the set of all instances of all statements and the set of all instances of writes (assignments). Moreover, the execution order on instances is a simple extension of the lexicographic order $\ll$ on iteration vectors [16], so $\ll$ is overloaded to mean both in the rest of this paper.

The goal of Instance-wise reaching definition analyses (IRDAs) is, for every *instance* of a statement R containing a reading reference r, to compute the set of instances of all assignments S, such that there is a program path from an instance of S to the instance of R being free of any modification of r. These analyses are sometimes iterative [14], but more often based on integer linear programming [12,25,4]. A more comprehensive study is presented in [13]. Notice that IRDAs handle any program, but a previous phase of the compiler is supposed to have eliminated gotos [3] (perhaps at the cost of some code duplication

```
a[1] = 0                          a[1] = 0
for i = 1 to n                    for i = 1 to n
  for j = 1 to n                    for j = 1 to n
    A1[i+j] = ...                      A1[i+j] = ...
    A3 = φ(a,A1,A2) (φ spurious)       A2[i] = ... if j ≥ 2
    A2[i] = ... A3[i+j-1]                       then A1[i+j-1]
  end for                                       else if i ≥ 2
end for                                              then A1[i+j-1]
                                                     else a[1]

                                  end for
                                  end for
```

(a) Array SSA without IRDA.   (b) Array SSA with IRDA.

Fig. 6. Array SSA without IRDA (a) and with IRDA (b) for Program sjs. Thanks to IRDA, we know the exact single array element to be read and, therefore, no run-time desambiguation (ϕ) is needed.

---

in the rare cases where the control graph is not reducible [1]). Arrays with *any* subscripts are handled, but not pointers.

The set of (instance-wise) definitions reaching reference r in $\langle R, r \rangle$ is denoted with $\mathbf{RD}(r, \langle R, r \rangle)$. When the reference r is clear from the context, $\mathbf{RD}(r, \langle R, r \rangle)$ is simply written $\mathbf{RD}(\langle R, r \rangle)$. As an example, let us consider an *instance*, parameterized with i and j, of the read reference a[i+j-1] in example std in Figure 1. Then, the definition $\mathbf{RD}(\langle S, i, j \rangle)$ reaching $\langle S, i, j \rangle$ is given by:

$$
\begin{aligned}
&\text{if } j \geq 2 \qquad\qquad\qquad\qquad\qquad\qquad\qquad (2)\\
&\text{then } \{\langle S, i, j-1 \rangle\}\\
&\text{else if } i \geq 2\\
&\qquad \text{then } \{\langle S, i', j' \rangle \, 1 \leq i' < i \wedge 1 \leq j \leq n\\
&\qquad\qquad\qquad\qquad\quad \wedge \, i' + j' = i + j - 1\}\\
&\qquad \text{else } \{\bot\}
\end{aligned}
$$

where $\bot$ conventionally denotes the undefined value.

4   Array SA and Array SSA: Definitions and Comparison

4.1   Definitions of (S)SA Forms

The formal definition of (scalar) SSA is quite simple because, in the scalar case, all run-time instances of a statement write in the same memory cell: the cell indicated by the l-value. Array SSA gets intricate because we need to work element-wise: Two different instances of the same statement do access the same variable (the same array), but they may access two distinct elements of this array.

Let M (resp. M') denote the map from writes to memory locations in the original program (resp., in the transformed program). Expanding (the data structure associated with) two writes w_1 and w_2 is denoted with $M(w_1) = M(w_2) \land M'(w_1) \neq M'(w_2)$: the memory locations written by the two references were equal, but are not the same any longer in the transformed program.

Array SSA form is defined as:

$$\forall S_p \in I, S_q \in I, \; w_p \in D(S_p), w_q \in D(S_q) :$$
$$(S_p \neq S_q) \Rightarrow (M'(\langle S_p, w_p \rangle) \neq M'(\langle S_q, w_q \rangle))$$

The Array SA form is defined as follows:

$$\forall S_p \in I, S_q \in I, w_p \in D(S_p), w_q \in D(S_q) :$$
$$(S_p \neq S_q \; \lor \; w_p \neq w_q) \Rightarrow (M'(\langle S_p, w_p \rangle) \neq M'(\langle S_q, w_q \rangle))$$

For the sake of comparison, we also define Array Privatization and Maximal Static Expansion [5] in the same framework. Array Privatization is defined as:

$$\forall S_p \in I :$$
$$(\forall w_p \in D(S_p), S_q \in I, w_q \in D(S_q), \langle S_p, w_p \rangle \in \mathbf{RD}(\langle S_q, w_q \rangle) \Rightarrow w_q = w_p)$$
$$\Rightarrow (\forall w_p, w'_p \in D(S_p) : M'(\langle S_p, w_p \rangle) \neq M'(\langle S_p, w'_p \rangle))$$

stating that the data structure written by S_p are expanded if all reached uses belong to the same iteration.

A Static Expansion is defined as:

$$\forall \langle S_p, w_p \rangle, \langle S_q, w_q \rangle \in \mathcal{W} :$$
$$(\exists z \in \Omega, \; \langle S_p, w_p \rangle \in \mathbf{RD}(z) \land \langle S_q, w_q \rangle \in \mathbf{RD}(z) \land M(\langle S_p, w_p \rangle) = M(\langle S_q, w_q \rangle))$$
$$\Rightarrow (M'(\langle S_p, w_p \rangle) \neq M'(\langle S_q, w_q \rangle))$$

A static expansion M' is maximal if, for any static expansion M'', $\forall u, v \in \mathcal{W} : M'(u) = M'(v) \implies M''(u) = M''(v)$.

4.2   Construction of Array SSA and Array SA Forms

For expository reasons, we make the following restrictions: The input program has only one array A and only one statement R having one single reference r reading A. These assumptions can be removed easily: programs with several statements, each having possibly several read references to array A, are handled by subscripting ϕ- and φ-functions with the reference identity r. Multiple arrays are handled separately.

Array SSA Let us consider a statement R with iteration vector r reading an array A. Statement R is of the form:

$$\ldots := \ldots \; \mathtt{A[}\, g(r) \,\mathtt{]} \; \ldots$$

Let statements $S_1..S_n$ be the definitions reaching R. Each statement S_p, with $1 \leq p \leq n$, with iteration vector w_p has the form:

$$\mathtt{A[}\, f_p(w_p) \,\mathtt{]} \; := \; \ldots .$$

By definition of reaching definitions, we have:

$$\forall p, 1 \leq p \leq n \quad : \quad \exists w_p, \exists r \text{ s.t. } \langle S_p, w_p \rangle \in \mathbf{RD}(\mathtt{A}[\, g(r)\,], \langle R, r \rangle).$$

Conversion to Array SSA intermediate representation proceeds as follows. Statements $S_1..S_n$ become:

$$\mathtt{A}_p[\, f_p(w_p)\,] \; := \; \ldots$$

for all p, $1 \leq p \leq n$. Arrays $\mathtt{A}_p$ match $\mathtt{A}$ in type, size and dimensions.

To each statement S_p writing in new array $\mathtt{A}_p$, we associate function @$\mathtt{A}_p$ mapping an element $\mathtt{A}_p[\, x\,]$ to its last definition by S_p. That is:

$$@\mathtt{A}_p[\, x\,] = \max_{\ll} \{w_p \; : \; x = f_p(w_p) \tag{3}$$
$$\wedge \; \mathsf{exec}(\langle S_p, w_p \rangle) = \mathbf{true}\},$$

where $\mathsf{exec}(\langle S_p, w_p \rangle)$ denotes that $\langle S_p, w_p \rangle$ actually executes. Obviously, this predicate is not known at compile-time, and this is one reason a reaching definition analysis yields sets. However, (3) defines a single value since @$\mathtt{A}_p[\, x\,]$ is evaluated at run-time and $\mathsf{exec}(\langle S_p, w_p \rangle)$ is then known.

On the other hand, due to non-deterministic branching structure of the control-flow graph, preserving the data flow requires some run-time mechanism. This mechanism is called a ϕ-function (which, admittedly, is not a real function according to the strict mathematical definition). A ϕ-function returns an array consistent with the data flow. ϕ returns an array $\mathtt{A}_0[1..n]$ such that, for all $\mathtt{A}_0[\, x\,]$, $1 \leq x \leq n$, there is an instance $\langle S_k, w_k \rangle$, such that $\mathtt{A}_0[\, x\,] = \mathtt{A}_k[\, x\,]$, and:

$$\langle S_k, w_k \rangle = \max_{\ll} \{\langle S_p, w_p \rangle \; : \; w_p = @\mathtt{A}_p[\, x\,] \tag{4}$$
$$\wedge \; \langle S_p, w_p \rangle \ll \langle R, r \rangle \}$$

(Recall that $\ll$ is overloaded to statement instances.) We see that predicate $\mathsf{exec}(\langle S_p, w_p \rangle)$ does not need to be stored. Only @$\mathtt{A}$ is stored and updated on the fly. The read reference $\mathtt{A}[\, g(r)\,]$ in Statement R is replaced by a reference to the ϕ-function:

$R:$ $\ldots := \ldots \phi(\mathtt{A}_1, .., \mathtt{A}_n)\,[\, g(r)\,] \; \ldots$

Since the same function ϕ may be use at different places, it is more efficient to create a new array and to initialize this array by function ϕ at merge point in the control flow graph. Traditional SSA then replace statement R above with the following two statements:

$R_1:$ $\mathtt{A}_0 \; := \; \phi(\mathtt{A}_1, .., \mathtt{A}_n)$
$R_2:$ $\ldots := \ldots \mathtt{A}_0[\, g(r)\,] \; \ldots$

thus making explicit the array $\mathtt{A}_0$ defined above.

Array SA Array SA considers, for a given R, the same statements $S_1..S_n$. Transformation to Array SA, however, proceeds in a different way.

Each statement $S_p, 1 \leq p \leq n$, becomes:

$$A_p [w_p] := \dots$$

That is, for each S_p, there is a one-to-one correspondence between the elements of the new array A_p and the iteration domain of S_p.

For reasons explained above, some run-time restoration of data flows has to be performed using auxiliary functions. These functions are very similar to ϕ-function, but to stress the difference, we'll use the alternative Greek letter φ. Thus, the right-hand side of R could become:

$$\dots := \varphi (\{A_p[w_p] : \langle S_p, w_p \rangle \in \mathbf{RD}(\langle R, r \rangle)\}) .$$

However, since the argument of φ just depends on R and r, we construct φ with $\langle R, r \rangle$ as the argument.

Formally, the semantics of φ is given by

$$\varphi(\langle R, r \rangle) = A_k [w_k],$$

where:

$$\langle S_k, w_k \rangle = \max_{\ll} \{\langle S_p, w_p \rangle : \langle S_p, w_p \rangle \in \mathbf{RD}(\langle R, r \rangle)$$
$$\wedge f_p(w_p) = g(r)\} \tag{5}$$

I.e., φ returns the array element defined by the last executed reaching definition instance. It is easy to see that ϕ and φ compute the same values: For a given $\langle R, r \rangle$, just take $x = g(r)$ in (4) and inline (3) in (4). φ is computed on the fly too, as explained in the next section.

5   Conversion to Array SA Form

We present here an algorithm to perform conversion into Array SA form. Let us first define $\mathsf{Stmt}(\langle S, w \rangle) = S$ and $\mathsf{Ind}(\langle S, w \rangle) = w$.

1. isAffine = **yes** if all array subscripts are affine, **no** otherwise.
2. For each assignment S (whose iteration vector is w and the left-hand side is $A[f(w)]$):
   (a) Create an array D_S whose shape is (the rectangular hull of) $D(S)$.
   (b) Let w be an index in $D(S)$. The control structures surrounding S, such as conditionals or loops sweeping over w, are left unchanged.
   (c) If there is a read u such that $\mathbf{RD}(u)$ is not a singleton and $\langle S, w \rangle \in \mathbf{RD}(u)$. Then, just after S, insert assignment
      i. Last $[u]$ = max$_\ll$ (Last $[u], \langle S, w \rangle$), if isAffine = **yes**.
      ii. Last $[u, f(w)]$ = max$_\ll$ (Last $[u, f(w)], \langle S, w \rangle$), if isAffine = **no**.
      (Last computes the result of the φ function on the fly.)
   (d) Replace the left-hand side with $D_S [w]$.

3. For each statement S, replace each read reference r to A[$g(r)$] with Convert(r), where:

   – If $\mathbf{RD}(\langle S, w\rangle) = \{u\}$, then Convert(r) = $D_{\text{Stmt}(u)}$ [Ind(u)].
   – If $\mathbf{RD}(\langle S, w\rangle) = \{\bot\}$, then Convert(r) = r (the initial reference expression).
   – If $\mathbf{RD}(\langle S, w\rangle)$ is a non-singleton set, then Convert(r) = $\varphi_r(\langle S, w\rangle)$.
   – If $\mathbf{RD}(\langle S, w\rangle) =$ if p then r_1 else r_2, then
     Convert(r) =if p then Convert(r_1) else Convert(r_2).

4. For each φ_r, output: if isAffine = **yes**:

appropriate_type $\varphi(w)$ {
return $D_{\text{Stmt}(\text{Last}[w])}$ [Ind(Last[w])]}

if isAffine = **no**:

appropriate_type $\varphi(w)$ {
return $D_{\text{Stmt}(\text{Last}[w,g(r)])}$ [Ind(Last[$w, g(r)$])]}

In both cases, output use the initial reference if the value stored in Last is $\bot$.

Let us apply this algorithm to Example std in Figure 1. The instance-wise reaching definitions are given by (2). We first create an array A[1..n,1..n]. The left-hand side is turned into A[i,j], a 2-D array since the iteration domain is two-dimensional. The read reference in the right-hand side is changed according to (2).

Let us now generate the function φ. All instances of $\langle S, i', 1\rangle$, $2 \le i' \le n$ have a non-singleton set of reaching definitions. We thus define an array Last [2..n,1]. If $\langle S, i, j\rangle \in \mathbf{RD}(\langle S, i', 1\rangle)$, then $i' = i + j$. Therefore, we insert the assignment:

$$\text{Last } [\,i + j, 1\,] \;=\; \max(\text{ Last } [\,i + j, 1\,], (i, j)\,)\,.$$

For a read $\langle S, i, 1\rangle$, $2 \le i \le n$, function φ is then:

$$\texttt{integer } \varphi(i, 1) \{ \texttt{ return A[Last}[i, 1]\texttt{]} \; ; \; \}$$

The resulting code appear in Figure 1.(c) (The second dimension of Last has been dropped since it is defined for 1 only).

Notice that our technique does not include any "pseudo-assignments" of φ-functions to intermediary arrays. The benefit is that placing φ-nodes is simple. The drawback is that, when the same φ-function is used several times, our scheme generates several instances of the same function. Notice also that, when iteration domains are not bounded at compile-time, the data structures D_S we allocate are not bounded either; we thus have to allocate them dynamically, or to tile the iteration space.

6 Related Work

Other Work on Array (S)SA Our method to convert programs with arrays
to single-assignment form, adapted from [16,17], uses the result of a reaching
definition analysis on arrays to get the SA intermediate representation. Recent
work by Knobe and Sarkar [18], on the other hand, does not make this separation.
So, is this an important issue?

We believe the answer is yes. Cutting the conversion to (S)SA into two phases
(IRDA *then* transformation of the internal representation) has several benefits:

- A ϕ- or φ-function is needed only when the (compile-time) analysis fails
  to find the unique instance-wise reaching definition. In [18], ϕ-functions are
  inserted even for affine programs, whereas well-known analyses such as [16]
  can easily prove that ϕ-functions are not necessary. This has practical applications for compiler writers: When a useless ϕ-function has been inserted in
  a program, we know what to blame: The reaching definition analysis.
- The program may not be converted to single-assignment, perhaps because ϕ-
  and φ-functions are considered too expensive. A maximal static extension [5]
  may be preferred instead, on top of the reaching definition analysis.

Notice that the work by Knobe and Sarkar is, in our mind, complementary,
since they prefer a robust "safety net" to more elaborate methods. How to use
an instance-wise reaching definition analysis to improve array SSA has been
described in this paper.

Other Work on SSA and Privatization Chow et al. [9] proposed an algorithm
to derive (scalar) SSA without involving iterative dataflow analysis nor bit vectors. Interestingly enough, the same holds for our algorithm for Array SA. The
Array SA we presented takes benefit of structured control-flow, and is therefore
related to the work by Brandis and Mössenböck [8]. However, and on the contrary to what is often stated, the techniques presented here are not limited to
structured counted loops nor to arrays with affine subscripts. Array privatization
by Tu and Padua [23,24] also expose parallelism from programs and is based on
data-flow analysis too. They, too, handle non-affine subscripts and detect private
arrays whose last value assignments can be determined statically (which is related to avoiding spurious ϕ or φ functions). Their data-flow analysis, however,
is not instance-wise. Moreover, their array expansion is limited to privatization,
whereas our framework allows to use a wider set of expansions ranging from
MSE [5] to Array SA.

Extending SSA to other data structures, such as languages with pointers,
has been addressed in [10,20].

7 Preliminary Experimental Results

Preliminary experiments were made for Program std in Figure 1 on an SGI
Origin 2000. Code in Array SA has been generated according to the algorithm

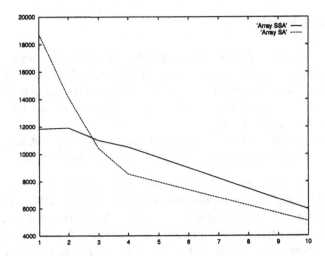

Fig. 7. Performance measures for Example `std` on an Origin 2000. The X-axis displays the number of processors. The Y-axis gives execution times, in milliseconds.

in Section 5. This form of code suits PCA, the automatic parallelizer for C. However, to be sure not to measure possible overhead or improvement due to PCA and not to Array SA, the generated codes were augmented by hand with directives from the `mp` library. Because of the lack of space, the reader is refered to the tech report [11] for details about the generated code.

Execution times appear in Figure 7. The experiment was done with $n = 9600$, from 1 to 10 processors, and the chosen predicate P was $P(i) = odd(i)$. These results are not surprising: with few processors, the parallelism in the Array SA version does not compensate for the overhead due to the management of bigger arrays and to the φ function. On the other hand, the Array SA version scales better. Comparing performances on a more meaningful set of programs is left for future work, so as to analyse which architecture-dependent parameters the choice of expansion should be based upon.

8   Extending Algorithms Based on SSA Form

SSA form has been very successful, as demonstrated by the large number of algorithms based on it. This success is due in part to the ability of SSA to express the semantic equality of expressions. So how can this success carry over to arrays?

An instance-wise reaching definition analysis gives accurate use-def relationships at the array-element- and statement-instance- level. Therefore, element-wise reaching definition analysis directly allows some optimizations, without the need for SA or SSA form. For instance, element-wise dead code elimination is simply given by eliminating the set of operations $\{u : \nexists v, u \in \mathbf{RD}(v)\}$.

The main benefit of instance-wise reaching definition analyses, however, is due to the following observation: If two references have the same single instance-wise definition, then their values are equal[1]. (Note that we don't know what this value is, but the value numbers are the same [20].) Array SA exactly captures the information given by an instance-wise reaching definition analysis (which Array SSA does not) and, therefore, allows to syntactically express value equalities.

On the other hand, it has been shown [19] that the value-flow graph is a representation of semantic equivalence superior to (classical scalar) SSA. It would thus be interesting to try and extend the work of Knoop et al. to programs with arrays.

Extending classical optimization algorithms (detection of common subexpression, redundancy elimination, construction of value flows [6], etc) to arrays, and comparing the respective benefits of Array SA and Array SSA, is definitely a very important future work.

9   Conclusion

We formally defined Array SSA and Array SA in a uniform way, and compared the two frameworks. We have shown that both Array SSA and Array SA require an instance-wise reaching definition analyses on arrays to avoid, when possible, the run-time overhead of restoring data flows. Moreover, we cannot express with Array SSA that two array elements having the same name have the same value. In addition, in the context of automatic parallelization, Array SSA fails to extract all the parallelism from programs.

This last point, however, may not be a drawback, since for some programs extracting all the parallelism implies a lot of ϕ- or φ-functions, with the associated overhead. The question is: "When choose Array SSA for my favorite programs? When choose Array SA? When choose maximal static expansion [5]?". The intuitive answer is: Let the compiler make an instance-wise reaching definition analysis first, because it will be needed anyway. Then, the more (and the larger) the reaching definition sets are, the more costly the ϕ- and φ-functions will probably be. Much more experimental studies are needed to assess this intuition and to allow expansion tuning.

Acknowledgment The author is supported by the CNRS (National Center for Scientific Research) and, in addition, by INRIA (Project A3) and a German-French project Procope. Access to the SGI Origin 2000 was provided by the University Louis Pasteur, Strasbourg. Many thanks to G.-R. Perrin and P. Brua for their help. This work benefited from fruitful discussions with D. Barthou, L. Bougé, A. Cohen, P. Feautrier, J. Knoop, F. Irigoin, V. Lefebvre, and L. Vibert.

---

[1] Therefore, iteration-wise reaching definition analyses allow to detect equal values, in a more general way (because arrays are handled element-wise) and more precise way (because loop iterations are considered separately) than most classical meet-over-paths dataflow analyses.

References

1. A. V. Aho, R. Sethi, and J. D. Ullman. *Compilers: Principles, Techniques and Tools.* Addison-Wesley, Reading, Mass, 1986.
2. B. Alpern, M. N. Wegman, and F. K. Zadeck. Detecting equality of variables in programs. In *ACM Symp. on Principles of Programming Languages (PoPL)*, pages 1–11, January 1988.
3. B. S. Baker. An algorithm for structuring programs. *J. of the ACM*, 24:98–120, 1977.
4. D. Barthou. *Array Dataflow Analysis in Presence of Non-affine Constraints.* PhD thesis, Univ. Versailles, February 1998.
5. D. Barthou, A. Cohen, and J.-F. Collard. Maximal static expansion. In *ACM Symp. on Principles of Programming Languages (PoPL)*, pages 98–106, San Diego, CA, January 1998.
6. R. Bodík and S. Anik. Path-sensitive value-flow analysis. In *ACM Symp. on Principles of Programming Languages (PoPL)*, pages 237–251, San Diego, CA, January 1998.
7. R. Bodík and R. Gupta. Partial dead code elimination using slicing transformations. In *ACM SIGPLAN Conf on Prog. Lang. Design and Implem. (PLDI)*, pages 159–170, Las Vegas, Nevada, January 1997.
8. M. M. Brandis and H. Mssenbck. Single-pass generation of static single-assignment form for structured languages. *ACM Trans. on Prog. Languages and Systems*, 16(6):1684–1698, November 1994.
9. F. Chow, S. Chan, R. Kennedy, S.-M. Liu, R. Lo, and P. Tu. A new algorithm for partial redundancy elimination based on ssa form. In *ACM SIGPLAN Conf on Prog. Lang. Design and Implem. (PLDI)*, pages 273–286, Las Vegas, Nevada, June 1997.
10. F. Chow, S. Chan, S.-M. Liu, R. Lo, and M. Streich. Effective representation of aliases and indirect memory operations in ssa form. In *Int. Conf on Compiler Construction (CC'96)*, pages 253–267, 1996.
11. J.-F. Collard. Array SSA: Why? how? how much? Technical report, PRISM, U. of Versailles, 1998.
12. J.-F. Collard, D. Barthou, and P. Feautrier. Fuzzy array dataflow analysis. In *ACM SIGPLAN Symp. on Principles and Practive of Parallel Prog. (PPoPP)*, pages 92–102, Santa Barbara, CA, July 1995.
13. J.-F. Collard and J. Knoop. A comparative study of reaching definitions analyses. Technical Report 1998/22, PRISM, U. of Versailles, 1998.
14. E. Duesterwald, R. Gupta, and M.-L. Soffa. A practical data flow framework for array reference analysis and its use in optimization. In *ACM SIGPLAN'93 Conf. on Prog. Lang. Design and Implementation*, pages 68–77, June 1993.
15. P. Feautrier. Array expansion. In *ACM Int. Conf. on Supercomputing, St Malo*, pages 429–441, 1988.
16. P. Feautrier. Dataflow analysis of scalar and array references. *Int. Journal of Parallel Programming*, 20(1):23–53, February 1991.
17. M. Griebl and J.-F. Collard. Generation of synchronous code for automatic parallelization of while loops. In S. Haridi, K. Ali, and P. Magnusson, editors, *EURO-PAR '95*, Lecture Notes in Computer Science 966, pages 315–326. Springer-Verlag, 1995.
18. K. Knobe and V. Sarkar. Array SSA form and its use in parallelization. In *ACM Symp. on Principles of Programming Languages (PoPL)*, pages 107–120, San Diego (CA), January 1998.

19. J. Knoop, O. Rüthing, and B. Steffen. Code motion and code placement: Just synonyms? In *Proceedings of the 7th European Symposium on Programming (ESOP'98)*, volume 1381, pages 154–169, Lisbon, Portugal, May 1998.

20. C. Lapkowski and L. J. Hendren. Extended SSA numbering: Introducing SSA properties to languages with multi-level pointers. In K. Koskimies, editor, *Compiler Construction CC'98*, volume 1383 of *LNCS*, pages 128–143, Lisbon, Portugal, March 1998. Springer-Verlag.

21. B. K. Rosen, M. N. Wegman, and F. K. Zadeck. Global value numbers and redundant computations. In *ACM Symp. on Principles of Programming Languages (PoPL)*, pages 12–27, 1988.

22. A.V.S. Sastry and R. D. C. Ju. A new algorithm for scalar register promotion based on SSA form. In *ACM SIGPLAN Conf on Prog. Lang. Design and Implem. (PLDI)*, pages 15–25, Montreal, Canada, June 1998.

23. P. Tu and D. Padua. Automatic array privatization. In *Proc. Sixth Workshop on Languages and Compilers for Parallel Computing*, number 768 in Lecture Notes in Computer Science, pages 500–521, August 1993. Portland, Oregon.

24. P. Tu and D. Padua. Gated SSA-Based demand-driven symbolic analysis for parallelizing compilers. In *ACM Int. Conf. on Supercomputing*, pages 414–423, Barcelona, Spain, July 1995.

25. D. G. Wonnacott. *Constraint-Based Array Dependence Analysis*. PhD thesis, University of Maryland, 1995.

Dependency Analysis of Recursive Data Structures Using Automatic Groups

D. K. Arvind and T. A. Lewis

School of Computer Science, The University of Edinburgh
Mayfield Road , Edinburgh EH9 3JZ, Scotland

Abstract. A framework is described for the static analysis of less regular, pointer-based data structures which have been augmented with explicit structural information. The framework has three distinct parts to it - the specification of structural information, their translation into an internal representation as automatic groups, and the dependency analysis. The application of the method to a case study in fluid flow simulation is described.

1 Motivation

This paper deals with the static analysis of dependencies in complex, pointer-based data structures, which are augmented with explicit structural information. The method of analysis can handle structures which can be represented as an automatic group [1]. The proposed framework, illustrated in Figure 1, can be divided into three distinct parts - the specification of structural information in the data structure, their translation into an internal representation and the analysis of dependencies. This paper is principally concerned with the latter two parts.

The idea of a graph of nodes and pointers being the Cayley graph of a group was introduced in [4]. The nodes represented group elements and the edges/pointers represented the action of one element on another. We have extended this idea to enable programmers to specify the structure within the group; we therefore require a class of groups where patterns of linkages could be expressed. These specifications also need to be manipulated so that equality of group elements (the *word problem*) could be decided. Automatic groups (AG) fit these requirements well. We are not strict about the group structure of these data structures; for example, we do not require every pointer to have a corresponding 'inverse' pointer. The group is used primarily as an underlying representation of linkages within a structure.

The manual creation of such automatic group representations is potentially awkward and prone to error, even for simple linkages. We believe that a more

S. Chatterjee (Ed.): LCPC'98, LNCS 1656, pp. 353–366, 1999.

suitable approach would be to use established 'front-end' description languages to specify the structures and then automatically convert them to an AG representation. In such a framework, expressions denoting dependencies can be automatically converted to produce an equivalent AG with the correct properties. We will demonstrate that this provides a sufficiently general and powerful framework for dependence analysis.

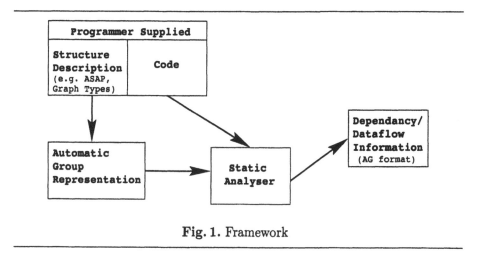

Fig. 1. Framework

2   Definitions

This section provides a brief introduction to Automatic Groups, in the context of understanding the method of analysis. (The reader is directed to [1], for a more detailed exposition of automatic groups.) An automatic group is a structure where each node is named by a string of symbols called a *path name*: it describes the path of pointers from the root of the structure. These symbols are the *generating* directions and correspond to the underlying tree pointers of the data structure. For example, consider a simple binary tree, where the two sub-trees at each node are labelled l and r. The nodes can be described by a string of l and r symbols, indicating the path taken from the root node at the top of the tree.

We may, in addition, have *link* directions. For instance, in a binary tree, we may want to link the nodes in each level of the tree into a doubly-linked list. Then each node will have two link directions - n for the next (eastwards) and p for the previous (westwards) nodes. The nodes can still be uniquely described by strings of l and r symbols. A description exists, for each additional link direction, in the form of a two-variable, finite state automaton (FSA), which specifies the set of nodes which are linked by this direction. The *two-variable* FSA attempts to accept a pair of strings and inspects one symbol from

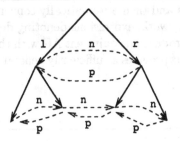

```
Generator l, r;
Link n, p;
{l:  }
{r:  }
{n:
   States 2;     Start 1;     Accept 2;
   Transitions[
            [(l,l)->1;(r,r)->1;(l,r)->2;]        //From state 1
            [(r,l)->2;]                          //From state 2
   ]
}
{p: (n)^}
```

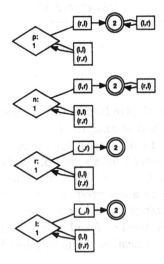

Fig. 2. A binary tree with additional 'next' and 'previous' pointers, with its source code description. The graphical representation of the AG description is shown below. The diamonds are start nodes and are labelled with the direction name e.g. (l). Other states are circles and are labelled with the state number. The boxes hold the pair of symbols for that transition. Double borders indicate an accept state.

each of them at each transition. It can also be viewed as a one-variable FSA, but with the set of symbols extended to pairs of symbols - the set $\{A \times A\}$. There is a subtlety, however, in that we may wish to accept strings of unequal lengths, so the shorter one is padded with the additional '−' symbol (we do not, however, allow the double padded symbol $(-, -)$). This makes the actual set of symbols $((A \cup \{-\}) \times (A \cup \{-\}))\backslash(-, -)$: for example, for our binary tree structure with two generators l and r, the set of symbols will be $\{(l, l), (l, r), (l, -), (r, l), (r, r), (r, -), (-, l), (-, r)\}$.

The description with each link direction, d, is a two-variable finite state automaton, called the multiplier of that link, and denoted M_d. There is also a word acceptor automaton, W, that accepts the path names that correspond to valid parts of the data structure.

Consider the task of producing the multiplier FSA for the n link direction. When moving eastwards from a node with a pathname ending in a l symbol, the last l is changed to a r, to obtain the name of the target node. For a name that ends with a r symbol, $x.r$ say, the target node can be defined in a recursive manner: if the node next to x is known, then a l symbol is appended to it, to produce the final target node. This information can be expressed by stating that the next direction links nodes of the format $x.l.r^p$ to nodes given by $x.r.l^p$, where p is any integer (or zero), and x is any path name. This description can be converted to a FSA along with others for the l, r and p directions. The generator FSAs (l and r) are simpler to understand, since they accept pairs of paths that are indentical up to the the point where the first terminates and the second has an additional symbol (either an l or r). These generator descriptions do not need to be described by the programmer.

Automatic groups are a good choice of description, since they can be readily manipulated by using existing regular language theory. In particular, we can produce FSAs for words of directions from the individual FSAs for each direction. We can perform basic logical operations (AND, OR, NOT, $\forall$ and $\exists$) with the FSAs, and by extension, on the sets of nodes that they represent. Other constructions from Automatic Group theory can be used; for instance, given FSAs for individual directions, one may wish to combine the multiplier FSAs into a multiplier for words of directions that appear in the code, e.g. to find those parts of the structure which are accessed by the word, a.b, when given the appropriate FSAs for a and b. This can be naturally performed in the AG approach - given two FSAs, $\mathcal{F}_1$ and $\mathcal{F}_2$, their composition is denoted by $\mathcal{F}_1.\mathcal{F}_2$ - see [1] for the details of its construction. The inverse FSA, denoted by $\mathcal{F}^{-1}$, is built by swapping the pair of letters in each transition of $\mathcal{F}$.

3   The Programming Model

The automatic groups representation will be illustrated by applying it to an example involving a pair of simple recursive functions (Fig. 3) over a particular structure. Fig.2 illustrates a binary tree, each node of which has a left and right subtree, and in addition the nodes in each level are connected as a doubly-linked list, with 'next' and 'previous' pointers. The description declares each direction as either a generator or a link, followed by the definitions of each. The l and r directions are generators, and so do not require an explicit FSA description. The n direction is given as a FSA with two states - *start* and *acceptance*, followed by a list of transitions from each state. The p direction is defined as the inverse of the n direction, with the syntax '(n)$^\wedge$'. Fig. 2 gives the structure of the AG representation which is built automatically from this description.

The implementation analyses a fairly restricted programming language that manipulates these structures. The code accesses one global data structure. Data elements are accessed via pathnames, which are used as a replacement for conventional pointers. The code consists of a number of possibly mutually recursive functions. These functions take one parameter w (a pathname), and return void. It is assumed that the first (main) function is called with the root path name. Each function may make possibly recursive calls to other functions using the syntax 'FuncName(w.g)' where g is any generator.

It should be clarified at this stage that the analysis assumes that the code does not recurse in a direction that is not a generator; otherwise the construction of the map from control words to pathnames ceases to be representable by a regular language. This is a restriction of the method. One can still produce some information, however, by *unrolling* the recursion, and analysing within the function. Another related problem is when a function calls another one with the parameter w, *e.g.* 'FuncName(w)'. This can be handled provided that it does not occur within a mutually recursive set of functions, *i.e.* the function can only be called a finite number of times.

The basic statements of the code are *reads* and *writes* to different parts of the structure. A typical statement would be of the form 'Struct(w.a) = Struct(w.b)' where w is a variable and a and b are words of directions. This statement denotes the copying of an item of data from w.b to w.a, within the structure Struct.

Another observation about these static control programs is that if run-time dependencies are disallowed in the code, then one may as well run the program and trace its dataflow directly. Therefore, variable sized structures are allowed, delimited by NULL pointers. Conditional statements of the form 'if (pathname == NULL) then ...' or 'if (pathname != NULL) then ...' are also allowed. This however restricts the type of analysis that can be done. For example, any dataflow analysis has the potential to become inaccurate when one cannot decide statically if a statement is executed or not. One can still find sets of nodes accessed by a particular statement and deduce coarser-grained parallelism.

4   The Analysis

The recursive functions given in Fig. 3 operate over a binary tree structure. The function Traverse moves down the left-hand side of the tree, copying values to adjacent nodes. It then calls Update on the right-hand sub-tree, which updates each node in that whole tree by copying from a nearby node.

```
Traverse(w) {
        if (w ==NULL) return;
    A: Update(w.l);
    B: Struct(w) = Struct(w.p);
    C: Traverse(w.r);
}
Update(w) {
        if (w ==NULL) return;
    D: Struct(w) = Struct(w.p.l.n);
    E: Update(w.l);
    F: Update(w.r);
}
```

Fig. 3. Sample recursive functions. The A, B, C, D, E, F are statement labels and not part of the original code.

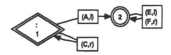

Fig. 4. FSA that maps control words to values of w.

The descriptions for single directions can be used to build composite directions. For instance, the 'read' in statement D requires the composite *read word*: $p.l.n$. Each runtime statement can be labelled by a *control word*, a word from the set given by the regular expression $(A|C|E|F)^*.(B|D)$. Each time the function is called recursively from statement A, a l direction is appended to the parameter w, and similarly for statement C, a r is appended. The same is true for statements E and F. This information can be captured in a FSA that converts a given control word into the value of the parameter, w, for that function call. This FSA is given in Fig. 4.

One can append, for each *read* statement, the statement symbol and the read word for that statement. This produces a FSA $\mathcal{F}_r$ that maps from any control word to all the nodes of the structure that can be read by that statement. Similarly, we can produce a FSA that maps from control words to nodes which are written, denoted by $\mathcal{F}_w$. These read and write FSAs are given in Fig. 5.

We can now describe all the nodes which are read from and written to, by any statement. By combining the FSAs for read and write, a new FSA is created that links statements when one writes a value that the other reads, *i.e* the statements *conflict*. The conflict FSA $\mathcal{F}_{conf}$ is given by $\mathcal{F}_r.(\mathcal{F}_w)^{-1}$. The FSA in Fig.5 is the conflict FSA which has also been combined (ANDed) with an FSA $\mathcal{F}_{causal}(X, Y)$ which accepts control words X, Y, only if Y occurs before X in the sequential running of the code. This removes any false sources that actually occur after the statement.

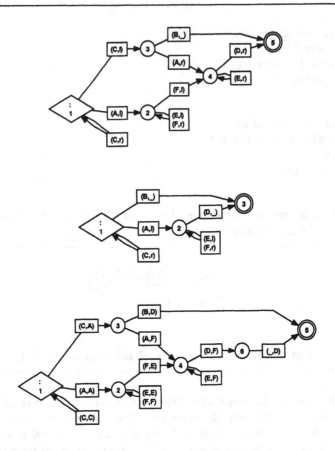

Fig. 5. Read (Top) Write (Middle) and Conflict (Bottom) FSAs.

The final step would be to extract dataflow information. If the statement X depends on Y and Z, and Z occurs after Y, then one can remove Y as a potential source. Removing all such sources, will provide the dataflow information. One can prune these false sources by splitting the conflict FSA up into components - one for each read statement, and then removing multiple sources. Consider the FSA for the potential sources for statement B in Fig.6, in particular, the (C, A) and (C, C) transitions from the start node. For a given sink with a C statement, the (C, C) transition will always produce a potential source later than the (C, A) transition, and will therefore overwrite the value. The earlier (C, A) transition can now be removed. In general, in any state with transitions, (X, Y) and (X, Y'), with $Y < Y'$, (X, Y) can be removed. We can then minimise the resulting FSA, by possibly removing unreachable states. The resulting dataflow when this is performed on the entire FSA FSA is shown in Fig.6.

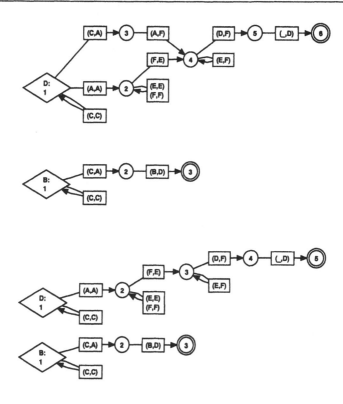

Fig. 6. (Above) Potential sources. (Below) Pruned to produce dataflow sources.

5   Conditional Statements

One cannot always predict at compile time whether a statement will actually be executed. This means that full dataflow information cannot be produced, since we cannot prune the FSA as mentioned in the last section. This section describes how one could incorporate some knowledge into our model.

We assume that the function begins with a *terminating condition*, a statement of the form, if T(w) then return, where T(w) is a predicate on the function parameter w. We restrict T to be a regular language with an associated FSA which we will denote by $\mathcal{T}$. Note that we do not require the programmer to supply these FSAs explicitly, and for certain simple classes of predicate (such as the ones that select paths of length greater than a fixed constant) we could generate them automatically. We do restrict these predicates, and require the property: $T(x) \Rightarrow T(x.y)\forall y$. This is needed so that we can determine whether a particular control word is executed without having to examine all shorter words for the one that has terminated the recursion.

In addition, each statement or function call C can have a *conditional guard* P_C, which determines if the statement is executed. For a statement C, this is equivalent to the code fragment 'if (P(w)) then C;'.

Our aim is to combine this conditional information into one FSA, $\mathcal{E}$, that decides whether the statement corresponding to a given control word is executed. Firstly, we need to convert the FSAs that operate on path names to ones that operate on control words. Then we merge the conditionals that guard the recursive calls into the termination FSA. Finally, we create the FSA, $\mathcal{E}$, by combining the termination and conditional guards of the read/write statements.

5.1   Merging call guards and the termination FSA

Our recursive function has a set of recursive call statements labelled RC_i of the form:

$$\text{if} \quad (RP_i(w)) \quad \text{then} \quad F(w.g_i)$$

We convert the $\mathcal{RP}_i(w)$ to $\mathcal{RP}'_i(W)$ that operate on control words, by applying S and then applying NOT, so that it accepts the words that halt the recursion. We now append $S(g_i)$ to this FSA to produce $\mathcal{RP}''_i(W)$, so that $\mathcal{RP}''_i$ accepts $W.S(g_i)$ if, and only if, $\mathcal{RP}''_i$ accepts W. The set of $\mathcal{RP}''_i$ now acts as additional termination conditions, and can be ANDed together with T.

5.2   Completion of the executing FSA

To determine whether a statement corresponding to a particular control word does get executed at runtime, we need to ensure that the actual recursive call is executed, and the conditional guard for that particular statement is true. For each statement labelled C_i, we convert the conditional guard P_i to P'_i using S. We append the label C_i to both P_i and T and then AND the pair. Finally, the executing FSA $\mathcal{E}$ is produced by ORing all these FSAs together.

6   Front-End Description Languages

The paper so far has described the analysis of the dependences in the framework of AG descriptions of structural information. In this section we will briefly touch on a couple of description languages - ASAP [2] and Graph Type [3] - which can be integrated in the framework. This will be achieved by augmenting the AG description with extra information, *i.e.* two further FSAs are defined - $\mathcal{F}_a$ and $\mathcal{F}_d$ to hold the aliasing and disjointedness information, respectively.

6.1   Integrating ASAP description

Linkage information in a structure is expressed in ASAP via a series of axioms. The axioms come in two basic types, which describe when the nodes are *equal* or *unequal*. The *equal* axioms describe aliasing information, the *unequal* ones - disjointedness.

There are three kinds of axioms:

$$1) \quad \forall p \quad p.RE1 \neq p.RE2$$
$$2) \quad \forall p \neq q \quad p.RE1 \neq q.RE2$$
$$3) \quad \forall p \quad p.RE1 = p.RE2$$

where p, q are any path names and $RE1, RE2$ are regular expressions over A^*.

Given a regular expression, $RE1$, it is trivial to convert it into a two variable 'appended' FSA that accepts $(p.RE1, p)$ for all p, and is denoted by Ap_{RE1}. In addition, using $\mathcal{F}_{\neq}$ (the FSA that accepts a pair of paths if they are not equal) we can produce expressions that convert axioms of each type to FSAs that accept the equivalent pairs of words.

$$1) \quad \mathrm{Ap}_{RE1}.(\mathrm{Ap}_{RE2}^{-1})$$
$$2) \quad \mathrm{Ap}_{RE1}.\mathcal{F}_{\neq}.(\mathrm{Ap}_{RE2}^{-1})$$
$$3) \quad \mathrm{Ap}_{RE1}.(\mathrm{Ap}_{RE2}^{-1})$$

We then build $\mathcal{F}_d$ by ORing together all the FSAs produced from axioms 1 and 2, and $\mathcal{F}_a$ by ORing the ones from axiom 3.

6.2   Graph Types

One cannot automatically convert from a Graph Types description to the AG one. We have instead focussed on extending our system to handle structures that can be described using this formalism. We need to introduce the idea of different types at each node. As it stands, the structures that have been considered are *homogeneous*, with the allowed number and type of pointers at each node being identical. We extend the descriptions to allow each pointer direction to be of a different type, and introduce the concept of type variant. Each of these is encoded into the path name, so that queries on type variants can be expressed. Consider the case of a binary tree with linked leaf nodes in C language.

```
union TreeNode {              struct Internal {
      Internal* intern;              int ival;
      Leaf*    leaf;                 TreeNode *left;
};                                   TreeNode *right;
struct Leaf {                      };
      int lval;
      TreeNode *next;
};
```

The path name for a node in the structure is then a word over the alphabet {*intern, leaf, left, right, next*}. Of course, some path names are invalid, *intern* must always be followed by either a *left* or *right*. Such properties can be readily expressed using FSAs and incorporated into the $\mathcal{W}$ part of the AG description, and derived automatically from the above style of code. In addition, we will need the programmer to supply descriptions of where the directions- {*left, right, next*}- actually point.

7 Complexity

Since finite state machines are the fundamental object being manipulated using this method, the complexity of our analysis relate to the complexity of the underlying FSA operations.

If n_g is the number of generating directions, n_l the number of lines in the code, then the size of the alphabet of each two-variable FSA is $(n_g + n_l + 1)^2 - 1$. For a reasonably-sized program, the number of lines in the code will dominate, making the complexity $O(n_l^2)$. The memory requirements for such a FSA with n_s states will be $O(n_s . n_l^2)$; storing the information sparsely will decrease this. However, the number of states can potentially increase dramatically: given two FSAs with n and m states, the FSA built by the operations AND, OR can have up to $n \times m$ states. When combining two FSAs to form a composite, the combined FSA can have up to $2^{n \times m}$ states. There is a potential to produce very large FSAs, with large memory requirements, and computation time.

In the case of FSAs obtained automatically from ASAP axioms, as described previously, the resulting FSAs can be significantly large. For example, the descriptions for a sparse matrix produce a disjointness FSA of approximately 150 states. Obviously, such large FSAs would pose a problem and impact on the analysis that could be carried out on real programs.

In practice, however, the number of states often remains manageable. For example, using the worst case estimates described previously, the combined word, $p.l$, required for analysis of the *read* in statement D in Fig. 3, could be expected to require 16 states. In fact it requires only 3. The reason is that these simple FSAs are sparse, there being only a couple of transitions from each state.

8 A Case Study: Fluid Flow Simulation

We have applied this description and analysis to the Fast Multipole Method Vortex algorithm which is used in fluid flow simulations.

A tree is data structure of choice, with l and r pointers at each node. We also have additional pointers, n and p, that link nodes at each level into a linked list, and a *spiral* pointer s, that joins the nodes in a spiral from bottom left of the tree to the root.

The nodes carry four items of data *psi*, *phi*, *theta* and *gamma*, all of which are multipole expansions of the energy potential due to various sets of vortices. The code shown in Fig. 7 has been simplified in two important ways:

- The summations represent more complex manipulations of these expansions.
- The code is a 'one-dimensional' version of the algorithm. In the two dimensional version there are four subtrees at each node, and the nodes in each level are linked into a grid, rather than a list.

Our method can handle all the complexities of the two dimensional version. We present the simplified version because it allows the essentials of the algorithm to be highlighted.

```
FindLeftmostLeaf(w) {
   if (w.l.l == NULL) PhaseTwo(w);
   FindLeftLeaf(w.l);
}
PhaseOne(w) {
   Struct(w.phi) = Struct(w.l.phi) + Struct(w.r.phi);
   if (w.m == NULL)
   PhaseOne(w.s);
}
PhaseTwo(w) {
    if (w == NULL) return;
  A: Struct(w.psi) = Struct(w.m.psi)
     + Struct(w.m.p.l.phi) + Struct(w.m.p.r.phi)
     + Struct(w.m.n.l.phi) + Struct(w.m.n.r.phi);
  B: if (w.l == NULL) Struct(w.theta) = Struct(w.psi)
                    + Struct(w.p.gamma) + Struct(w.n.gamma);
  C: PhaseTwo(w.l);
  D: PhaseTwo(w.r);
}
```

Fig. 7. Algorithm for fast multipole method

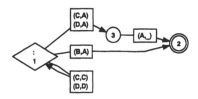

Fig. 8. FSA for dependency of the second phase of fluid simulation algorithm

If we analyse the function PhaseTwo, we get the FSA in Fig. 8, for the possible sources of statements. This shows that the *reads* that occur in statement B are produced by the *write* in statement A. Also the *read* in statement A uses the value produced in the previous function call.

We need a different approach to producing information for the function 'PhaseOne' since it recurses in a non-generator direction. We have 'unrolled' three of the function calls into the body of the loop, and have looked for dependencies within one call, rather than between all calls of the function. The resulting dependancy FSA is given in Fig. 9. The main observation is that there are only dependencies between calls that access the first three levels of the tree. In all the other levels the four statements are independant and can therefore be executed simultaneously.

```
PhaseOne(w) {
    A: Struct(w.phi) = Struct(w.l.phi) + Struct(w.r.phi);
       if (w.m == NULL) return;
    B: Struct(w.s.phi) = Struct(w.s.l.phi) + Struct(w.s.r.phi);
       if (w.s.m == NULL) return;
    C: Struct(w.s.s.phi) = Struct(w.s.sl.phi) + Struct(w.s.s.r.phi);
       if (w.s.s.m == NULL) return;
    D: Struct(w.s.s.s.phi) = Struct(w.s.s.s.l.phi) + Struct(w.s.s.s.r.phi);
       if (w.s.s.s.m == NULL) return;
       PhaseOne(w.s.s.s.s);
}
```

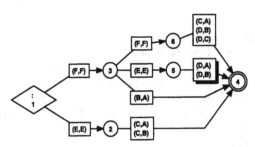

Fig. 9. PhaseOne of the algorithm, unrolled and the FSA for dependencies within one function call of this function.

9 Conclusion

This paper has described a framework based on an underlying Automatic Group representation for analysing the dependencies in complex, pointer-based data structures which are less regular. The approach assumes that the programmer supplies explicit structural information. We have given a flavour as to how description languages such as Graph Types and ASAP can be integrated into this framework.

We have demonstrated that this analysis can be carried out on a class of programs which consist of many possibly recursive functions of a single parameter. We are presently working towards extending this method to handle functions that recurse with multiple parameters, and to allow recursion in non-generator directions.

Our framework allows us to combine ASAP descriptions, with stricter AG descriptions. Thus we allow a broader range of information to be supplied by the programmer. In return, the dependency information given can be more detailed, with a finer grained resolution of dependencies between individual run-time statements.

Acknowledgements

Tim Lewis was supported by a postgraduate studentship from Engineering and Physical Sciences Research Council (EPSRC). We would like to thank Christian Lengauer for useful discussions - the visits to Passau were funded under British Council/ARC grant entitled *Formal Parallelisation of Program Specifications*.

References

1. David B. A. Epstein, J. W. Cannon, D. E. Holt, S. V. F. Levy, M. S. Paterson, and W. P. Thurston. *Word Processing in Groups*. Jones and Bartlett, 1992.
2. Joseph Hummel, Laurie J Hendren, and Alexandru Nicolau. A language for conveying the aliasing properties of dynamic, pointer-based data structures. In *Proceedings of the 8th International Parallel Processing Symposium*, April 1994.
3. Nils Klarlund and Michael I. Schwartzbach. Graph types. In *Proceedings of the ACM 20th Symposium on Principles of Programming Languages*, pages 196–205, January 1993.
4. Olivier Michel. Design and implementation of 81/2, a declarative data-parallel language. Technical Report 1012, Laboratoire de Recherche en Informatique, December 1995.

The I+ Test

Weng-Long Chang and Chih-Ping Chu

Department of Computer Science and Information Engineering, National Cheng
Kung University,
Tainan, Taiwan 701, R.O.C.
{changwl,chuch}@csie.ncku.edu.tw

Abstract. The I test is an efficient and precise data dependence method
to ascertain whether integer solutions exist for one-dimensional arrays
with constant bounds. For one-dimensional arrays with variable limits,
the I test assumes that there may exist integer solutions. In this paper, we
propose the I+ test—an extended version of the I test. The I+ test can
be applied towards determining whether integer solutions exist for one-
dimensional arrays with either variable or constant limits, improving the
applicable range of the I test. Experiments with benchmark cited from
EISPACK, LINPACK, Parallel loops, Livermore loops and Vector loops
showed that among 1189 pairs of one-dimensional arrays tested, 183 had
their data dependence analysis amended by the I+ test. That is, the
I+ test increases the success rate of the I test by approximately 15.4
percent. Comparing with the Power test and the Omega test, the I+ test
has higher accuracy than the Power test and shares the same accuracy
with the Omega test when determining integer solutions for these 1189
pairs of one-dimensional arrays, but has much better efficiency over them.

1 Introduction

One-dimensional array references with linear subscripts occur quite frequently
in real programs in light of an empirical study reported in [9]. That study shows
that one-, two- and three-dimensional array references account for 56 percent,
36 percent and 8 percent among array references examined, respectively. That
study also shows that about 60 percent of them have linear subscripts. The
major findings from these data are (1) one-dimensional array references are very
common, and (2) linear subscripts in one-dimensional array references emerge
quite frequently. Therefore, an efficient and precise method for testing linear
subscripts in one-dimensional array references is very important.

The question of whether one-dimensional array references with linear subscripts may be paralleled/vectored depends upon the resolution of those one-
dimensional array aliases. The resolution of one-dimensional array aliases is to
ascertain whether two references to the same one-dimensional array within a
general loop may refer to the same element of that one-dimensional array. This
problem in general case can be reduced to that of checking whether a linear equation with n unknown variables has an integer solution, which satisfies the bounds

S. Chatterjee (Ed.): LCPC'98, LNCS 1656, pp. 367–381, 1999.
© Springer-Verlag Berlin Heidelberg 1999

for each variable in the linear equation. It is assumed that a linear equation is written as

$$a_1 X_1 + a_2 X_2 + \cdots + a_{n-1} X_{n-1} + a_n X_n = a_0 \qquad (1)$$

where each a_j is an integer for $0 \le j \le n$. It is postulated that the limits to each variable in (1) are represented as

$$P_{r,0} + \sum_{s=1}^{r-1} P_{r,s} X_s \le X_r \le Q_{r,0} + \sum_{s=1}^{r-1} Q_{r,s} X_s \qquad (2)$$

where $P_{r,0}, Q_{r,0}, P_{r,s}$ and $Q_{r,s}$ are integers for $1 \le r \le n$.

If each of $P_{r,s}$ and $Q_{r,s}$ is zero in the constraints of (2), then (2) will be reduced to

$$P_{r,0} \le X_r \le Q_{r,0}, \text{where } 1 \le r \le n \qquad (3)$$

That is, the bounds for each variable X_r are constants.

There are several well-known data dependence analysis algorithms in practice. The *Banerjee inequalities* determines whether real-valued solutions exist for a linear equation (1) under the bounds of (3). The *Banerjee algorithm* ascertains whether there exist real-valued solutions for a linear equation 1 under the limits of (2) [1]. The I test is a combination of the Banerjee inequalities and the GCD test [6]. It figures out integer solutions for a linear equation (1) with the constraints of (3). More precise results are achieved by judging the consistency of a linear system of equalities and inequalities. The Power test is a combination of Fourier-Motzkin variable elimination with an extension of Euclid's GCD algorithm [13,12]. The Omega test combines new methods for eliminating equality constraints with an extension of Fourier-Motzkin variable elimination to integer programming [8]. Though both of the methods gain more accurate outcomes, they have exponential worst-case time complexity. For one-dimensional array references with nonlinear subscripts, the range test is used to test them [3].

The I test is extended to check whether a linear equation (1) together with the bounds of (1) has a relevant integer solution. A theoretical analysis explains that we take advantage of the trapezoidal shape of the convex sets derived from a linear equation under variable limits in a data dependence testing. An algorithm called the I+ test has been implemented and several measurements have also been performed (see Section 4).

The rest of this paper is proffered as follows. In Section 2, the problem of data dependence is presented. The GCD, Banerjee and I tests are briefly reviewed. In Section 3, the theoretical aspects and the time complexity for the I+ test are proposed. Experimental results showing the advantages to the I+ test are given in Section 4. Finally, brief conclusions are given in Section 5.

2   Background

In this section, we mainly introduce the concept of data dependence and cite some dependence testing methods.

2.1   Data Dependence

It is assumed that S_1 and S_2 are two statements within a general loop. The general loop is presumed to contain d common loops. Statements S_1 and S_2 are postulated to be embedded in $d+p$ loops and $d+q$ loops, respectively. An array A is supposed to appear simultaneously within statements S_1 and S_2. If a statement S_2 uses the array A defined first by another statement S_1, then S_2 is true-dependent on S_1. If a statement S_2 defines the array A used first by another statement S_1, then S_2 is anti-dependent on S_1. If a statement S_2 redefines the array A defined first by another statement S_1, then S_2 is output-dependent on S_1.

2.2   The GCD, Banerjee and I Tests

The GCD test is based upon a theorem of elementary number theory, which says that a linear equation (1) has an integer solution if and only if $gcd(a_1, \cdots, a_n)$ is a divisor of a_0. The Banerjee test (the Banerjee inequalities and the Banerjee algorithm) computes the minimum and maximum values for the expression on the left-hand side of (1) beneath constant limits or variable constraints. By the Intermediate Value Theorem, the Banerjee test infers that (1) has a real-valued solution if and only if the minimum value is less than or equal to a_0 and the maximum value is greater than or equal to a_0.

A linear equation (1) with the bounds of (3) will be said to be integer solvable if the linear equation (1) has an integer solution to satisfy the bounds of (3) for each variable in the linear equation (1). The I test deals with a linear equation by first transforming it to an interval equation. Definitions 1 and 2 simply describe the definitions of integer intervals and an interval equation [6].

Definition 1. *Let* $[\alpha_1, \alpha_2]$ *represent the integer intervals from* α_1 *to* α_2, *i.e., the set of all integers between* α_1 *and* α_2.

Definition 2. *Let* $a_1, \cdots, a_{n-1}, a_n, L$ *and* U *be integers. A linear equation*

$$a_1 X_1 + a_2 X_2 + \cdots + a_{n-1} X_{n-1} + a_n X_n = [L, U] \qquad (4)$$

which is referred to as an interval equation, will be used to denote the set of ordinary equations consisting of:

$$a_1 X_1 + a_2 X_2 + \cdots + a_{n-1} X_{n-1} + a_n X_n = L$$
$$a_1 X_1 + a_2 X_2 + \cdots + a_{n-1} X_{n-1} + a_n X_n = L+1$$
$$\vdots$$
$$a_1 X_1 + a_2 X_2 + \cdots + a_{n-1} X_{n-1} + a_n X_n = U$$

An interval equation (4) will be said to be integer solvable if one of the equations in the set, which it defines, is integer solvable. If $L > U$ in an interval equation (4), then there are no integer solutions for the interval equation (4). If the expression on the left-hand side of an interval equation (4) is reduced to zero items, then the interval equation (4) will be said to be integer solvable if and only if $U \geq 0 \geq L$. It is easy to see that a linear equation (1) is integer solvable if and only if an interval equation

$$a_1 X_1 + a_2 X_2 + \cdots + a_{n-1} X_{n-1} + a_n X_n = [a_0, a_0]$$

is integer solvable. The following definition and theorems, cited from [6], in detail state how the I test determines integer solutions of an interval equation under constant bounds.

Definition 3. *Let a variable* a_i *be an integer* $1 \leq i \leq n$. *The positive part* a_i^+ *and the negative part* a_i^- *of an integer* a_i *are defined by* $a_i^+ i = MAX\{a_i, 0\}$ *and* $a_i^- = MAX\{-a_i, 0\}$.

Theorem 1. *Given a linear equation (1) subject to the constraints of (3). Let* $a_1, a_2, \cdots, a_n, L$ *and* U *be integers. For each* r, $1 \leq r \leq n-1$, *let each of* $P_{r,0}$ *and* $Q_{r,0}$ *be either an integer or an unknown limit, where* $P_{r,0} \leq Q_{r,0}$ *if both* $P_{r,0}$ *and* $Q_{r,0}$ *are integers. Let* $P_{n,0}$ *and* $Q_{n,0}$ *be integers, where* $P_{n,0} \leq Q_{n,0}$. *If* $|a_n| \leq U - L + 1$, *then the interval equation*

$$a_1 X_1 + a_2 X_2 + \cdots + a_{n-1} X_{n-1} + a_n X_n = [L, U]$$

is $(P_{r,0} \leq X_r \leq Q_{r,0}; 1 \leq r \leq n)$*-integer solvable if and only if the interval equation*

$$a_1 X_1 + a_2 X_2 + \cdots + a_{n-1} X_{n-1} = [L - a_n^+ Q_{n,0} + a_n^- P_{n,0}, U - a_n^+ P_{n,0} + a_n^- Q_{n,0}]$$

is $(P_{r,0} \leq X_r \leq Q_{r,0}; 1 \leq r \leq n)$*-integer solvable.*

Proof. Refer to [6].

Theorem 2. *Given a linear equation (1) subject to the constraints of (3). Let* $a_1, a_2, \cdots, a_n, L$ *and* U *be integers. For each* r, $1 \leq r \leq n$, *let each of* $P_{r,0}$ *and* $Q_{r,0}$ *be either an integer or an unknown limit, where* $P_{r,0} \leq Q_{r,0}$ *if both* $P_{r,0}$ *and* $Q_{r,0}$ *are integers. Let* $g = gcd(a_1, \cdots, a_{n-1}, a_n)$. *The interval equation*

$$a_1 X_1 + a_2 X_2 + \cdots + a_{n-1} X_{n-1} + a_n X_n = [L, U]$$

is $(P_{r,0} \leq X_r \leq Q_{r,0}; 1 \leq r \leq n)$*-integer solvable if and only if the interval equation*

$$(a_1/g)X_1 + (a_2/g)X_2 + \cdots + (a_{n-1}/g)X_{n-1} + (a_n/g)X_n = [\lceil L/g \rceil, \lfloor U/g \rfloor]$$

is $(P_{r,0} \leq X_r \leq Q_{r,0}; 1 \leq r \leq n)$*-integer solvable.*

Proof. Refer to [6].

3   The Extension of the I Test

A data dependence problem is considered where one-dimensional array references are linear in terms of index variables. Bounds for one-dimensional array references are presumed to be variable. (Note: constant limits are a special case of variable constraints, so variable bounds actually contain constant limits.) Given the data dependence problem as specified, the I+ test examines a linear equation (1) with the constraints of (2) and deduces whether the system has integer solutions. In this section, the theoretical aspects and the time complexity for the I+ test are provided.

3.1   Interval-Equation Transformation

A linear equation (1) under the constraints of (2) will be said to be integer solvable if the linear equation (2) has an integer solution to satisfy the constraints of (2) for each variable in the linear equation (1). In the following, Definition 4 states the definition of the set of all integer intervals. Definition 5 describes the definition of the set of all interval equations. Definition 6 introduces the definition of the set for the length of the right-hand side interval on every interval equation in the set of all interval equations.

Definition 4. *Suppose that the constraints of X_r for $1 \leq r \leq n$ are equal to the bounds of (2). Let $[b_0 + \sum_{r=1}^{n} b_r X_r, c_0 + \sum_{r=1}^{n} c_r X_r]$ represent the set of all the integer intervals for every X_r to satisfy the bounds of (2), where b_0, c_0, b_r and c_r for $1 \leq r \leq n$ are integers. The set of all the integer intervals Φ is denoted to be equal to*

$$\{[b_0 + \sum_{r=1}^{n} b_r y_r, c_0 + \sum_{r=1}^{n} c_r y_r] | P_{r,0} + \sum_{s=1}^{r-1} P_{r,s} y_s \leq y_r \leq Q_{r,0} + \sum_{s=1}^{r-1} Q_{r,s} y_s$$
$$\text{for } 1 \leq r \leq n\}.$$

Definition 5. *Suppose that the constraints of X_r for $1 \leq r \leq n$ are equal to the bounds of (2). Let $L = b_0 + \sum_{r=1}^{n} b_r X_r$ and $U = c_0 + \sum_{r=1}^{n} c_r X_r]$, where $L \leq U$, and b_0, c_0, b_r and c_r for $1 \leq r \leq n$ are integers. The following equation*

$$a_1 X_1 + a_2 X_2 + \cdots + a_{n-1} X_{n-1} + a_n X_n = [L, U] \tag{5}$$

will be used to denote the set of all the interval equations inferred from every variable X_r under the bounds of (2). The set of all the interval equations Ψ is denoted to be equal to

$$\{a_1 y_1 + \cdots + a_n y_n = [b_0 + \sum_{r=1}^{n} b_r y_r, c_0 + \sum_{r=1}^{n} c_r y_r] |$$
$$P_{r,0} + \sum_{s=1}^{r-1} P_{r,s} y_s \leq y_r \leq Q_{r,0} + \sum_{s=1}^{r-1} Q_{r,s} y_s \text{ for } 1 \leq r \leq n\}.$$

If $b_0 + \sum_{r=1}^{n} b_r y_r \leq \sum_{r=1}^{n} a_r y_r \leq c_0 + \sum_{r=1}^{n} c_r y_r$ in the variable interval equation (5), then the corresponding constant interval equation exists. Otherwise, the corresponding one does not exist.

Definition 6. *Suppose that the constraints of X_r for $1 \leq r \leq n$ are equal to the bounds of (2). Let K represent the left-hand-side expression $\sum_{r=1}^{n} a_r X_r$, $L = b_0 + \sum_{r=1}^{n} b_r X_r$ and $U = c_0 + \sum_{r=1}^{n} c_r X_r$ in the equation (5), where $L \leq K \leq U$, and b_0, c_0, a_r, b_r and c_r for $1 \leq r \leq n$ are integers. The set Ω for the length of the right-hand side interval on every interval equation in the equation (5) is denoted to be equal to*

$$\{1 + (c_0 - b_0) + \sum_{r=1}^{n}(c_r - b_r)y_r | P_{r,0} + \sum_{s=1}^{r-1} P_{r,s}y_s \leq y_r \leq Q_{r,0} + \sum_{s=1}^{r-1} Q_{r,s}y_s$$
$$\text{for } 1 \leq r \leq n\}.$$

If each of b_r and c_r is zero for $1 \leq r \leq n$, then the set of all the interval equations Ψ only contains one interval equation. The set Ψ will be said to be integer solvable if one of the interval equations in the set Ψ is integer solvable. If $b_0 + \sum_{r=1}^{n} b_r y_r > c_0 + \sum_{r=1}^{n} c_r y_r$ in every interval equation in the set Ψ, then there are no integer solutions for the set Ψ. If $\sum_{r=1}^{n} a_r y_r < b_0 + \sum_{r=1}^{n} b_r y_r$ or $\sum_{r=1}^{n} a_r y_r > c_0 + \sum_{r=1}^{n} c_r y_r$ in every interval equation in the set Ψ, then there are no integer solutions for the set Ψ. If all of the integers in between the intervals of the interval equations in the set Ψ are not divisible by the greatest common divisor of the left-hand-side coefficients of 5, then the variable interval equation will be integer unsolvable. If the expression of the left-hand side for one of the interval equations in the set Ψ is zero items, in the processing of testing, then the set Ψ will be said to be integer solvable if and only if $b_0 + \sum_{r=1}^{n} b_r y_r \leq 0 \leq c_0 + \sum_{r=1}^{n} c_r y_r$. It is easy to see that a linear equation (1) is integer solvable if and only if the only interval equation in the set

$$\{a_1 X_1 + a_2 X_2 + \cdots + a_{n-1} X_{n-1} + a_n X_n = [a_0, a_0]\}$$

is integer solvable.

The I+ test involves a number of interval equation-to-interval equation transformations. In the following, Lemmas 1 and 2 are extensions of Theorem 1. Lemmas 1 and 2 will be employed towards doing interval equation-to-interval equation transformations.

Lemma 1. *Suppose that the constraints of X_r for $1 \leq r \leq n$ are equal to the bounds of (2). Let $L = b_0 + \sum_{r=1}^{n} b_r X_r$ and $U = c_0 + \sum_{r=1}^{n} c_r X_r$, where $L \leq U$, and b_0, c_0, b_r and c_r for $1 \leq r \leq n$ are integers. If $a_k > 0, 0 \leq b_k \leq a_k, 0 \leq c_k \leq a_k$, and the value for a_k is less than or equal to the length of the right-hand side interval on one of the interval equations in the equation (5), where $1 \leq k \leq n$, then the equation (5) is*

$$(P_{r,0} + \sum_{s=1}^{r-1} P_{r,s}X_s \leq X_r \leq Q_{r,0} + \sum_{s=1}^{r-1} Q_{r,s}X_s \text{ for } 1 \leq r \leq n) \text{ -integer}$$
$$\text{solvable}$$

if and only if the equation

$$a_1 X_1 + \cdots + a_{k-1} X_{k-1} + a_{k+1} X_{k+1} + \cdots + a_n X_n =$$
$$[b_0 + \sum_{r=1}^{n} b_r X_r + (b_k - a_k)(Q_{k,0} + \sum_{r=1}^{k-1} Q_{k,s}X_s),$$

for $r \neq k$ *is*
$$c_0 + \sum_{r=1}^{n} c_r X_r + (c_k - a_k)(P_{k,0} + \sum_{r=1}^{k-1} P_{k,s} X_s)]$$
$(P_{r,0} + \sum_{s=1}^{r-1} P_{r,s} X_s \leq X_r \leq Q_{r,0} + \sum_{s=1}^{r-1} Q_{r,s} X_s$ *where* $1 \leq r \leq n$ *and* $r \neq k$)-
integer solvable.

Lemma 2. *Suppose that the constraints of* X_r *for* $1 \leq r \leq n$ *are equal to the bounds of (2). Let* $L = b_0 + \sum_{r=1}^{n} b_r X_r$ *and* $U = c_0 + \sum_{r=1}^{n} c_r X_r$, *where* $L \leq U$, *and* b_0, c_0, b_r *and* c_r *for* $1 \leq r \leq n$ *are integers. If* $a_k < 0$, $a_k \leq b_k \leq 0$, $a_k \leq c_k \leq 0$, *and the negative value for* a_k *is less than or equal to the length of the right-hand side interval on one of the interval equations in the equation (5), where* $1 \leq k \leq n$, *then the equation (5) is*

$(P_{r,0} + \sum_{s=1}^{r-1} P_{r,s} X_s \leq X_r \leq Q_{r,0} + \sum_{s=1}^{r-1} Q_{r,s} X_s; 1 \leq r \leq n)$-*integer solvable*

if and only if the equation

$$a_1 X_1 + \cdots + a_{k-1} X_{k-1} + a_{k+1} X_{k+1} + \cdots + a_n X_n =$$
$[b_0 + \sum_{r=1}^{n} b_r X_r + (b_k - a_k)(P_{k,0} + \sum_{r=1}^{k-1} P_{k,s} X_s),$
for $r \neq k$ *is*
$$c_0 + \sum_{r=1}^{n} c_r X_r + (c_k - a_k)(Q_{k,0} + \sum_{r=1}^{k-1} Q_{k,s} X_s)]$$
$(P_{r,0} + \sum_{s=1}^{r-1} P_{r,s} X_s \leq X_r \leq Q_{r,0} + \sum_{s=1}^{r-1} Q_{r,s} X_s$ *where* $1 \leq r \leq n$ *and* $r \neq k$)-
integer solvable.

The set of all the interval equations Ψ at least contains one interval equation in light of Definition 5. The set Ω for the length of the right-hand side interval on every interval equation in the set Ψ at least consists of one element according to Definitions 5 and 6. If the set Ω only includes one element, then the only element is equal to $c_0 - b_0 + 1$ due to Definition 6. Otherwise, every element in the set Ω is equal to $1 + (c_0 - b_0) + \sum_{r=1}^{n}(c_r - b_r) y_r$ according to Definition 6. Lemmas 1 and 2 can be used to determine integer solutions of the equation (5) if there is the coefficient a_k for one item in the equation (5) with a small enough value to justify the movement of the item to the right. If $a_k > 0$, $0 \leq b_k \leq a_k$, $0 \leq c_k \leq a_k$, and the value for a_k is less than or equal to one of the elements in the set Ω in light of the assumption of Lemma 1, then the value is actually equivalent to the small enough value to justify the movement of the item to the right. If $a_k < 0$, $a_k \leq b_k \leq 0$, $a_k \leq c_k \leq 0$, and the negative value for a_k is less than or equal to one of the elements in the set Ω in light of the assumption of Lemma 2, then the negative value is actually equivalent to the small enough value to justify the movement of the item to the right. On the other hand, Lemmas 1 and 2 are inapplicable towards ascertaining integer solutions of the equation (5) if the absolute values of the coefficients for all the items in the equation (5) are greater than the maximum element in the set Ω. The Banerjee algorithm can be employed to determine the maximum element in the set Ω.

The I+ test generates three possible results when it is used to determine integer solutions of the equation (5) with the bounds of (2). The first generated result of "yes" means that the equation (5) has integer solutions, and the second generated result of "no" means that there are no integer solutions for the equation (5). The third generated value of "maybe", on the other hand, shows that the equation (5) has a solution which satisfies the limits on all the variables which the I+ test has managed to move to the right-hand side of the equation (5), and might still have a solution which satisfies the limits on the rest of the variables.

The I+ test produces a result of "maybe" because there are no longer any coefficients with small enough values to justify their movement to the right. In the case, it is prudent to complete the "step-by-step *Banerjee algorithm*" anyway, i.e., to complete the computation of the Banerjee bounds, L_b and U_b, and to test for $[L_b, U_b] \cap [L, U] = \emptyset$, where $[L, U]$ is the right-hand side of the equation (5) after Lemmas 1 and 2 have been applied as many times as possible. This is to imply that the I+ test is always at least as efficient and accurate as the Banerjee algorithm.

The I+ test can be viewed as involving the term-by-term computation of the Banerjee bounds. That is, the Banerjee-bound-computation components to the I+ test cost at most the cost of a *single* Banerjee algorithm. If the I+ test arrives at a definitive result before all terms have been moved to the right-hand side of the equation (5), then the Banerjee-bound-computation components for the I+ test cost even less.

We now use the following example to explain the enhanced power of the I+ test over the I test, when it is applied to deal with a data dependence problem for a linear equation with variable bounds.

Consider the equation

$$X_1 - X_2 + X_4 = 0 \tag{6}$$

subject to the bounds

$$2 \leq X_1 \leq 100, \; 2 \leq X_2 \leq 100, \; 1 \leq X_3 \leq -1 + X_1, \text{ and } 1 \leq X_4 \leq -1 + X_2.$$

The equation (6) are rewritten as the interval equation

$$X_1 - X_2 + X_4 = [0, 0] \tag{7}$$

If Theorem 1 is used to resolve the problem, then the term $-X_2$ in the interval equation (7) is moved to the right-hand side of (7) to gain the new interval equation

$$X_1 + X_4 = [2, 100] \tag{8}$$

Now the length of the right-hand side interval has been increased to 99, so Theorem 1 is again employed to move the term X_1 in the interval equation (8) to the right-hand side of (8) to acquire the new interval equation

$$X_4 = [-98, 98] \tag{9}$$

Now the length of the right-hand side interval has been increased to 197. Theorem 1 is inapplicable to deal with the interval equation (9) because the constraints for X_4 are variable bounds. Therefore, the I test assumes that there exist integer solutions.

If I+ test is used to resolve the same problem, then according to Definition 5 the set of all the interval equations Ψ is equal to

$$\{X_1 - X_2 + X_4 = [0,0]| \text{ every varaible } X_r \text{ satisfies its bounds for } 1 \leq r \leq 4\}.$$

The set Ω for the length of the right-hand side interval on every interval equation in the set Ω is $\{1\}$. Therefore, the maximum element in the set Ω is one. It is obvious from Definition 5 that the set Ψ is integer solvable if the only interval equation in the set Ψ is integer solvable. The coefficient for X_4 satisfies the assumption of Lemma 1: (1) $1 > 0$, (2) $1 \geq 0 \geq 0$, (3) $1 \geq 0 \geq 0$ and (4) the value of the coefficient is equal to one. Lemma 1 is applied towards moving the term X_4 to the right-hand side of the only interval equation in the set Ψ. The new set Ψ_1 in light of Lemma 1 and Definition 5 is

$$\{X_1 - X_2 = [1 - X_2, -1]| \text{ every varaible } X_r \text{ satisfies its bounds for } 1 \leq r \leq 2\}.$$

Now the set Ω_1 for the length of the right-hand side interval on every interval equation in the set Ψ_1 is equal to $\{X_2 - 1|2 \leq X_2 \leq 100\}$. The maximum element computed by the Banerjee algorithm in the set Ω_1 is 99. When the maximum element is 99, the value for X_2 is equal to 100. Because $X_2 = 100$ and $2 \leq X_1 \leq 100$, so $1 - X_2 \leq X_1 - X_2 \leq -1$ hold. Therefore, there exists a constant interval equation in the set Ψ_1 satisfying the given limitations. The coefficient for X_2 satisfies the assumption of Lemma 2: (1) $-1 < 0$, (2) $0 \geq -1 \geq -1$, (3) $0 \geq 0 \geq -1$, and (4) the negative value of the coefficient is less than 99. Lemma 2 is employed toward moving the term $-X_2$ to the right. The new set Ψ_2 is

$$\{X_1 = [1, 99]|2 \leq X_1 \leq 100\}.$$

Now the set Ω_2 for the length of the right-hand side interval on every interval equation in the set Ψ_2 is equal to $\{99\}$. Meanwhile, there exists a X_1 such that $1 \leq X_1 \leq 99$ hold. Therefore, the maximum element in the set Ω_2 is 99. The coefficient for X_1 satisfies the assumption of Lemma 1: (1) $1 > 0$, (2) $1 \geq 0 \geq 0$, (3) $1 \geq 0 \geq 0$ and (4) the value of the coefficient is less than 99. Lemma 1 is again used to move the term X_1 to the right. The new set Ψ_3 is

$$\{0 = [-99, 97]\}.$$

The expression of the left-hand side on the only interval equation in the set Ψ_3 is reduced to zero items. The only interval equation in the set Ψ_3 is integer solvable because $-99 \leq 0 \leq 97$ is true. Hence, the I+ test concludes that there are integer solutions.

3.2   Interval-Equation Transformation Using the GCD Test

It is obvious from Lemmas 1 and 2 that one variable in the equation (5) can be moved to the right if the coefficient of the variable has a small enough value to justify the movement of the variable to the right. If all coefficients for variables in the equation (5) have no sufficiently small values to justify the movements of variables to the right, then Lemmas 1 and 2 can not be applied to result in the immediate movement of a variable to the right. In the following, Lemma 3 is an extension of Theorem 2. While every variable in the equation (5) can not be moved to the right, Lemma 3 describes the new transformation using the GCD test which always enables one or more additional variables to be moved.

Lemma 3. *Suppose that the constraints of X_r for $1 \leq r \leq n$ are equal to the bounds of (2). Let $L = b_0 + \sum_{r=1}^{n} b_r X_r$ and $U = c_0 + \sum_{r=1}^{n} c_r X_r$, where $L \leq U$ and $b_0, c_0, a_r, b_r,$ and c_r for $1 \leq r \leq n$ are integers. Let $g = gcd(a_1, \cdots, a_{n-1}, a_n)$. The equation (5) is*

$(P_{r,0} + \sum_{s=1}^{r-1} P_{r,s} X_s \leq X_r \leq Q_{r,0} + \sum_{s=1}^{r-1} Q_{r,s} X_s; 1 \leq r \leq n)$ - *integer solvable*

if and only if the equation
$(a_1/g)X_1 + (a_2/g)X_2 + \cdots + (a_{n-1}/g)X_{n-1} + (a_n/g)X_n = [\lceil L/g \rceil, \lfloor U/g \rfloor]$
is $(P_{r,0} + \sum_{s=1}^{r-1} P_{r,s} X_s \leq X_r \leq Q_{r,0} + \sum_{s=1}^{r-1} Q_{r,s} X_s; 1 \leq r \leq n)$ - integer solvable.

Lemma 3 guarantees to always perform at least as well as (and sometimes better than) a combination of the GCD test and the Banerjee algorithm at no more than their cost (and sometimes at a lower cost). In the worst case, the I+ test consists of n GCD tests, where n is the number of variables in the equation (5). In actual practice, it requires frequently no more than one.

We now use the following example to explain the enhanced power of Lemma 3 over Lemmas 1 and 2.

Consider the equation

$$2X_2 - 2X_3 = 0$$

subject to the bounds

$$1 \leq X_1 \leq 100, 1 \leq X_2 \leq 100, 1 + X_1 \leq X_3 \leq 100 + X_1, \text{ and}$$
$$1 + X_2 \leq X_4 \leq 100 + X_2.$$

If the I+ test is applied towards resolving the problem, then the set of all the interval equations Ψ according to Definition 5 is

$\{2X_2 - 2X_3 = [0, 0] | \text{every variable } X_r \text{ satisfies its bounds for } 1 \leq r \leq 4 \}$.

It is obvious from Definition 5 that the set Ψ is integer solvable if the only interval equation in the set Ψ is integer solvable. The set Ω for the length of the right-hand side interval on the only interval equation in the set Ψ is $\{1\}$. The value of the coefficient for X_2 is greater than one, and the negative value of the coefficient for X_3 is greater than one. Therefore, Lemmas 1 and 2 are inapplicable to treat the only interval equation because there are no sufficiently small coefficients. However, if we employ Lemma 3, then we gain the new set Ψ_1

$\{X_2 - X_3 = [0, 0] | \text{every variable } X_r \text{ satisfies its bounds for } 1 \leq r \leq 4 \}$.

The set Ω_1 for the length of the right-hand side interval on every interval equation in the set Ψ_1 is $\{1\}$. The coefficient for X_3 satisfies the assumption of Lemma 2: (1) $-1 < 0$, (2) $0 \geq 0 \geq -1$, (3) $0 \geq 0 \geq -1$, and (4) the negative value of the coefficient is equal to one. Lemma 2 is applied to move the term $-X_3$ in the only interval equation in the set Ψ_1 to the right. The new set Ψ_2 is

$$\{X_2 = [1 + X_1, 100 + X_1] | 1 \leq X_1 \leq 100, \text{ and } 1 \leq X_2 \leq 100\}.$$

Now the set Ω_2 for the length of the right-hand side interval on every interval equation in the set Ψ_2 is equal to $\{100\}$ and there exists a X_2 such that $1 + X_1 \leq X_2 \leq 100 + X_1$ hold. The coefficient for X_2 satisfies the assumption of Lemma 1: (1) $1 > 0$, (2) $1 \geq 0 \geq 0$, (3) $1 \geq 0 \geq 0$, and (4) the value of the coefficient is less than 100. Lemma 1 is employed to move the term X_2 to the right. The new set Ψ_3 is

$$\{0 = [-99 + X_1, 99 + X_1] | 1 \leq X_1 \leq 100\}.$$

According to Definition 5, the set Ψ_3 is equal to $\{0 = [-98, 199]\}$. The expression of the left-hand side on the only interval equation in the set Ψ_3 is reduced to zero items. The only interval equation in the set Ψ_3 is integer solvable because $-98 \leq 0 \leq 199$ is true. Therefore, the I+ test concludes that there are integer solutions.

3.3   Time Complexity

The main phases to the I+ test for figuring out integer solutions of the equation (5) are: (1) finding a small enough coefficient to justify the movement of a term to the right-hand side of the equation (5), (2) changing the expression of the right-hand side on the equation (5) due to the movement of a term to the right and (3) using the GCD test to reduce coefficients of each variable in the equation (5). A small enough coefficient is easily found according to Lemmas 1 and 2. It is obvious that the worst-case time complexity to searching such a coefficient is $O(n^2 + yn)$ in light of Lemmas 1 and 2, where n is the number of variables in the equation (5) and y is a constant. The number of looking for all small enough coefficients in the equation (5) is at most n times because the number of terms moved in the equation (5) is at most n terms. Thus, the worst-case time complexity to finding all small enough coefficients in the equation (5) is at once concluded to be $O(n^3 + n^2 y)$.

The expression of the right-hand side on the equation (5) is changed according to Lemmas 1 and 2 because an item on the left-hand side of the equation (5) is moved to the right. The cost of changing the expression of the right-hand side on the equation (5) according to Lemmas 1 and 2 is actually equivalent to a *single* term computation of the *Banerjee algorithm*. The worst-case time complexity to a single term computation of the Banerjee algorithm is $O(n)$. Thus, the worst-case time complexity to the I+ test to modifying the expression of the right-hand side on the equation (5) is at once deduced to be $O(n)$ due to the movement of a term to the right. The number to modifying the expression of the right-hand side on the equation (5) is at most n times because the number of terms moved in the equation (5) is at most n terms. Therefore, the worst-case time complexity for the I+ test for changing all the expressions of the right-hand side on the equation (5) is right away concluded to be $O(n^2)$. If all coefficients in the equation (5) have no absolute values of 1, then Lemma 3 employs the GCD test to reduce all coefficients to obtain a small enough coefficient to justify the movement of a term to the right. In the worst cases, the I+ test contains n GCD tests. That study [9] shows that a large percentage of all coefficients have absolute values of 1 in one-dimensional array references with linear subscripts in real programs. Therefore, the GCD test is not always applied to reduce all coefficients in the equations inferred from one-dimensional array references with linear subscripts in real programs because all coefficients in the equations have at least an absolute value of 1. The worst-case time complexity to the I+ test to testing those one-dimensional array references with linear subscripts in real programs is immediately derived to be $O(n^3 + yn^2 + n^2)$. The worst-case time complexity of the I test is $O(n^2y + ny)$ [6]. The I+ test slightly decreases the efficiency of the I test because the number of variables, n, in the equation tested is generally very small.

4   Experimental Results

We tested the effect of the I+ test through performing experiments on Personal Computer Intel 80486 to the codes cited from five numerical packages EISPACK, LINPACK, Parallel loops, Livermore loops and Vector loops [10,2,5,7,4]. The codes include about 37000 lines of statements involving 205 subroutines and 1189 pairs of one-dimensional array references. The I test detected that there were *definite* (*yes* or *no*) results for 788 pairs of one-dimensional array references with constant bounds. The I+ test is only applied to those one-dimensional arrays with linear subscripts under variable constraints, and it found that there were 183 pairs with *definite* results. Therefore, there were 971 *definite* results obtained based on interval testing approach.

The improvement rate of the I+ test can be affected by two factors. First, the frequency of one-dimensional array references with linear subscripts subject to variable limits. Second, the "success rate" of the I+ test, by which we mean how often the I+ test detects a case where there is a definite result. Let b be the number of the one-dimensional arrays found in our experiments, and let c be the number that is detected to have definite results from the one-dimensional arrays with linear subscripts subject to variable limits. Thus the success rate is denoted to be equal to c/b. In our experiments, 1189 pairs of one-dimensional array references were found, and 183 of them were found to have definite results. So the improvement rate of the I+ test over the I test in our experiments was about 15.4 percent.

In our experiment the Power test and Omega test were also tested to resolve those 1189 pairs of one-dimensional array references. The Power test concluded that there were 971 *tentative* results. This indicates the Power test is not as accurate as the I+ test. In terms of testing performance, let us compare the

	Speed-up	Total number of subroutines involved
K_P/K_I	8.0 – 10.0	21
	11.0 – 12.0	145
K_P/K_E	7.0 – 10.0	5
	14.0 – 21.0	34

Table 1. The speed-up of the I test and the I+ test when compared with the Power test

execution efficiency for these test approaches as follows. Suppose that k_I, k_E, and k_P are the execution time to treat data dependence problem of a one-dimensional array for the I test, the I+ test, and the Power test, subsequently. Table1 shows the speedups the I test and the I+ test over the Power test for those 971 pairs of array references with results. It is very clear the I test and the I+ test are much superior to the Power test in terms of testing efficiency.

	Speed-up	Total number of subroutines involved
K_O/K_I	3.5 – 10.0	154
	16.0 – 17.0	12
K_O/K_E	3.5 – 13.0	36
	19.0 – 27.0	3

Table 2. The speed-up of the I test and the I+ test when compared with the Omega test

The Omega test, based on its computing principles, were obviously to give the same accurate results as the I test and the I+ test when it was used to handle dependence testing of one-dimensional array references under either constant bounds or variable bounds. As for the testing efficiency, Table2 shows the comparison of testing efficiency with the I test and the I+ test, where k_O represent the execution time to treat data dependence problem of a one-dimensional array for the Omega test.

5   Conclusions

The I+ test proposed in this paper extends the dependence testing range of one-dimensional array references to linear subscripts with variable bounds, enhancing significantly data dependence analysis capability of the I test. The I+ test defines some conditions under which dependence equations of linear subscripts with variable bounds can be continuously tested if integer solutions exist. In short, the I+ test is exactly equivalent to a version of the I test which combines the GCD test and the Banerjee algorithm, because the Banerjee algorithm can deduce integer bounds to a linear expression of which the variables are with variable constraints [1].

The Power test is a combination of Fourier-Motzkin variable elimination with an extension of Euclid's GCD algorithm [13,12]. The Omega test combines new methods for eliminating equality constraints with an extension of Fourier-Motzkin variable elimination to integer programming [8]. The two tests have currently the highest precision and the widest applicable range in the field of data dependence testing. However, the cost of the two tests is very expensive because the worst-case of Fourier-Motzkin variable elimination is exponential in the number of free variables [13,12,8]. Triolet [11] found that using Fourier-Motzkin variable elimination for dependence testing takes from 22 to 28 times longer than the Banerjee inequalities. According to our experiments, the efficiency and the precision of the I+ test are much better than those of the Power test. Whereas, the I+ test shares with the Omega test the same accuracy but is with much better efficiency.

The I+ test extends the applicable range of the I test and, according to the time complexity analysis, only slightly decreases the efficiency of the I test. Therefore, the I+ test seems to be a practical scheme to analyze data dependence for one-dimensional arrays with linear references.

References

1. U. Banerjee. *Dependence Analysis for Supercomputing*. Kluwer Academic Publishers, Norwell, MA, 1988.
2. W. Blume and R. Eigenmann. Performance analysis of parallelizing compilers on the perfect benchmark $S^{©}$ programs. *IEEE Transactions on Parallel and Distributed Systems*, 3(6):643–656, 1992.
3. W. Blume and R. Eigenmann. The range test: a dependence test for symbolic, non-linear expressions. In *IEEE Supercomputing*, pages 528–537, Washington, D.C., 1994.
4. D. Callahan, J. Dongarra, and D. Levine. Test suite for vectorizing compilers. Technical report, Argonne National Laboratory, Apr. 1991.
5. R. Dongar. Test suite for parallel compilers. Technical report, Dec. 1991.
6. X. Kong, D. Klappholz, and K. Psarris. The i test. *IEEE Transactions on Parallel and Distributed Systems*, 2(3):342–349, 1991.
7. J. Levesque and J. Williamson. *A Guidebook to Fortran on Supercomputing*. Academic Press, New York, NY, 1989.
8. W. Pugh. A practical algorithm for exact array dependence analysis. *Communication of the ACM*, 35(8):102–114, 1992.
9. Z. Shen, Z. Li, and P.-C. Yew. An empirical study of Fortran programs for parallelizing compilers. *IEEE Transactions on Parallel and Distributed Systems*, 1(3):356–364, 1992.
10. B. Smith et al. *Matrix Eigensystem Routines-Eispack Guidge*. Springer, 1976.

11. R. Triolet, F. Irigoin, and P. Feautrier. Direct parallelization of call statements. In *Proceedings of SIGPLAN Symposium on Compiler Construction*, pages 176–185, Palo Alto, CA, July 1986.
12. M. Wolfe. *High Performance Compilers for Parallel Computing*. Addison-Wesley Publishing Company, Reading, MA, 1996.
13. M. Wolfe and C.-W. Tseng. The power test for data dependence. *IEEE Transactions on Parallel and Distributed Systems*, 3(5):591–601, 1992.

Author Index

Lecture Notes in Computer Science

For information about Vols. 1–1584
please contact your bookseller or Springer-Verlag